The Jew in
Christian Theology

Dedicated to my beloved wife Ursula and
to the memory of my friends, Janet and Selig Adler,
Zellman Notarius and Milton Plesur,
and to "The Righteous Gentiles" who gave their lives
during the Nazi tyranny so that their Jewish brethren could live.

"To save a single life is to save the world."
—Talmud; Mishnah Sanhedrin 4

"No greater love has any man than that he gives his life for another."
—The New Testament

The Jew in Christian Theology

Martin Luther's Anti-Jewish
Vom Schem Hamphoras, *Previously
Unpublished in English, and
Other Milestones in Church
Doctrine Concerning Judaism*

GERHARD FALK

McFarland & Company, Inc., Publishers
Jefferson, North Carolina, and London

Author's Notes and Acknowledgments On a wintry night a week before Christmas in 1989 I drove past a church in front of which glowed three words written in lights: "God is Love." This was a message I had seen many times before and had taken for granted.

I had just finished a book about murder, so I knew that many who participated in the murder of European Jews between 1933 and 1945 were raised as Christians and that others who claimed to be Christians approved of these executions. It struck me as a paradox that those who taught that message on the church door could also teach hatred of the Jewish people into which was born the Founder of Christianity. The present book attempts to explain the paradox of these two attitudes, the Christian message of "good will to men" and hatred for Jews, by citing the very words of Christian theologians, Christian synods and Christian preachers relating to the Jews.

This is not a book about anti–Semitism. Nor is it a book about Jews. It is a book about Christian beliefs, written in the spirit of William I. Thomas, who reminded us that the consequences of beliefs are real. One of the consequences of anti–Jewish beliefs was the Holocaust. It is to be hoped that a consequence of the new Christian theology concerning the Jews will be that Christianity may get closer to an ideal first found in the Jewish scriptures: "love your neighbor as yourself."

My thanks go to my friend Ms. Marjorie Lord who helped me so many times by obtaining the most unusual books in every language from "the four corners of the earth" and to my friend Dr. George Tomashevich for his invaluable aid in the work of translation and in acquainting me with writers essential to this study.

The present work is a reprint of the library bound edition of The Jew in Christian Theology: Martin Luther's Anti-Jewish Vom Schem Hamphoras, Previously Unpublished in English, and Other Milestones in Church Doctrine Concerning Judaism, *first published in 1992 by McFarland.*

LIBRARY OF CONGRESS CATALOGUING-IN-PUBLICATION DATA

Falk, Gerhard, 1931–
    The Jew in Christian theology: Martin Luther's anti–Jewish Vom Schem Hamphoras, previously unpublished in English, and other milestones in church doctrine concerning Judaism / Gerhard Falk.
       p.   cm.
    Includes bibliographical references and index.

    ISBN 978-0-7864-7744-9
    softcover : acid free paper ∞

    1. Judaism (Christian theology)—History of doctrines. 2. Christianity and antisemitism. 3. Judaism—Controversial literature—History and criticism. I. Luther, Martin, 1483–1546. Vom Schem Hamphoras und von Geschlecht Christi. English & German. 1992. II. Title.
BT93.F35 2014   231.7'—dc20   91–48242

BRITISH LIBRARY CATALOGUING DATA ARE AVAILABLE

© 1992 Gerhard Falk. All rights reserved

No part of this book may be reproduced or transmitted in any form or by any means, electronic or mechanical, including photocopying or recording, or by any information storage and retrieval system, without permission in writing from the publisher.

Cover image © iStock/Thinkstock

Manufactured in the United States of America

McFarland & Company, Inc., Publishers
  Box 611, Jefferson, North Carolina 28640
  www.mcfarlandpub.com

Table of Contents

Introduction   xi

One: The Contribution of Christian Theology to the Fate of the European Jews

The Catholic Contribution
1. The Early Church Fathers   3
2. Christian Synods and Christian Law   27

The Contributions of Protestants and Others
3. Erasmus and Luther   49
4. From Calvin to Soloviev: The Devil Through Four Centuries   81

Two: Toward a New Christian Theology of Judaism

5. The Jews in Early 20th Century Christian Theology   103
6. After the Holocaust: A New Christian Theology   129
7. Great Expectations: From Conflict to Unity   153

Appendices

A. *Vom Schem Hamphoras und vom Geschlecht Christi*, by Martin Luther (1543), in English translation   163

B. *Vom Schem Hamphoras und vom Geschlecht Christi* (original German version)   225

C. Pastoral Letter on the Occasion of the 25th Anniversary of the Proclamation of the Conciliar Declaration "Nostra Aetate" (January 1991)   277

D. Resolution 3–09, "To Clarify Position on Anti-Semitism," of the Missouri Synod of the Lutheran Church (July 1983)   281

Bibliography   283
Index   291

Introduction

The fate of the Western Jews was of necessity tied to the view of them held by the vast Christian majority during all those centuries of Jewish life in Europe. Such is the case even at this writing, not only for the Jews of Europe but also for the Jews elsewhere and for any minority living among a large majority from which it differs in ethnicity, religion, race or any other visible manner, social or congenital.

It is therefore important to record the impact Christian theology has had upon the Jews, for better or for worse, because as William I. Thomas has so eloquently reminded us, "If men define situations as real, they are real in their consequences." Holding to this precept, the present study seeks to show how beliefs about Jews, as taught by Christian theologians and as formulated in Christian laws, created all those conditions which placed the Jews into about the same position between the fourth and the twentieth centuries as the "blacks in Mississippi before the Civil Rights Movement" (Heller: *On the Edge of the Abyss*).

The Holocaust, which finished the thousand-year history of the German and Eastern European Jews, was therefore the outcome, the extension of theological teachings and Christian laws. This is not to say that Christianity is exclusively responsible for these horrors. On the contrary, this book argues that Christians were, and in some cases still are, anti-Jewish. Nazis and their allies were and are anti-Semitic. Therein lies a vast difference, since anti-Semitism is a racial theory holding that Jews are by nature inferior and that they have inherited a form of blood which makes them the world's parasites. Hence, Christians with one Jewish grandparent were treated as Jews by the Nazi killers. Not so among Christians. Christianity has sought conversion; anti-Semitism seeks the death of Jews as no Jew can be redeemed from his "blood" according to that theory.

It is another thesis of this book that Christianity grew to maturity upon renouncing anti-Judaism in the early 1960s. This new policy makes

Christianity independent for the first time in its existence and therefore assures Christianity a future without using the Jews as a foil for promoting its superiority. Thus, both Christians and Jews have benefited and will continue to do so. Both religions appear to have a great future as they finally join in working for a common cause: "Peace on earth, good will toward men."

In writing this book, I have used primary sources wherever possible. This means that I have examined the speeches, sermons and writings of those most responsible for formulating Christian beliefs throughout the centuries, whether they exist in English or in any other language. In short, the book is based on the verbatim statements of the Christian leadership concerning the Jews. This is not a history of the Jews. The book deals only with the theology behind that history, since there is surely no shortage of such histories. There is however no succinct examination of the theological foundations of Christian attitudes toward the Jews. This does not mean that it cannot be found. There are many sources. However, most of these either are not in the English language or have been ignored. Many receive only scant mention in books devoted to Jewish history, Christian history or the Holocaust. This book seeks to close that gap by featuring what is generally overlooked. I have translated from medieval German Martin Luther's entire manuscript *Vom Schem Hamphoras*, which is here presented in English for the first time.

In addition to all this I have analyzed the pronouncements of Christian theologians and church councils toward the Jews from the sociological point of view. Using functional analysis I show the uses which Christian society made of its anti-Jewish polemics and explain what advantages it gained from teaching its followers anti-Judaism.

These explanations can also be used, and have been used, to understand many other forms of intergroup relations. But they have never before been applied to Christian anti-Judaism because historians deal in the consequences but not the origins of events as understood by sociologists.

ONE: The Contribution of Christian Theology to the Fate of the European Jews

The Catholic Contribution

1

The Early Church Fathers

I

In the second century of the Christian era, there lived in Alexandria, Egypt, a Jew named Barnabas. When he accepted the new religion, Christianity, Barnabas became a bitter enemy of his erstwhile co-religionists and thereby introduced into Jewish history a feature of Jewish existence which has troubled Jews in every century and in every generation. This is the enmity of Jewish apostates, who have been the worst enemies of the Jewish people and have at all times and in all ages done everything possible to torture and destroy the people from whom they came.

Barnabas survives in *The Epistle of Barnabas*, written about 100 C.E. (Common Era). Though some scholars dispute Barnabas's authorship of the work, it is significant that this polemic "is unique in the literature of the early Church for its radical anti–Jewish attitude."[1]*

It introduced into Christian literature and theology a number of themes which were repeated thereafter for centuries and which constitute the core of Christian arguments against Jews and Judaism.[2]

The first of these arguments is that the Jewish law is no longer incumbent upon the Jews because it has been abolished by God. Here Barnabas writes, "He has therefore abolished these things, that the new law of our Lord Jesus Christ, which is without the yoke of necessity, might have a human oblation [an offering or gift to a deity]." This and additional arguments against the temple sacrifices suggested that "instead of the outward sacrifices of the law, there is now required a dedication of man himself."[3]

The implication is that inner dedication cannot coexist with outer manifestation of religion as exhibited in the ancient animal sacrifices.

Looking at this argument from the sociological viewpoint, we may ask

---

*Notes to this chapter begin on page 22.

just what is meant by theology and by religion. These two words need to be explained here so that we can recognize the direction of Christian attitudes toward Jews and their eventual outcome.

Cicero, writing in *De Natura Deorum*, argues at one point that the word religion is derived from "relegere," to read again and again. Yet he also uses the word as if derived from "religare," to bind together. These original meanings do indeed give us some idea as to the function of religion. However, sociologists have identified a number of the anticipated consequences of religion so that a summary definition of religion could be stated thus: Religion is a systematic explanation of the relationship of man to man and man to the universe. Such a definition would of course include such religions as pure Buddhism, which has no god, as well as the god-centered religions such as Judaism and Christianity.[4]

Theology, as the word implies, is the study of God. Such a study depends of course on the supposition that a god or gods exist and that these deities or the sole deity can be subjected to human analysis. It is interesting to reflect here upon the Judeo-Christian view that God is beyond human understanding and not at all human, and the additional view that a theology is possible. Religion is not subject to dispute by sociologists, since the Thomas theorem teaches that "If men [people] define situations as real, they are real in their consequences."[5] Therefore, for our purposes, it need only be kept in mind that Christian antagonists to Judaism sought to advance themselves and prove their faith's superiority to the older religion by stressing their relationship to the Jewish God while asserting that the same God had abandoned the Jews. Thus, Barnabas argued in Greek that the Jews had misunderstood the Law by interpreting it literally. This is an argument against the Jews which we will meet many times again and which, at a minimum, taught its adherents the contempt for Jews which finally led to acceptance of mass murder. Barnabas goes on to discuss other aspects of Judaism that displease him. He claims, for instance, that "the fasts of the Jews are not true fasts, nor acceptable to God."[6]

Here Barnabas lists numerous virtues such as "restore to liberty them that are bruised; tear to pieces every unjust engagement; feed the hungry with thy bread; clothe the naked when thou seest him; bring the homeless into thy house; not despise the humble ... and not turn away from members of thy own family" ... etc. The implications here are clear. Barnabas seeks to convince his reader that Jews adhere to empty legalities but that Christians are devoted to all these good deeds.

Becoming even more specific, Barnabas lists "Jewish errors" in his next chapters and lectures his readers to the effect that the Jews have lost the Covenant, which according to Barnabas's views is now Christian but not Jewish. He writes, "But they [the Jews] thus finally lost it, after Moses had already received it. For the Scripture saith, 'And Moses was fasting in the mount forty days and forty nights, and received the covenant from the Lord, tables of stone written with the finger of the hand of the Lord,' but turning away to idols they lost it."

It would serve no purpose to discuss here what is meant by the Covenant. That is not the thrust of this inquiry. It suffices to recognize that Barnabas, and after him innumerable Christian interpreters, concluded that Christianity had supplanted Judaism and that therefore Judaism and its followers, the Jews, were not legitimate.

We touch here on the Principle of Legitimacy.[7] All religions seek to legitimize their views by claiming higher authority. Such authority for a belief is not always derived from a deity as not all religions have a deity. Tradition can legitimize many beliefs, as can group cohesion or agreement concerning conduct as well as beliefs or suppositions.

Since the early Christians were either Jews themselves or were well aware of the Jewish origin of their own faith, it was important to them to delegitimize Judaism by declaring that God had rejected that mode of worship and had rejected the Jews accordingly.

Barnabas, eager to show this to be the case, tells us, "Moses understood the meaning of God, and cast the two tables out of his hands; and their covenant was broken, in order that the covenant of the beloved Jesus might be sealed upon our heart, in the hope which flows from believing in Him."[8]

In an *Epistle of Ignatius to the Magnisians* the writer declares that "it is absurd to speak of Jesus Christ with the tongue and to cherish in the mind a Judaism which has now come to an end. For where there is Christianity there cannot be Judaism ... and those that were of a stony heart have become the children of Abraham." Here we learn that the writer does not merely confine himself to promoting his own religious views but that he further finds it necessary to malign the Jews and to insist that Christianity and Judaism cannot exist together.

Perhaps the greatest change in Christian attitudes toward Judaism and the Jews of the post–Holocaust era has been the willingness of both the Catholic and Protestant branches of Christianity to recognize that both religions can flourish side by side and that Christianity need not supplant Judaism in order to prosper.

This, however, was not the view of Ignatius. Said he: "If anyone preaches the one God of the law and the prophets, but denies Christ to be the Son of God, he is a liar, even as is also his father the devil...."[9]

Here we find for the first time the Christian habit of associating Jews with the devil—a belief which was as ancient as it was untenable by the beginning of the twentieth century. Nevertheless, a large number of people believe this even at the end of the twentieth century.

A number of the early Church fathers wrote letters and tracts designed to promote their views and refute those of the Jews, but Ignatius resorted to name calling and slander.

The "most important Christian apologist of the second century," however, was Justin, who wrote the first anti–Jewish polemic in Greek. It has been almost entirely preserved in *The Dialogue with Tryphon*.[10]

Justin was also known as Justin Martyr. Born about 100 C.E. in Samaria, he was a Samaritan in the geographic sense but was not a member of that sect. On the contrary, he makes it a point to state that he was "one of the uncircumcised" who came to Ephesus.[11]

Ephesus was at that time one of the centers of the Greek religion located in present-day Turkey near the coast of the Aegean Sea, slightly south of the 38th parallel.

Here stood the Temple of Artemis (or Diana), built five centuries before the Christian era. According to Pliny, it took 220 years to complete the temple. Enormous riches were stored there. Its size made it one of the Seven Wonders of the Ancient World. It was 425 feet long, 225 feet broad and supported by 127 columns of Parian marble each 60 feet high and weighing 150 tons. In 356 B.C.E. it was burned by Erostratus, a man otherwise unknown to history.

The temple was rebuilt at that time but was finally burned by the invading Goths in 263 C.E., 619 years later.[12]

That Ephesus was of great importance in the Greek world is further visible in that the fifth of Paul's epistles was written to the Ephesians. This letter, famous for its exhortation to unite Jews and gentiles, compares Christians to soldiers engaged in the battle of salvation.

It is therefore understandable that Justin would visit Ephesus, where he claims to have met a Jew named Tryphon. Seeking to discredit Judaism, Justin uses a method later adopted by other enemies of the Jewish people—he quotes the Jewish scriptures as evidence of the correctness of his views. Accordingly, Justin presents a long list of Christian beliefs of which he hopes to convince Tryphon, though he will not succeed. Justin begins by discussing Isaiah, using that Jewish prophet's alleged writings to show how mundane Judaism is and how kind, helpful and truthful Christianity has become. Although Justin mentions a number of Jewish religious leaders, he seeks to show that Jews have deliberately altered the text of the Bible so as to dominate others.[13]

Justin then makes some charges against the Jews which would be thereafter repeated by many of the Church fathers and hence by subsequent Christian writers. These charges, which were believed true, led to the massacre of Jews throughout the ages and are undoubtedly responsible for the millions of Jews butchered in Europe from the time of Constantine to Hitler. The main charges Justin leveled against the Jews were that they speak ill of Jesus, malign Christians and malign the Nazarenes.

In the ancient world, the Nazarenes were identified with Christians or were in fact regarded the same as Christians, hence the complaints concerning the attitude of Jews toward them. Whatever the beliefs of Justin on this subject, our concern is to show that these writings were viewed as justification to persecute and murder Jews throughout Christian history.

Justin proceeds now in his *Dialogue with Tryphon* to discredit Judaism. He argues that the Jews themselves violate the eternal law and misinterpret the Law of Moses. He claims to have found that the prophet Isaiah, who lived from 750 to 695 B.C.E., "teaches that sins are forgiven through Christ's blood." The story of Elijah, another Jewish prophet who lived more than 700 years before the beginning of the Christian era, is also employed by Justin to promote his arguments against the Jews. Most important, however, as justification of Christian persecutions of Jews is Justin's argument that any misfortunes that befell the Jews after the Roman emperor Constantine became a Christian were the fault of the Jewish victims and not the perpetrators of crimes against them.

Sociologists classify the blaming of the victim as one of the techniques of neutralization used by both delinquent children and adult criminals in explaining their deeds without suffering from a sense of guilt.

For example, writing about the Jewish custom of circumcision, Justin remarks, "For the circumcision according to the flesh, which is from Abraham, was given for a sign; that you may be separated from other nations, and from us; and that you alone may suffer that which you now justly suffer; and that your land may be desolate, and your cities burned with fire; and that strangers may eat your fruit in your presence, and not one of you may go up to Jerusalem."[14]

Justin refers here to the edict by the emperor Hadrian (76–138 C.E.) prohibiting Jews from entering Jerusalem "on pain of death." It has of course always been a Christian contention that the exclusion of Jews from Jerusalem was just punishment for the "crime" of killing Christ and refusing to accept the Christian messiah. This doctrine has been largely reversed by the restoration of Israel in our own century.

Justin continues his attack upon the Jews by claiming Jews have persecuted Christians far more than any other nation and that the Jewish Law applies only to Jews and not gentiles because "of your transgressions and the hardness of your hearts."[15]

Justin announces that the Jews have forsaken God, that the observance of the Passover is not pleasing to God, and that the prophets Zechariah and Malachi predicted the Christian outcome of history and how the prophecies of these Jewish prophets referred not to Jews among whom the prophets lived, but to Christians. From all this, Justin concludes that "Christians are the Holy People promised to Abraham"; that Christians were promised to Isaac, Jacob and Judah and that Christians are "the Sons of God."[16]

Here we also find that Christians are encouraged to pray for the Jews, who are labeled "hard hearted" and repeatedly accused of killing "the Christ." Finally, Justin exhorts the Jews that Christ is their king and that they must convert since otherwise they "hope for salvation in vain."

The views of Clemens of Alexandria and his contemporary Origen, later the Bishop of Caesaria in Israel, were by no means as malicious as the writings we have met so far. Evidently, there were among the Church fathers those who could present arguments in favor of their views without attacking the opposition ad hominem. "Origen carefully avoids, in his polemic, offensive expressions."[17]

Nevertheless, Clemens also belabors the Jewish religion by using such devices as the defense of Christianity by a "chief of the people," Gamaliel, who allegedly was "secretly our brother in the faith." This technique evidently succeeded in preventing violence after Clemens spoke to a crowd of Jews and "foretold to them the overthrow of the temple."[18]

Clemens also recites the history of the early Christian experience and the rejection of their claim that the Messiah had come. Thus he competes for followers, but he does not confuse the issue of religious zeal with a zeal to defame and persecute.

The same attitude prevails in the writings of Origen. In his *Commentary on Matthew*, Origen, although he disputes at length the contentions of his Jewish contemporaries concerning a number of beliefs, nevertheless does not resort to invective. He discusses "Chastity and Prayer," "Why the Pharisees Asked a Sign from Heaven," and other matters, always staying with the issue at hand. His principal argument in all of these polemics is that "Jesus had passed over from things material to things spiritual, and from things sensible to those which are intellectual."

Nevertheless, Origen had no hope for the Jews. "We may thus assert in utter confidence," said he, "that the Jews will not return to their earlier situation, for they have committed the most abominable of crimes, in forming this conspiracy against the Saviour of the human race ... hence the city where Jesus suffered was necessarily destroyed, the Jewish nation was driven from its country, and another people was called by God to the blessed election."[19]

Origen's writing illustrates that Christianity can be interpreted in the light of those who promoted their religion but did not promote hate. This has evidently been done since the early 1960s without any loss to the Christian position. Also significant here is Christianity's heavy reliance on Judaism for its interpretation of its own worth. Even the Church fathers were interpreters, not of their literature, but of Jewish literature and Jewish theology. In addition to those Church fathers already mentioned, others who were also active in writing anti–Jewish material may be briefly listed.

Bishop Appolinaris of Hierapolis wrote a polemic against the Jews in about 175 C.E., and Tertullian wrote the first anti–Jewish tract in Latin, *Adversus Judeaus*, in 175. At the beginning of the third century, Hippolytus of Rome wrote *Contra Judeaus*, attributing the miserable condition of the Jews in Rome to their rejection of the Christian faith, a view which continued to receive wide acclaim in all of Christendom even when in the 1940s Jews were gassed by the millions and lampshades were produced from the skins of Jewish babies.[20]

> All prisoners with tatooing on them were ordered to report to the dispensary.... After the prisoners had been examined the ones with the best and most artistic specimens were killed by injections. The corpses were then turned over to the pathological department where the desired pieces of tattooed skin were detached from the bodies and treated further. The finished products were turned over to Koch's wife, who had them fashioned into lamp shades, and other ornamental household articles. [From: *U.S. Department of Justice, Nazi Conspiracy and Aggression, Washington, D.C., Government Printing Office, Vol. VI, pp. 122–123.*]

"Now, then, incline thine ear to me, and hear my words, and give heed, thou Jew," begins the *Expository Treatise Against the Jews* by Hyppolytus. "Many a time doest thou boast thyself, in that thou didst condemn Jesus of Nazareth to death, and didst give Him vinegar and gall to drink; and thou dost vaunt thyself because of this. Come therefore and let us consider together whether perchance thou doest not boast unrighteously, O Israel, (and) whether that small portion of vinegar and gall has not brought down this fearful threatening upon thee, (and) whether this is not the cause of thy present condition involved in these myriad troubles."[21]

Lactantius, author of *The Divine Institutes*, summarizes in his writings all of those polemics against the Jews and the Jewish religion which all other Christian writers against the Jews have reproduced over and over again. Here we find the accusation that "the Jews"—i.e., any Jew, living at any time—committed the crime of deicide. In addition we find the Christian view, by no means a Jewish one, that there are two "Testaments" of which the Jews recognize only "the Old" while Christians also recognize "The New Testament." Jews of course have no "Old Testament" since the Five Books of Moses, the Prophets and the Writings are all part of the Torah in the Jewish view. In fact, the very word Testament is a Latin word and is foreign to Judaism. Nevertheless, it is assumed by Christian writers and by many Christians today that Jews "have" the Old Testament.

Here is a significant quotation from Lactantius, not because Lactantius is the most important of the Church fathers, but because this statement summarizes so well all the subsequent arguments whereby Christian assumptions were superimposed upon Jewish beliefs.

In a work entitled "Of the Departure of Jesus into Galilee after his Resurrection; and the two Testaments, the Old and the New," Lactantius writes the following:

> Therefore He went into Galilee, for He was unwilling to show Himself to the Jews, lest He should lead them to repentance, and restore them from their impiety to a sound mind. And there He opened to His disciples again assembled the writings of Holy Scripture, that is, the secrets of the prophets; which before His suffering could by no means be understood, for they told of Him and of His passion. Therefore Moses, and the prophets also themselves, call the law which was given to the Jews a testament: for unless the testator shall have died, a testament cannot be confirmed, nor can that which is written in it be known, because it is closed and sealed. And thus, unless Christ had undergone death, the testament could not have been opened; that is, the mystery of God could not have been unveiled and understood.
>
> But all Scripture is divided into two Testaments. That which preceded the advent and passion of Christ—that is, the law and the prophets—is called the Old; but those things which were written after his resurrection are named the New Testament. The Jews make use of the Old, we of the New: but yet they are not discordant, for the New is the fulfilling of the Old, and in both there is the same testator, even Christ, who, having suffered death for us, made us heirs of His everlasting kingdom, the people of the Jews being deprived and disinherited....[22]

The sum of this message is that (1) Jesus, having been resurrected, would not give the Jews an opportunity to "repent," (2) the Jewish scriptures cannot be understood without their Christian interpretation, (3) the Jewish scriptures are a "testament," thus constituting the will of one deceased, Jesus, and (4) the so-called "Old" testament is void in view of the so-called "New" testament.

Since Jews recognize no testament, either old or new, it is significant that Christians decided as early as the second century what the Jewish religion is or should be, not permitting Jews to decide that for themselves.

The unknown author of *Constitutions of the Holy Apostles* writes in the same vein, arguing that the Jews have been dispersed from their land because they would not recognize the Christ and therefore are unable to carry out their religious law and therefore are cursed by God.[23] The historian Eusebius (260–340 C.E.) repeated all of these charges against the Jews in his monumental *Preparatio Evangelica* and *Demonstratio Evangelica*.

II

It is quite evident from this partial review of Christian arguments that the Jewish religion itself was used first to justify the suppression of Judaism, and eventually, in the twentieth century, to justify some of those cruelties collectively known as the Holocaust.

These measures began in the days of the first Christian Roman emperor, Constantine, and continued past the days of Hitler. Constantine lived only 31 years, from 306 to 337 C.E., during which time he made Christianity the state religion and called the first ecumenical council at Nicea in 325 C.E.[24]

Thereupon the savage persecution of the Jews became commonplace in all of the Roman empire, both east and west, and continued to our own day. It is true that Constantine included the Jews in the Edict of Milan in 331 C.E., granting them sufferance but not civil equality with either pagans or Christians.

He called Jews "a nefarious and perverse sect" (*feralis, nefaria secta*), banished the rabbis, forbade Christians to associate with Jews, and made the marriage of a Jew and a Christian a capital offense.[25]

The German law of 1933 entitled *Law for the Protection of German Blood and Honor* had a similar purpose and prohibited such marriages again, 1,600 years later.[26]

Constantine also removed Jews from the Roman army, where they had been both fighting men and officers, because the Christian clergy demanded that the emperor remove Jews from these and other influential positions including any administrative appointments. While these restrictions were at first confined to major positions at court, they were later extended to even lower-ranking positions in the empire.[27]

Exactly the same laws were enacted by the National Socialist German Workers Party after their leader, Adolf Hitler, became chancellor of Germany in January of 1933. Thus, on April 4, 1933, the *Reichsgesetzblatt* (or *Federal Law Journal*) announced that as of that date, civil servants not of "Aryan" descent were to be pensioned or dismissed outright.

In addition, Jewish lawyers were excluded from the professions by German law on the grounds of being of "non–Aryan" descent. Innumerable other laws followed this one, all designed to keep Jews from earning a livelihood.[28]

The demands of the Christian clergy in fourth century Rome were derived from the view that Jews were guilty of "Christ killing" so that the very word Jew became synonymous with the phrase "Christ killer." This served as an argument against the employment of Jews in any occupation that gave them any ascendancy over non–Jews and permitted any excess and cruelty against them.

For example, in 405 C.E. a Christian mob attacked the Jews then living in Antioch, Syria. Inflamed by the religious hatred preached by St. John Chrysostom, "The Golden Mouth," the mob destroyed the synagogues in that city, tearing them down stone by stone. Jewish homes were pillaged. In

Alexandria, where Jews had lived for 700 years, all Jews were driven out by Christian devotees who viewed themselves as elected to commit these crimes by their interpretation of their religion and considered it their duty to murder the "Christ killers."[29]

> There was a room ... perhaps five times as large as this one. Perhaps it was only four times as big as the one in which I am sitting now. And Jews were inside. They were to strip and then a truck arrived where the doors open, and the van pulled up at the hut. The naked Jews were to enter. Then the doors were hermetically sealed and the car started ... and then I saw the most breathtaking sight I have ever seen in my life.
> The van was making for an open pit. The doors were flung open and corpses were cast out as if they were some animals-some beasts. They were hurled into the ditch. I also saw how the teeth were being extracted. [*From the testimony of Adolf Eichman in Joachim von Lang and Claus Sybill, eds.* Eichmann Interrogated *New York, Farrar, Strauss and Giroux, 1983, p. 77.*]

Jews then and later "were outlawed and labeled as people who had no right to exist no matter how they behaved."[30]

It should be noted that not only Jews but others who were viewed as damnable by the Bible were brutally murdered. Thus, "many old women ... were burned at the stake because a witch shall not be suffered to live."[31]

John Chrysostom, who was mainly responsible for the riots at Antioch, was born in 349 C.E. in that Syrian city. Founded by Greek-speaking peoples, Antioch was a large metropolis in the time of John Chrysostom and contained a large Jewish minority.[32]

Chrysostom became a public speaker in favor of his Christian religion and in his lifetime was Patriarch of Constantinople. Christian tradition holds that he was "driven from the patriarchate of Constantinople by the evil scheming of the empress Eudoxia and the self-serving plots of Theophilus, the patriarch of Alexandria. He was abandoned to die in lonely exile in a forsaken village on the eastern edge of the Black Sea."[33]

In his days in Antioch, however, his zeal in promoting Christianity led him to write and preach on the Jews in a manner which has been called "the most horrible and violent denunciations of Judaism to be found in the writings of a Christian theologian."[34] Another modern writer, Malcolm Hay, writes, "The violence of the language used by St. John Chrysostom in his homilies against the Jews has never been exceeded by any preacher whose sermons have been recorded.... These homilies filled the minds of Christian congregations with a hatred which was transmitted to their children and to their children's children for many generations.... Priests were taught to preach with St. Chrysostom as their model—where priests were taught to hate, with St. Chrysostom as their model."[35]

In a series of eight polemics delivered in 387 C.E., Chrysostom calls Jews and so-called Judaizers (Christians who continued to participate in Jewish customs) a disease infecting the Church.

"But if those who are sick with Judaism are not healed now when the Jewish festivals are near, at the very door, I am afraid that some, out of misguided habit and gross ignorance, will share in their transgressions...."

Jews are also described by Chrysostom as beasts and wolves. Said he, "Again those sorry Jews, most miserable of all men, are about to hold a fast and it is necessary to protect the flock of Christ.... Today the Jews, more troublesome than any wolves, are about to encircle our sheep, it is necessary to arm ourselves for battle...."

Chrysostom also viewed Jews as drunks. "The fast of the Jews—or should I say the drunkenness of the Jews—is past. It is possible to be drunk without wine.... Drunkenness is even more pitiful than other illnesses because the drunken man does not realize he is drunk, just as men who do not realize they are insane.... Similarly, the Jews who are now drunk do not realize they are drunk...."

According to John Chrysostom, "They [the Jews] are truly wretched and miserable for they have received many good things from God yet they have spurned them and violently cast them away."

He also accuses Jews of simultaneously rejecting the Law and observing it. "Nothing is more miserable than those who kick against their salvation. When it was required to keep the law, they trampled it under foot; now when the law has been abrogated, they obstinately observe it."

A favorite technique of Chrysostom and anti-Jewish orators since then has been to cite a New Testament passage against the Jews and a passage of the Christian "Old Testament" which, at least in the view of the speakers, contains the same anti-Jewish message. This technique includes "exaggeration, insinuation, guilt by association. Chance phrases in the Bible are singled out because they merge easily with the rhetorical language."[36]

John Chrysostom is best remembered, however, for inflicting the charge of "Christ killers" upon the Jews of his day and upon all Jews living subsequently.

The phrase "Christ killers" was used before Chrysostom in *The Constitutions of the Holy Apostles* and by several of the early Church fathers. Here the Jews are called "the synagogue of 'Christ killers' or the assembly (synagogue) of evil doers."[37] However, these references dealt only with the Jews living at the time of Jesus. Chrysostom for the first time used the phrase to refer to the Jews living 300 years later, in his own time, a reference which was refuted by Christians only in the second half of the twentieth century.

Chrysostom became the father of this canard: "We must return again to the sick. Do you realize that those who are fasting have dealings with those who shouted, 'Crucify him! Crucify him!' [*Luke 23: 21*] and with those who said, 'His blood be on us and on our children' [*Matthew 27: 25*]? ..."

The sum of this teaching was a blunt message to the Jews: "God hates you."[38]

It is of course immaterial whether anyone ever said this or anything whatever about the Christian savior. Important is once more the Thomas theorem—"If men define situations as real, they are real in their consequences"—together with the interpersonal and emotional results such teaching had for both Christians and Jews over the centuries.

Chrysostom argues further that "You have no chance for atonement, excuse or defense.... You Jews did crucify him. But after he died on the cross he then destroyed your city; it was then that he dispersed your people; it was then that he scattered your nation over the face of the earth. In doing this, he teaches us that he is risen, alive and in heaven."[39]

In short, Chrysostom taught that God revenged himself upon his killers, a message perpetuated in all of Christendom from then until the middle of the 1960s.

One of the unspoken but evident reasons for the anti-Jewish conduct of Chrysostom and all who followed and preceded him in their Christian anti-Judaism was the fear that Judaism would attract converts of its own, not only from among the pagan population, but particularly from among Christians. In Chrysostom's day, as in the 1990s, there were persons who became Jewish. In addition, there were in the fourth century (as today) practicing Christians who also participated in Jewish rites. For example there are Christians who observe the Passover; Christians, such as members of the New Covenant Church, who hold worship services on Friday night, the beginning of the Jewish Sabbath; and Christians who are in fact Sabbatarians—that is, they consider Saturday a holy day. There are even Christians who observe a number of Jewish holy days.

All of this "Judaizing" may be only a matter of religious liberty in the United States of the 1990s without having any political significance. In view of the American attitude toward religious liberty and the constitutionally guaranteed protection of free religious choice, all of this is a private matter. In addition, it is extremely unlikely that any of these activities threaten Christianity.

In the fourth century and for many years thereafter, however, "Judaizing" was viewed with fear and alarm by those Christians who believed that Judaism was a very attractive religion and that some Christians might become converts to Judaism.[40]

This fear became particularly acute among the Christians living during the reign of the Emperor Julian (Flavius Claudius Julianus). The nephew of the emperor Constantine, Julian had been raised in Constantinople where he was born in 332 C.E. He studied in Athens and there returned to the Greek religion, becoming an opponent of Christianity. Called "Julian the Apostate" by Christians, he ascended to the throne of Rome in 355 as joint ruler with Constantine. Upon becoming emperor in 361 when Constantine died, he announced his intention to rebuild the temple in Jerusalem and to return the city of Jerusalem to the Jews. This caused immense anxiety among Christians as they saw such a move as a challenge to their superiority over the Jews and a denial of the Christian view that the Jews would never see their temple rebuilt, nor return to Jerusalem, as punishment for their rejection of the Christian savior.

So Christians greatly rejoiced when Julian died in battle after only two years as Emperor and Jovian assumed the throne, particularly as Jovian restored to the Christians all the funds that had been allocated to the "pagans" during the reign of Julian.[41]

It is important to remember that Christianity depends on Judaism for its very existence. Not only is Christianity the direct descendant of Judaism, but it has until recently needed a downtrodden and defeated Judaism as a measurement, a yardstick, a comparison against which to prove the triumph of Christianity. This is well illustrated on the walls of many a medieval church. These churches usually contain a statue of "The Synagogue," as for example in Trier, Germany. These statues are always blindfolded, have dejected features, a loose and falling crown and other symbols of defeat. Such statues can be seen to this day all over Europe.

Aurelius Augustine, best known as St. Augustine (354–430), was and continues to be one of the leading theologians and philosophers in Christianity. His views concerning the Jews are therefore definitive of Christian teachings and cannot be overlooked. Augustine considered the Jews a foil for the glory of Christianity, proving by their misery the truth of the victorious Christian religion. In *The City of God* Augustine repeats the then-well-established Christian argument that the Jewish nation was destroyed by Rome as punishment for Jewish refusal to believe in the divinity of Jesus.[42]

Shortly before his death, Augustine returned to the subject of the Jews and in either 428 C.E. or 429 C.E. wrote his *Tractatus Adversus Judaeos*.[43]

This polemic has been summarized by the Austrian scholar Bernhard Blumenkranz as follows:

> 1. Augustin dealt with the Jews at considerable length. Few of his writings do not mention this theme at least once.
> 2. Amidst these expressions there are some objective descriptions of the contemporary Jews concerning their lives, their manners and customs and their legal position etc.

3. Beyond that however, a very severe polemic against Jews and Judaism is found, particularly when Augustin addresses his believers and followers.

4. Augustin does defend the Judaism prior to Jesus when speaking with pagans and heretics. However, Judaism after the time of Jesus is portrayed by him as rejected.

5. Augustin repeats every one of the arguments against Judaism already supported and used by his many predecessors. However, he also promotes the original idea that Israel has been dispersed as a means of witnessing the truth of Christianity.

6. Augustin was not involved in immediate anti-Jewish actions or anti-Jewish measures of the day. Nevertheless, he sufficiently proved his enmity for the Jews. In view of the high esteem in which he was held his views concerning Jews were passed on together with all of his other teachings with highly detrimental consequences for the Jews.[44]

In an earlier essay, *Of True Religion*, Augustine had written, "It [the Catholic Church] makes use of the nations as material for its operations, of heretics to try its own doctrine, of schismatics to prove its stability, of the Jews as a foil to its own beauty."

He held a similar view concerning Jewish law. Here we are told that "The moral precepts under the old Law are lower and in the Gospel higher...."[45] a view which Emile Durkheim recognized as one of the most important functions of religion—social control.[46]

This means that any group, Christians included, needs to draw a line, set a boundary beyond which a member may not go without forfeiting membership in his group. To achieve such a boundary and secure the group from possible disintegration, hell, the devil, witches and Jews have been used at various times in Christian history. The Jews in particular have served the function of being all of these things, thus securing for orthodox Christians all the benefits of membership in the human race as contrasted with the "Christ killers," who not only forfeited such membership, but could be used with impunity by Christians for the commission of any crime, the expression of any cruelty and the gain which comes to those who may persecute without inhibition.

"All over the world the Jews are in all respects treated as if they were of a different species." So wrote Bishop Newton in 1765 and so wrote the early Church fathers who founded these views.[47] In the fourth century, St. Gregory of Nyssa called the Jews "Slayers of the Lord, murderers of the prophets, adversaries of God, haters of God, men who show contempt for the law, foes of grace, enemies of their father's faith, advocates of the devil, brood of vipers, slanderers, scoffers, men whose minds are in darkness, leaven of the Pharisees, assembly of demons, sinners, wicked men, stoners, and haters of the righteous."[48]

To this he added that Judaism is "a degraded superstition," that the Jews "insulted our Lord's bodily presence by their wanton unbelief," and that the Jews are "condemned."[49]

From these writings we learn that the Jews have served Christian society in the same function over the years that witches have. From the fourteenth to the seventeenth century, about 500,000 so-called "witches" were murdered in Europe and America. The accusations of witchcraft, entirely the product of imagination, served to tightly control the Puritan communities of New England as did the murderous anti–Jewish measures of the Nazi government in Europe between 1933 and 1945.[50]

While Chrysostom preached his anti–Jewish sermons after the death of Julian (353), the dangers of "Judaizing" were by no means alleviated as far as the Christian leadership could see. In fact, this need to defend against reputed Jewish ensnarements continued to the time of Luther (1483–1546), and is met again in the speeches of Adolf Hitler (1889–1945), 400 years later.

While the views of theologians may have been incendiary in any case, and did indeed lead to innumerable forms of violence against Jews, the laws and decrees by which Medieval man was governed caused the Jews far more grief than ecclesiastic preachments ever could.

III

Until the American revolution, and even thereafter, religious freedom was hardly known. It is therefore important to remember that the ascent of Christianity in Rome brought on not only private bigotry but also public persecution for all dissenters and particularly the Jews. This public persecution was institutionalized by the various Church councils and thereby attained significance in the entire Christian world.

A number of Christian Church councils took place before the age of Constantine. These, however, had only local significance until their various decisions concerning the Jews became public law for the whole Roman Empire, both Eastern and Western, by means of the codes of Theodosius and Justinian.

The Spanish Council of Elvira, meeting in 306, prohibited marriage and all sexual intercourse between Jews and Christians and even prohibited Christians from accepting Jewish hospitality.[51]

When the Council of Nicea in 325 established the date for Easter, they could not refrain from making its decision another occasion for attacking the Jews. Writing to all not present at the Council, the emperor Constantine explained the decision this way: "It was declared particularly unworthy for this, the holiest of all festivals, to follow the custom [calculation] of the

Jews, who had soiled their hands with the most fearful of crimes, and whose minds were blinded.... We ought not, therefore, to have anything in common with the Jews...."[52]

This effort to divorce Easter from Passover was strengthened when the Council in Trullo approved of Canon VII and went so far as to proclaim that "If any bishop, presbyter, or deacon, shall celebrate the holy day of Easter before the vernal equinox, with the Jews, let him be deposed."

At the Synod of Laodicea, occurring around 363 C.E., Canon 38 declared that "It is not lawful to receive unleavened bread from the Jews, nor to partake of their impiety" meaning the Passover celebration. At the Council of Chalcedon in 451, Christian "readers and singers" are prohibited from marrying Jews.

The Canon of the Council in Trullo, held in 692 and also called the Quinisext Council, included Canon XI to the effect that Christians must not only refuse to eat the unleavened bread (Matzoh), but must also avoid "familiar intercourse with them [the Jews], nor summon them in illness, nor receive medicines from them, nor bathe with them...." The right to appear in court and accuse citizens of crimes was denied Jews in Canon 129 of the so-called "African Code" as the Council issuing these decrees met at Carthage. The Apostolic Canons threatened excommunication: "If any bishop, presbyter or deacon, or anyone of the list of clergy, keeps fast or festival with the Jews, or receives from them any of the gifts of their feasts, as unleavened bread, or any such things, let them be deposed. If he be a layman, let him be excommunicated."

On January 17, 395 C.E., the Roman Empire was divided for a second and final time between East and West. On that day, Theodosius died and his sons, Honorius, emperor of the West, and Arcadius, emperor of the East, ended the unity of the Empire forever.

In 408, at the death of Arcadius, Theodosius II assumed the throne of the Eastern empire and Honorius continued as emperor of the West.[53]

It was during the reign of these two emperors that the Theodosian Code became the law of Rome, for the most part, in both the East and West. This may seem strange inasmuch as the empire was governed by two separate emperors at the time of Theodosius II. However, the evidence indicates that "These laws were valid in the entire Empire, so that a law legislated in one half of the Empire needed to be explicitly repealed in order not to be in force in the other half."[54]

In the reign of the emperor Justinian in the East, the Code of Justinian continued this tradition. "The Code enacted orthodox Christianity into law."[55]

The deadly consequences of an alliance between the church and the state are well illustrated. There are of course innumerable other examples of this hideous mismatch, some of which we will see as we progress in this discussion, while others fall outside the limitations of this book. What appears most astonishing in this matter is that there are still so many Americans who seek to use the state to force their religious views upon an unwilling public, despite the long history of horrors which must result from such a policy.

In Rome the Jews, and other non–Christians, became outsiders in the empire both East and West. Jews had been Roman citizens before the promulgation of these codes, but such citizenship now became dependent on belief in the state religion, Christianity. The unwillingness of Jews to accept the new faith not only made them unacceptable to Christian zealots, as we have already seen, but now also cast doubt on their patriotism, a condition which continued to haunt them until the Nazi persecutions of the 1930s and 1940s removed even their humanity.

On the 29th of December, 534, the Justinian Code took effect in the Eastern empire while the West, no longer an empire, continued to be governed by the Theodosian Code until the twelfth century.[56] Both codes dealt with the Jews in three ways. First, there were laws concerning the relations of the Jews with the government; second, laws dealing with the relations of Jews with non–Jews; and third, laws dealing with the relations of Jews with other Jews.[57]

With respect to the laws concerning the Jews and the government, it is obvious that the Theodosian Code permitted the Jews some autonomy and protected their religious rights even into the Christian era. Although we will see that eventually Christians allowed Jews few rights, the early Christian emperors and church leaders were willing to continue the privileges Jews had acquired during pagan Roman rule. In fact, the need to keep Jews alive as a reminder to Christians of the "sin" of rejecting Jesus made it impossible for any Christian government to wipe out all Jews. It was precisely this need to use the Jews as witnesses to the truth of Christianity, and the need to adhere to at least some of the demands of the Ten Commandments and other Judeo-Christian teachings, that inhibited some Christians at all times from committing the worst forms of genocide which the non–Christian Nazis, despite their Christian antecedents, finally achieved.

In any event, in 393 C.E. Theodosius wrote, "It is sufficiently established that the sect of the Jews is prohibited by no law."[58]

In a law of the year 412 C.E. the Western emperor Honorius "recognized the right of Jews not to be summoned to court on a Sabbath or holiday," adding that this right was recognized because it was traditional and had been recognized by earlier emperors. These rights were later included in the Code of Justinian in the Eastern Empire and in the Breviarium, a code of law in the Western Visigoth kingdom.

Further, from the year 330 C.E. in the reign of Constantine through the year 404 C.E., during the reign of the Eastern emperor Arcadius, Jewish religious life was repeatedly recognized as legal and *equal to that of the Christian law*.[59]

Despite these favorable rulings enjoyed by Jews at the hands of the Christian Roman emperors, the Christian clergy was unwilling to permit Jews the freedom of religion that had been theirs in the empire. In 423 C.E., because of "pressure of fanatical Christians," the Eastern Emperor Theodosius II prohibited the establishment of new synagogues, although he permitted the maintenance of existing synagogues. This was of course an effort to control the growth of Judaism. These laws pertaining to synagogues were continued in the Code of Justinian (534 C.E.).[60]

In the political sphere, Jews suffered legal discrimination beginning in the sixth century. Prior to that, legal restrictions on Jewish office holders were rare or not enforced. Even in the sixth century the prohibitions against Jews holding high office were not well enforced. But the laws restricting the political rights of Jews did exist as evidenced by a law enacted in both the Eastern and Western empires in 438 C.E. Accordingly, Jews were forbidden to serve in the imperial administration or to hold offices of dignity in the municipal government. The construction of new synagogues was once more prohibited and Jews were also forbidden to proselyte either slaves or free persons.[61]

In 1933, similar laws were enacted by Germany's Nazi government. On April 7 of that year, all Jews were dismissed from the German civil service. Innumerable other laws made Jewish life in Germany untenable, and, on the night of November 10–11, 1938, all synagogues in Germany and Austria were destroyed.[62]

Considering now the relationship of Jews to non–Jews as reflected in the codes of Theodosius and Justinian, the evidence indicates that conversion to and from Judaism concerned the authorities a great deal. Seven laws issued between 329 C.E. and 553 C.E. were designed to entice Jews to become Christians. For example, in 426 C.E. Jewish parents were forbidden to disinherit Jewish converts to Christianity. Likewise, in 329 C.E. a law protected apostates from Judaism from attack by Jews by threatening the death penalty for such conduct. This law was included in both the Code of Theodosius and the Code of Justinian. The law as shown in the Justinian Code reads as follows: "We want the Jews, their principals and their patriarchs informed, that if anyone—once this law has been given—dare attack by stoning or by other kind of fury one escaping from their deadly sect and raising his eyes to God's cult, which as we have learned is being done now, he shall be delivered immediately to the flames and burnt with all his associates. But if one of the people shall approach their nefarious sect and join himself to their conventicles, he shall suffer with them the deserved punishments."[63]

In the year 388 C.E., marriage between a Jew and a Christian was prohibited by Theodosius. This law, also applicable in the West, continued in force by inclusion in the Codex Theodosius, the Visigothic Commentary, the Breviarium, the Roman Law of the Burgundians and the Code of Justinian. These codes reflected earlier laws such as the decree of the Council of Eliberti and the aforementioned Council of Elvira, which also prohibited Christians from eating with Jews.

The penalty for such intermarriages was the same as the penalty for adultery. The legislation concerning adultery dated from 18 B.C.E. and provided for capital punishment in some cases and for loss of property and exile in most instances. Similarly, the Nazi "Law for the Protection of German Blood and Honor" sought to ensure the same results in 1935.[64]

Finally, Roman law pertaining to Jews involved the relations of Jews with one another. Here, the most important legislation dealt with "the continuous contraction of the scope of Jewish autonomy" as seen "by a comparison of the Theodosian and Justinian Codes." One of these codes deals with the judicial powers of the Jewish authorities on the grounds that as Roman citizens, Jews would have to live by Roman and not Jewish law and that synagogues could no longer collect taxes from such citizens.[65]

All told, there were 45 laws pertaining to Jews in the Theodosian Code and a total of 66 laws concerning Jews in all of Roman law. The first was a law of the year 138 C.E. permitting Jews to circumcise their own sons but not the sons of non-Jews; the last was a law in 553 C.E. in which Justinian permitted Jews to use all languages in a synagogue while prohibiting the study of the Mishna. (The Mishna, a word derived from the Hebrew root word Shanah, to repeat, constitutes one of the three parts of the Talmud, an immense work of learning and instruction developed by the Rabbis of the first and second centuries. The Mishna is also called the Code of Oral Law.[66])

In his preface to *The Jews in Roman Imperial Legislation* Linder writes, "Historians are unanimous in recognizing the important contributions of Roman law to the evolution of the attitudes adopted by non-Jewish society towards Jews since the second century."[67]

This is surely visible in what followed as the Christian synods over the centuries increasingly restricted the rights of the European Jews and thereby laid the foundations for the abominations of Martin Luther and the "Final Solution of the Jewish Question" by the Hitlerites of our own century.

> There was now only one truck waiting. A German soldier got into the truck behind the wheel and drove it closer to the hospital building wall. There was silence for a moment. No one could figure out what was going to happen next.

> There were now about six or eight soldiers standing around the truck plus about eighteen people more positioned around the rope.... Suddenly, two Germans appeared in an upper story window and pushed it open. Seconds later, a naked baby was pushed over the ledge and dropped to its death directly into the truck below.
>
> We were in such shock that at first few of us believed it was actually a live, new born baby. We thought it was an object of some kind until we saw another and another being hurled out the window into the waiting truck....
>
> The SS seemed to enjoy this bloody escapade. Just then the youngest of the bunch asked his superior if it was all right to catch one of these "little Jews" on his bayonet as it was coming down. His superior gave him permission, and the young SS butcher rolled up his sleeve and caught the very next infant on his bayonet. The blood of the infant flowed down the knife unto the murderer's arm and into his sleeve. He tried his talent once more, and again he was successful in catching the wailing child on his sharp bayonet. He tried a third time but missed and gave up the whole game, complaining it was getting too messy. [*From: Martin Gilbert,* The Holocaust, *New York, Hill and Wang, 1979, p. 33.*]

By the end of the fourth century of the Christian calendar, attitudes of the vast Christian majority in Europe towards the Jews had been developed on the basis of Christian theology. These attitudes were maintained *in the form of law* for 1600 years and were based on a number of beliefs upon which Christian theologians elaborated again and again, promoting unrelenting hatred of Jews and culminating in the Holocaust of the period 1933–1945. These beliefs were as follows:

1. That Chrisitianity has supplanted Judaism
2. That Jews are instruments of the devil
3. That Jews deliberately alter the texts of the Bible
4. That Jews are themselves to blame for all their misfortunes
5. That Jews are God killers
6. That there can be no salvation for Jews
7. That the Jewish scriptures are "Old"
8. That Jews are disinherited
9. That Jews deserve legal disabilities
10. That God hates the Jews and they are cursed by Him
11. That Jews serve as an example to unbelievers
12. That Jews are less than human.

Notes

1. *The Encyclopedia Judaica,* Vol. 1 (Jerusalem, Keter, 1971).
2. Alexander Roberts and James Donaldson, eds., *The Ante-Nicene Fathers,* Vol. 1 (Grand Rapids, Mich., Eerdmans, 1885), p. 138.

3. See note, *ibid.*, p. 138.
4. Ralph Ross and Ernest van den Haag, *The Fabric of Society* (New York, Harcourt Brace, 1957), p. 311.
5. William I. Thomas, "The Relation of Research to the Social Process," in *Essays on Research in the Social Sciences* (Washington, D.C., The Brookings Institution, 1931), p. 168.
6. Roberts and Donaldson, *op. cit.*, Vol. 1, p. 138.
7. Emile Durkheim, *The Elementary Forms of the Religous Life* (1912; reprint, New York, The Free Press, 1948). See also: Ernest Gellner, *Legitimation of Belief* (London, The Cambridge University Press, 1974).
8. Roberts and Donaldson, *op cit.*, Vol. 1, p. 139.
9. *Ibid.*, p. 82.
10. *Encyclopedia Judaica, op cit.*, p. 551.
11. S. Krauss, "The Jews in the Works of the Church Fathers," *The Jewish Quarterly Review*, Vol. V and VI, 1893/1894 in: *Judaism and Christianity*, Jacob B. Agus, ed. (New York, Arno, 1973), p. 123.
12. Georg Wissowa, ed., *Realencyclopedie der Classischen Altertumswissenschaft* (Stuttgart, Alfred Druckenmuller Verlag, 1905), pp. 2810–2811.
13. Krauss in Agus, *op. cit.*, p. 129.
14. Roberts and Donaldson, *op. cit.*, Vol. 1, p. 202.
15. *Ibid.*, p. 203.
16. Justin, *Dialogue with Tryphon*, in Roberts and Donaldson, *op. cit.*, Vol. 3, pp. 261–266.
17. S. Krauss, *op. cit.*, p. 140.
18. Allen Menzies, "Recognitions of Clement," in Roberts and Donaldson, *op. cit.*, Vol. 10, p. 92.
19. "Origin Against Celsus," Chapter XXII, p. 506, and "Origens Comments on Matthew," in Menzies, *op. cit.*, p. 452.
20. *Encyclopedia Judaica, op. cit.*, p. 552.
21. Roberts and Donaldson, *op. cit.*, p. 219.
22. Lactantius, *The Divine Institutes*, in Roberts and Donaldson, *op. cit.*, Chapter XXI, p. 122.
23. "Constitution of the Holy Apostles," in Roberts and Donaldson, *op. cit.*, p. 461.
24. Max Margolis and Alexander Marx, *A History of the Jewish People* (New York, Meridian, 1958), p. 229.
25. Heinrich Graetz, *History of the Jews*, Vol. II (Philadelphia, The Jewish Publication Society, 1967), p. 562. See also: Saul Baron, *A Social and Religious History of the Jews*, Vol. I (New York, Columbia University Press, 1951), p. 266.
26. Bruno Blau, *Das Ausnahmerecht für die Juden in Deutschland* (Düsseldorf, Verlag Allgemeine Wochenzeitung der Juden in Deutschland, 1965), p. 33.
27. Rudolf Pfisterer, *Im Schatten des Kreuzes* (Hamburg, Reich Verlag, 1966), p. 24.
28. Blau, *op. cit.*, p. 35.
29. Nathan Asubel, *The Book of Jewish Knowledge* (New York, Crown, 1964), p. 113. See also: Simon Dubnov, *The History of the Jews*, Vol. 2 (London, Thomas Yoseloff, translated by Moshe Spiegel, 1968), pp. 172–173. Also Paul W. Harkins, trans., *Saint John Chrysostom, Discourses Against Judaizing Christians* (Washington, D.C., The Catholic University of America, 1977).
30. Nora Levin, *The Holocaust* (New York, Schocken, 1973), p. 47.
31. Herbert J. Muller, *The Uses of the Past* (New York, Oxford University Press, 1952), p. 91.

32. Robert L. Wilken, *John Chrysostom and the Jews* (Berkeley, The University of California Press, 1983), pp. 34–65.
33. *Ibid.*, p. 29.
34. James Parkes, *Prelude to Dialogue* (London, Vallentine, Mitchel and Co., 1969).
35. Malcolm Hay, *Thy Brother's Blood, The Roots of Christian Anti-Semitism* (New York, Hart, 1975), p. 27.
36. Wilken, *op. cit.*, p. 124.
37. *Ibid.*, p. 125.
38. Hay, *op. cit.*, p. 32 and Harkins, *op. cit.*
39. Wilken, *op. cit.*, p. 126.
40. Wilken, *op. cit.*, pp. 158–160.
41. Will Durant, *The Age of Faith* (New York, Simon and Schuster, 1950), pp. 3–21. See also: Graetz, *op. cit.*, p. 566.
42. Augustine, *The City of God*, Whitney J. Oates, *Basic Writings of Saint Augustine*, Vol. 2 (New York, Random House, 1948), p. 455.
43. Roy Joseph Deferrari, ed., *The Fathers of the Church*, Vol. 12, *Saint Augustine, Treatises on Marriage and Other Subjects* (New York, Fathers of the Church, 1955), pp. 387–414.
44. Bernhard Blumenkranz, *Die Judenpredigt Augustins* (Basel, Switzerland, von Helbing und Lichtenhahn, 1946), pp. 210–212.
45. Aurelius Augustine, "On True Religion," in John S. Burleigh, *Augustin: Early Writings* (Philadelphia, Westminster, 1953), pp. 231 and 241.
46. Durkheim, *The Elementary Forms of Religious Life* (1912; reprint, New York, Free Press, 1965), pp. 371, 378–379.
47. Hay, *op. cit.*, p. 23.
48. Hay, *op. cit.*, p. 26.
49. Phillip Schaff and Henry Wace, eds., *A Select Library of Nicene and Post Nicene Fathers of the Christian Church*, Vol. 5 (Grand Rapids, Wm B. Eerdmans, 1892), pp. 59–60 and 490.
50. Kai T. Erikson, *Wayward Puritans: A Study in the Sociology of Deviance* (New York, Wiley, 1966).
51. Parkes, *op. cit.*, p. 174.
52. Henry R. Percival, ed., *The Seven Ecumenical Councils*, in Vol. XIV, Schaff and Wace, *op. cit.*, p. 54.
53. Durant, *op. cit.*, p. 103.
54. Amnon Linder, *The Jews in Roman Imperial Legislation* (Detroit, Wayne State University Press, 1987), p. 27.
55. Durant, *op. cit.*, p. 113.
56. Linder, *op. cit.*, p. 47.
57. *Ibid.*, p. 67.
58. "Iuadeorum sectam nulla lege prohibitam satis constat," *ibid.*, p. 190.
59. *Ibid.*, pp. 69–70 and 221. Note that in the law of 404 C.E. given by Arcadius with Honorius, the Jewish patriarch was still addressed as "excellent" and viewed as having the highest rank. The emperor wrote, "Cuncta privilegia, quae viris spectabilibus patriarchis vel his ... suum robur tenere censemus."
60. *Ibid.*, p. 74.
61. *Ibid.*, p. 325.
62. Blau, *op. cit.*, p. 54.
63. Linder, *op. cit.*, pp. 79–80 and 126–127.
64. *Ibid.*, p. 178, and Raul Hilberg, *The Destruction of the European Jews* (New York, Octagon, 1978), pp. 5–6. See also: Blau, *op. cit.*, p. 30. The two paragraphs in

the German law citing *Reichsgesetzblatt, Teil I,* Seite 1146 read as follows: "Eheschliessungen zwischen Juden und Staatsangehörigen deutschen oder artverwandten Blutes sind verboten... Ausserehelicher Verkehr zwischen Juden und Staatsangehörigen deutschen oder artverwandten Blutes ist verboten."
65. Linder, *op. cit.*, p. 88 and pp. 215–217.
66. *Ibid.*, pp. 99 and 402.
67. *Ibid.*, p. 9.

2
Christian Synods and Christian Law

I

A synod is a gathering or assembly. Such meetings, called conventions in American usage, exist when an organization becomes formal in its relationships because it cannot rely only on face-to-face contacts, exceeds the geographic area whose points are all reachable in one day, and seeks to perpetuate itself beyond the present generation. This description also fits what sociologists call a "secondary group," i.e., a group which needs a division of labor to survive and perpetuates itself also by clearly defining the limits of membership into in-groups and out-groups.

The Christian Church had become such a secondary group by the fourth century of its existence and was by then so organized that it could survive by using the European Jews as the means of indicating the limits of membership and the boundary of normality in that society. This clear demarcation of membership served Christian unity for centuries, even after Christianity suffered its first formal schism into Greek and Latin observances in 1054 C.E.

This "Great Schism" was of course far older than the eleventh century. In fact, the struggle between the Greek and Roman aspects of Christianity had always been a part of the Christian drama and became visible in the fourth century when the first Christian emperor of Rome, Constantine, moved his capital to Byzantium and called it Nova Roma, only to find that everyone else called it Constantinople (330 C.E.).

That cleavage in the Christian experience was of course not the only one the universal or Catholic Church had to endure. Many others followed so that the Church was forever trying to ensure Christian unity by force or by persuasion.

In this effort it did not succeed. Even at the first ecumenical synod called by Constantine in 325 C.E., the Church fathers had to deal with the "Arian heresy." Additional heresies threatened Christian unity at all times and became a torrent of dissent in the sixteenth century, a time generally labeled the Protestant Reformation.

Because Christianity was unable to achieve internal consensus it needed to rely on external threat to survive. This external threat came from the European Jews, not because the Jews had any political, military or economic power, but because they were readily available to furnish Christians with a visible enemy.

Thus the Jewish people, from the fourth century to the twentieth century, served Christian Europe as a means of segregating the "normal" from the abnormal, the legitimate from the illegitimate, the sinners from the saints.

It is fruitless to seek the causes of Christian anti–Judaism in anything done or not done, believed or not believed, by the Jews. Anti–Judaism was and is a Christian phenomenon which serves Christian needs. Christians have needed Jews for centuries in order to mark the limits of Christianity, the boundaries of "in-group" behavior and the bonds which hold an otherwise loose and shaky alliance together.

In 1895, the great French sociologist Emile Durkheim recognized the uses of punishment for wrong-doers in any society. Durkheim wrote that protection and social solidarity are the goals of punishment and that all societies reaffirm their values by punishing the wrong-doers. Therefore, according to Durkheim, the goal of such punishment is really not to change the wrong-doer at all.

Said Durkheim: "Imagine a society of saints, a perfect cloister of exemplary individuals. Crimes, properly so-called, will there be unknown; but faults which appear venial to the layman will create there the same scandal that the ordinary offense does in ordinary consciousness. If then, this society has the power to judge and punish, it will define these acts as criminal and will treat them as such."[1]*

Throughout the more than 1,600 years that elapsed from the Council of Nicea to the extermination camps of the Nazis, and to this day in Eastern Europe, Jews were and are defined as criminals in the consciousness of European Christians and punished again and again for such acts, beliefs or lifestyles as Christian society chose to define as criminal and chose to treat accordingly.

Providing a definition of criminality, then, was the function of the European Jews as illustrated by Christian laws concerning them among both Eastern and Western Christian churches.

---

*Notes to this chapter begin on page 45.

II

The Orthodox Church, whose membership is principally found in Russia and other Eastern European nations, relies upon 85 Apostolic canons or rules to establish the theological base upon which the dogma of the Church rests.

This means that the seven ecumenical or worldwide synods of the Orthodox Church as well as the canons of the regional synods are deemed to conform to these 85 apostolic canons. It is therefore necessary to review those Apostolic Canons affecting the Jews, not only because these canons in part determined the fate of the millions of Jews living at one time in Russia and other Eastern European lands, but also because all subsequent canons issued by the seven ecumenical synods concerning Jews reflected the 85 apostolic canons.[2]

Only three of the Apostolic Canons deal with Jews. The first is Canon LXV, which reads as follows: "If any Clergyman or Layman enter a synagogue of Jews or of heretics to pray, let him be both deposed and excommunicated." The "Interpretation" following this canon relies on the views of St. Justin and St. Chrysostom to the end that "[a] Christian is violating the law who prays along with the crucifiers of Christ." Further, the "Interpretation" holds that "any church of heretics, or any religious meeting of theirs, ought not to be honored or attended, but rather ought to be despised and rejected, on the ground that they believe things contrary to the beliefs of Orthodox Christians."[3]

Canon LXX refers to "Christ killing Jews," an expression which has undoubtedly led to more bloodshed than any other accusation made by Christians against the Jewish population of Europe. Here we learn that "anyone at all who is on the list of clergymen" may not fast together with Jews, celebrate a holiday with them or accept any gifts or favors from them on pain of being removed from office. Laymen are threatened with excommunication for the same offense. Canon LXXI augments this by threatening the same punishment for offering oil to or lighting a lamp for "a synagogue of Jews" on the grounds that such an action may give the appearance that the participant believes these Jewish rituals to be true.[4]

> To please the Russians, he [King Sigismund of Poland] agreed that Jews shall not be permitted in the realm of Moscow for trade or for any business and shall be forbidden altogether. [*From* A History of Russia, *by Jesse Clarkson, New York, Random House, 1961, p. 140.*]

During the reign of the emperor Justinian II, in 691 C.E., an ecumenical council met in the palace called Troullos in Constantinople and there expressed 102 canons or rules which the Orthodox Church considered binding until recent years. This council is considered the 6th Ecumenical Synod by orthodox Christians.

It should be understood in this connection that although Orthodox Christians view the decisions of their synods as infallible, this "infallibility" is circumscribed by the assumption that "wherever there is infallibility there also is validity."[5] Thus, we read in *The Rudder* that "The seven holy Ecumenical Councils are found to have been in all respects God-inspired and infallible and valid." That same authoritative volume also states, however, that "over and above the voice of the Councils there is the word of the Holy Scriptures to serve as the criterion of truth...." This disclaimer makes it possible for the Orthodox Church to change former beliefs even if based on canons originally promulgated by one of the seven synods. Therefore, as we shall see later, the Orthodox Church as well as the Roman Catholic and Protestant churches in the last quarter of the twentieth century have largely abandoned the anti–Jewish attitudes with which we are here concerned.[6]

In any case, Canon XI of the 6th Ecumenical Council held that no Orthodox Christian, whether clergy or layman, was allowed to eat unleavened bread or wafers (*matzohs*) sent him by Jews, "nor indeed be in any way friendly with Jews," nor use medicines prescribed by Jews, nor bathe with them. Once more, clergy who violated this canon were to be deposed from office and laymen excommunicated. Canon LXX of that same council refers to Christians as the "Children of Israel," disputing the Jewish claim to that distinction and joining the Roman Catholic view, later adopted also by Protestants, that Christianity had supplanted Judaism and Christians had taken the place of Jews in the eyes of God.[7]

> Beginning the very day of the issue of the October Manifesto, pogroms were unleashed in over a hundred cities; ... in Odessa alone several hundred [Jewish] lives were lost in a brutal four day masacre. [*From Clarkson, p. 386.*]

The seventh ecumenical council recognized by the Orthodox Church met in Niceae in 783. It passed 22 canons, of which only Canon VIII dealt with the Jews. Here the council warns Orthodox Christians not to accept as converts Jews who secretly keep the Sabbath or other Jewish customs and who continue in what is called "Jewish superstition." Further, the council ordered that no Jew was to own a Christian slave and that Jews accused of a crime or owing a debt should not be accepted as converts, lest such conversion be only a subterfuge for evading the consequences of such accusations.[8]

These then were the canons of the ecumenical councils recognized by the Orthodox Church and bearing upon the position of the Jews. In addition, however, two regional councils and two saints of the church dealt with the Jews in canons they respectively promulgated and which were accepted as valid by Orthodox Christians. These were, first, Canon I of the Regional Council convened in Antioch, Syria, in 341 C.E.; second, Canons XXIX, XXXVII and XXXVIII of the regional council held in Laodicea in Phrygia (Turkey) in 364 C.E.; third, Canon IX of Peter of Alexandria; and finally, Canon XXXV of John the Faster.

Accordingly, the following views concerning Jews became part of Orthodox Christian belief: that anyone "who should dare to celebrate Easter with the Jews" is deposed from office (if clergy); that no Christian should rest on Saturday, but that Christians should work on that day lest they become "Judaizers"; that Christians must not accept gifts from Jews or celebrate holidays with them; that Christians must not have unleavened bread; that the Jews not only killed Jesus Christ but also several Christian saints; and that sexual intercourse between Christians and Jews is prohibited.[9]

> In 1871, a frightful pogrom occurred in Odessa; for three days the troops did not interfere with rioting and looting mobs. After the assassination of Alexander II, anti–Semitism was given free rein. In 1881 violent pogroms took place in Elizavetgrad in New Russia, at Kiev and in a number of other towns and villages. [*From: Jesse D. Clarkson*, A History of Russia, *New York, Random House, 1961, p. 332.*]

That these admonitions to avoid Jews were taken seriously by Orthodox Christians is underscored by the "Orthodox Church's Attitude Toward Freemasonry," reported in *The Rudder* in 1948.

This prohibition to join the Freemasons was even then based on the belief that "In the international organization the first place of influence and importance belongs to the Jewish membership." No evidence for this claim is presented, nor does that admonition give any reason for the need to avoid such an organization on those grounds. Presumably, the followers of the church were expected to take avoidance of Jews for granted thus legitimizing anti–Jewish beliefs and actions to this day.[10]

> Early in the morning of Sept. 9, in the holy Russian city of Zagorsk, a priest was murdered with a precise swing of an ax to the back of his neck as he walked along a wooden path to the train that would take him to his church. ... This was no ordinary crime, and the Rev. Alexander Menn 55, was no ordinary priest. Father Alexander, as he was usually known, was born a Jew. ... "It goes without saying that this crime is connected with the growing wave of anti–Semitism in Russia," the Rev. Gleb Yakunin, a fellow priest ... said.... Speculation about the killers centered immediately on ultra-conservative forces in the KGB and on Pamyat, the neo–Nazi, fanatically nationalistic Russian movement that blames Soviet Jews

for all the Soviet Union's problems. [*Recounted by Yevgenia Albats and James Yuenger*, Chicago Tribune, *Sept. 22, 1990.*]

III

The hostility of the Orthodox Church toward the Jews was matched by similar attitudes on the part of the Roman Catholic Church.

In the year 306 C.E. a Christian synod met in Elvira and decreed, among other concerns, that Christians were not to marry Jews, that Jews were not permitted to bless a field[11] owned by a Christian (Canon XVI) and that the Christian clergy and others were to avoid close contact with Jews (Canon L).[12]

Canon XII of the Synod of Vennes, France, which met in 465, prohibited Christian clergy from eating with Jews, a prohibition which the Synod of Epaon extended to laymen in the year 517. Thereafter, the third Synod at Orlean in 538 confirmed this rule. In 692, the Synod of Trullane added that "no Christian, whether layman or cleric may eat the unleavened bread of the Jews, deal with them in confidence, take medicine from them or bathe with them. The clergy who do this will be deposed and the layman excommunicated." In 888 the Synod of Mainz in Germany ruled that "No Christian may eat or drink with a Jew nor accept anything edible from him," and finally the Synod of Nabonne in France similarly held that "No Christian may stay in a house with a Jew or eat with him."[13]

It was in 535 that the Synod at Carthage also ruled that no Jewish man may marry a Christian woman nor a Jewish woman a Christian man and that on penalty of excommunication such marriages must be dissolved. This had of course already been decided in 306 at Elvira and was affirmed repeatedly thereafter by other synods and councils.

Hefele, whose *Conciliengeschichte* is the most definitive account of the Catholic councils and their work, claims that Jost, a German historian, considered the Jews to have become so numerous and powerful in first century Spain, that "they believed they could dare attempting the Judaization of the whole country."[14] Heferle believed that Jews had settled in Spain a hundred years before the beginnings of Christianity and that they were engaged in proselyting the entire peninsula. Further, he believed that at that time a good number of Christians in Spain "were Judaized" to a high degree.

Whatever their number, it appears that Jews lived in relative equality with other Roman citizens in Spain and were not oppressed at that time. Nevertheless, the Christian legislation concerning them which was only then appearing at various synods throughout the empire, both East and West, was designed to drive a wedge between the Christian and Jewish populations. Successive councils indeed succeeded in this. Therefore, segregation with all its consequences was one of the principal aims of these councils with reference to the Jews, a segregation which was first enforced on a local level, was then enforced in the whole empire and was in turn imitated by those local synods who had not passed such resolutions until the worldwide (i.e., ecumenical) councils ordered segregation at the instigation of those who already had it.

Additional Christian legislation segregating Jews from Christians and preventing Jews from gaining any position of superiority or advantage over Christians continued for centuries. Thus, Canon XIV passed by the Synod of Macon in the year 581 ruled that Jews could not be seen on the street during Holy Week (the week before Easter), that they must pay attention to the wishes of Christian clerics and that they must not sit in the presence of such clerics unless permitted to do so. That same synod, according to its Canon XV, held that Jews could not be judges or tax collectors over Christians nor hold Christian slaves. Throughout the ancient world, slavery was the only manner in which agriculture could be carried on, so that anyone who could not own slaves could not work the land. This fact prevented Jews for centuries from engaging in agriculture until it became folk wisdom that Jews are by nature incapable of farming. That belief was of course disproven more recently as Jews have farmed in the Dakotas and Wyoming since the nineteenth century and have made agricultural settlements the very basis of Israeli society in the twentieth century.

Returning to the effort of the Christian synods to segregate Jews from Christians, we see that the fourth synod at Toledo in 633 prohibited converted Jews from having dealings in any manner with other Jews (their relatives, of course) and that no Jew could lie with his Christian wife unless he converted to Christianity. Children of such unions were to be forced to become Christians and live with the Christian parent alone if the Jewish parent would not convert.[15]

Twenty laws against the Jews were confirmed by the 12th synod of Toledo in the year 681 C.E. These laws had been decreed by King Erwig and added to the "Leges Wisigoth," the Visigothic code of law. These laws were as follows:

1. that the old laws against the Jews were renewed;
2. that Jews not insult the trinity;
3. that Jews not withdraw themselves, their sons or their male servants from baptism, i.e., conversion;
4. that they not celebrate the Passover in their manner, conduct circumcisions or divert a Christian from his beliefs;
5. that they not celebrate their Sabbaths or festivals;
6. that they stay away from work on Sunday;
7. that they not make any distinctions among foods;

8. that they not advise relatives;
9. that they not attack the Christian religion or defend their sect;
10. that they not emigrate so as to apostate again (apostanai=to rebel);
11. that no Christian accept a gift from a Jew which could injure his beliefs;
12. that no Jew read books rejected by the true faith (Christianity);
13. that no Jew hold Christian slaves;
14. that Jews not pretend to be Christians so as to keep their Christian slaves;
15. the law concerning the creed of converted Jews and the oath they must give;
16. the law concerning those Christians who were slaves of Jews and who did not consider themselves Christians;
17. that no Jew, unless authorized by the king, rule over or punish a Christian;
18. that slaves of Jews be freed if they converted to Christianity;
19. that no Jew rule as landlord over a Christian family of serfs; and
20. that every Jew entering the country notify the bishop or a priest of that locality and that the bishop call the Jews to appear before him on certain days.[16]

In the seventh century, the 16th Synod of Toledo ruled that every law against the Jews must be followed exactly, as this was thought to force the Jews to convert. In addition, the synod underscored that Jews who did convert would no longer have to pay the special tax all Jews had to pay and that the converts would have the same rights as all other subjects of the king. This inducement evidently did not convince very many Jews to become Christians, since the following year, 694 C.E., that same synod of Toledo ruled that Jews should be robbed of their fortunes, that the king should make them into slaves and that their children should be removed from them in their seventh year and be married to Christians. Further, the synod expressed the opinion that Jews are guilty of all sorts of crimes and that they seek to ruin the fatherland (Spain) and the people and that they must be punished accordingly.[17]

Thus, the seventh century ended on a note of hostility toward the European Jewish population on the part of the Christian majority expressed in laws that led to segregation, contempt and fear.

IV

The measures taken by Christian councils and synods against the Jews by the end of the seventh century were of course followed by yet more stringent laws of later ages. They sufficed, however, to start Christian-Jewish relations upon a path of discrimination which followed all those levels of discriminatory conduct identified by sociologists as antecedents to mass murder (i.e., genocide).

Discrimination is usually analyzed by sociologists at five levels: verbal expression, avoidance, exclusion, physical abuse and massacres or genocide.

As we have already seen, the Christian synods and legislation from other sources promoted the first three of these levels of discrimination against the European Jews on theological grounds and, as we shall see later in this book, led predictably to the last two levels.[18]

For example, St. John Chrysostome and others preached sermons against the Jews, sometimes causing their listeners to become enraged and to hold the Jews of their own time and place responsible for the death of Jesus. Such crowds then burned synagogues, assaulted Jews in their homes and on the streets and at a minimum practiced avoidance and exclusion of Jews from their own circle of friends and neighbors.

Anti–Jewish pamphlets were circulated in almost all Christian communities for centuries, culminating with the writings of Martin Luther, who in the 16th century published the most violent anti–Jewish tracts produced to that time, *On the Jews and Their Lies* and *Vom Schem Hamphoras*.

In the ninth century, Agobard, the Archbishop of Lyon, France, brought before the synod meeting in that city in 829 two letters dealing with "the Jewish danger." One of these letters was also signed by Archbishop Bernard of Vienne and Bishop Eaof of Chalons.

The first letter complained about the increasing number of Jews near Lyon. The archbishop asked the synod to discuss how best to prevent Christian maids from celebrating the Sabbath with Jews and how to prevent them from eating with Jews.

Agobard argued that no Christian should buy meat from a Jew or drink wine bought from them.

Agobard's second letter demands a sharp separation between Christians and Jews. Arguing that Judaism is most revolting, Agobard thought he could prove his point by citing the Church fathers, a number of French Councils and even the Talmudic teaching of the Jews themselves.[19]

Here, then, we have examples of verbal expression, avoidance and exclusion as practiced by the Church fathers, by the early Christians and by the Christians of the first ten centuries. Avoidance and exclusion are evident in the list of measures taken at the 12th Synod of Toledo in 681 and thereafter in other synods.

A good example of physical abuse was the ruling of the Synod of Toulouse in 883. Here discussion concerning the Jews led to the conclusion that the Jews called the "Saracens" (i.e., Moslems) to Gallica or France. To atone for this supposed affront, the synod ruled and the emperor confirmed that on every Christmas, Good Friday and Ascension Day a Jew was to be given a powerful slap in the face in front of the church door and that the Jew receiving the slap was to shout three times, "It is just that the Jews must bend their neck under the beatings of Christians, as they are unwilling to submit to Christ."[20]

In 1179 the 11th General Synod affirmed once more that Jews could not own Christian slaves, could not live with Christians and could not testify in court against a Christian, although the testimony of Christians against Jews had to be accepted by a court.[21]

The fourth canon of the Synod of Avignon in 1209 went further. Jews were now forced not to work on Sundays and were prohibited from eating meat on Christian Holy Days. In addition, Jews were prohibited from taking usurious interest, although this was the only business to which Jews were admitted. Yet, by decree of Pope Innocent III, they were forced to return usurious interest to those from whom they received it.

"The mere expression, 'Jewish usury' has caused the greatest misery" says Guttman, "because it created a totally false impression, for the most limited amount of interest was labeled 'usury' in the middle ages because the taking of interest of any kind was prohibited by the church."

This prohibition for Christians could be maintained only because Jews were encouraged to enter the money-lending business. As soon as this was no longer the case, Christians did enter that business since lending was as necessary then as it is now.[22]

Thomas Aquinas argues that although it is a sin to induce anyone to take interest or enter the money-lending business, it is not a sin to borrow money from someone already in the business since such money can be used for good purposes. In short, Aquinas uses the well-worn argument that the ends justify the means.[23]

Perhaps the most important medieval council concerning the Jews was the Fourth Lateran Council, which met in 1215. The decree prohibiting Christians to deal with Jews sexually or to marry them as first passed by the Synod at Carthage was now repeated as the Council ruled that Jews and "Saracens" had to wear different clothes from Christians so that "because of ignorance, no fleshly mixup between them and female Christians and in reverse, between Christian men and female Jews can occur. In some provinces, this difference in clothing already exists. It must be installed everywhere."[24]

This was promptly done as evidenced by a number of such decrees such as the one passed by the Synod at Vienna in 1267 whose Canon 17 reads as follows: "When a Jew is caught in fornication with a Christian woman, he must be kept in a tough prison until he has paid at least ten marks. The Christian woman, who has chosen such damnable association is to be whipped out of town and to be chased away without any hope of ever being allowed to return."[25]

These same laws were passed by the German government during the National Socialist (Nazi) regime. On September 15, 1935, the following law, entitled "Law for the Protection of German Blood and German Honor," took effect in Germany.[26]

> 1) Marriages between Jews and citizens of German or kindred blood are prohibited. Marriages which are undertaken nevertheless are void even if, in order to evade this law, they are undertaken in a foreign country.
> 2) Extramarital affairs between Jews and citizens of German or kindred blood are prohibited.

Additionally, a police directive of September 1, 1941, directed Jews to wear a special insignia so that they could be easily recognized and not be confused with non-Jews. The order reads as follows:

> 1) Jews who have completed the sixth year are prohibited from appearing in public without the Jewish star.
> 2) The Jewish star consists of a six-pointed star of yellow cloth with a black boundary and the black inscription "Jew." This must be visibly sewn to the left breast of the garment.[27]

The Fourth Lateran Council also repeated and made universal the prohibition against Jewish office holders already in effect, as we have seen, in several local jurisdictions. Recalling the Synod of Toledo, Canon LXIX of Fourth Lateran then decreed that "Jews may not receive public office which permits them to gain power over Christians...."[28]

This too was ordained by the National Socialist government of Germany on April 7, 1933, when all Jews were dismissed from the German civil service as the "Law for the Reconstruction of the Professional Civil Service" went into effect.[29]

Blaming the victim is a common technique of neutralization. Sociologists have shown that this technique permits the offender to victimize the victim without his conscience worrying him as he holds himself guiltless and converts the victim into the aggressor.[30]

Using this rationale, the Synod at Narbonne decreed in Canon IV that every Jewish family must pay six dinars to the pastor's church and must also relinquish any interest due them, particularly if the money were owed by a crusader. These rules were also confirmed by the Council of Lyon in 1245 and the Synod of Beziers in 1246.[31]

This too was ordained by Nazi decree when on November 12, 1938, the Jews of Germany were forced to pay collectively 1 billion mark to the government for damage done by the Nazi gangs themselves as they smashed Jewish stores, burned synagogues and destroyed Jewish property all over Germany on the night of November 9–10, 1938.[32]

The last order of business of the Fourth Lateran Council was the Crusade decreed by Pope Innocent III for the year 1217. This was the fifth crusade. Two more were to occur in 1228 and in 1248.[33] As in the earlier crusades, these efforts to Christianize the Holy Land became an invitation to massacre the Jews living in Christian lands. Thus, from 1095 on, when Pope Urban II preached the first crusade, the fifth level of discrimination against the European Jews was reached by the Christian crusaders who thought it easier to massacre the defenseless Jewish infidels living among them than to take on the powerful Moslems in the far-off Holy Land. We have seen that hatred of Jews had been sanctioned by innumerable decrees and canons of the Church since 325 C.E. Hatred of Jews was not only the canon law of the Church, but also state policy everywhere in Europe. In addition, attacks on Jews were profitable. The crusaders, like so many other Europeans after them, were more than happy to seize the property of the Jews they had murdered all along the Rhine as the "Knights of the Cross" slaughtered so many Jewish families that popes Innocent IV and Gregory IX expressed their revulsion at the killings.[34]

Christians were always ambivalent about the use of physical force in attempting to convert Jews to Christianity. While some rushed to slaughter, others thought persuasion should be used. It was this milder attitude which led the Dominicans to attempt the conversion of Jews by means of sermons.

V

Sermons to the Jews were tried as early as the ninth century when the archbishop of Lyon, Agobard, indicated in his "Epistola de baptizandis Hebraeis" (Letter to the Baptized Hebrews) that the clergy of that city preached at the Jews inside their synagogues every Saturday. Attendance was compulsory.

James the First of Aragon mentions conversion sermons again in 1242. The practice continued through the 13th century in Spain and became more general when these sermons received papal approval in 1278. Thereafter the Jews in the papal states were forced to listen to conversion sermons all the time. "Beadles armed with rods saw to it that they paid attention and examined their ears to ensure that they were not plugged."[35]

From Rome, the conversionist sermons passed to all of Italy. Such sermons were preached in the churches of Florence, Ferrara, Padua and other places until the French Revolution in 1789. Jews were of course forced to attend these churches. What the Jews thought of these sermons is best captured by the poet Robert Browning in his poem "Holy Cross Day" or by the fact that hardly anyone was converted by these efforts.[36]

V

Born in 1225 at Aquinas, in southern Italy, St. Thomas was undoubtedly the foremost interpreter of Christian theology in the Middle Ages. His influence was not great in his own day but grew in later centuries as evidenced by the large number of books and articles published every month about him as late as the last decade of the twentieth century. His great work on theology and his many other writings contain only two references to the Jews. The first is his treatment on "Disbelief" and the other a letter he wrote to the Duchess of Brabant entitled "De Regime Judaeorum ad Ducissam Brabantiae," or "On Ruling the Jews for the Duchess of Brabant." This is part of his *Summa Theologica*.[37]

It is of course not possible for St. Thomas to have influenced the councils and the synods of the Church before he was born. The anti–Jewish beliefs and legislation promoted by the Church fathers on these many occasions reflected commonly accepted beliefs which St. Thomas later confirmed in part, but rejected in other areas. As a teacher in the Catholic Church he did not see himself as a reformer, but accepted and integrated into his system the conclusions of the various councils and synods concerning the Jews.[38] His influence surely supported later actions concerning Jews although the degree or extent of such influence is a source of endless controversy. It is my view that St. Thomas had little influence on the treatment of Jews in his own day but much more influence thereafter. It is important to present his views here because he was later recognized as Christendom's most important voice since St. Augustine. Furthermore, Thomas contributed to the anti–Jewish polemics of his own day and later times, not because he added anything to the level of anti–Jewish hatred already in existence in Europe, but because he lent his name and his work to the anti–Jewish measures already in force. Later anti–Jewish deeds could also be justified by pointing to the philosophical composure with which Thomas accepted the general conduct towards the Jews.[39]

In short, no discussion of any aspect of Christianity in the Middle Ages is possible without consulting the views of St. Thomas Aquinas including his views concerning the Jews.

Thomas's discussion of the Jews begins as a part of his essay on "Disbelief in General."[40] He writes in Article 6, entitled "Is the infidelity of heathens and pagans worse than that of others?", that "Among heresies the more hateful are those which contradict the truth of faith on more numerous and important points, thus that of Arius, who split the Godhead, was more detestable than that of Nestorius, who split Christ's humanity from the person of the Son of God. Now heathens depart from the faith on more numerous and important points than do Jews or heretics, for they do not accept the faith at all. Their unbelief, then, is the worst." Additionally, "heathens" are held to be the worst of "sinners" as compared to Jews and heretics. Says Thomas: "Again, every good lessens evil. Yet, there is good in the Jews for they profess that the Old Testament is from God, and also heretics, for they honor the New Testament. Therefore they sin less grievously than heathens, who detest both Testaments."[41]

In another respect St. Thomas holds that Jews and heretics are worse than heathens. He refers to the notion that "heathens have never known the way of justice, whereas Jews and heretics have abandoned it after having known it in some sense. Therefore theirs is the more grievous sin."

In his "Reply" to this proposition, Thomas says that "The infidelity of those who in effect attack by corrupting the Gospel faith they profess is more serious than that of the Jews who have never embraced it. Yet, since these on their part have received it figuratively in the Old Law, which they corrupt by their false interpretations, their unbelief is more grievous than that of heathens who have not accepted the Gospel faith in any way at all."

The second element relates to the corruption of matters of faith. "In this respect since heathens err on more heads than Jews, and Jews on more heads than heretics, the unbelief of heathens is more grave than that of Jews and that of Jews more grave than that of heretics . . . the unbelief of heretics is the very worst."[42]

By setting up a hierarchy of unbelievers, Thomas makes the assumptions of Christianity much more believeable and true than if there were only one category of unbelievers. If the world were to consist of only two categories of mankind, Christians and unbelievers, the two categories would be equal. But by having four such categories, heretics, Jews and heathens, as well as Christians, arranged in a hierarchial order, Christians triumph on the top and their Truth is even more pronounced and visible than would otherwise be the case. We see by this arrangement, however, that these three groups, Jews included, are pushed firmly into the "out-group" and are not given the same consideration as those who live by the Truth. For if ever there was a medieval argument for religious discrimination it was the view that Error must not have the same rights as Truth. Evidently no one considered that one man's Truth is another man's Error or that there is no truth nor error in the realm of belief.

Yet St. Thomas, like all Christian theologians before him, believed that the so-called Sinaitic legislation, the Old Testament, was completely appropriate for the time . . . as a striking symbol of the coming salvation under the 'new' covenant."[43]

Thirteenth century Europe knew slavery. In fact, as we have already seen, church law prohibited Jews from keeping Christian slaves, making it impossible for Jews to cultivate land and enter agriculture. St. Thomas agreed with this policy and wrote, "When the slave of a Jew becomes a Christian he should forthwith receive his freedom without paying a price....

"The church does no injustice here, since such Jews are themselves the subjects of the Church, and she can dispose of their possessions...."

St. Thomas also opposed cohabitation between Jews and Christians. "The Church permits Christians to work on lands belonging to Jews, because this does not entail their living together.... Nevertheless, if there be reason to fear the undermining of the faithful from such participation and intercourse it should be altogether forbidden."[44]

We have already seen that many synods and councils of the Church demanded that Jewish children be baptized Christians even against the will of their parents. St. Thomas opposed this practice. He presents the arguments for such practices in Article 12 of his *Summa* concerning disbelief. These arguments are chiefly that it would be a sin to refuse help to someone in danger of spiritual death, inasmuch as everyone is obliged to help those in danger of physical death.

Another argument for such practices, according to Thomas, is that children of slaves are themselves slaves and Jews are all "slaves of kings and princes." Hence the church can have Jewish children baptized against the will of their parents because "no injustice would be done" in having them baptized even though the parents are unwilling. In his "Reply" concerning this question, St. Thomas concludes however that "Never was it the usage of the Church to baptize Jewish children against their parents' will ... and, that it is a danger to the faith that a Jewish child be baptized against the parents' will" because they would influence him to change his mind on his maturity, and because "the custom would be repugnant to natural justice.... According to natural law a child ... is under the charge of his parents."[45]

In his letter "On Ruling the Jews," Thomas Aquinas concurs with the then-common Christian view that "Inasmuch as the Jews are the Church's serfs, it has the power to dispose of their wealth." (Nec in hoc injuriam facit ecclesia cum ipsi Judaei sint servi Ecclesiae, potest disponere de rebus eorum.) He further advises the duchess that Jews "were punished with eternal serfdom for their own guilt [for killing Jesus] according to canon law; the rulers were therefore entitled to take the Jews' money as if it were their own."[46]

In that same letter, Thomas also answers the question of the Duchess of Brabant as to whether she may force Jews to wear special clothes. In this Thomas concurs and supports his argument in favor of special Jewish clothing on the grounds that the Jews of the Old Testament followed the commandment to wear special fringes on their garments.[47]

Despite these opinions, St. Thomas wrote that "The Jews are also linked to the Church by the meaning of the ritual they practice, but they do not know what they are doing; consequently, no force may be applied to make Christians of them."[48]

Thomas Aquinas emphasized the "voluntary character of conversion." He was opposed to using force in order to spread the faith.[49] However, as we have seen, he was of the opinion that Jews were servants or slaves of the Christian Church and could therefore be deprived of their slaves without compensation. He thought Jews were ecclesiastical property. Jews thereby served two important functions for Christians. As infidels, unbelievers, they demonstrated the limits of acceptable conduct for Christians, and as symbols of all that is materialistic and acquisitive they also served as symbols of evil as contrasted with Christian "good." As we have seen before, Jews were used as vital examples for all Christians of "evils to be avoided."[50]

It is important to remember that thirteenth century Europeans never questioned the right of St. Thomas or anyone else to sit in judgment as to what constitutes "unbelief" or sin, to categorize the beliefs on anyone as good or bad or to comment on the religious views of others. Evidently the idea of the separation of religion from other human concerns was utterly unknown. Thirteenth century Europeans did not consider belief a private matter not to be discussed in polite society. On the contrary, the Church frequently staged "disputations" or public discussions between Christian and Jewish theologians, such as the one which took place in Paris in 1240 and led to the burning of the Talmud. St. Thomas never questioned the right of the church to conduct such a disputation or to burn the books. Thomas held the view that such disputations were useful if they served the purpose of rectifying "errors."[51]

In Article 7 of the same polemic, St. Thomas asks, "Should we enter into public debate with unbelievers?" He quotes the words of St. Paul: "Contend not in words, for it is to no profit, but to the subverting of the hearers." By this he meant to show that if a disputation with Jews were held by someone not learned in Christianity or uncertain of his belief, then it was to be avoided.[52]

Finally, it is worth noting that St. Thomas took considerable notice of Jewish philosophers who preceded him. He repeatedly mentions Isaac Israeli, Solomon ibn Gabirol and particularly and at great length Moses ben Maimon.[53]

Liebeschutz in his analysis of the influence of St. Thomas on the fate of the European Jews says, "It had not the slightest impact on the fate of Jewry."[54]

VI

The Jews of Europe never recovered from the Crusades. After the thirteenth century, Jewish life in Europe was precarious as Christian synods, councils and governments permitted them to live only to serve as an example and reminder "to all men that they are descended from the lineage of those who crucified our Lord Jesus Christ." So stated the Castilian Code of Alfonso X and so thought Christians everywhere as illustrated by the actions of the synods yet to come.[55]

Five local synods dealt with the Jews during the thirteenth and fourteenth centuries. The first of these was the Synod of Vienna, which in 1267 ordered that Jews had to wear a special "horned hat" in addition to other special clothing, that Jews could not enter a public bath house or tavern, that Jews could not employ Christian domestics and that Jews could not be tax collectors. Sexual contact between the religions was also prohibited. In addition, Jews and Christians were forbidden to eat with one another, Jews were told to return money collected from usurious loans and Jews were forced to stay off the streets on Good Friday or at any time that the sacrament was carried past their houses, a time when they were to close all their doors and windows. Jews were forbidden to build new synagogues or enlarge old ones, and finally Jews were warned not to convert Christians to Judaism.

The Hungarian National Synod in 1279 imitated the decree of the French King Louis IX of 1269 by ordering that Jews had to wear a red ring both on the front and back of their clothing and that in case they did not do so, they were to be fined, while their denunciator was to receive their garments. The German Synod of Aschaffenburg in 1292 confirmed all of these decrees as did the Synod of Mainz or Mayennece in 1310. This synod added that any Jew who became a Christian could never return to Judaism; those who did would be turned over to the Inquisition to be dealt with as a heretic. This was to be the case even if the Jew accepted baptism only because he feared otherwise to be killed. The Synod of Prague in 1349 added to these laws that no new synagogues could be built and that the old ones could not be enlarged.[56]

In 1434 the Council of Florence and Basel concerned itself once more with the Jews. It reaffirmed that Jews had to wear special clothing and could not work on Christian Holy Days nor on Sunday. Additionally, this council ordered that the universities should teach Hebrew, Chaldaic, Arabic and Greek so that special preachers could be trained to preach Christianity to the Jews who were to be forced to enter churches and hear these sermons. This was indeed done.[57]

One of those attending the Council of Basel was Nicholas of Cusa, also known as Nicholas Krebs (1401–1464). Born in Germany, he had become a cardinal and was well known for his extensive writings in theology, mathematics and philosophy.[58]

Remarkable among his writings is his book *De Pace Fidei*, or *Peace Among the Faiths*. "While maintaining the superiority of Christianity over other religions, he tried to reconcile their differences. Beneath their oppositions and contradictions he believed there is a fundamental unity and harmony, which, when it is recognized by all men, will be the basis of universal peace."[59]

De Pace Fidei is written as if the author had a dream in which Christ holds a great meeting of saints who report concerning the difficulties that agreement on religious matters produced. Men of several nationalities and religions participate and state their views. This even includes Jews whose opinions Cusanus, as he is commonly known, reports with good will. In fact, straying far from normal Christian attitudes of the times, he attributes to Jews sincerity and true religious commitment.

For example: "Jews are often willing to endure death in order to fulfill the law and its sanctity. If they did not believe that after death they will gain salvation because they prefer zeal for the law to life itself, they would not die. The belief of the Jews does not imply that there is no eternal life and that they cannot attain it. Otherwise, no one would die for the law. The fortune which they expect they do not expect on the grounds of works of the law, since that law does not promise it to them, but on the basis of belief, which presupposes Christ, as can be found above."[60]

Like Thomas Aquinas before him, Cusanus's efforts to take a more positive attitude towards the Jews and other non–Christian religions was ignored by his contemporaries. Instead, the position of the European Jews worsened when in the year 1452 the synod at Augsburg in Germany and the provincial synod at Cologne once more dealt with a Jewish concern. The principal discussion concerning Jews this time was their books. The well known controversy regarding the Talmud came before these meetings as the theological faculty at Cologne agreed with the Jewish apostate Johann Pfefferkorn that the Talmud should be destroyed on the grounds that it contains anti–Christian materials while the Christian Hebraist Johann Reuchlin defended the Talmud and succeeded in convincing Pope Leo X to defend Reuchlin's position, only to have the decision reversed four years later. By now, the powerful words of Martin Luther (1483–1546) entered this dispute as he had become the dominant force in European Christianity as leader of the Reformation.

There can be no doubt that the most important synod of the Church since Nicea was the Council of Trent, meeting from 1545 to 1547 in that Austrian city. That council dealt with the Reformation and the rebellion of Luther. It said nothing about the Jews, nor did it need to do so. The fate of the Jews had been sealed by all that had been said and done already.

It is remarkable that in 1556 Pope Pius V in his Catechism of the Council of Trent for Parish Priests stated that the guilt for the death of Christ "seems more enormous in us than in the Jews, since according to the testimony of the same Apostle, 'If they had known it, they would never have crucified the Lord of Glory' [*Corinthians 2:8*] while we, on the contrary, professing to know Him, yet denying Him by our actions, seem ... to lay violent hands on Him."[61]

Principally, the Christian clergy had succeeded in divorcing the European Jews from normal relationships with their European Christian neighbors. That this divorce needed constant reinforcement is evident from the numerous decrees or canons issued by councils and synods for years. Evidently, this was deemed necessary because the daily lives of Christians and Jews led to constant friendly relationships between them so that only the heavy weight of religious decree succeeded in bringing about the social distance which normal human intercourse would not permit.

We have every reason to believe that given a different theology, or no comment concerning Jews at all, Christian-Jewish relations between the third and the twentieth centuries in Europe would have been, and evidently frequently were, friendly, pleasant and productive. But theologians would have it otherwise even after the Protestant Reformation in the sixteenth century had created a rift in Christianity which has never healed. Beginning with the Lutheran revolt it was the turn of the Protestant Christians to deal with the Jews. Moreover, the Catholic Church did not hold another ecumenical council until 1870 at the Vatican. That council did not discuss the Jews at all. It was only at Vatican II that, on October 28, 1965, Pope Paul signed a historic Declaration on the Jews which sought to place the church in opposition to persecution and hatred of Jews for the first time in its history. Of that we will speak later.

Thus, we now turn to the Protestant reaction to Judaism and the Jews and begin with Desiderius Erasmus who, although not a Protestant, was the most influential Catholic of his day as his views greatly influenced the Reformers.

Notes

1. Emile Durkheim, *The Rules of the Sociological Method* (1895; reprint, Glencoe, Ill., The Free Press, 1950), pp. 68–69.
2. D. Cummings, trans., *The Rudder* (Pedalion) of the Metaphorical Ship of the One Holy Catholic and Apostolic Church, Chicago, The Orthodox Christian Educational Society, 1957, pp. lx and lxi.
3. *Ibid.*, p. 113.
4. *Ibid.*, pp. 127–128.
5. *Ibid.*, p. xvi.

6. *Ibid.*, pp. xv–xix.
7. *Ibid.*, pp. 383 and 385.
8. *Ibid.*, pp. 438–439.
9. *Ibid.*, pp. 534, 564, 567, 568, 747 and 951.
10. *Ibid.*, p. 600.
11. See: James George Frazier, *The Golden Bough*, Chapter 5 (1922; reprint, New York, Macmillan, 1960) and Edward Burnett Tyler, *Religion in Primitive Culture*, Chapter 18 (New York, Harper & Bros., 1958) for a discussion of the widespread belief in the effect of blessings and prayers upon agricultural and human fertility.
12. Carl Joseph von Hefele, *Concilgeschichte*, Vol. 1 (Freiburg, Germany Herder'sche Verlagshandlung, 1873), p. 178. The English version of this work is William Clark, trans., *A History of the Councils of the Church* (Edinborough, T. and T. Clark, 1896).
13. *Ibid.*, Vol. 2, pp. 594, 683, 776; Vol. 3 (1877), p. 332 and Vol. 4, pp. 546 and 757.
14. *Ibid.*, p. 146 ... dass sie Versuche zur Judaisirung des ganzen Landes wagen zu dürfen glaubten.
15. *Ibid.*, Vol. 3 (1877), p. 37.
16. *Ibid.*, p. 318.
17. *Ibid.*, p. 353.
18. See: Gordon Allport, *The Nature of Prejudice* (Reading, Mass., Addison, Wesley, 1954), p. 251; Robin Williams, *The Stranger Next Door* (Englewood Cliffs, N.J., Prentice-Hall, 1964), p. 150; James W. Van der Zanden, *American Minority Relations* (New York, Ronald Press, 1972), pp. 460–469; and a host of other publications concerning research in this area.
19. Hefele, *op. cit.*, Vol. 4 (1879), pp. 70–71.
20. *Ibid.*, p. 544.
21. Canon 26, Eleventh General Synod, *Ibid.*, Vol. 5, p. 716.
22. J. Guttmann, *Das Verhältniss des Thomas von Aquinos zum Judenthum und zur jüdischen Literatur* (Göttingen, Vandenhoeck & Ruprecht's Verlag, 1891), p. 9. "Schon der blosse Ausdruck, 'jüdischer Wucher' hat, durch die falschen Vorstellungen, die er erweckt, das grösste Unheil angerichtet, denn bekanntlich wird im Mittelalter, weil nach Bestimmungen des kanonischen Gesetzes jedes Zinsnehmen untersagt war, auch der massigste Zins als Wucher bezeichnet."
23. *Ibid.*, p. 10.
24. Hefele, *op. cit.*, Vol. 5, p. 899.
25. *Ibid.*, Vol. 6, p. 104.
26. Reichsgesetzblatt Teil I, Seite 1146 in Bruno Blau, *Das Ausnahmerecht für die Juden in Deutschland* (Düsseldorf, Verlag Allgemeine Wochenzeitung der Juden in Deutschland, 1965), p. 30.
27. Reichsgesetzblatt Teil I, Seite 547 in *Ibid.*, p. 89.
28. Hefele, *op. cit.*, Vol. 5, p. 900.
29. Blau, *op. cit.*, p. 13.
30. Gresham Sykes and David Matza, "Techniques of Neutralization: A Theory of Delinquency," *American Sociological Review*, Vol. 22 (1957), pp. 664–670.
31. Hefele, *op. cit.*, pp. 1119 and 1144.
32. Blau, *op. cit.*, p. 53, Reichsgesetzblatt I, p. 1579. Also see: Martin Gilbert, *The Holocaust* (New York, Henry Holt, 1985), pp. 66–75.
33. James Westfall Thompson and Edgar Nathaniel Johnson, *An Introduction to Medieval Europe* (New York, W.W. Norton, 1937), pp. 515–560.

34. Solomon Grayzel, *A History of the Jews* (Philadelphia, The Jewish Publication Society of America, 1947), pp. 339–358.
35. Solo Whittmayer Baron, *A Social and Religious History of the Jews*, Vol. 9 (New York, Columbia University Press, 1965), pp. 79 and 274, and Vol. 14, pages 60–61. See also: Solomon Grayzel, *The Church and the Jews in the Thirteenth Century*, Kenneth R. Stone, ed. (Detroit, Wayne State University Press, 1989, Vol. 2), pp. 1254–1314.
36. Robert Browning, *The Poems and Plays of Robert Browning* (Bennet A. Cerf and Donald Klopfer, eds., New York, The Modern Library, 1934), pp. 176–179.
37. Etienne Gilson, *The Christian Philosophy of St. Thomas Aquinas* (New York, Random House, 1975). See also: Thomas Aquinatis, *Opera Omnia* (Parisiis, Luduviccum Vives, 1889).
38. Guttmann, *op. cit.*, p. 2.
39. *Ibid.*, p. 2.
40. St. Thomas Aquinas, *Summa Theologicae* (New York, McGraw Hill, 1975), pp. 53–57 and 71–77.
41. *Ibid.*, p. 55.
42. *Ibid.*, p. 57.
43. H. Liebeschutz, "Judaism and Jewry in the Social Doctrine of Thomas Aquinas," *The Journal of Jewish Studies*, Vol. 13, 1962, p. 58.
44. *Ibid.*, p. 71.
45. *Ibid.*, p. 77. See also: Guttmann, *op. cit.*, p. 3.
46. Salo Wittmayer Baron, "'Plenitude of Apostolic Powers' and Medieval Jewish Serfdom," in *Ancient and Medieval Jewish History: Essays*, Leon A. Feldman, ed. (New Brunswick, N.J., Rutgers University Press, 1972), p. 295.
47.a. This refers to Numbers, xv, 37–41, which reads in the Hebrew text as follows: "Veosuh lochem Tzitzit al kanfay bigdayhem"; i.e., "and order them to make fringes in the corners of their garments." This is done to this day by orthodox Jewish men, who wear a special undergarment at all times which holds these fringes. In addition, Jewish men, and now some Jewish women, wear a prayer shawl at religious services which holds the mandated fringes.
   b. The entire text of "De Regimine Judaeorum" ("On the Governance of the Jews") may be found in English and Latin in J.G. Dawson, trans., *Aquinas: Selected Political Writings* (New York, Barnes and Noble, 1959), pp. 84–95.
48. Liebeschutz, *op. cit.*, p. 63.
49. Guttmann, *op. cit.*, p. 3.
50. *Ibid.*, pp. 64–74.
51. Guttmann, *op. cit.*, p. 5.
52. Thomas Aquinas, *Summa Theologica* II, 2 qu. 10 art. 7. "Ex parte vero audientium considerandum est, utrum illi, qui disputationem audiunt, sunt instructi et firmi in fide, aut simplices et in fide titubantes."
53. Guttmann, *op. cit.*, p. 15.
54. Liebeschutz, *op. cit.*, p. 81.
55. Nathan Ausubel, *The Book of Jewish Knowledge* (New York, Crown, 1964), p. 273.
56. *Ibid.*, Vol. 6, pp. 501 and 688.
57. Hefele, *op. cit.*, p. 589. See also: Ausubel, *op. cit.*, p. 130.
58. *The Encyclopedia of Philosophy* (New York, Macmillan, 1967), pp. 496–498.
59. *Ibid.*, p. 498.
60. Nicholaus von Kues, *Philosophische-Theologische Schriften*, Leo Gabriel, ed. (Vienna, Verlag Herder, 1967), p. 776. "Iudaei pro observantia legis et eius

sanctimonia morti saepe se tradunt. Unde nisi crederent se felicitatem post mortem ex eo assecuturos, quia zelum legis praeferunt vitae, non mererentur. Non est igitur fides Iudaeorum non esse vitam aeternam, ac quod illam assequi non possint. Alias nemo omnium mereretur pro lege. Sed felicitatem quam expectant non expectant ex operibus legis—quia ille legis illam non promittunt—, sed es fide, quae Christum praesupponit, ut supra dictum reperitur."

61. McHugh and Callan, eds., *Catechism of the Council of Trent for Parish Priests* (New York, Joseph F. Wagner, 1923), pp. 50–61 and 362–365.

The Contributions of
Protestants and Others

3

Erasmus and Luther

Desiderius Erasmus (1469–1536)

I

Geert Geerts or Gerhard Gerhards was the original name of "The Desired Beloved" as he called himself. Widely acclaimed as a humanist, Erasmus satirized the Catholic Church, incessantly pointed at abuses within it, insisted on an increase in human knowledge for the benefit of mankind, promoted the influence of reason upon religion, translated the Greek classics into Latin and lived and died a Catholic.

Although Erasmus was not the founder of any Protestant movement, his views concerning the Jews is of great importance to the Protestant cause since his opinions on all subjects, particularly on theological issues, influenced Martin Luther and other reformers considerably and remain influential to this day.

Hocking says that "Humanism can be fulfilled only in a world that sustains the zest of doing one's human job as a religious observance."[1]* This definition describes the efforts of Erasmus, who remained a Christian all his life and was a humanist, in not the agnostic but the Christian sense.

"It is widely acknowledged," says Markish, "that north of the Alps humanism differed from the Italian version in the sharp expression of its religious coloration. For the English, French and German humanists Christian faith and Christian piety were not just the rules of the game but rather the games' essence and meaning. For exactly this reason Erasmus was first and foremost a Christian theologian."[2]

*Notes to this chapter begin on page 76.

II

Only two writers have devoted entire books to the views Erasmus had of the Jews.

In 1969 Guido Kisch published *Erasmus' Stellung zu Juden und Judentum* or *Erasmus' Attitude Toward Jews and Judaism*, and in 1986 the Russian writer Shimon Markish published the English version of *Erasmus and the Jews*.[3]

Kisch concludes that Erasmus was an anti–Semite, but Markish disagrees despite the thorough and exhaustive treatment he gives to Erasmus's anti–Jewish polemics.

The scholar Arthur A. Cohen believes that Markish judged the views of Erasmus from the vantage point of Russian experience and therefore found Erasmus less vicious than would be thought from the American point of view where, according to Cohen, "traditions of anti–Semitism are no more distinguished and publicly endorsed than any other mode of ethnic contempt."[4]

The second reason for the difference in evaluation of Erasmus's attitude between Kisch and Markish may well be Markish's failure to distinguish between anti–Judaism as expressed by Erasmus and anti–Semitism, an attitude not known in Erasmus's day and not fully developed until practiced by the Germans of the late nineteenth and early twentieth centuries.

The phrase "anti–Semitism" was invented in 1873 by the German journalist Wilhelm Marr. Marr also founded the League of Anti-Semites after publishing a best-selling book entitled *The Victory of Judaism over Teutonism*. These efforts by Marr, which changed religious anti–Judaism to racial hatred, were unknown to Erasmus, who lived 350 years earlier. Therefore, it is ipso facto inaccurate to call Erasmus an anti–Semite. Anti–Judaism is not anti–Semitism because the latter claims, in Nazi terminology, "Die Religion ist einerlei—in der Rasse liegt die Schweinerei"; i.e., "Religion is indifferent—the swinishness is in the race." Anti–Jews permit Jews an escape from persecution if they are willing to become Christians. Anti–Semites allow no such escape since they view Jewishness as an inborn racial condition to which believing Christians and other non–Jews are also subject so long as they have one Jewish grandparent.

Therefore, the anti–Jews seek Jewish conversion. The anti–Semites seek Jewish death. For them, nothing less will do since they view Jews as "Ungeziefer," vermin whose nature cannot change and whose "crimes" are the consequence of racial characteristics.[5] Examining now the writings of Erasmus we turn to the *Colloquies* because these "Conversations" were censured by the Church as they contained "heresies" and ridiculed many an established belief. Thus, Erasmus challenged innumerable orthodoxies and was charged with "indecencies and irreverence."[6]

Yet, when it comes to the Jews, Erasmus was indeed orthodox in his writings and enhanced rather than reduced hatred of Jews by repeating all of the prejudices and invidious distinctions which we met already in the fourth century. Moreover, Erasmus claimed that he had written the *Colloquies* especially for the instruction of the young to whom he therefore imparted all of the hatreds and demeaning bigotries which his comments on the Jews had to produce in any reader.

Erasmus even blamed the Jews of his day for the disturbances the Reformation had caused in Europe and claimed that the violence stemming from the rebellion of the peasants in Germany came about because the participants were largely Jews, "who hate Christ."[7]

III

The Godly Feast was published by Erasmus in 1522 and contains the common rhetoric to the effect that Judaism is only sterile ritualism while Christianity is an advanced state of true understanding and love. "God rejects the Jews," says Erasmus. "Saturated with greed, pride, theft, hatred, envy and other sins, they thought God much in their debt because they frequented the Temple on holy days, offered burned sacrifices, abstained from forbidden foods, and fasted occasionally." The Christian belief that "God rejects the Jews" is here related to the Jewish food laws, a relationship which Christians have produced since Appolinaris wrote *Adversus Judeaus* in 175 C.E. (see Chapter 1). The Jewish Sabbath observance also does not escape unscathed by Erasmus. "The Jews rescued an ass if it fell into a ditch on the Sabbath," complains Erasmus, "yet reviled Christ for healing a man on the Sabbath."

Since stories concerning the Christian savior have no meaning to Jews and are unknown to them, this complaint evidently sought to arouse anti-Jewish attitudes in Erasmus's readers in the same sense as Luther sought later to arouse such sentiments by perpetuating the view that Jews are mere ritualists without any sense of charity or kindness.

The charge of deicide is also not foreign to Erasmus. In *An Examination Concerning Faith* Erasmus lets a fictional Aulus say, "Do you believe he was really seized by the Jews, bound, assailed and beaten, spit upon, mocked, scourged," etc.[8]

Here we also read the same accusations against Judaism made since the days of the early Church fathers, in that Erasmus seeks to distinguish Judaism from Christianity by holding that the "Jewish distinction of foods" has been abrogated by God, that God "abominates the feast days of the Jews," that Jews have a "superstitious reverence for the Law," and that the "New" testament has of course supplanted the "Old."[9]

To all this are added numerous discussions of the Jewish food laws, all designed to show that Christianity needs no food laws because it is of the spirit while Judaism is empty ritual.

"Judaism I call not Jewish impiety, but prescriptions about external things, such as food, fasting, clothes...."[10]

Erasmus's obsession with "Jewish ceremonies" is repeated throughout his work. In 1517 Erasmus accused the monks of slipping into Judaism because of their supposed interest in the Jewish "ceremonies," and in 1521 he wrote, "I followed no other goals than to resurrect the humanities, which among us are almost consigned to the grave; further, to rouse the world, sunk in Jewish ceremonies, to take trouble about true evangelical piety...."[11]

Obsessed with the view that Judaism is empty and wrong, Erasmus wrote in 1523, "Just as we justifiably view the religion of the Jews as empty and wrong because they treat the Book of their Law with peculiar reverence, place the cleanest linen under it, fall down before it and pray to it, touch it only with the cleanest hands, while godlessly ignoring that which the Law prescribes in the first place, so we must be careful that we are not pious worshipers of the gospel and its ceremonies...."[12]

Erasmus knew a good deal about the Jewish Law and despised it because he saw in it a form of legislation which was only interested in gaining salvation though the observance of minute details concerning food, dress, prayer, feasts and fasts.

He also worried that the sixteenth century interest in Hebrew would lead some Christians to return to Judaism, which Erasmus viewed as a catastrophe.

As to the synagogue, Erasmus endlessly repeats the phrase, "synagogue of Satan," first used in *Revelation 2:9* and *3:9*. Support for such opinions of Jews and the synagogue is of course already visible in the New Testament as seen in *St. Luke 19:48* or *St. Mark 11:18*, both of which deal with the theme of Christ misunderstood and rejected by the Jews. The belief that the Jews were degraded and denounced by God himself is however *not supported by the Gospels*, despite the frequent assertion of this theme among so many Christian theologians of the past. Thus, in *Romans 11:1* St. Paul says, "Has God rejected his people? By no means." In *Acts of the Apostles 4:27* it appears that both the Romans and the Jews are held responsible for the death of Jesus: "There were gathered together against thy holy servant Jesus, whom thou didst anoint, both Herod and Pontius Pilate with the gentiles and the people of Israel." This passage does not call for the kind of "Christ killer" mentality which led to so much bloodshed for so many centuries after the crucifixion.

Nevertheless, Ersamus chose to interpret Judaism in the most bigoted terms despite the evidence that the New Testament allows a far more favorable interpretation. This was undoubtedly the consequence of the century old theological interpretations concerning Jews begun in the main by St. John Chrysostom and St. Augustine and continued ever after.[13]

Kisch argues that Erasmus was aware of the expulsion of the Jews from Spain (1492) and that this event and the general disdain for Jews common in all of Europe in Erasmus's lifetime made Erasmus's attitude toward Jews almost inevitable.

Anyone, however, who still does not see the anti–Jewish bigot in Erasmus need only look at the list of epithets he heaps upon Jews as quoted by Markish from Erasmus's *Desiderii Erasmi Roterodami Opera Omnis emendatiora et auctiora* or "All of the Works of 'The Desired Beloved' of Rotterdam, Improved and Increased." Jews are marked by faithlessness and blindness and are "envious, stubborn, ungrateful, corrupt, impious, superstitious, arrogant, malicious, suspicious, slanderous, coarse and stupid, savage, rabid, jealous and of a hopelessly base nature." Furthermore they are "despised by all people (*contempti ab omnibus nationibus*) and pitiful, abject and sterile."[14]

Erasmus's letters are used by Guido Kisch to highlight Erasmus's views regarding the Jews.

"In a relatively early letter," says Kisch, "Erasmus praises France because 'it alone is free of heretics, Bohemian schismatics, Jews and half jewish Marranos [swine]....'"[15]

In another letter, written to Wolfgang Capito, Erasmus worries that the resurgence of Hebrew studies and Judaism could lead to a renewed interest in this "pest" and that there is nothing more antagonistic or dangerous for the Christian faith than Judaism.

This negative attitude toward Judaism and Jews seems out of place in Erasmus because all of his biographers have repeatedly pointed to his religous tolerance, his struggle for freedom of religion, his ethics and his reputed rejection of all dogmatisms.

IV

Kisch compares Erasmus's attitude toward the Jews with those of Ulrich Zasius and Johann Reuchlin. Zasius was a leading jurist of his time[16] whose views concerning the Jews are best understood by this passage: "The Jews are exceedingly ungrateful to the Christians, curse them each day publicly with curses and maledictions, exploit them through their usury, refuse them their help, ridicule our clearly understandable beliefs and besmirch them constantly. They turn against our Savior publicly with the most shameful blasphemies. Most hideous however is that the Jews yearn for the blood of Christians and thirst for it day and night.... Why then should the princes not be entitled to kick out such grim beasts [truculentas bestias], why not drive them out of the territory of the Christians? One must permit this most revolting excrement to sink into the bilging darkness."[17]

Having delivered this hate tirade, Zasius then ruled that Roman law pertaining to slaves also pertained to Jews and concluded that it would be legal and justifiable to convert Jewish children, while still minors, against the will of their parents. He even declared that a prince had the right to remove a small child from his Jewish parents and to baptize it.

Johann Reuchlin was a sixteenth century Christian student of Hebrew who used his knowledge of that language to defend the Talmud against the accusations of the apostate Pfefferkorn who sought to have the Talmud burned so as to protect Christians against the alleged anti-Christian contents of those books.

Reuchlin was no friend of the Jews. He studied Hebrew because he believed that this would permit him to convert the Jews to Christianity. Nevertheless, he did not make accusations concerning the drinking of Christian blood; nor did he, like Luther, who also knew some Hebrew, suggest the destruction of the Jewish communities in Germany if the Jews would not convert.

In 1539, a commission of preachers including the Strasbourg theologian Martin Bucer published an "Opinion on Whether a Government Can Allow Jews to Live Among Christians." This came as a result of a petition by Jews to the Landgrave of Hesse asking to be permitted to do business in his principality. The commission recommended against Jewish settlement and "reached back to Roman Civil Law and canon law to rediscover the limits for tolerating Jews." Bucer added a letter which argued that Jews could not be allowed to practice any craft which relied on shared trust. He also complained about the alleged Jewish power over everyone else on the grounds of their domination of the "money-trades." He did not of course remember that Jews were forced into the money trades because they were not permitted any other trade, nor did he comment on the large Christian-owned banks then already far wealthier than the Jews of Europe.

These polemics were outdone in their irrationality and hate by the Catholic Dr. Johann Eck as Eck was consulted by the bishop of Eichstatt concerning a blood accusation. This event had reputedly taken place in the bishop's jurisdiction. Eck published a pamphlet entitled *Ains Judenbuchlins Verlegung (Refutation of a Jew-book)* in which Eck claimed that he listed every anti-Jewish diatribe and hate-induced fairy tale against Jews that he could find. Moreover he claimed to have personally seen the Jews of a small German town commit such crimes. This book by Eck has been called "the worst book by a truly first-rate mind in the Reformation era."[18]

In sum, then, we see that Erasmus—like Zasius, Reuchlin, Bucer, Eck and Luther—was a son of his times. Like Nicholas Cusanus, yet another "great thinker of the late middle ages,"[19] Erasmus limited his humanism to Christians. Although he was able to critique his church and call for changes in morals and thought among his European contemporaries, he could not and would not rise above the most abject bigotries of his and every age since the beginnings of Christianity. He thereby became one of the unwitting contributors to the legitimization of the Holocaust.

That Erasmus had a tremendous influence on Luther, the founder of all that may be called Protestant Christianity, is best understood by noting that when Martin Luther was excommunicated in 1520, the papal nuncio (ambassador) Jerome Aleander, who posted the bull of excommunication, accused Erasmus of being the hidden fomenter of Luther's revolt and threatened him with the same possible penalty.[20]

Nevertheless, Erasmus never went as far as Luther in his militancy against the Catholic Church, which Erasmus never abandoned, or in his violent outbursts against the Jews which earned Luther the reputation of being the forerunner of Nazi bloodshed and the supporter of religious hate such as the Christian world had not seen before.

Martin Luther (1483–1546)

I

The contributions of Martin Luther to Christian history and theology are so vast and of such importance that the literature concerning him and his work encompasses entire libraries in every European language, particularly in German. For Luther was not only a major figure in the history of Christianity, but also surely a principal and dominant shaper of German history. Any discussion of the fate of the European Jews must therefore include the views of Luther concerning them, in particular since there are those who believe that the mass murder of the European Jews between 1933 and 1945 was the direct outcome of Luther's teaching and that it is possible to trace a linear connection from Luther to Hitler.[21]

Luther thus becomes a pivotal character in any discussion of the fate of the European Jews, not only because of his great influence upon the course of Christian-Jewish relations in Germany, but also because he represents very well all the accumulated hatred which Christians for 1,300 years before his birth had vented upon the Jews of every generation by expulsions, killings and tortures of every kind.

While it is undoubtedly true that religious sentiment constituted a principal motive in committing these cruelties, it is also true that greed and robbery motivated many of those who participated in the medieval pogroms and mass expulsions "which defiled the cities of Spain, France and Germany with blood."[22]

As a result of these pogroms, "When Martin Luther began lecturing on the Psalms at the University of Wittenberg in 1513, those Jews left in the empire were clinging to survival in small territories often controlled by a bishop or an abbot. The large territories and most of the imperial cities had expelled their Jews some years earlier. Only on rare occasions did Luther encounter Jews; he never lived in close proximity to them, but he inherited a tradition, both theological and popular, of hostility toward them. He lived within a larger community, Western Christendom, which saw the Jews as a rejected people, guilty of the murder of Christ and capable of murdering Christian children for their own evil purposes. And he lived within a community that had expelled its Jews some ninety years earlier."[23]

All of these events influenced the views of Luther, a born Catholic and founder of the Protestant Reformation. For in him we can see all that occurred before him and all that occurred after him in this sorry chapter of man's inhumanity to man.

It is of course a grave mistake to attribute to any one person, however influential, a solitary power to define the events of his time or subsequent events, entirely because of his own personality or his own abilities. On the contrary, as Leo Tolstoy contends in the epilogue to his monumental novel *War and Peace*, "the wielder of power" cannot alone determine the outcome of history.[24]

Luther, of course, had no power. He had instead a tremendous influence. Yet influence is circumscribed by the same limitations which restrict the power to coerce the behavior of others, namely the culture base.

The phrase culture base refers to the history of a people to the present. Thus, Christian and German history to the day of Luther not only influenced his thinking and his deeds, but made it possible for him to lead the Protestant movement of his day and to prescribe the treatment of the Jews both in his own time and thereafter.

A leader, obviously, is someone who has followers. Followers in turn are those who have reason to think that the leader says and does something that is in agreement with their interests and their beliefs. Anyone whose views are not in accordance with at least the major contentions of his day cannot expect to lead his followers into new ways of thinking because his arguments will go unrecognized and will therefore be rejected. There are of course many instances in which a social or a physical innovation has been proposed and rejected in the day of the proponent, only to be acclaimed at a later date. When George Boole (1815–1864) invented an algebra that now carries his name, his invention was viewed as a private curiosity—but in the twentieth century, his invention became the basis for the development of computer science. A similar fate befell Louis Pasteur (1822–1895) and Joseph Lister (1827–1912). Both Pasteur, who discovered bacteria, and Lister, who sought to apply Pasteur's discoveries to the practice of surgery, were rejected by contemporaries who did not understand the importance of their findings.

On the other hand, Albert Einstein (1879–1955) had little trouble finding acceptance for his discoveries in the field of physics because the culture base upon which he worked had been accepted by the physicists of his day.

Likewise, social inventions such as the Reformation needed a culture base in order to succeed. This is best illustrated by the fate of John Wycliffe (1320–1384) who translated the Latin version of the Bible into English a hundred years before Luther and who was posthumously condemned by the Church because, like Luther, he denied absolute papal authority and even rejected the doctrine of transsubstantiation.

These examples serve to illustrate that the conduct and the writings of Luther concerning the Jews found so much favor among his followers in both the sixteenth and the twentieth centuries because the ground had been well prepared to permit the growth of these hatreds. Thus Luther in some respects did not differ from his Christian predecessors, contemporaries or progeniture in his anti–Jewish attitude.

It is important to remember here that hatred of Jews existed in the fifteenth and sixteenth centuries in all of European Christendom. In 1492, when Luther was nine years old, Ferdinand and Isabella expelled all Jews from Spain in order to remove them from their converted relatives. These measures were taken in order to lessen the chance that these "New Christians," also called Marranos, or swine, would be tempted back into Judaism.[25]

A few years before these events occurred at one end of Europe, the Jews of Poland had been deprived of the privileges King Casimir had granted them earlier, as the clergy, the nobility and the people agitated against the Jews as "infidels" until Casimir in 1454 revoked the Statute of Nyeshava, which had given Jews protection against groundless charges, protection against physical attack and communal and judicial autonomy.[26]

Anti–Judaism was not Luther's only message concerning the Jews. In his early career, he proposed friendship with the Jews of his day and even objected to the treatment they had received.

Let us see what that earlier message was, and how Luther came to change his mind in his later years so that he is now widely charged with being a forerunner of the Nazi spirit.[27]

There are of course many examples of anti–Jewish writings dating to the Nazi epoch in German history. It is less well known that even before the National Socialist German Workers Party was able to capture the German government, large numbers of German Christians had already subscribed to an anti–Jewish attitude which was widely disseminated by leading Christian speakers and writers, such as the Lutheran court pastor of Kaiser Wilhelm II, Adolf Stöcker. Stöcker lost no opportunity to attack the Jewish citizens of Germany while blaming his victims for the defamations he rained upon them.[28]

Innumerable anti–Jewish writings and deeds can be recorded in Germany in every year since Luther's death, reaching a particular crescendo in the nineteenth century when the famous historian and professor Heinrich von Treitschke became a leader in the defamation of Jews generally.[29]

In 1972, the University of Munich published a large volume entitled *Luther's Attitude Toward the Jews in the Light of his Interpreters*.[30] In addition to a long list of earlier anti–Jewish authors who based their views on Luther, this book shows the manner in which Nazi newspapers and Nazi ideologues generally used Luther as a source for their anti–Jewish theses. The hate sheet *Der Stürmer*, devoted entirely to anti–Jewish propaganda, published innumerable anti–Jewish articles citing Luther.

For example, as early as 1925, eight years before the appointment of Hitler to the position of German chancellor and at a time when the editor of *Der Stürmer*, Julius Streicher, had no official government position, that paper cited Luther as an outspoken Jew hater. In March of 1928, *Der Stürmer* called upon Luther's spirit as one who sought to free the German people of the Jewish "pestilence." After attaining power in Germany, this Nazi sheet continued to cite Luther yet more often. In March of 1937 there appeared an article in *Der Stürmer* entitled "Judaism against Christianity" and in February of 1938 another article, "Luther and the Jews! Protestant Clergy! Open Your Eyes!" Both made much of Luther as a fighter for Christianity against Jewish domination and Jewish "power." In 1943, editor Streicher devoted an entire issue to Luther entitled "The Great Warner, Martin Luther," in which Streicher argues that Luther was not really interested in converting the Jews to Christianity, but fought them as a matter of self-defense in view of the "Jewish Danger" and their alleged destructiveness.[31]

It was also Streicher who used Luther's writings against the Jews as a defense at his trial before the Nuremberg War Crimes Tribunal.[32]

II

In the year 1523, when Martin Luther was 40, he published a pamphlet entitled *Das Jesus Christus ein Geborener Jude Sei* (*That Jesus Christ Was Born a Jew*). Written in German, the book ran through nine editions and was then translated into Latin so that it might receive international circulation.[33]

It must be understood that Luther's first and principal motive in writing this pamphlet was to refute the allegation that he had denied the virginity of Mary both before and after the birth of Christ. This report about Luther's possible apostasy was circulated by Catholics and consisted also of the allegation that Luther had denied the presence of the body and the blood at the Mass.[34]

In addition, Luther hoped to convert the Jews to Christianity by showing friendliness to those still adhering only to what Christians, but not Jews, call the Old Testament.[35]

It is important to keep in mind here, that Christian writers to this day frequently fail to recognize that many of the terms and much of the language used by them in relationshiip to Jews are of Christian making and are unknown in Judaism. One of these terms is "Old Testament." There is no "Testament" in Judaism either old or new. The Latin word testament, derived from the two words for witness and hand refer to the ancient practice of swearing by the male reproductive glands. Thus, the word "testis" means both "witness and "testicle."[36]

Although a custom resembling this practice did exist among the Hebrews, the Five Books of Moses, all of the Scriptures and all of the Jewish sacred tradition are together called the Torah by Jews, meaning "The Way."

In any event, Luther hoped to convert the Jews to Christianity by publishing this pamphlet which among other things said

> Those fools, the Papists, bishops, sophists, monks, have formerly so dealt with the Jews, that every good Christian would rather have been a Jew, and, having seen such stupidity and such blockheads reign in the Christian Church, I would rather have been a pig than a Christian. They have treated the Jews as if they were dogs, not men, and [as] if they were fit for nothing but to be reviled. They are blood relations of our Lord; therefore, if we respect flesh and blood, the Jews belong to Christ more than we.
>
> I beg therefore, my dear Papists, if you become tired of abusing me as a heretic, that you begin to revile me as a Jew.
>
> Therefore it is my advice that we should treat them kindly but now we drive them by force, treating them deceitfully or ignominiously, saying they must have Christian blood to wash away the Jewish stain, and I know not what nonsense. Also we prohibit them from working amongst us, from living and having social intercourse with us, forcing them, if they would remain with us, to be usurers.[37]

Luther believed, as have many Christians before and after him, that the conversion of the Jews to Christianity would herald the second coming of the Christian savior, Jesus. He also believed that the "Paraclete" or Holy

Ghost would soon appear inasmuch as the year 1558 was believed to be the "last year of human history."[38]

This belief was derived from the belief held by many Jews and Christians in Luther's day, and for some time before and since, in a form of Biblical numerology which to them contains hints as to future developments in human history. The Book of Daniel contains a phrase that some Christian believers thought referred to the fall of Constantinople to the Turks (1453) and to a period of 105 years succeeding that event. Luther thought the conversion of the Jews would "confirm his speculation" and permit him to see the Second Coming.[39]

The year in which Luther expressed these sentiments favorable to the Jews needs to be remembered. For in 1523, when he wrote these words, he was not yet well established, was still a rebel and had not yet won his great fight.[40]

In 1523 Luther sent a letter to a converted Jew named Bernard. Here he expressed his worry about the difficulty in converting the Jews, not only because so few were willing to convert, but also because the few who did were apparently not sincere in their new beliefs. In addition he believed that the Catholic Church would never succeed in converting the Jews since in his view the Church was itself living in error. His hope that many other Jews would follow Bernard's example was of course never realized. Here is part of that letter as translated from the Latin. This letter and many of Luther's other Latin writings were translated into German to give them wider circulation in Germany after Latin ceased to be the universal language it had been in Luther's day.

> Grace and peace from the Lord. The conversion of the Jews is in bad odor almost everywhere, not only among Christians but also among the Jews. The latter say that no one goes over from Judaism to Christianity in good faith, but that anyone who attempts it is guilty of some crime and cannot stay among the Jews. The Christians say that experience shows that they either return to their vomit [Judaism] or only pretend to have deserted Judaism. ... I think the cause of this ill repute is not so much the Jews' obstinacy and wickedness, but rather their absurd and asinine ignorance and the wicked and shameless life of popes, priests, monks and universities. ... They find fault with the Jews because they only pretend to be converted, but they do not find fault with themselves because they only pretend to convert them; nay, they seduce them from one error to another which is worse.
> But when the golden light of the Gospel is rising and shining, there is hope that many of the Jews will be converted in earnest.[41]

The endless hope and effort, particularly on the part of the Reformers and Protestants, to convert Jews to Christianity can also be seen by looking at a pamphlet from the year 1524 and published in German.[42]

The pamphlet is entitled *A Discussion Between a Christian and a Jew*. The unknown author depicts a discussion between a Jew and a Christian at an inn where both are guests overnight. The discussion lasts all night and when the Jew finally leaves in the morning, the Christian continues the discussion with the landlord. The sum of these two "discussions" illustrates the general Protestant point of view concerning Jews as taught first by Luther. Here too, the views of Luther as first encountered in *That Jesus Christ Was Born a Jew* find expression.

The author begins by listing all of the same old anti-Jewish canards that all earlier centuries had emphasized—the beliefs that Jews damn all Christians in Jewish prayers, poison the supply of drinking water, murder Christian children in order to drink their blood, are incessantly motivated by greed, hate all authority and have too much influence on the government and the judiciary.[43]

All of this Luther had denied in his essay of 1523, and the Christian in the *Discussion Between a Christian and a Jew* echoes his view: "If we want to help them [the Jews] then we must treat them with Christian love and be friendly to them and let them trade and work so that they may have cause to be among us and with us and hear our Christian teachings and see our Christian life."[44]

Having spoken well of the Jews in his own pamphlet, Luther now expected them to convert to the Christian point of view.

In this Luther was of course disappointed. In addition, he was indeed reviled as a "Judaizer" as were the Humanists because they wished to study Hebrew. The Calvinists accused the Unitarians of "Judaizing"; the Catholics, or Papists as Luther called them, lost no time calling him a "Judaizer," and he was in addition held responsible for the "Judaizing" reputedly attempted by the Ana-baptists and the Sabbatarians. Finally, Luther's enemies published their suspicions that Luther was in fact himself a Jew even as he labeled his opponents Jews. Luther fought various Christian scholars of Hebrew and accused translators of the Bible of following the Hebrew text too closely, thus "Judaizing."

Not only other Christians but Jews as well at first believed that the Protestant interest in the Hebrew language and their efforts to study Cabbalistic mysticism were indications that the Reformers sought to become Jews. It may well be that Luther went to extraordinary lengths to show his hatred and disdain for Judaism, as did almost all other leaders of the Reformation, in order to defend himself against this charge.[45]

Whatever the reason, this accusation of "Judaizing" was used by Luther's enemies against him, by Luther against his enemies and by almost all of the Christian participants in the religious disputes of the sixteenth century. Thus, Johann Reuchlin was attacked as "Judaizer" by everyone because he was a student of Hebrew. Melanchthon, whose German name had been Schwarzerde, was accused of Judaizing and deriving everything from Moses, and Martin Luther was called "Semi–Judaeus" by Catholics and others. When a sect of Luthero-Papists sought to bring conciliation between these several views of Christianity, they too were denounced by all sides as Judaizers as were the Sabbatarians, as professors of Hebrew in the various universities.[46]

What is important here is that not only Luther but also his fellow reformers and antagonists shared the fear of Jewish influence upon Christianity and, almost without exception, viewed Judaism as a great threat and Jews as less than human.

Luther himself made every effort to prove to the Jews of his time that Christianity was true and Judaism false. His arguments were several. He insisted that *Isaiah 7:1* predicted that Jesus would be born of a virgin, and therefore insisted that the Hebrew word "Almah" did not mean "young woman" as the Jews have consistently maintained, but "virgin." This issue of translation is of course very important to all who use the Bible as a source of religious inspiration, since translation is indeed interpretation.

Luther knew this very well. He was accused in his own time of deliberately neglecting or denying Jewish interpretations of the Bible which he translated from the Hebrew into the German. Yet "Luther never mastered Hebrew, having a deep-seated distaste for Hebrew grammar, which he asserted was a concoction of the Rabbis, studiously to be avoided; not a knowledge of grammar, but of 'holy things' is necessary, he says, to translate the Hebrew Scriptures."[47]

In making his translations, Luther chose only passages in the Bible which were in accord with his his own views. This is of course what translators have always done, although all of them did not necessarily admit as Luther did that their translations were more the product of belief than of accuracy. Despite these admissions, however, Luther accused the Jewish critics of his translations of "wishing for a second time to obscure the text."[48]

Luther's principal purpose in translating the Old Testament into German was his hope to convert the Jews. He interpreted the Hebrew Bible christologically and "saw all promises by God in ... the Hebrew Bible as referring to Christ."[49]

In addition, it should be considered that one of the principal differences between the Protestant and the Catholic viewpoint was then and still is the interpretation of the Bible. "For to the Protestant spirit," says Grant, "the Bible is not a book of law like the American Constitution, interpreted by judicial decision which possesses binding force. It is a book of life through which God speaks directly to the human soul. The spirit of the Reformation is diametrically opposed to the authoritative interpretation of the Bible."[50]

Luther's translation of the Old Testament from the Hebrew to the German was begun in 1522 with the translation of the Pentateuch or the Five Books of Moses and ended in 1532 when he translated the prophets.

In making this translation Luther was guided by the principles he described in his pamphlet *Über das Übersetzen (On Translating)*. He wrote that it is not possible to translate a foreign idiom into one's native tongue but that the spirit of the foreign language be rendered. "I do this with such care in translating Moses, that the Jews accuse me of rendering only the sense and not the precise words. In rendering Moses I make him so German that no one would know he was a Jew."

Although Luther was weak in Hebrew grammar, he believed that he nevertheless understood the true meaning of the Hebrew better than those who knew the language very well. He believed that he already knew the sense of the Old Testament no matter what a grammatically correct translation may have meant. For him "words follow sense." Therefore he translated with the idea that "without the New Testament you could not understand the Old and that therefore all Hebrew texts really foretold the coming of Christ."[51]

Since the Jews evidently did not convert to Christianity despite Luther's efforts, his conduct toward them appeared to change dramatically with the publication of several tracts which dealt with Luther's view of the Jews, culminating in 1542 in his pamphlet *Über die Juden und Ihre Lügen (About the Jews and Their Lies)*. He continued his anti–Jewish attacks in another pamphlet published the following year, *Vom Schem Hamphoras*.[52]

In all of these writings the theme is always that the Jews are a rejected people but that they nevertheless could have undue influence on Christians if the author Luther, did not correct their false interpretations of scripture.

Jews, Luther thought, were the enemies of Christ not only because they were unable to understand such mysteries as the Trinity, but also because their rabbis did understand this but deliberately falsified their teachings when, according to Luther, they knew that they were wrong and Christianity right.

In an essay entitled "Neue Vorrede auf den Propheten Hesekiel" ("New preface concerning the prophet Ezekiel") Luther skewered the rabbis for allegedly "tearing apart and torturing scripture in their explanations, just as gross swine tear up and turn upside down a garden."[53] Fearing Jewish influence, Luther counseled Christians not to deal with Jews and went so far as to urge Christians not to use Jewish physicians.[54]

Luther's change in attitude toward the Jews as evidenced by comparing his early pamphlet *That Jesus Christ Was Born a Jew* and the last mentioned pamphlet viewing Jews as liars was only apparent. In fact there was never a change in Luther's views. His only concern toward the Jews had always been his wish to convert the Jews to Christianity, and his only motive in writing his earlier pamphlet was his wish to achieve their conversion.

In this wish he was in no way unique. Luther indeed represented sixteenth century Christianity so thoroughly that we can see in his utterances and writings all those beliefs, prejudices and worldviews which motivated the Christian population of his day everywhere and which reflected Christian thinking to that day.

Every age and every society rests upon the culture base of all that preceded it. It would therefore be both unjust and impossible to believe that Luther should have had anything but anti–Jewish attitudes, since as a Christian he and all of Christianity of his day and all preceding him had always been taught the two principal tenets of Christian belief, the two pillars upon which Christianity had always rested: Love for all mankind and hatred for the Jews.

III

The misery in which Jews lived for centuries was in fact used by Luther and by all Christian theologians for their contention that the Jews had been discarded by God, were "Christ killers" and were justly excluded from their land and from the company of decent people for the "sin" of rejecting the Christian savior. "The theologian knows that the church has stepped into the place of the synagogue and has inherited all of her books; the Jewish people have been discarded because of their infidelity and replaced by the Christian people who thereby became the People of God."

The Church repeats unendingly, "your people, your family, etc. These expressions emerge already in the most ancient liturgy; their purpose is to emphasize that Christians have taken the place of the Jewish people." So said Luther.[55]

Further, the Church viewed itself as the sole successor of Israel. Thus, the Jews brought their discard upon themselves by crucifying Christ; they thereby lost their erstwhile election and no longer constituted His people. According to this Lutheran conception, the Church is therefore the new true Israel and has replaced the Jews in the "election" which had been their patrimony.

The crime of deicide was thought to have separated the living God from this people. This catchword was a significant Christian contribution to the already existing anti–Judaism. With such language the emotions of the masses could be easily and quickly excited.

Since the Jews, according to this opinion, were no longer God's people, what then was their role? They could only testify to the anger of God. St. Augustine believed that the Jews must be witnesses of the messages proclaimed by the prophets. They were a judgment for themselves, for Christians evidence of the truth of the evangelium (from Greek *ev*, "good," *angelum*, "message"). Referring to the letter of Barnabas, Luther disputed the right of the Jews to the Old Testament, which he believed was denied them: "The Old Testament is our truth; the Jews have for ever lost the Testament received by Moses." Christianity more and more related to the first Jews who were not gripped by the gruesome rejection of the Jews then living. "The ancient Jews, in their hope for the intended redeemer Christ were already Christians. That is why the Jews must be viewed as apostates because they are guilty of breaking THE LAW in that they would not recognize Christ." From the relationship between Jacob and Esau, the ante-Nicene Father, Tertullian, derived the following statement which Luther repeats: "The older and larger people, that is the Jews, must serve the younger people, that is, the Christians and the younger people must exceed the older." Augustine said, "The Jews exist only in order to carry our books for their own confusion.... The books that the Jew carries [are] the basis of Christian belief. They are the mailcarriers like a slave who runs behind his master and carries his books. The senior must be the slave of the younger. Thus, the Jews are slaves in relation to Christians."

By these means the church supported the social degradation of the Jews, a degradation Luther believed was fully deserved. We have already seen that this degradation began as soon as the Church had received official recognition from the state (325 C.E.) so that its influence upon related measures against the Jews could make itself felt.[56]

Removal of Jews from Christian society had a deeper cause. Once Christianity had become the state religion, anyone who would not take part in the sacraments of the Church was not considered a member of the national community, so Jews and other non–Christians became merely tolerated residents of the empire, living only at the edge of a society whose limits were best understood by participation in these sacraments.[57]

From then on segregation between Jews and Christians became inevitable and continued into our own time. In 1215, at the Fourth Lateran Council, so named because it met at the Palace and Church of St. John Lateran in Rome, the Church finally ordered that all Jews had to wear special clothes and a yellow star to make certain that Christians would not deal with them.

As a consequence of this demonization of the Jews through social distance, many Christians, including Luther, saw Jews as fearsome and, upon this fertile ground of fear and misgivings, came to believe that Jews murdered Christian children so as to use their blood in their Passover rituals and for other purposes, that Jews poisoned the wells and that Jews tortured the "Host"—the sacred wafer used in the Mass. The consequences of the fears that these beliefs aroused climaxed with the horrors of the Holocaust but were responsible, long before then, for other gruesome excesses over the years.

In particular, there was the accusation of killing Christian children so as to use their blood in Jewish rituals, a view which was taught by both Catholic and Protestant theologians. Even the most bitter enemies of Martin Luther among the Catholic writers of his day agreed with him and he with them, that Jews were indeed devoted to all these crimes.

> The climax of these post-war killings came on July 4, 1946. Three days earlier, an eight year old Polish boy from Kielce, Henryk Blaszczyk, disappeared from his home. Two days later he returned, claiming that he had been kept in a cellar by two Jews who had wanted to kill him, and that only a miracle had enabled him to escape. In fact, he had been to the home of a family friend in a nearby village. The friend had taught him what to say after his return.
>
> On July 4, a crowd of Poles, aroused by rumors of Jews abducting Christian children for ritual purposes, attacked the building of the Jewish Committee in Kielce. Almost all the Jews who were inside the building, including the chairman of the committee, Dr. Seweryn Kahane, were shot, stoned to death, or killed with axes and blunt instruments. Elsewhere in Kielce, Jews were murdered in their homes, or dragged into the streets and killed by the mob. Forty two Jews were killed in Kielce that day. Two ... were children. Four were teenagers.... Three were officers in the Polish army.... Seven could not be named. One ... was a survivor of Birkenau....
>
> No Polish town was free from such incidents.
>
> [*From Martin Gilbert,* The Holocaust, *New York, Henry Holt, 1985, pp. 818–819.*]

It is remarkable that Luther attacked every obsolete prejudice except prejudices against Jews—and even those when it suited his purpose. We have already seen that Luther knew better since his earliest essay concerning Jews, *That Jesus Christ Was Born a Jew*, makes precisely the argument that these stories were utter fabrications. Yet, when he had given up all hope that Jews in great numbers would convert to his version of Christianity, he associated himself with the views of the notorious Catholic hatemonger, Dr. Johann Eck, a man who had vilified Luther many times. Despite this, Luther not only supported Eck in his outbursts against the Jews but even superseded him.[58]

He claimed that Jews were related to the devil. This belief was underscored in medieval society by depicting the devil wearing the clothes assigned to Jews by medieval law.

To give sufficient vent to his hatred of Jews, Luther wrote the aforementioned book *Concerning the Jews and Their Lies*. In it Luther accused the Jews of four "lies" which he sought to disprove. Before presenting his proofs he writes as follows: "Next to the devil, Christians have no enemy worse than a Jew ... so that everyone will suffer the most from these devil's children and offspring of snakes.

"Whoever enjoys protecting, feeding and honoring such poisonous snakes ought to be truly attracted to these Jews. He may then pride himself on having been kind, [having] strengthened the Devil and his young devils in cursing our dear Lord and the sacred blood so that we Christians may be redeemed."[59]

Luther, as well as many of his contemporaries, believed that there were "devil children" in this world. These were believed to be animated lumps of flesh without a soul. Luther believed that these "devil children" should be killed along with witches and Jews.

These were the four "lies" Luther attributed to the Jews:

> 1. that the Jews claimed to be of noble descent by reason of the patriarchs, Abraham, Isaac and Jacob;
> 2. that the Jews believed themselves to be "chosen" by God by reason of circumcision;
> 3. that the Jews boasted that God had given them the Law; and
> 4. that the Jews boasted they had received the land of Canaan and the city of Jerusalem.

Luther wrote that far worse than these four so-called "lies," however, was the Jews' refusal to believe that the Messiah had already come and their anticipation that a Messiah would yet appear.[60]

To put it concisely, Luther wrote in 1542, "The Jews still believe in vain in a God who promises a Messiah, although their fathers once correctly believed this."[61]

Lest it be thought that Luther's views had little influence, it should be noted that four "witches" were burned at Wittenberg (where Luther lived) on June 29, 1540, when witch executions were rare in Germany.

Luther was so obsessed with the Devil that he believed the Pope worshiped the Devil, that the Catholic Church was the Devil's invention, that suicides were murders committed by the Devil, that "heretics" are forced by the Devil to speak falsehood, that "lunatics" are possessed by the Devil and that he personally had encountered the Devil many times.[62]

Having abused the Jews in as obscene a manner as the age permitted, Luther then proceeded to advise his contemporaries that they

> should throw brimstone and pitch upon them; if one could hurl hell fire at them, so much the better ... and this must be done for the honor of Our Lord and of Christianity, so that God may see that we are indeed Christians. Let their houses also be shattered and destroyed ... let their prayer books and Talmuds be taken from them, and their whole Bible too; let their rabbis be forbidden on pain of death, to teach henceforth anymore. Let the streets and highways

be closed against them. Let them be forbidden to practice usury, and let all their money and all their treasures of silver and gold be taken from them and put away in safety. And if all this be not enough, let them be driven like mad dogs out of the land."[63]

> One mother threw a small child wrapped up in a pillow from the wagon, shouting: "Take it, that's some money to look after it." In no time an SS man ran up, unwrapped the pillow, seized the child by the feet and smashed its head against a wheel of the wagon. this took place in full view of the mother, who was howling in pain. [*From Martin Gilbert,* The Holocaust, *New York, Henry Holt, 1985, p. 399.*]

Even in his letters to his wife Luther repeatedly attacked the Jews, as in a letter written in 1546 in which he complains that a Count Albert of Eisleben had "exposed the Jews in his territory to shame," that no one was willing to do anything about them but that "I have expressed my opinion today, roughly enough etc."[64]

Using all the techniques of neutralization that aggressors have always used to justify their crimes, Luther blamed the Jews themselves for the misery in which they lived. For example, he wrote the following in 1542:

> "Listen Jew, are you aware that Jerusalem and your sovereignty, together with your temple and priesthood, have been destroyed for 1,460 years?" For this year, which we Christians write as the year 1542 since the birth of Christ, is exactly 1,468 years, going on fifteen hundred years, since Vespasian and Titus destroyed Jerusalem and expelled the Jews from the city.[65]

This argument was of course not of Luther's invention. In fact, it had been used for centuries to "prove" that God had rejected the Jews and put the Church in their place.

It therefore was, and continues to be, difficult for some Christians to accept the return of Israel to Jerusalem and to accept Jewish sovereignty over the city, which was achieved in 1967. For this Jewish rule of Jerusalem flies into the face of that erstwhile Christian theology.

In fact, as a consequence of the re-establishment of Israel and the unification of Jerusalem under Jewish rule, modern Christian theologians have given up the notion of Israel's rejection and have altered their stance to now allow that the covenant between God and Israel is permanent and that the Christian covenant is an addition to but not a substitution for, the earlier covenant.

Arrogance and pride of descent and race are a second accusation Luther makes against the Jews. He claims to know that Jews "boast before

God" and demand special privileges on the grounds of their descent from Abraham.[66]

Next, Luther claims that circumcision is believed by Jews to be a special mark of nobility for Jews alone. Correctly observing that Moslems too are circumcised, he concludes that Jews have no monopoly on this practice and therefore no right to boast of it. It was of course Luther, not the Jews, who believed that circumcision was grounds for Jewish boasting in the first place. Luther's extensive harangue concerning circumcision is of particular interest in light of psychoanalytic theory.

Luther's third argument against the Jews stems from their presence at Mount Sinai and their reception of the Ten Commandments. While not denying this event, Luther argues that the Jews do not observe the Ten Commandments but "must be the multitude of the whoring and murderous people.... Their boast of lineage, circumcision and law must be accounted as filth."[67]

Having accused the Jews of boasting about these beliefs, Luther becomes particularly vitriolic as he discusses the refusal of the Jews to believe in the Christian Messiah.

Here Luther finds it offensive that the Jews ask God for a Messiah when, according to him, the Jews know very well that the Messiah has already come. To prove his point Luther quotes extensively from a variety of Hebrew verses and claims to know that their origin supports his position. For example, he claims that the German word *schild* (shield) is derived from the Hebrew word *shlit* meaning "prince." This interpretation is not supported by any evidence and is held wrong by modern etymologists.[68]

Calling upon a vast variety of Hebrew sources, Luther then proceeds to prove to his satisfaction that "No doubt it is necessary for the Jews to lie and to misinterpret in order to maintain their error...."

He further claims to know that Jews insult the Christian Trinity and other holy concepts and are particularly cruel in labeling Mary and Jesus in an offensive manner. He then concludes that Jews are the enemies of God and "of us accursed Goyim, to curse us and to strive for our final, complete and eternal ruin."

Finally, Luther makes several recommendations as to what Christians should do "with this rejected and condemned people, the Jews."

His first exhortation is "to set fire to their synagogues or schools and to bury and cover with dirt whatever will not burn so that no man will ever again see a stone or cinder of them."[69]

It is to be noted that the National Socialist government of Germany did just that on the night of November 9–10, 1938. On that night, 119 synagogues and innumerable Jewish-owned shops and homes all over Germany were burned to the ground. The windows in Jewish-owned stores and department stores were deliberately broken and Jews driven into concentration camps where they were murdered.[70]

> After a while, the Stromtroopers were joined by people who were not in uniform; and suddenly, with one loud cry of, "Down with the Jews," the gathering outside produced axes and heavy sledgehammers. They advanced toward the little synagogue which stood in Michael's own meadow, opposite his house. They burst the door open, and the whole crowd, by now shouting and laughing, stormed into the little House of God.
> Michael, standing behind the tightly drawn curtains, saw how the crowd tore the Holy Ark wide open; and three men who had smashed the ark, threw the Scrolls of the Law of Moses out. He threw them — these Scrolls, which had stood in their quiet dignity, draped in blue or wine-red velvet, with their little crowns of silver covering the tops of the shafts by which the Scroll was held during the service — to the screaming and shouting mass of people which had filled the little synagogue.
> The people caught the Scrolls as if they were amusing themselves with a ball game — tossing them up into the air again, while other people flung them further back until they reached the street outside. Women tore away the red and blue velvet and everybody tried to snatch some of the silver adorning the Scrolls.
> Naked and open, the Scrolls lay in the muddy autumn lane; children stepped on them and others tore pieces from the fine parchment on which the Law was written — the same which the people who tore it apart had, in vain, tried to absorb for over a thousand years. . . . The children had lit a little bonfire and the parchment of the Scrolls gave enough food for the flames to eat up the smashed-up benches and doors, and the wood, which only the day before had been the Holy Ark for the Scrolls of the Law of Moses. [*From Dr. Arthur Flehinger, 'Flames of Fury,' Jewish Chronicle, 9, November 1979, page 27, in Gilbert, op. cit. p. 72.*]

Luther's second recommendation is that the house of the Jews should be razed and destroyed and that all their prayer books and Talmudic writings be taken away from them.

His third recommendation is that the rabbis be forbidden to teach henceforth "on pain of loss of life and limb." Here Luther compares the teachings of the rabbis with the pope who, according to Luther, also teaches lies.

In Luther's words, "he [the pope] did not teach in accord with the word of God, and therefore he forfeited the right to teach."

Luther's fourth recommendation is that "safe conduct on the highways be abolished completely for the Jews." This step was also taken by the Nazi government in that the German Jews could no longer acquire a driver's license after 1935 and could not get a German passport but instead were issued a *Judenkennkarte*, a Jew identification card, whose purpose was to alert any country to which a Jew might flee that its bearer was a Jew and not really a human being.

Although Luther knew very well that Jews were forced to lend money at interest because they were forbidden most other occupations (see *That Jesus Christ Was Born a Jew*), he recommended that Jews be prohibited that occupation also and underscored his argument by referring to the Law of Moses which he claimed the Jews were violating at all times.

He next recommends that Jews be forced into physical labor. This recommendation was also carried out by the Nazi government in innumerable concentration camps during the years 1933–1945 when a considerable number of Jews were worked and starved until they died. This served to reinforce the myth that Jews had theretofore never worked but, in Luther's words, "idled away their time behind the stove, feasting and farting, and on top of all, boasting blasphemously of their lordship over the Christian by means of our sweat...."[71]

Luther continues ranting against the Jews for yet another 100 pages. As William Shirer, author of *The Rise and Fall of the Third Reich*—himself a Protestant—has said, "The great founder of Protestantism was both a passionate anti-Semite and a ferocious believer in absolute obedience to political authority."[72]

It is legitimate to ask here why it was that despite the undoubted anti-Jewish attitudes which existed in all of Europe for so long, it was particularly Germany which gave rise to Hitler and organized the mass murders which finally came to be known as the Holocaust.

The answer to this riddle was given by the famous German author Thomas Mann, himself a Lutheran, in his essay "Deutschland und die Deutschen" ("Germany and the Germans"), delivered in Germany as a speech after the end of the Second World War. Said Mann: "[He], Luther, understood nothing about freedom. I do not mean the freedom of a Christian, but political freedom, the freedom of the citizen; this not only left him [Luther] cold, but their movements and demands were deeply disgusting to his very soul."[73] Thus Luther supported authoritarian government and helped as much as anyone to make Germans followers of authoritarians and dictators so that some would have it that in that respect Luther was again an example in word and deed of all that which made the Nazi movement possible. *Bonis exemplis, magis impetramus, quam bonis verbis*— "A good example achieves more than good words." And so does a bad one.

Thus, Luther is accused not only of instigating anti-Jewish hatred or at least supporting it where he found it, but also of furnishing Germans with an attitude toward authority which permitted the worst gangsters to impose themselves and their crimes upon the German people in the name of obedience to secular authority.[74]

IV

As we have already seen, Luther's, *On the Jews and Their Lies* was not his only effort to vilify the Jews. He also called Jews a good number of vile names in his book *Against the Sabbatarians*, which was directed at Christians who preferred to view Saturday, not Sunday, as the Sabbath. Here too Luther reviles the Jews at length although his essay is neither as long nor as vitriolic as *On the Jews and Their Lies*.[75]

In view of this teaching it is by no means surprising that the brutal treatment of the German Jews, begun by the Nazi government in 1933, was widely approved by the German Christian population. When Nazi troopers marched through the streets singing *"Und wenn das Judenblut vom Messer spritzt, dann geht's nochmal so gut"* ("When Jew blood squirts from the knife, things will go twice as well"), Protestant and Catholic clergy marched ahead of the column convinced in their self-righteousness that the Jews themselves were to blame for their decimation and torture.[76]

In March of 1543, Martin Luther published yet another treatise concerning the Jews, *Vom Schem Hamphoras*.[77] The phrase *Schem Hamphoras* is Hebrew and means the "Hidden Name." The word *schem* means "name" and the word *meforashe* is translated as "explicit"; thus *hameforashe* would be "inexplicit." Both English words are derived from the Latin *ex + plicare*, "to unfold" or "to be evident," hence "inexplicit" or not unfolded, not known, not evident or hidden. In this case it is reasonable to interpret the phrase to mean "unpronounced."

Note that Luther has changed the word so that in his spelling it ends in "S" and not in "Sh." It is of course understood that it is impossible to portray the Hebrew sound accurately by using English, or for that matter German, letters.

Some translators use the English word "ineffable," so unusual a word that it is hardly recognized by many English speakers. "Ineffable" is derived from the Latin *ef + fari*, meaning "to speak," and *abilis*, "to be able."

This "ineffable" name can be found in the Pentateuch, or the Five Books of Moses, only a few times despite the immense number of references to God in these books. It appears, for example, in *Exodus 15:18*, which reads, "YHVH shall reign for ever and ever." (*YHVH yimloch leolom voed.*) *Numbers 23:21* reads in part, "YHVH his God is with him...." (*YHVH Alowhoff eemow.*) The phrase also appears several times in *Deuteronomy*, chapters 33 and 34, as in the line "YHVH came from Sinai...." (*YHVH Meeseenai bow).*[78]

These four letters were called the "Tetragrammaton" in Greek because *Tetra* means four and *grammaton* means letters. According to the *Encyclopedia Judaica* the pronunciation of this four-letter name of God was avoided since the third century B.C.E., and the word *Adonoi*, "Lord," substituted. The pronunciation "Jehovah" was introduced by Christian scholars in Europe who did not really know how the original pronunciation of the tetragrammaton sounded.

There is a real possibility that the pronunciation is "Yahwe" because the syllable "Yah" is repeatedly used in Hebrew to indicate the name of God, as in "Hallelujah," meaning "let us praise [*hallelu*] God [*jah* or *yah*]." Additionally, YHVH is used in other books of the Bible.[79]

Let us then briefly review the content of Luther's *Vom Schem Hamphoras* as it is relevant to the present discussion.

Written in 1543 in the antiquated German of the time, a German which today seems ungrammatical, the book begins at once with such offensive language that it soon becomes evident how much the author hates and despises the Jewish objects of his derision.

In the very first sentence of this essay the Jews are called mad and wretched (*rasenden, elenden Juden*) and are accused of insulting God. Luther goes on to say that Jews have hearts of stone and that they claim God is a liar. Furthermore, the Jews are accused of saying that they are always right no matter how miserable their lives may be as a consequence of this attitude.

Quoting now from the first chapter of a book by the Latin writer Porchetus, Luther finds further ammunition in his attack against the Jews. Here he agrees with Porchetus that "the Jews were so averse to the miraculous deeds of Christ that they attributed them to the prince of the devils, Beelzebub...."[80]

Among these reputed miracles, reported by Porchetus and evidently accepted by Luther as facts, was the Jewish belief that when Jesus came to Jerusalem, he found a stone upon which the Ark of the Lord had been set. The words *Schem Hamphoras* were reportedly written upon this stone, and it was believed that whosoever learned and understood the letters and the name it spelled could do whatever he pleased.

There follows a further verbatim citation from the work of Porchetus, the thrust of which is the guilt of the Jews in killing the Christ.

Luther cites Psalm 81 to the effect that the Jews had at one time been elected to be "God's mouth" but that the Jews covered their mouths, eyes, ears, noses and hearts and all their energy (against this election). Then, reports Luther, the Devil came and the Jews opened their eyes, their throats, their ears, their hearts and all their senses. They even ate the Devil's excrement, according to Luther. Consequently, the Jews crucified Jesus and shouted, "His blood come upon us and our children" an event which had already occurred, according to Luther as he sought to interpret the misfortunes of the Jews in terms of this theology.[81]

Luther writes at length that anyone who may consider the possiblity of becoming Jewish will have to believe the most irrational teachings of the rabbis, all of which are nonsense and utterly false. Even if God says otherwise, claims Luther, Jews believe what their rabbis teach.

"*Sie mussen ihren Rabinen gleuben, wenn dieselben gleich sagten die rechte Hand wäre die Linke*"; i.e., "they must believe their rabbis even if these should say that the right hand is the left hand."[82]

At this point Luther arrives at his principal argument. He claims that the Jews will attribute miraculous powers to the *Schem Hamphoras*, the name of God, but will not accept Jesus, when any reasonable person can see that four dead letters could not possibly be useful in bringing about miracles.[83]

Jews are called devils by Luther and are also accused of worshiping the Devil.

Examining the concept of *Schem Hamphoras* again, Luther discusses the numerology of these Hebrew words, a superstition which many Jews shared with Luther at that time. Luther's language in portraying the Jews becomes pornographic as he accuses them not only of false belief and of deliberately pretending not to know the truth but also of falsifying their own books to hide their activities.

According to Luther, Jews are prisoners of the Devil who claim to make gods and angels themselves. Jews are further accused of damning all non-Jews and refusing to listen to the word of God, listening to devils instead. Luther resorts to quotations from the Pentateuch as well as the New Testament to prove to himself how right he is concerning the Jews. The Jews, says Luther, know very well that Christianity is right. However, obstinacy and sheer hatred for God and the Truth lead them to pretend otherwise.

Finally Luther claims that the Jews are not even knowledgeable concerning their own religion, but misconstrue the teachings of Moses and the prophets who all predicted the coming of the Christian Messiah, a fact which the malicious Jews now will not accept.[84]

In sum, Luther repeats in *Vom Schem Hamphoras* what he and so many other Christian theologians had preached for centuries, namely, that the victim was at fault. The misery imposed on Jews by Christians was the fault of the Jews whom God wished to punish for rejecting Jesus and refusing to become Christians. "Blaming the victim" is of course a well-known technique of neutralization used by offenders everywhere.[85]

These techniques have been thoroughly analyzed and documented by sociologists and are used not only by Christian apologists, but also by others who are accused of crimes of every kind. Thus, the Nazi defendants at the Nuremberg trials made extensive use of these techniques, particularly since they were then so old and well established as excuses for anti-Jewish excesses.[86]

These techniques are the following:

1. Denial of responsibility. Luther and other anti–Jewish apologists argue that not they but the Jews themselves are responsible for Jewish misery.

Luther says in *Vom Schem Hamphoras*, "But your judgment is right. 'Iustus es Domine.' Yes, so shall Jews, and otherwise no one else be punished, as they have despised, ridiculed, insulted and damned your word and your works for so long. They, [the Jews] should not go to the upper hell as do heathens, ... nor into the middle hell, but into the very abyss of hell as no one can fall lower."[87]

2. Denial of injury. Luther and others before and since his day insisted that the Jews had injured them and that the complaints of the Jews concerning their persecution were wholly unjustified.

Luther accuses Jews of murder, robbery and other crimes and even claims that the Jews of his day were not descendants of ancient Israel but "foreign rabble and Gypsies" (*"zugelauffenen, frembden buben oder Zigeuner"*) who circumcised themselves as if they were Jews."[88]

3. Denial of the victim. Not only were the Jews not victims, but according to Luther and his later followers, the Jews were the victimizers. Jews were accused of killing Christian children and drinking their blood so as not to smell. Jews were also accused of baking their Passover bread (Matzohs) with the same blood and of poisoning the drinking supply.

This accusation was first made in the twelfth century but continued at intervals into the twentieth century when such accusations were made in Russia and in Germany.[89]

4. Condemnation of the condemner. No matter how brutal the treatment of Jews, those who objected to such treatment were themselves accused of every crime and condemned as far worse than the persecutors themselves. Even defenders of the Hebrew language were accused of "Judaizing" despite the fact that Johann Reuchlin, "the foremost Christian scholar of Hebrew in Germany," was by no means a friend of the Jews but rather sought the early conversion of the Jews by learning their language and their customs.[90]

5. Appeal to higher loyalties. No technique of neutralization was used more often in the long history of anti–Jewish abuse than appeal to God himself, who, it was said, demanded of Christians that they abuse Jews as he too had rejected them. Christians were showing their loyalty to God by making Jewish life miserable.

This attitude is already visible in the writings of the early Christians, whose work on behalf of the new religion took place before the Council of Nicea met in 325 C.E. and institutionalized all those cruelties and oppressive measures which Christians felt were necessary to prevent Jews from having any influence upon the newly Christianized population.[91]

Typical of such anti–Jewish writings is the statement of Justin, who lived from 110 to 165 C.E. and who wrote extensively about the Jews as did the anonymous author of "the Epistle of Mathetes to Diognitus. In the Epistle of Ignatius to the Magnesians we even read that "Judaism ... has now come to an end"—prediction which even 1,600 years of the most ardent persecution could not fulfill.[92]

It is therefore not surprising that other Reformation theologians also proposed various forms of persecution for Jews since they were acting from a tradition which rested largely on the assumption that their own religion could only survive if it could use the Jews and their religion as a foil with which to achieve comparisons favorable to themselves and unfavorable to the Jews. Thus, Christianity became dependent on Judaism and the state of misery in which the Jewish population of Europe was forced to live. At every turn, Christians "proved" their superiority and their veracity by pointing to the errors of the Jews and the consequences which these "errors" had precipitated.

Luther was convinced, as Christian theologians were until recently, that Jews could never again govern themselves in their own land until they became converts to Christianity. He makes that point in *Vom Schem Hamphoras* when he claims to know that "Jews will never govern themselves again but will always live an uncertain life." "*Aber sollen doch kein Eigen Herrschafft kriegen, sondern auf ungewjissem Fusse sitzen,*" he predicts in the antiquated German of the sixteenth century.[93]

"It would be tempting to dismiss these writings as aberrations, as medieval remnants, or as the consequences of old age. But we cannot do this. The anti–Jewish writings must be taken seriously as an accurate expression of Luther's views and as an integral part of his own theological understanding."[94]

In addition to the two tracts dealing with Jews already mentioned, Luther returned to the subject again in his essay *On the Last Words of David*, published in 1543. There he once more repeated his charges, always emphasizing the Jewish rejection of Jesus.

Notes

1. William Ernest Hocking, *Types of Philosophy*, 3rd ed. (New York, Scribner's, 1959), p. 320.
2. Shimon Markish, *Erasmus and the Jews* (Chicago and London, The University of Chicago Press, 1986), p. 5.
3. Guido Kisch, *Erasmus Stellung zu Juden und Judentum* (Tübingen, J.C.B. Mohr, 1969), and Markish, *op. cit.*
4. Arthur A. Cohen, in Markish, *op. cit.*, p. 153.
5. Marjorie Lamberti, *Jewish Activism in Imperial Germany* (New Haven, Yale University Press, 1978), p. 36.
6. Craig R. Thompson, *The Colloquies of Erasmus* (Chicago, The University of Chicago Press, 1965), p. xxix.
7. Kisch, *op. cit.*, p. 8.
8. Thompson, *op. cit.*, pp. 61–63.

9. Thompson, *op. cit.*, pp. 183, 188, 210 and 320–322.
10. Markish, *op. cit.*, p. 23.
11. *Ibid.*, p. 24.
12. Kisch, *op. cit.*, p. 8.
13. Jules Isaac, *Has Anti–Semitism Roots in Christianity?* (New York, National Conference of Christians and Jews, 1962), pp. 58–60.
14. *Ibid.*, p. 65.
15. Kisch, *op. cit.*, pp. 6–8.
16. Kisch, *op. cit.*, p. 30.
17. Kisch, *op. cit.*, pp. 30–31. "Die Juden sind den Christen im höchsten Masse undankbar, verfluchen sie täglich und öffentlich mit Fluchen und Verwünschungen, beuten sie durch ihren Wucher aus, verweigern ihnen ihre Dienstleistungen, verspotten unseren gelauterten Glauben, und besudeln ihn ständig. Gegen unseren Erlöser wenden sie sich öffentlich mit den schädlichsten Blasphemien. Was aber am entzsetslichsten ist, die Juden dursten nach Christenblut, nach welchem diese blutdurstigen Blutsauger Tag und Nacht lechtzen.... Warum also sollte es den Fürsten nicht gestattet sein, so ausgesprochene Feinde, so grimmige Bestien auszustossen, warum sie nicht aus den Gebieten der Christen auszutreiben? Man muss jenen ekelhaftesten Auswurf in kimmerische Finsterniss versinken lassen."
18. Steven Rowan, "Luther, Bucer and Eck on the Jews," *The Sixteenth Century Journal*, Vol. XVI, No. 1, Spring 1985.
19. Kisch, *op. cit.*, p. 39.
20. Will Durant, *The Reformation* (New York, Simon and Schuster, 1957), p. 430.
21. Heiko A. Oberman, *Wurzeln des Antisemitismus im Zeitalter der Renaissance und der Reformation* (Berlin, Severin und Siedler, 1981).
22. Klaus Haberkamm, "Die alte Dame in Andorra. Zwei Schweizer Parabeln des Nationalsozialistischen Antisemitismus," in Hans Wagener, ed., *Gegenswartliteratur und Drittes Reich* (Stuttgart, Philipp Reclam, Jr., 1977), p. 105.
23. Mark Edwards and George Tavard, *Luther, A Reformer for the Churches: An Ecumenical Study Guide* (Philadelphia, Fortress, 1983), p. 77.
24. Leo Tolstoy, *War and Peace*, Louise and Aylmer Maude, trans. (New York, Norton, 1966).
25. Solomon Grayzel, *A History of the Jews* (Philadelphia, The Jewish Publication Society, 1947), p. 412.
26. S. M. Dobnow, *History of the Jews in Russia and Poland, from the Earliest Times to the Present Day*, I. Friedlaender, trans. (Philadelphia, The Jewish Publication Society of America, 1916), pp. 62–63.
27. See Eberhard Mannack, "Luther—Ein Geistiger Ahnherr Hitlers?" in Ferdinand von Ingen and Gerd Labraisse, *Luther Bilder im 20ten Jahrhundert* (Amsterdam, Rodopi, b.V., 1984), pp. 167–185.
28. Leopold Cordier, *Die Evangelische Jugend und Ihre Bunde Schwerin in Mecklenburg* (Friedrich Bahn Verlag, 1927), pp. 236–237.
29. Werner Jochmann, "Struktur und Funktion des Deutschen Anti-semitismus," in *Juden in Wilhelminischen Deutschland 1890–1914*, Werner E. Mosse, ed. (Tübingen, J.C.B. Mohr, 1976), p. 390.
30. Johannes Brosseder, *Luthers Stellung zu den Juden im Spiegel seiner Interpreten* (Munich, Max Hueber Verlag, 1972).
31. *Ibid.*, pp. 182–198.
32. *Der Prozess gegen die Hauptkriegsverbrecher*, or *The Trial of the Major War Criminals*, Vol. XII (Nuremberg, 1947), p. 346.

33. Abram Lipsky, *Martin Luther, Germany's Angry Man* (New York, Frederick A. Stokes, 1933), p. 267.
34. Martin Brecht, *Martin Luther: 2. Band, Ordnung und Abgrenzung der Reformation* (Stuttgart, Calwer Verlag, 1987), p. 116.
35. Mark Edwards and George Tavard, *op. cit.*, p. 77.
36. See Otto Gradewitz, *et al.*, *Vocabularium Jurisprudentiae Romanae* (Berlin, Savigny Stiftung, 1903); Charlton T. Lewis, *A Latin Dictionary* (Oxford, Clarendon, 1980), p. 1863; and Louis de Wolzogue, *Dictionnaire Universelle de Philosophie Sacrée* (Paris, 1846). Note also that *Genesis 24:2* and *47:29* use the phrase: Yodchah tachat yerachi" which means "[place] your hand under my thigh" and refers to oaths sworn by sons before their fathers.
37. Heinrich Graetz, *History of the Jews* (Philadelphia, The Jewish Publication Society), Chapter XIV.
38. Carl Cohen, "Martin Luther and His Jewish Contemporaries," *Jewish Social Studies*, Vol. 25, No. 3, July 1963, p. 197.
39. Cohen, *op. cit.*, p. 197.
40. George F. Abbott, *Israel in Europe* (New York, Macmillan, 1907), p. 219.
41. Preserved Smith and Charles M. Jacobs, *Luther's Correspondence and Other Contemporary Letters* (Philadelphia, The Lutheran Publication Society, 1918), pp. 185–187. This English version of Luther's letter is in the "Preserved Smith Collection" at the Concordia Publishing House in St. Louis, Mo. The German version was published by that publisher in 1890 in *Dr. Martin Luther's Sämmtliche Schriften*, Dr. Joh. Georg Walch, ed. This German edition is somewhat less antiquated than Luther's own writing and therefore more accessible to modern German readers.
42. Otto Clemen, *Flugschriften aus den Ersten Jahren der Reformation* (Nieuwkoop, Netherlands, B. de Graaf, 1967), pp. 375–377 (transl. by the author).
43. *Ibid.*, p. 378.
44. *Ibid.*, p. 380.
45. Abbott, *op. cit.*, p. 219.
46. Louis Israel Newman, *The Jewish Influence on Christian Reform Movements* (New York, Columbia University Press, 1925), pp. 617–618.
47. *Ibid.*, pp. 622–623.
48. *Ibid.*, p. 625.
49. Edwards and Tavard, *op. cit.*, p. 79.
50. Robert M. Grant, *A Short History of the Interpretation of the Bible* (New York, Macmillan, 1963), p. 128.
51. Abram Lipsky, *op. cit.*, pp. 166 and 268.
52. Martin Brecht, *Martin Luther: Die Erhaltung der Kirche, 1532–1546* (3ter Band, Stuttgart, Calwer Verlag, 1987), p. 336.
53. "...sie zerreissen und zermartern die Schrift in ihren Auslegungen, wie die unflätigen Säue einen Lustgarten zerwühlen und umkehren." See Martin Brecht, *op. cit.*, Vol. 3, p. 335.
54. *Ibid.*, pp. 332–335.
55. Rudolf Pfisterer, *Im Schatten des Kreuzes* (Hamburg, Herbert Reich Evangelischer Verlag, 1966), pp. 21–63.
56. Pfisterer, *op. cit.*, p. 22.
57. Wilhelm Maurer, *Kirche und Synagogue* (Stuttgart, 1953), p. 53, as quoted in Pfisterer, *op. cit.* (transl. by the author).
58. Heinrich Graetz, *op. cit.*, Vol. IV, pp. 546–548.
59. Pfisterer, *op. cit.* p. 22 (transl. by the author).

60. Selma Stern, *Joel Rosenheim*, Gertrude Hirschler, trans. (Philadelphia, The Jewish Publication Society of America, 1965), pp. 188–189.
61. Heinrich Bornkamm, *Luther and the Old Testament*, Eric W. Gritsch and Ruth C. Gritsch, trans. (Philadelphia, Fortress, 1969), p. 1.
62. Lipsky, *op. cit.*, pp. 134–135.
63. Luther, *Werke*, Erlangen Edition, 1827, as quoted by Will Durant in *The Reformation* (New York, Simon and Schuster, 1957), p. 422.
64. Theodore G. Tappert, ed., *Luther: Letters of Spiritual Counsel* (Philadelphia, Westminster), pp. 104–107.
65. Martin Luther, *On the Jews and Their Lies*, in Helmut Lehman, gen. ed., Franklin Sherman, ed., *Luther's Works*, Vol. 47, "The Christian in Society" (Philadelphia, Fortress, 1971), p. 138. Luther believed that Jerusalem was destroyed by the Romans in the year 74 C.E. as evidenced by his tabular outline of the history of the world entitled *Suppotatio annorum mundi (Reckoning of the Years of the World)*. Present scholarship has determined that the year of Jerusalem's destruction was 70 C.E.
66. *Ibid.*, p. 147.
67. Luther, in Lehman and Sherman, *op. cit.*, p. 167.
68. *Ibid.*, p. 180.
69. *Ibid.*, pp. 267–269.
70. William Shirer, *The Rise and Fall of the Third Reich: A History of Nazi Germany* (New York, Simon and Schuster, 1960), p. 430.
71. Gerhard Falk, *Murder: An Analysis of Its Forms, Conditions and Causes* (Jefferson, N.C., and London, McFarland, 1990), pp. 58–66. See also the extensive Holocaust literature.
72. Shirer, *op. cit.*, p. 236.
73. Thomas Mann, *Politische Schriften und Reden* (Dritter Band, Frankfurt, a.M., Fischer Bücherei, 1960), p. 167. "...denn er [Luther] verstand nichts von Freiheit. Ich meine jetzt nicht die Freiheit des Christenmenschen, sondern die politische Freiheit, die Freiheit des Staatsbürgers, -die liess ihn nicht nur kalt, sondern ihre Regungen und Ansprüche waren ihm in tiefster Seele zuwider."
74. Oscar L. Arnal, "Luther and the Peasants: A Lutheran Reassessment," *Science and Society*, Vol. XLIV, No. 4, Winter 1980, p. 451.
75. Martin Luther, *Against the Sabbatarians*, in Lehman and Sherman, *op. cit.*, pp. 65–98.
76. Werner Jochmann, "Von der Ausgrenzung zum Pogrom," in *Offene Wunden, Brennende Fragen, Juden in Deutschland von 1938 bis Heute*, Gunter Gorschenek and Stephan Reimers, eds. (Frankfurt a.M., Joseph Knecht, 1989), pp. 35–57.
77. Doctor Martinus Luther, *Von Schem Hamphoras und vom Geschlecht Christi* (D. Martin Luther's Werke, Kritische Gesammtausgabe, Weimar, Herman Bohlhaus, Nachfolger, 1920), pp. 579–648. This book is part of the so-called "Weimar Edition" of Luther's works, begun in 1883. This book is not part of the Fortress Press Edition of 1971 which does not include all of Luther's writings. (See note 25, above.) Since *Vom Schem Hamphoras* has not been published in English, the present discussion is based on the author's translation.
78. *The Pentateuch and Haftorahs*, 2nd Ed., C.H. Hertz, ed. (London, Soncino Press, 1961), pp. 273, 676 and 909.
79. *The Encyclopedia Judaica* (Jerusalem, Keter Publishing House, 1971, Vol. 7), pp. 679–682.

80. Luther, *Vom Schem Hamphoras*, p. 580. "Subsequenter per ordinem videndum est, qualiter Iudei Christi miraculis invidentes Beelzebub, principi demoniorum, ea primitus ascripserunt."
81. Luther, *op cit.*, p. 587.
82. *Ibid.*, p. 586.
83. *Ibid.*, p. 591.
84. *Ibid.*, p. 646-648.
85. Gresham Sykes and David Matza, "Techniques of Neutralization: A Theory of Delinquency," *American Sociological Review*, Vol. 22, 1957, pp. 664–670.
86. See *The Trial of the Major War Criminals* in *Nazi Conspiracy and Aggression* (Washington, D.C., Government Printing Office, 1951–1952).
87. Luther, *Vom Schem Hamphoras*, p. 605. "Aber recht ist dein Gericht. 'Iustus es Domine.' Ja, so sollen Juden und sonst niemand gestrafft werden, die dein wort und wunderwerck so lange zeit on unterlas verachtet, verspottet, gelestert und verdampt haben, Das sie nicht fallen mussen wie andere menschen kinder, Heiden, und wer sie sind inn sunde und tod, nicht oben in die Helle, nicht mitten in die Helle, sondern in den Abgrund der Helle, da man nicht tiefer fallen kan." Please note that the spelling, grammar and sentence structure is that of Luther. The entire manuscript is written in this style which appears to be grammatially incorrect and spelled in a manner quite different from what would be acceptable spelling today.
88. *Ibid.*, p. 614.
89. See Grayzel, *op. cit.*, pp. 143, 352–53, 391, 449, 522, 605, 609, 634, 635, 644 and 710.
90. *Ibid.*, p. 423.
91. Alexander Roberts and James Donaldson, *The Ante-Nicene Fathers* (Grand Rapids, Mich., Eerdman's, 1885).
92. *Ibid.*, Vol. I, pp. 201 and 63.
93. Luther, *Vom Schem Hamphoras, op. cit.*, p. 615.
94. Edwards and Travard, *op. cit.*, p. 80.

4

From Calvin to Soloviev: The Devil through Four Centuries

Catholic Policy, 1555–1593

In view of the foregoing discussion of Catholic theology concerning Jews and Judaism, it is not surprising that the long-range consequence of these beliefs was the unrelenting persecution of Jews by both Catholic and non–Catholic Christians for the 400 years preceding the Holocaust.

There are innumerable examples of this persecution which constitute a great part of Jewish history and are not the topic of this book. It is instructive, however, to review the attitude of the sixteenth century popes toward the Jews, not only because it illustrates Catholic theology until 1965, but also because such attitudes determined Christian-Jewish relations in such a way as to contribute greatly to the fate of the European Jews.

It is evident that the contributions of Pope Paul IV and other popes to that fate were as influential as the contributions made by the Protestant Martin Luther and other Protestant theologians, for Paul IV relegated the Jews by edict to the ghetto and limited their occupational activities. This segregation, by no means solely achieved by that edict alone, had all the numerous consequenes which accomany all segregation.

In a most comprehensive discussion of this matter, Kenneth Stow has reviewed these papal policies beginning with the papal bull *Cum nimis absurdum* ("Since it is absurd," etc.) issued by Paul IV on July 17, 1555.[1]*

Stow successfully argues that the purpose of these policies was to "convert the Jews en masse' by using considerable pressure on the Jews and by expanding Catholic resources devoted to that end. Stow shows that conversion "was the core to which all of Jewry policy was united" a statement which, as we shall see, applied to non–Catholic Christians as well.[2]

*Notes to this chapter begin on page 98.

Here is a quote from *Cum nimis*:

> Since it is absurd and improper that Jews—whose own guilt has consigned them to perpetual servitude—under the pretext that Christian piety receives them and tolerates their presence, should be ingrates to Christians, so that they attempt to exchange the servitude they owe to Christians for dominion over them; we—to whose notice it has lately come that these Jews, in our dear City and in some other cities, lands and places of the Holy Roman Church, have erupted into insolence: they presumed not only to dwell side by side with Christians and near their Churches, with no distinct habit to separate them, but even to erect homes in the more noble sections and streets of the cities, lands and places where they dwell, and to buy and possess fixed property, and to have nurses, housemaids, and other hired Christian servants, and to perpetrate many other things in ignominy and contempt of the Christian name— considering that the Roman Church tolerates the Jews in testimony of the true Christian faith and to the end that they, led by the piety and kindness of the Apostolic See should at length recognize their errors, and make all haste to arrive at the true light of the Catholic faith, and thereby to agree that, as long as they persist in their errors, they should recognize through experience that they have been made slaves while Christians have been made free through Jesus Christ, God and our Lord, and likewise recognize that it is iniquitous that the children of the free women should serve the children of the maidservant,—and, desiring to make sound provisions as best we can— with the help of God—in the above matter, we sanction, by this our perpetually valid constitution, that [ghettos be established, etc.][3]

The foregoing summarizes almost all of the anti–Jewish decrees of the numerous Catholic councils and synods already reviewed and makes explicit what had always been the policy of the Church and later the policy of the Protestants, namely the conversion of the Jews to Christianity. All of the measures and efforts by Christians concerning Jews have been to that end for nearly 2,000 years, and continue to be so governed by some Christians to the present day.

Relying on the Fourth Lateran Council (1215; see Chapter 2) for inspiration in these matters, Paul IV merely repeated the decrees of that council concerning employment of Christians in Jewish homes and the wearing of special clothes by Jews. But, as Stow points out, the rulings of Fourth Lateran were designed to make the Jews aware that they were slaves and not masters of Christians. The purpose of *Cum nimis*, however, was to bring about the conversion of the Jews. Thus, the same words were put to a different end in 1555. The pope believed, and this was henceforth Catholic theology, that Jews would eventually recognize that they were slaves because of their apostasy and would therefore convert.[4]

Stow shows that there were several earlier efforts by sixteenth century popes to convert the Jews. He mentions 63 letters by popes Paul III and Julius III to that effect.

These earlier letters promise privileges to Jews who convert. *Cum nimis,* however, states that the Jews are tolerated only so that they may convert. According to Stow, Paul IV meant to achieve conversion of the Jews by concrete steps rather than by rhetoric. Thereafter, succeeding popes continued the policies and beliefs of Paul IV. Thus, Pius IV in 1562 continued this policy, as did Pius V, who extended the policies of Paul IV beyond Rome to cover all areas where Jews might be living, thus bringing the ghetto to all of Europe. The European Jews were imprisoned in these ghettos until the days of Napoléon Bonaparte.

Jean Chauvin (a.k.a. John Calvin) and Martin Bucer

I

There are those who claim that Calvin's "influence was even greater than Luther's."[5]

Such a claim may be defensible in other areas of concern, but it was surely not the case in Christian theology as it affected the Jews of the sixteenth century and thereafter.

In fact, Calvin (1509–1564) wrote very little about the Jews because he could not have met Jews in Geneva, inasmuch as the Jews were forced to leave that city on December 28, 1490, in the middle of the winter.[6]

It is true that Calvin accepted common Christian teachings concerning the position of Jews as outsiders, enemies of God and Christ killers. But compared to the excesses of hatred which Luther spewed forth for years, Calvin's attitudes toward the only non–Christians permitted to live in Christian Europe seemed mild and ordinary.

Baron, in his comprehensive essay "John Calvin and the Jews,"[7] shows that Calvin knew few Jews personally and that the constant friction between Christians and Jews stemming from money lending did not disturb Calvin as much as others because his ambiguous attitude toward money lending led Calvinists to enter banking themselves. Calvin did abuse the Jews on this account in a number of his sermons influenced mainly by Martin Butzer, also known as Bucer, who was a bishop in Strasbourg in Calvin's time. A prolific theologian and a pronounced Jew hater, Butzer was closely associated with Calvin for many years.[8]

Like Luther, Calvin was accused by his enemies of Judaizing and returned that same accusation against them. He denounced Jewish teachings with vehemence and accused Jews of seeking the Messiah only so as to attain personal wealth. Like all Christian theologians of his and earlier times, Calvin believed that ancient Judaism was a preparation for Christianity and that present Judaism was a relic. "The Jews' greatest crime consists in their lack of faith," argued Calvin. Further he accused the Jews of being responsible for a lack of peace in the world because "the Jews through their perversity show that they wish to have no peace with God." He also recited once more the canard that the Old Testament forefathers of the Jews had sinned many times and that "their cumulative sins over the generations accounted for the sufferings of the people of Israel...."[9] Calvin's attitude toward the Jews may also be seen in a pamphlet including 23 questions which were asked by a hypothetical Jew and answered by Calvin.[10]

All of these questions are designed to expose the paradoxes in the Gospels and seek to bring Christians into a state of confusion and uncertainty. For example, the eighth question is, "Why do Christians feel unhappy on the day of their Master's crucifixion, since they believe they are rescued from Hell because of it?" Another of these questions is, "If we are in exile because of our attitude toward Jesus, what has become of the verse 'Father, forgive them, for they know not what they do?'" All of these questions were answered by Calvin with this judgment: "Their [the Jews'] rotten and unbending stiffneckedness deserves that they be oppressed unendingly and without measure or end and that they die in their misery without the pity of anyone."[11] Calvin also supported the thesis that the Jews themselves were responsible for their misery because they were as a people guilty of deicide.

In his *Commentaries on the Epistles of Paul the Apostle to the Romans*, Calvin discusses the Jews once more, but that is the extent of his comments concerning the Jews. Unlike Luther, Calvin, despite his evident hostility toward Jews as just cited, nevertheless holds out the hope that the Jews will yet accept the Christian view and believes that some Jews at least, might yet be saved. Calvin comments on the following text from *Romans 11:11*:

> I say then, Did they stumble that they might fall? God forbid: but by their fall salvation is come unto the Gentiles, for to provoke them to jealousy. Now if their fall is the riches of the world, and their loss the riches of the Gentiles; how much more their fulness? But I speak to you that are Gentiles. Inasmuch then as I am an Apostle of the Gentiles, I glorify my ministry: if by any means I may provoke to jealousy them that are my flesh, and may save some of them. For if the casting away of them is the reconciling of the world, what shall the receiving of them be, but life from the dead?

Calvin regards this passage as evidence that all of Israel is not lost but that only those Jews are lost "who are obstinately offended by Christ in such a way that their destruction was universal, with no hope of repentance remaining." Calvin also believed that jealousy of the advantages gentiles gained from holding to the truth would lead Jews to turn to Christianity because Israel and the Church belong together. Further he writes that "the salvation of the Gentiles is so annexed to the salvation of the Jews that the same means is able to advance both." Finally, in his commentary on *John 1:47* Calvin writes, "For a true Christian and a true Israelite are one and the same."

Calvin also holds that Jews and gentiles are equally guilty before God and that the mercy of God is available to both, thus giving both access to salvation.[12]

It would serve no useful purpose to discuss here whether any of the assumptions made by Calvin have merit. Such phrases as "grace" and "salvation" may be nothing more than the verbal expression of Calvin's imagination. It may well be that the entire structure of Christian belief is imaginative only. It is nevertheless a fact that Calvin was by no means as malicious as Luther with reference to the European Jews, as is reflected in the conduct of his followers.

Baron writes that "Calvin escaped the danger of becoming linked up with the rising European nationalism ... in part his non-involvement stemmed from Geneva's small size. More importantly, ... in its large following among the English 'dissenters' it commanded allegiance among persecuted religious minorities.... Calvinism represented an international movement ... very much resembling in its socio-religious structure that of the persecuted Jewish minority."[13]

II

Closely associated with Calvin, when Calvin was living in Strasbourg, was Martin Butzer (or Bucer), bishop of that city. In 1538, Bucer (1491–1551) published a pamphlet entitled *RATSCHLAG: ob Christlicher Oberkait geburen muge, das sye die Juden unter den Christen zu wonen gedulden, und was sye zu gedulden, wolcher gestalt und mass* (or, "ADVICE: whether Christian government must be held reponsible for permitting the Jews to live among Christians, and what is to be tolerated, in which form and to what extent"). Medieval in its grammar, spelling and sentence structure, the book is a veritable encyclopedia of bigotry beginning with the assertion that the Christian government is responsible for the welfare of the true (Christian) religion. Bucer even holds that government ought either to expel or otherwise punish those who attach themselves to a different religion.[14]

Given this assertion, there arises the question concerning the treatment of Jews, who are certainly non–Christians. Citing the Roman Codex

Justiniani (see Chapter 1), which Bucer claimed was a divine law reflecting the will of God, Bucer recommended that Jews ought to be allowed their synagogues but should be expelled if they were to attempt the conversion of Christians or ridicule the Christian faith. According to Bucer, Jews were not to have any honors or administrative positions among Christians. He further recommended that Jews be treated in such a manner that they would be reminded of the anger of God over their unwillingness to convert.

Bucer viewed Jews as strangers who needed to be punished for their disbelief. He supported the expulsion of Jews from innumerable towns, principalities and countries. Nevertheless, Bucer did not condemn those nobles who permitted Jews in their territory on the ground that *jre wurzell heilig jst* ("their root is holy").

According to Bucer, the "Jewish Question" was not a matter for the present but for the last days, the days of judgment. God, Bucer believed, would preserve a small remnant of these Jews and would then choose a few of them. Meanwhile, it appeared to Bucer, Christians were to do all they could to win the Jews to the Truth. Consequently, Christians were to live an exemplary life so as to serve as a model for the yet unconverted Jews. However, since God sought to punish the Jews, Bucer thought it fitting that Christians do so in this world. Jews were to have no access to "clean and honest professions." Listing a number of obnoxious and dangerous jobs, Bucer recommended that Jews be assigned to them. In addition he also recommended that Jews be forced to listen to *Judenpredigten*, the Jew sermons we have encountered before.

Bucer also proposed that mercantile and financial occupations as well as the self-administration of Jewish villages or ghettos be prohibited the Jews. He also supported the widespread custom of having Jews pay a *Schutzpfennig*, a good-sized amount all Jews had to pay for "protection." It is difficult not to be reminded of similar demands made by organized crime in our own century in our own country.

All told, Bucer is convinced that God has assigned the Jews "the tail among the peoples among whom they live. That they should be the least and the last...."[15]

Nevertheless, Bucer also recommends that Jews be treated with kindness by Christians and that Christians be friendly at all times so that Jews will find love among Christians.

All of the hardships Bucer sought to impose on Jews were to be examples to any other non-believers as to the punishment God would impose for such unbelief.

On receiving objections to the harsh treatment he recommended from the Count of Hesse, to whom he had sent his views, Bucer renewed his insistence that Jews not be allowed trade or commerce of any kind.[16] Finally, Bucer recommended that Jews not be permitted the possession of the

Talmud, that great series of books derived from the discussions of the Jewish academies flourishing in Babylon and Israel in the first century C.E.

Hoping to avert the consequences of Bucer's recommendations, the Jews of Hesse evidently asked that they not be forced to pay a yet greater sum for protection than had already been extorted from them.

Unlike Luther, Bucer viewed the Old Testament as co-equal with the New Testament. Nevertheless, Bucer advised that Jews would become Christians only if treated in a manner that would impress on them their status of dishonor and their condition of deserved punishment. Using his view of the Old Testament status of "strangers," Bucer held that Jews should be treated accordingly in Christian countries—i.e., as strangers in their native lands. However, Bucer did not believe that Jews should be driven out of their homes and out of their countries as Luther taught.

Consequently, the Jews of Hesse were not evicted, as some Christian leaders had demanded, as Bucer succeeded in persuading the count to refrain from that measure.

English Theologians (1489–1556)

I

There were no Jews in England from their expulsion during the reign of Edward I in 1290 until their re-admission, albeit by the back door, during the rule of Oliver Cromwell in 1655.[17]

Therefore, the views of English theologians concerning the Jews before 1655 and after 1290 could not have been based on English experience with Jews, except insofar as some Englishmen undoubtedly met Jews outside of England itself.

It is remarkable that even Christian communities which had no Jews, such as Spain after 1492 and Poland after the mass murders during the Second World War, have repeatedly shown great antagonism to the mythical Jews with whom they had no real experience. William Shakespeare's classic call for hatred of Jews, *The Merchant of Venice*, and *The Jew of Malta* by Marlow, which created truly sardonic pictures of Jews, were both written by authors who had never seen a Jew but were influenced by the popular bigotry which was as common in the England of 1594 as it was everywhere else in the Christian world.

These plays were written during the reign of Elizabeth I. Since she supported the Church of England as established by her father, Henry VIII, it is reasonable to view briefly the attitude of the first archbishop of

Canterbury, Thomas Cranmer, concerning the Jews—not only because Cranmer never met a Jew in England, but also because he became a martyr to his religion in 1556.

Throughout his career, Cranmer evidently preached only one sermon revealing his beliefs concerning Jews. This sermon agreed with the common Christian attitude that the cruelties imposed by Christians upon Jews were the fault of the Jews themselves and were indeed imposed by God.[18]

Further he believed that the misery to which Jews had been subjected was to be a lesson to Christians who would not live according to the Gospel, all leading to divine punishment.

Several paragraphs of Cranmer's opinions concerning Jews illustrate those same sociological mechanisms which we have already met in earlier chapters and which served Cranmer as well as they had previously served other theologians. Said Cranmer: "But such as rejoice and brag in such things, utterly deceive themselves. Whoso listeth to read the histories of the heathen people and greatest idolaters, he shall not find among them all any region, people, or nation that was so scourged by God, so oft brought into servitude, so oft carried into captivity, with so divers, strange and many calamities oppressed, as were the children of Israel...."

There is no indication that it occurred to Cranmer that those who forced the Jews into captivity or oppressed them with "calamities" were responsible for these actions. To him, the victim is entirely at fault. Quoting St. Paul, Cranmer continues:

"Thou art called a Jew, and dost trust in the law, and makest thy boast of God, and knowest his will, and allowest the things that be best, and are informed by the law, and thinkest that thou art a guide to the blind, a light to them that are in darkness, a teacher to them that be ignorant, a doctor to them that be unlearned, which has the true form and knowledge of the truth by the law. But yet thou which teaches another teaches not thyself...."[19] Cranmer continues: "Thus the apostle St. Paul charging the Jews, chargeth us also...." Here Cranmer seeks to apply the lesson concerning the Jews to his Christian congregants whom God, as Cranmer viewed things, would punish also if they too were to exhibit "rebellion," which was the topic of his sermon.

This was also the topic of the preface to Thomas Becon's *Prayers*, in which he deals with the destruction of Jerusalem and reminds his readers that "The Jews have ever lived like most vile vagabonds and abominable abjects, having no certain country, no commonweal, no kingdom, no priesthood...." This condition Becon, who was Cranmer's chaplain, attributes to "their unfaithfulness and disobedience (I mean the Jews), neither will he spare 'the wild olive tree,' (I mean us that are gentiles), if we commit like offenses."[20]

Cranmer himself was charged with all of these "crimes" and burned at the stake when "Bloody Mary," the Roman Catholic queen, succeeded Edward VI. It is significant that the same mechanisms which permitted Christians of various denominations to persecute Jews for so long were also used to create all those religious horrors by which Christians persecuted one another. Secular power is a far more important reason for such persecution than other-wordly participation in the affairs of men. The proposition that God punishes the other fellow is, after all, not one which Christians applied only to the disagreeing Jews. Kaiser Wilhelm II of Germany coined the motto *"Gott strafe England"* ("God punish England"), and his successor Adolf Hitler had his troops wear a belt buckle which announced, *"Gott Mit Uns."*

Cranmer, then, did not deviate from the theological assumptions concerning Jews which were held everywhere in his day. Nevertheless, Cranmer was no Luther. There is no evidence that he made a special effort to castigate the Jews of his time nor that he initiated any new theology concerning them. Since there were no Jews in England, except perhaps those who as converts or pseudo-converts were living there, Cranmer could hardly have been aroused to deal with them in any manner.[21]

The sixteenth century was of course a time of great religious debate and ferment throughout all of Europe, including England.

The writings of John Foxe (1516–1587), author of *The Book of Martyrs*, are of interest here because Foxe, who escaped to Strasbourg during the reign of "Bloody" Mary, exhibits a view very typical of sixteenth century English Protestants with regard to the Jews. This is most important, because he was so very much concerned with religious martyrdom. We may justifiably ask whether Foxe was capable of recognizing the suffering of the Jews at the hands of Christians, in view of his great interest in the suffering of Christians at the hands of Christians.[22] That Jesus was the victim of the Jews is repeated many times in Foxe's martyrology. Thus, we learn that "In the reign of Tiberius, the Lord Jesus, the Son of God, in the four-and-thirtieth year of his age, which was the sixteenth of this emperor, by the malice of the Jews suffered his blessed passion...."[23]

In recording the destruction of the Jewish nation by Vespasian and Titus, Foxe does list that "eleven hundred thousand" were slain by these emperors and that others were sold into slavery and yet others "devoured of wild beasts." His conclusions concerning these events are however the same as those of Cranmer. Says Foxe: "By whose case all nations and realms may take example, what it is to reject the visitation of God's verity being sent, and much more to persecute them which be sent of God for their salvation."[24]

Here again is the old theme that those who disagree are victimized by God. Jews of course have held the same view, pointing out that those who have attacked them were punished by God.

Foxe mentions that the Jews betrayed Hegesippus because he was a Christian so that he was crucified by the Romans.[25] Evidently the same fate befell Polycarp of Smyrna. Again Foxe makes it a point to show that not only Romans but "Jews with their usual malice" were responsible for the martyr's death.[26]

Foxe also accuses Jews of inducing the emperor of Persia to persecute Christians, who are always depicted as innocent victims. We have already seen that in describing the victimization of Jews, the Jewish victim was generally himself held at fault. Therefore it is surprising that Foxe describes the conduct of the crusaders of the first Crusade (1095) in these terms: "But as the object of their undertaking was to extirpate the enemies of the christian faith, Jews as well as infidels fell a sacrifice to their fury. . . . The most horrible atrocities were committed against these unhappy outcasts, whose only chance of safety consisted in professing themselves Christians, and renouncing their religion."[27]

It is surprising indeed that Foxe could bring himself to make so sympathetic a remark concerning Jews, for in subsequent descriptions of anti-Jewish behavior and even the most heinous cruelties inflicted on Jews, Foxe returns to blaming the victim.

Discussing the events of 1189, when a large number of Jews were murdered in London and York, Foxe concludes that the Jews deserved this hideous persecution because "Every year commonly their custom was, to get some Christian man's child from the parents, and on Good Friday to crucify him, in despite of our religion."[28]

Foxe takes as fact the legend that in August of 1255 "the wicked Jews at Lincoln had cruelly crucified, whipped, and tormented a certain child, named Hugo" and that the Jews of Norwich had done the same, 20 years earlier.[29] He also recites that the Jews of London had intended to burn the city down but that "divers of them were taken and burned at the time of Lent. . . ."

The Jews of Lincoln are mentioned once more as Foxe describes how the Barons "spoiled the Jews" there, entered a synagogue, tore up the books of "their law," and burnt them and all other writings and "obligations which they could buy." Discussion of the Jews concludes with the statement that they were "utterly banished this realm of England at the same time, for which the commons gave to the king a fifteenth &c."[30]

Thus, while Foxe made no efforts to castigate the Jews whom he did not know, his teachings concerning them were in the Christian tradition. Hugh Latimer, the Bishop of Worcester, was another martyr of the Anglican Church, burned at the stake in 1555 by "Bloody" Mary. A major contributor to the Reformation in England, Latimer was a great preacher and a member of the ecclesiastical court. In the latter capacity he participated in voiding the marriage of Henry VIII to Catherine of Aragon.[31]

Latimer accused the Jews of Jesus's day and of his own day of seeking to rule the whole world, an accusation which we see continued even now and which featured prominently in the nineteenth century forgery known as *The Protocols of the Elders of Zion*. Said Latimer:

> Here is to be noted the error of the Jews, which believed that this Saviour should be a temporal king and ruler, and deliver them out of the hands of the Romans; subdued by Pompeius, the great and valiant captain, as Josephus, a great and learned man among the Jews, and Titus Livius do witness. Therefore they believed that this Saviour should not only set them at liberty, but should subdue all nations; so that the Jews only, with their Saviour, should be the rulers of all the whole world, and that the world should serve them. This was at the same time, and is yet still, the opinion of the Jews....

He further preached that "they [the Jews] were cursed in the sight of God"—an opinion he buttressed, as did so many others, with examples derived from Jewish history. He too blamed the victims. Latimer agreed with all other Christian theologians that "Though Jerusalem be builded again, yet the Jews shall have it no more"[32]—an opinion shared by James Calfhill, bishop of Worcester, who not only attributed the aborted effort of the Jews to rebuild their temple during the reign of Julian the Apostate to divine intervention, but also had information to the effect that God placed the sign of the cross upon Jewish clothing. "And the Jews' apparel was filled with the sign of the cross."[33]

Similar views were held by all the other Protestant theologians of the day, including John Bale, bishop of Usury, James Pilkington, bishop of Durham, Lancelot Andrews, bishop of Winchester and George Berkely, bishop of Cloyne.[34]

John Knox (1505–1572), the founder of the Scottish Presbyterian church, held similar views. Nevertheless, Knox made no angry accusations against Jews; nor did he villify them. Of course he held the Jews in error with respect to the Messiah, making these observations: "Ye shall understand that the Jews had a fleshly opinion of this promised Seede: for they understood that the Messiah which was promised to them, should rule temporally as David did; and establish his realme in great quietness and rest, with all pleasure and voluptuousness...."[35]

Knox also used the fate of the Jews as a warning to Christians who in his day disagreed with his interpretation of Christian teachings.[36] We can make certain observations then, about the teachings of English theologians during the sixteenth century, the century which saw the establishment of Protestantism in that country.

First, it is evident that English theologians treated Jews mainly in a historical, disembodied manner. There were no Jews in England and therefore only the Jews whose activities were read in Christian scriptures were useful examples to the Christian theologians of that time and place. It may well be that it was for this reason that we do not find the extreme hatred expressed so often on the continent, a hatred fueled by the imagination and by segregation. Nor do we find special laws against Jews in England, for the same reason.

Second, there was great interest in 16th century England in the Mosaic Law and third, the English Reformation, like the Reformation on the continent, sought to return to its Hebraic roots. There were those who believed that Hebrew had supernatural qualities, that it was or should be the universal language, that "the lost ten tribes" were found in Scotland, that the "millennium" or Second Coming was at hand and that the Jews had a role to play in the eschatological (*estkahatos* = "last," Gr.) events about to come.[37]

All of this led to an attitude toward the Jews among English Christians which Katz has described as "philo–Semitic" and which we prefer to call "pro–Jewish" as the word "Semitic" is hardly useful in describing Jews. The consequence of this positive estimation of Jews, despite the theology already discussed, was the readmission of Jews to England in 1660. Of course, the readmission revealed that a number of Jews had lived in England for some time but had been ignored as Jews so as not to violate the official stance that no Jews were to live there. Thus, it became state policy to bring Jews into England during the rule of Oliver Cromwell and beyond, so that despite the continued conviction that God was still punishing Israel for refusing to recognize the Christian Messiah, the English thought it just that they too should harbor some of the people dispersed among the nations. In short, if it was true that God had scattered the Jews among all nations, "Why not let some into England?"[38]

This spirit of toleration is best expressed in the *Letter Concerning Toleration* written by the great British philosopher John Locke (1632–1704) in 1689.[39]

Here Locke actually wrote the following:

> Neither pagan nor Mahometan nor Jew, ought to be excluded from the civil rights of the commonwealth because of his religion. The Gospel commands no such thing. The church which judges not those that are without, wants it not. And the commonwealth, which embraces indifferently all men that are honest, peaceable and industrious, requires it not. . . . If we allow the Jews to have private houses and dwellings among us, why should we not allow them to have synagogues? Is their doctrine more false, their worship more abominable, or is the civil peace more endangered by their meeting in public than in their private houses?"[40]

Thus, the Jews returned to England and have prospered there ever since. This is not to say that Christian theology among English-speaking people did not include prejudices and negativisms against Jews. The great theologian Jonathan Edwards, who was an Englishman born in America (1703–1758), accused the Jews of Jesus's day of being arrogant unbelievers.[41] But unlike the peoples of the European continent, and despite all prejudices, the English did not persecute or annihilate any Jewish community since the return of the Jews in the seventeenth century. Instead, the condition of the English Jews improved steadily since then so that the leading Jewish communities of our own day are found in the United States and in England, Canada, and other countries at one time associated with the British Commonwealth of Nations.

II

Returning now to the European continent, where the majority of the world's Jews lived before the Second World War and where their ultimate fate would eventually be decided, we need to take a brief look at the teachings of Christian theology in Germany concerning Jews. This is important because the Germans were the final arbiters of Jewish fate, not only in Germany but in all of Europe outside of England and a few neutral countries not invaded by the German armies during the Second World War.

With the exception of Lessing (1729–1791), the author of *Nathan der Weise* (*Nathan the Wise*), German theologians were unwilling to accommodate Jews in European society.

A playwright in his mature years, Lessing, the son of a Lutheran pastor, wrote theological treatises in his younger years. In 1753 he published *Letter of a Jew to a Philosopher*, arguing that governments should alleviate the misery of the Jews. He cites the example of England, where, he says, Jews could buy homes and farms. He further shows that in Holland and England Jews could enter the professions, and that no harm has come to anyone as a result of these policies. The letter promises that any nobleman who would free the Jews would find them most grateful.[42]

It is once more necessary to emphasize that these sentiments were the rare exception. Instead we find that the principal theologian-philosophers of Germany during the centuries between Luther and Hitler were so anxious to remove Jews and Judaism from the Christian world that they even tried to suppress the Jewish ancestry of Jesus and the Jewish origins of Christianity. This trend was not as pronounced in Catholic theology which, despite its hostility to Judaism, never denied this connection.

German Protestantism, however, was bolder. Johann Gottlieb Fichte (1762–1814), whose *Addresses to the German Nation*[43] sought to connect the

Christian faith to the German soul, doubted the Jewishness of Jesus, which, he thought, could not possibly have anything to do with "the dead religiosity of Judaism."[44]

His two contemporaries, Schleiermacher and Hegel, likewise continued the anti–Jewish tradition in German theology and philosophy. Friedrich Schleiermacher (1768–1834) has been called "the Kant of modern Portestantism" and as such determined the course of that faith in Germany for two centuries.[45]

Schleiermacher did not write lengthy polemics against Jews and Judaism; his comments on the subject were few. His views were that "The rule may be set up that almost everything else in the Old Testament is, for our Christian usage, but the husk or wrapping of its prophecy, and whatever is more definitely Jewish has least value."[46]

One of the greatest of German philosophers, Georg Wilhelm Friedrich Hegel (1770–1831), wrote an entire treatise called *The Spirit of Judaism* as part of his *The Spirit of Christianity and Its Fate*.[47]

The importance of Hegel to German philosophy can hardly be exaggerated. Though trained as a theologian, Hegel did not practice the ministry, but became a critic of orthodox Christianity. To Hegel, reason was God, and the Deity pure reason.

The Spirit of Judaism is based on Hegel's interpretation of the life of Abraham as recorded in Genesis. Hegel concedes that Judaism had risen above oriental religions by viewing God as spirit and as "conscious subject and absolute power."[48]

His criticism of Judaism, however, reinforced all those ancient bigotries which in his day were so institutionalized that his theological education would have made any other attitude impossible. Hegel sees Abraham, and hence all his spiritual descendants (i.e., the Jews), as wanting *not* to love. Here is a very common prejudice enjoyed by Christians for centuries, holding that Christianity is a religion of love, but Judaism a religion devoted not to love but to cold legalisms. Thus Abraham and, by extension, Jews, are "strangers to the soil and men alike. He [Abraham] persisted in cutting himself off from others. He was suspicious and resorted to cunning and duplicities."[49]

Lest anyone doubt that Hegel meant to describe the Jews of his own time and all Jews who came thereafter, Hegel wrote, "With Abraham, the true progenitor of the Jews, the history of this people begins, i.e., his spirit is the unity, the soul, regulating the entire fate of his posterity."[50]

Abraham is depicted as seeking every means to avoid love and human relationships. "Love alone was beyond his power," says Hegel as he teaches that "mastery was the only possible relationship in which Abraham could stand to the infinite world opposed to him." The claim of Abraham and his posterity to a singular God is "horrible," according to Hegel, while the sons of Jacob act "with satanic atrocity" in connection with the rape of their sister.

Continuing his review of Jewish Biblical history, Hegel finds that Jews, even in Moses's time, did not exit from Egypt because of a "heartfelt hatred of oppression, ... but in certain tricks with which Moses baffled them."[51]

The Exodus from Egypt leads Hegel to the conclusion that Egypt suffered from the Jews who, unwilling to do anything to gain their freedom, merely took advantage of what was done for them. The Jews are cowards whose only emotion is malice and whose only achievement is theft. Hegel leads his reader to believe that the Egyptians were the victims of the malicious Jews, not the other way around. "Amid the general lamentation they [the Jews] withdraw, driven forth by the hapless Egyptians (*Exodus 12: 33-34*) but they have only the malice the coward feels when his enemy is brought low by someone else's act."[52]

We learn from Hegel that Jews are utter materialists who wish for no more than physical existence with no understanding of beauty or truth. They see in everything only matter coupled to a total passivity. "The Jews," says Hegel, "had no share in anything eternal." Instead their religion is "born of misfortune and made for misfortune."

The strength of Jews rested on hostility alone, according to Hegel, and their independence prior to 70 C.E. was a state of "total ugliness." The Jews "turned against its own vitals the same rabid lovelessness and godlessness which formerly it had turned against other nations...."[53]

The fate of the Jews, Hegel concludes, "can rouse neither terror nor pity.... It can rouse horror alone."

Thus Hegel legitimized once more all those beliefs which led his successors, including Karl Marx on the German left and the Nazis on the right, to use him as a source of inspiration and reference for all those hatreds which Hegel surely did not invent but which he incorporated into his system to the edification of movements which he could not foresee but which he bolstered nonetheless.

It would be the rare communist or Nazi, or victim of either, who could not have identified Hegel as the father of these ideologies and their consequences. Centuries of Christian theology, however, colored Hegel's views concerning the Jews in such a manner as to make him a participant in that gruesome Jewish fate which his philosophical descendants had in store.

III

Although the position of the Jews in Christian theology remained fixed during the centuries after Luther and before the middle of the twentieth century, it can be shown that here and there some Christian theologians relieved the universal hostility toward Judaism with some measure of acceptance. We have already seen this to be true of Lessing and find it again at the end of Hegel's century in the Russian theologian Vladimir Sergeyevich Soloviev (1858–1901). Despite his announced wish to convert the Jews to Christianity, Soloviev discusses the so-called "Jewish question" in a manner surprising for one who was born a century before the ecumenical efforts of *The New Delhi Report* and the *Documents of Vatican II on Non–Christians* were even considered.

Referring to the possible conversion of Israel (the Jews) to Christianity, Soloviev writes this concerning "A Christian Solution to the Jewish Question": "Our trouble does not stem from an excessive influence of the Talmud but from an insufficient influence of the Gospel. On us, ourselves, and not on the Jews, depends the desired solution of the Jewish question. We cannot make the Jews renounce the laws of the Talmud but it is always in our power to apply to Jewry the commands of the Gospels. One of the two! Either the Jews are not our enemies, and, in that case, the Jewish question does not exist at all, or they are our enemies, and, in that case, treat them in the spirit of love and peace—that is the only solution to the Jewish question."[54]

There is of course no Jewish question. The proposition that Jewish existence ought to be questioned is ipso facto the problem for which the solution can only be an attitude change on the part of Christians. This even Soloviev did not see. We can nevertheless credit him with willingness to recognize the part Christianity had played in the condition of the Jews until then, a recognition best understood by citing the following:

> The reciprocal relations between Judaism and Christianity in the course of many centuries of combined, intermingled living in each other's midst represent a remarkable circumstance. The Jews have always looked upon Christianity and treated it in accordance with the precepts of their religion, their faith and their law. The Jews have always treated us in accordance with Judaism; we the Christians, however, have until now not yet learned to treat Judaism in accordance with Christianity. In relation to us they have never violated their religious law, while we have, in relation to them, constantly been violating and continue to violate the commands of the Christian religion.[55]

IV

A review of these contributions of Martin Luther and other reformers to Christian-Jewish relations leaves no room to doubt their hatred for Jews and the Jewish religion. This does not mean, for several reasons, that

Protestants living at the end of the twentieth century are therefore obliged to hate Jews or to participate in anti–Jewish conduct. That is true for several reasons.

First, it is evident that Christian theology before the Reformation was just as condemnatory of the Jews as were the Reformers, and that their defamatory statements were a reflection not only of beliefs current in the fifteenth and sixteenth centuries, but of a current in Christian societies since and even before the Council of Nice. The writings of the Ante-Nicene Fathers make very plain that the Jewish religion and Jews were always the foil upon which Christianity proved its veracity and that the need to defame Jews and Judaism had been so essential an aspect of Christian theology since its inception that until the last half of the twentieth century, Christianity without anti–Judaism was as inconceivable as the conception of good without evil or the belief in Heaven without a belief in Hell.

Dualism thus pervades the essence of Christianity and gives it a Zoroastrian aspect which is generally overlooked as the doctrines of trinitarian monotheism are emphasized. That is the principal message in Christian anti–Judaism and its offshoots, anti–Semitism and anti–Zionism.

Since the early 1960s, however, all branches of Christianity have, in the face of the Holocaust, attempted to reject this dualiasm with ever-increasing effort so as to rid Christianity of the scandal deriving from Christian association with the Nazi crimes. In the ever more secularized and industrialized world in which all faiths must exist at the end of the twentieth century, it is ever more apparent that secular humanism, not the Jewish religion, is the enemy of faith and belief no matter what its label. To put it bluntly, Christians have learned that the extermination of Judaism is impossible, that there is little if any chance of Judaism rivaling Christianity and that total indifference to *any* religion is the real threat to believers who had hoped at least to hang on to their children if they could not convert the whole world.

Before turning to the Christian attitude concerning Jews in the twentieth century, both before and after the Holocaust, consideration will be taken of the manner in which the Jews of Europe, and particularly Germany, lived their lives during the century and a half between the French Revolution and the advent of Hitler.

One must consider the usual daily existence of the Jews in Christian Germany because it was in Germany that the Holocaust originated, although it collected its victims from all parts of the European continent. The fact is that the Jews of Europe continued a medieval existence until the French Revolution and that this great event determined their lives until the coming of World War II. Then another great change was in store for them, leading to major changes in Christian thinking which will be explored later.

Notes

1. Kenneth R. Stow, *Catholic Thought and Papal Jewry Policy* (New York, The Jewish Theological Seminary, 1977), p. 3.

   Cum nimis absurdum et inconveniens existat ut iudaei, quos propria culpa perpetuae servituti submisit, sub praetextu quod pietas christiana illos receptet et eorum cohabitationem sustineat, christianis adeo sint ingrati, ut, eis pro gratia, contumeliam reddant, er in eos, pro servitute, quam illis debent, dominatum vendicare procurent; nos, ad quorum notitiam nuper devinit eosdem iudaeos in alma urbe nostra et nonnullis S.R.E. civitatibus, terris et locis, in id insolentiae prorupisse, ut non solum mixtim cum christianis et prope eorum ecclesias, nulla intercedente habitus distinctione, cohabitare, verum etiam domos, in nobilioribus civitatum terrarum et locorum, in quibus degunt, vicis et plateis conducere, et bona stabilia comparare et possidere, ac nutrices et ancillas aliosque servientes christianos mercinarios habere, et diversa alia in ignominian er contemptum christiani nominis perpetrare praesumant, considerantes Ecclesiam Romanam eosdem iudaeos tolerare in testimoniam verae fidei christianae et ad hoc, ut ipsi Sedis Apostolicae pietate et benignitate allecti, errores suos tandem recognoscant, et ad verum catholicae fidei lumen pervenire satagant, et propterea convenire ut quamdiu in eorum erroribus persistunt, effectu operis recognoscant se servos christianos vero liberos per Iesum Christum, Deum et Dominum nostrum effectos fuisse, iniquumque existere ut filli liberae filiis famulentur ancillae. Volentes in praemissis, quantum cum Deo possumus, salubriter providere, hac nostra perpetuo valitura constitutione sancimus quod de detero....

2. *Ibid.*, p. 5.
3. *Ibid.*, p. 6.
4. *Ibid.*, p. 10.
5. Will Durant, *The Reformation* (New York, Simon and Schuster, 1957), p. 488.
6. Rudolf Pfisterer, *Im Schatten des Kreuzes* (Hamburg, Evangelischer Verlag, 1966), p. 72.
7. Solo Wittmayer Baron, "John Calvin and the Jews," in Feldman, *op. cit.*, pp. 338–352.
8. *Ibid.*, pp. 339–340.
9. *Ibid.*, pp. 341–348.
10. Jacques Courvoisier, *Calvin et les Juifs*, in Pfisterer, *op. cit.*, p. 72.
11. *Ibid.*, p. 72.
12. David W. Torrance and Thomas F. Torrance, eds., *Calvin's Commentaries on the Epistles of Paul the Apostle to the Romans* (Grand Rapids, Mich., Eerdmans, 1960), pp. 245–247.
13. *Ibid.*, p. 352.
14. Robert Stupperich, ed., *Martini Buceri Opera Omnia*, Series I, Vol. 7 (Paris Presses Universitaires de France, 1964), p. 325.
15. *Ibid.*, pp. 328–329.
16. *Ibid.*, p. 331.

17. David S. Katz, *Philo-semitism and the Readmission of the Jews to England* (Oxford, Clarendon Press, 1982).
18. Thomas Cranmer, "A Sermon on Rebellion," in *Letters of Thomas Cranmer*, John E. Cox, ed. (The Parker Society, Cambridge, The University Press, 1846), p. 198.
19. *Ibid.*, p. 198.
20. Thomas Becon, S.T.P. *Prayers and Other Pieces* (Cambridge, The University Press, 1844), p. 9.
21. Katz, *op. cit.*, pp. 1–244.
22. John Foxe, *The Acts and Monuments*, George Townsend, ed. (New York, AMS, 1965).
23. *Ibid.*, Vol. I, p. 90.
24. *Ibid.*, p. 91.
25. *Ibid.*, p. 116.
26. *Ibid.*, pp. 133–134.
27. *Ibid.*, p. 142.
28. *Ibid.*, p. 277.
29. *Ibid.*, Vol. II, p. 532.
30. *Ibid.*, p. 578.
31. Hugh Latimer, *Works* (Cambridge, The University Press, 1845).
32. *Ibid.*, p. 47.
33. James Calfhill, *An Answer to John Martiall's Treatise of the Cross* (Cambridge, The University Press, 1846), pp. 114–123.
34. See *The Publication of the Works of the Fathers and Early Writers of the Reformed English Church* (The Parker Society, Cambridge, The University Press, 1849).
35. John Knox, *The Works*, David Laing, ed. (Edinburgh, Bannatyne Club, 1854, and New York, AMS, 1966), p. 456.
36. *Ibid.*, Vol. 5, pp. 22–23.
37. Katz, *op. cit.* p. 5.
38. *Ibid.*, p. 243.
39. John Locke, *A Letter Concerning Toleration*, Mario Montuori, ed. (The Hague, Martinus Nijhoff, 1963).
40. *Ibid.*, p. 103.
41. Jonathan Edwards, *Original Sin* (New Haven and London, Yale University Press, 1970), p. 337.
42. Gotthold Ephraim Lessing, *Lessing's Werke*, Richard Gosche, ed. (Berlin, 1884), pp. 176–177.
43. Johann Gottlieb Fichte, *Addresses to the German Nation*, R.F. Jones and G.H. Turnbull, trans. (Open Court, 1922), pp. 93–94.
44. Allan Davies, "Racism and German Protestant Theology," *The Annals*, Vol. 450, July 1980, pp. 20–25.
45. Richard R. Niehbur, "Introduction," in Friedrich Schleiermacher, *The Christian Faith* (New York, Harper & Row, 1963), p. ix.
46. *Ibid.*, p. 62.
47. Friedrich Hegel, *On Christianity*, T.M. Knox, trans. (New York, Harper, Row Inc., 1948), pp. 182–205.
48. *Ibid.*, p. 183.
49. *Ibid.*, p. 186.
50. *Ibid.*, p. 182.
51. *Ibid.*, pp. 188–189.
52. *Ibid.*, p. 190.

53. *Ibid.*, pp. 201–202.
54. Vladimir Soloviev, in *Zhaba: Russkie Mysliteli o Rossii I Chelovechestve— Antologiia Russkoi Obshchestvennoi Mysli*, George Vid Tomashevich, trans. (Paris, YMCA, 1954), p. 247.
55. *Ibid.*, pp. 246–247.

TWO: Toward a New Christian Theology of Judaism

5

The Jews in Early 20th Century Christian Theology

I

The life of the European Jews during the 150 years from 1789 to 1939 was mainly a product of institutionalized Christian theology. The Jewish minority in Europe was forced to permit Christian opinion to intrude upon all facets of their lives both in Eastern Europe, where the Jews remained in small Jewish communities called *shtetls* until their mass murder during the Second World War, and in Western Europe, where the ghetto was abolished as the Napoleonic armies brought the message of "Liberty, Fraternity and Equality" to all parts of that continent.

While the vast majority of European Jews lived in the Eastern European Yiddish-speaking world, segregated by language, religion and custom from the Christian majority, the Jews of Western Europen entered European society after 1789 and believed, not without reason, that their emancipation would eventually lead to full equality in the lands of their birth.

Nowhere was this belief more prevalent than in Germany—the country which eventually succeeded in killing not only the German Jews but almost all of the Jews of Europe on racial, not theological, grounds. These racial beliefs were and are called "anti–Semitism."

It is true, as we have already seen, that Christian theology contributed to the anti–Semitic movement. Nevertheless, it is the thesis of this book that although Christian theology contributed to racial anti–Semitism, it was anti–Semitism and not Christian theology which finally led to the mass murders usually called the Holocaust.

This is true because Christians, even including Martin Luther, were willing to accept former Jews as equals if they converted to the Christian faith. For example, in a letter Luther wrote in 1523 to "Bernard" called "A

Converted Jew" he shows friendship and camaraderie with him and discusses the condition of the Jews of his day in some detail.[1]*

Furthermore, Christianity, claiming to be a universal faith, could hardly exclude converted Jews from equal treatment, not only because doing so would deny the message Christians sought to convey concerning the gospel of their founder, but also because such exclusion would jeopardize further conversion efforts toward other Jews.

For this reason, the popes intervened repeatedly when Christians of Jewish birth and descent were subjected to discrimination in sixteenth century Spain. There the Jews had been forced on pain of death to leave or convert in 1492. About half of the 200,000 Spanish Jews left. Those Jews who remained and practiced Christianity were nevertheless called *Marranos*, meaning swine, by the Spanish populace. Even second and third generation Christians of Jewish descent were so named.

No doubt that is an example of racial anti–Semitism, although the Spanish example falls far short of the events occurring in Germany between 1933 and 1945.[2]

Thus, while there have been and still are Christians who suffer from their own racial hatred against others, Christian doctrine and theology never taught racism, which is a contradiction, indeed a paradox, that can be incorporated neither into the view that all men are the same "in Christ," nor into the Jewish precept upon which Christianity rests: "You shall love your neighbor as yourself" (*Leviticus 19:18*).

It is therefore reasonable to hold that the mass murder of the European Jews would not have taken place had the government of Germany remained Christian between 1933 and 1945.

It was precisely the fact that the Nazi movement was anti–Christian that led to these murders despite the evidence that Christianity contributed to anti–Semitism in the manner already explored here in detail.

The great French philosopher Jean-Paul Sartre, who was himself a Catholic, shows in his remarkable book *Anti–Semite and Jew* that the anti–Semite attacks Christianity and its precepts by attacking the Jews who created the moral restrictions of the Judeo-Christian tradition in the first place, a view with which Sigmund Freud concurred when in his *Moses and Monotheism* he wrote, "The hatred of Judaism is at bottom hatred of Christianity."[3]

This distinction between anti–Judaism and anti–Semitism is therefore important and needs to be understood. Here, however, we are concerned only with the attitudes of Christian theology concerning the Jews and need therefore only to review the principal Christian theological theses developed concerning them.

Notes to this chapter begin on page 126.

II

Throughout all the centuries of Christian dominance in Europe and elsewhere, six theses have motivated Christian theologians in their writings concerning Jews. These theses are well summarized by Charlotte Klein, a German theology professor, in her remarkable book *Der Anti-Judaismus in der Christlichen Theologie.*[4]

According to Klein, the following views were still the principal assumptions of German Christian theologians concerning Judaism in the early 1970s:

1. Judaism has been superseded and replaced by Christianity.
2. Judaism has scarcely any right to exist.
3. In any case its teachings and ethical values are inferior to those of Christianity.
4. No effort is made by Christian theologians to ask how Jews see themselves. Jewish history is interpreted only from a Christian point of view.
5. The same authors will have a different view of Judaism when dealing with ecumenical issues than when dealing with theological issues.
6. The Christian theologian continues to assume that he has the right to pass judgment on Judaism, its destiny and its task in the world—or even that he is permitted to dictate this task.

All these attitudes have traditionally been the views of Christians concerning Jews and Judaism and continue to flourish despite the Holocaust and the mass murders to which these attitudes have so richly contributed.

Nevertheless, during the first third of the twentieth century these beliefs did not go unquestioned. While these beliefs did indeed give rise to anti-Semitism and were in turn reinforced by racial doctrines, and while in addition a good number of Christian theologians in Europe before the Holocaust actively participated in the Jew-baiting that had become endemic there, there were nevertheless some Christian theologians who had become uncomfortable with the persecution of the German Jews beginning in 1933. These theologians tried to disassociate Christianity from these crimes but were unable to refute clearly the doctrines just listed.

Thus, the great dilemma of Christian theology concerned Jews during and after the Nazi episode has been to hold on to the anti-Jewish teachings so long an essential part of Christian belief while rejecting the outcome of these doctrines—persecutions, racism and mass murder. This dilemma was visible in the writings of Christian theologians before the declarations on the Jews issued by the Protestant and Catholic churches in 1958 and 1965 and is once more evident in the thinly disguised anti-Jewish attitudes of some Christian churches which are now labeled "anti-Zionism."

III

Just prior to the rise of Nazi power in Europe, "there was scarcely any independent Catholic biblical study."[5] The writings of European, particularly German, Protestants will therefore be mentioned more in this connection than the works of Catholics.

Nevertheless, just prior to the Holocaust, the French Catholic theologian Jacques Maritain (1882–1973) dealt with "The Jewish Question," as he called it, in a most sympathetic manner while the influential German Protestant theologian Rudolf Bultmann included considerable discussion of Judaism in his *Jesus and the Word*.[6]

Maritain first wrote his "L'Impossible Antisemitisme" in 1937 as an article in *Les Juifs*. While his essay deals at length with the consequences of German anti–Semitism, a topic which does not concern us here, he also deals with the theological issue of "The Divine Significance of the Dispersion of Israel."

He begins with the Pauline dispensation to the effect that "Christians have been grafted onto the predestined olive tree of Israel in place of the branches which did not recognize the Messiah foretold by the prophets."[7]

Here, even the sympathetic Maritain takes it for granted that he has the right to comment upon a religion not his own.

The "Jewish Problem," says Maritain, "is an insoluble problem." To him the "problem" will "resemble a resurrection from among the dead." Accordingly, both the Church and Israel, here meaning the Jews, are each one, a "mystical body" that is in the world but not *of* the world. That, says Maritain, is the Christian point of view.

Maritain views the ambivalence of anti–Semites as yet another evidence of the mystery of Israel. He notes that almost all Jew haters claim to know at least one Jew personally who to them is "different" and whom they praise. This too he includes as evidence of the "Mystery of Israel."

Hatred of Jews Maritain attributes to the feeling that "they [the Jews] will always be outsiders in a spiritual sense.... It is the vocation of Israel which the world execrates.

"Hatred of Jews and Christians spring from a common source."[8] That common source, according to Maritain, is naturalism, the belief that supernaturalism is not needed. Thus, *omnes quidem peccaverunt, et egent gloria dei* ("all have sinned and need the glory of God"). He attributes the Nazi excesses of his day to naturalism and views those who adopt a racist mentality as "Hitler's messengers." His advice is this: "The only realism which a Christian has the right to profess in such a matter is the one that warns us that the least word which might convey the merest shadow of an indulgence or concession toward racism, runs the risk of bearing an ugly complicity and of dripping with innocent blood."[9]

Maritain quotes Pope Pius XI, who said in 1938, "Anti-Semitism is unacceptable. Spiritually we are all semites."

Such pronouncements may well include anthropological inaccuracies inasmuch as very few Jews are Semites. However, the meaning is clear. The pope was clearly trying to disassociate himself and his church from the Nazi measures already fully in effect in 1938 when he made this statement.

Commenting upon this view Maritain finally concludes that "the bitter zeal of anti-semitism always turns in the end into a bitter zeal against Christianity itself."[10]

"We do not wish to know that as a man our Lord was a Jew," says Maritain. That was indeed true, for Christian theology in the early part of the twentieth century included those who tried to deny the Jewish heritage of Jesus and in their hatred sought to prove his non-Jewish origins.

Among these was the German theologian Walter Grundmann. In 1940, in the midst of the Hitlerian madness, Grundmann produced his *Jesus der Galilaer und das Judentum*, whose purpose it was to prove that Jesus not only was not Jewish in his message, but was biologically descended from a Roman soldier and not a Jew.[11]

Similar claims were made then by Martin Dibelius (1883–1947) and Gerhard Kittel, author of *Die Judenfrage* (*The Jewish Question*), who wrote that Jews have an obligation to take upon themselves suffering and dispersal so as to please God.[12]

In addition to these theologians there were numerous other European and particularly German theologians who, in an effort to please the Nazis, wrote innumerable diatribes of "theology" during the years 1933–1945 which sought to utterly divorce Christianity from Judaism.

The theologian Rudolf Bultmann (1884–1976) was one of them. His views of Judaism and Jews came from an earlier source and sought to portray the Jews in the light of traditional teachings about Judaism but with a special contribution to that immense anti-Jewish polemic we have already reviewed.

But, as occurred so often in the long history of theology, Bultmann found yet one more means of denigrating Judaism in his *Jesus and the Word* published in 1934.[13]

Here we are told that Judaism rested on law, but a law that could "not be characterized as a moral code." Jewish law, according to Bultmann, is "a law which does not rest upon the ethical conception of man and humanity...." According to Bultmann, the Jewish conception of God views Him as an oriental ruler so that the Jewish people were obliged to give unconditional obedience to this invisible potentate.

Bultmann's criticism of Judaism concerns what he calls Israel's cultic religion, meaning the belief that "Israel's war is God's war, Israel's honor is God's honor, and Israel's country is God's country." This is no doubt the case. However, Bultmann lets his readers believe that it is only true of Israel and the Jews. Ethnocentrism, however, is surely not only a Jewish trait. It is universal and therefore not remarkable because it also occurs among Jews. It is particularly astonishing that Bultmann criticized Judaism for its ethnocentric attitudes at a time when the Nazi government of Germany was exhibiting a degree of nationalism and racism previously unknown anywhere.

Bultmann continues his critique of Judaism by claiming that the Jews obeyed their law, not because of its content but only because it was to be obeyed. "Not what was commanded determined the will of the person acting, but the fact that such and such was commanded."[14] Bultmann nevertheless agrees that the Old Testament contains ethical precepts useful to everyone at all times and that these precepts, such as the decalogue, had universal validity. But Bultmann remains of the opinion that "the commandments were kept because they were commanded" and not because they had any validity. It would appear that nothing fit the Prussian and National Socialist ideology better than the view that obedience was more important than any virtue, a view repeatedly used by Nazi criminals after the Second World War in defense of their brutal actions.[15]

Jewish morality is "definitely opposed to all humanistic ethics," said Bultmann, for "only obedience has significance." How Germanic Bultmann's Jews were!

Closely associated with Bultmann was Martin Dibelius, co-founder with Bultmann of the school of "Form-criticism."

In his book *Jesus*, published in 1939, Dibelius repeats the endless argument about Jewish legalism and even uses a typically Nazi term in claiming that the Jews saw God as "the party leader of the legalists."

A similar argument was used by Bultmann's student Gunther Bornkamm, whose well known *Jesus of Nazareth* repeats the view of Dibelius that God had become a party leader to the Jews and that Jewish history came to an end in the year 70 C.E.[16]

Bultmann and others thus remained largely within the standard interpretation of Judaism achieved by the beginning of the twentieth century. While by no means crude anti–Semites, Bultmann and Dibelius produced the kind of intellectual critique of Judaism which made anti–Judaism respectable on grounds that appeared most legitimate and therefore prepared the educated readers of this kind of theology for all the excuses they needed to tolerate the persecutions they were about to witness.

It was in the first third of the twentieth century that the great German scholar Max Weber (1864–1920) published his classic *The Theory of Social and Economic Organization*. Here Weber discussed forms of authority and legitimacy and included in that discussion what he called "Traditional Authority," meaning authority associated with status. Speaking of the "routinization" of authority Weber showed that acts and beliefs were often perpetuated in human societies because they were always done in a particular way. Anti-Jewish theology was therefore no exception. Those who interpreted everything Jewish in a negative manner were acting traditionally and reinforcing traditional authority. Thus, when the Holocaust came, many Christians could point to all of the writings of theologians from Barrabas to Bultmann as evidence of the legitimacy of Jewish suffering.[17]

At the same time, it can be demonstrated that there were even then European theologians who, like Maritain, denounced bigotry and anti-Jewish conduct and derived their views from the same Christian theology which led others to legitimize persecution.

One of these was Karl Barth (1886–1968), surely one of the most influential of German Protestant theologians. Writing in 1936, at a time when the Nazi government had already been in power for three years, Barth continues the usual polemic to the effect that the Jews rejected the Messiah Jesus, that Jesus was the King of the Jews and others "gratefully accepted and grasped" the gospel but the Jews would not.

However, he also taught that the "Church has made no convincing impression on the Jew as a whole."[18]

Specifically, Barth charged that the Church, meaning all of Chrsitianity, has "abandoned him [the Jews] to persecution without protest." "What is worse" says Barth, "it [Christianity] has made baptism an entrance card into the best European society." Here are some more observations by Barth which, together with the words of Maritain and others, foreshadow the developments in Christian theology after the Holocaust. Said Barth: "It [Christianity] still owes everything to those to whom it is indebted for everything. This failure, which is often unconscious, or perhaps concealed by all kinds of justifiable and unjustifiable countercharges against the Jews, is one of the darkest chapters in the whole history of Christianity and one of the most serious of all wounds in the body of Christ."[19]

Like Sartre after him, Barth viewed attacks on Jews as attacks on Christianity. "The recurrent Jewish question is the question of Christ and the Church" says Barth in the only comment on Judaism and Jews in his immense work.

Finally, Barth wrote in 1950, "The Jews are without any doubt at all the chosen People of God down to this day, in the same sense as they were from the beginning according to the Old and New Testaments. They have God's promise, and if we Christians from among the gentiles also have this promise, then we have it as those chosen along with them, as guests, come into their house, as branches grafted unto their tree.[20]

Dietrich Bonhoeffer (1906–1945) is perhaps the best known among the German protestant theologians of the early twentieth century. Murdered by the Nazis during the war, Bonhoeffer concerned himself extensively with "The Church and the Jewish Question" both in his sermons in the 1930s and in his exchange of letters with Karl Barth, dating to that period.[21]

Starting with Luther, Bonhoeffer holds that the Church cannot intervene in state activities or demand of the state any particular action. Bonhoeffer writes, "As long as the state continues to create law and order by its acts, even if it be a new law and order, the church of the Creator, the Mediator and the Redeemer cannot engage in direct political action against it." Bonhoeffer thought that the Church should object to actions taken by the state (i.e., the Nazi government) against baptized Jews and against efforts by the Church to missionize Jews.

Bonhoeffer saw no role for the Church, however, in helping the Jews persecuted by the Nazi government. Here Bonhoeffer supports the familiar Christian view that "'the chosen people,' who nailed the redeemer of the world to the cross, must bear the curse for its action through a long history of suffering." Though, surely an opponent of Nazi doctrine, Bonhoeffer nevertheless held to the classic view that "the conversion of Israel, that is to be the end of the people's period of suffering." In short, Bonhoeffer rejected anti-Semitism but proclaimed anti-Judaism. He believed that Jews deserved suffering and persecution but that the state had no right to persecute on racial grounds those Christians who had been converted from Judaism to Christianity. He called them "those of the people of Israel who have come home, . . . those who have come to believe in the one true God in Christ." These former Jews were of concern to him as members of his church.[22]

"Judaism is never a racial concept but a religious one," says Bonhoeffer. Bonhoeffer was a Lutheran in this matter, for Luther also argued that a Christian is anyone so baptized, including former Jews. Said Luther: "There is no other rule or test for who is a member of the people of God or the church of Christ than this: where there is a little band of those who accept this word of the Lord, teach it purely and confess against those who persecute it, and for that reason suffer what is their due."[23]

Bonhoeffer then was an anti-Jew but not an anti-Semite. As has been shown previously, there is such a distinction. Rejection on religious grounds does not have to result in racial theories. But Bonhoeffer, a firm opponent and victim of Nazis, did not understand that anti-Judaism has been and continues to be the legitimization of anti-Semitism and is its source.

When the German government by means of the "Aryan clause" removed Jewish Christians from the German churches, Bonhoeffer called for direct action against this move. In several letters to Karl Barth he denounced again and again any action taken against Jewish Christians and became vehement on this issue even in his correspondence with the Nazi government.

Yet the brutality of that government against the Jews themselves moved him only to say, "No nation can ever be commissioned to avenge on the Jews the murder at Golgotha." From this we can deduce that Bonhoeffer thought that while vengeance was in fact due, it was not for the German government to institute it, for "Vegeance is mine, says the Lord" (*Deuteronomy 32:35* and *Hebrews 10:30*).

Nothing illustrates the dilemma of the anti-Jewish Christian theologian more than these comments. Seeking to punish Jews for refusing the Christian religion, the Christian anti-Jew wants nevertheless to disassociate himself from the consequences of his own teaching by denouncing racial anti-Semitism even while clinging to his anti-Jewish doctrines. That this cannot be done was finally recognized in the 1960s and has led to profound changes in Christian theology concerning the role of Judaism in the world. A longer list of anti-Jewish Christian theologians can easily be presented. Their examples support our thesis that European Christian theology continued as the handmaiden of anti-Semitism well into the twentieth century and persisted in that role until the 1960s.

There was Leonhard Goppelt, who knew so little of Judaism that he not only wrote *Jesus, Paul and Judaism* but also concluded that Jewish history ended with the rejection of the gospel. The Catholic theologian Schmaus decided that Israel was obsolete and its existence meaningless while Bousset and Gressman in *Religion des Judentums* discovered that Israel ceased to exist in the sixth century B.C.E. and that Judaism was utterly uncreative and imitative.

Alfred Bertholet, Eduard Meyer and Emil Schurer continued the attack on Judaism. For Schurer "the religious ideas of Israel ... are on the one hand quite fantastic and on the other purely academic."

Similar views were expressed by Adolf von Harnack and Adolf Schlatter, whose violent language revealed him to be a common anti-Semite in the most pejorative sense of that word.[24]

It is significant that some of these authors and others wrote their anti-Jewish theology after the end of the Third Reich when the concentration camps had been opened by the Allies and the mountains of murder victims shown to all the world.

A leader in this anti-Jewish movement after the Second World War was the well known Pierre Benoit, who in his *Exégèse et Théologie* repeated every anti-Jewish accusation and canard already mentioned here and, as late as 1968, made a point of blaming the Jews for the death of Jesus and therefore for all their own suffering.

By then, however, the major trend in Christian theology had turned in a different direction with regard to Jews and Judaism culminating in the declaration of the World Council of Churches in New Delhi in 1961 and in the Ecumenical Council of the Catholic Church in the Vatican in 1965.

As we have already seen, there were always Christian theologians who sought to remember their Jewish heritage. These now came to the forefront of Christian thinking and have dominated Christian theology since the end of World War II.

IV

In all the centuries during which Christian theology fulminated against the Jews, some theologians alleviated this nearly universal antagonism by at least finding an occasional reason for Jewish existence and limiting the extent to which anti-Jewish measures could be carried out.

St. Thomas Aquinas in the thirteenth century, Nicholas of Cusa in the fifteenth century, Pope Pius V in the sixteenth century, Vladimir Soloviev in the nineteenth century and Jacques Maritain in the twentieth century are all examples of this moderating influence. In fact, theological developments in the early twentieth century concerning the Jews included a number of writers who wished to see Jewish emancipation even in Eastern Europe. In short, Maritain was not alone. The Protestant German theologian Oscar Cullmann, (1902–) promoted a more reasoned attitude towards the Jews even in his earliest writings, as did the Catholic theologian Hans Kung in Germany and Father George Tavard in France. The work of Dr. Gertrud Luckner in Germany during the Second World War needs to be mentioned here as well. Arrested by the Gestapo (Geheime Staatspolizei or Secret State Police) for aiding Jews, she was imprisoned in a notorious Nazi camp for women but survived. After the war she started a magazine called "Freiburger Rundbrief" whose purpose was to engage in free and equal discussion with Jews instead of viewing Jews only as objects of proselytism or persecution.[25]

These and other concerned Christians met in August of 1947 in the small Swiss town of Seeligsberg and there formulated a ten-point program aimed at "promoting fraternal love" toward the Jews:

> 1. To remember that it is the same living God who speaks to all, in the Old Testament as well as in the New.
> 2. To remember that Jesus was born of a Jewish virgin of the race of David of the people of Israel, and that his eternal love embraces his own people and the entire world.
> 3. To remember that the first disciples of Jesus, the apostles, and the first martyrs were Jewish.
> 4. To remember that the basic precept of Christianity, love of God and neighbor, promulgated in the Old Testament and confirmed afterwards by Jesus, obligates Christians as well as Jews in all their human dealings without exceptions.

5. To avoid using the word "Jew" in the exclusive sense of "enemy of Jesus," or the expression "enemies of Jesus" to designate the Jewish people.
6. To avoid presenting the Passion in such a way that the odium of the condemnation of Jesus falls only on the Jews....
7. To avoid referring to the maledictions of Scripture....
8. To withhold credence to the opinion that the Jewish people are reprobate, cursed, or destined to suffer.
9. To avoid speaking of the Jews as if they were not the first faithful of the Church.
10. To avoid debasing of Biblical or post–Biblical Judaism in order to elevate Christianity.[26]

It is this last statement, concerning the elevation of Christianity by means of debasing Judaism, which is of the greatest importance in achieving Christian maturity. Surely it is well known and evident that the need to debase others for the sake of improving the image of self is a signal of adolescence from which the Christian world is only gradually emerging at the end of the twentieth century. In addition to the endless misery which this Christian need meant for the Jews of Europe, it is now apparent that Christianity was unable to grow to its full potential while holding such a view. As we shall soon see, the renunciation of this attitude has opened entirely new opportunities for Christian theology and Christian influence upon the peoples of the world.

Since 1843, a French Catholic group known as The Congregation of Notre Dame de Sion has been concerned with maintaining a dialogue with the Jewish community in Europe. While originally interested only in the conversion of the Jews, this congregation began to alter its program after the Second World War. Having abandoned the effort to convert Jews, the Sisters, with 60 convents on four continents, now are "devoted to providing Catholics with information about Jews, in order to instill in them understanding and respect."[27]

In 1950, the proposals of Bad Schwalbach were drawn up by Catholic and Protestant theologians. Ten years later, the Institute of Judeo-Christian Studies at Seton Hall University made a similar proposal. Both had significant impact on the Church fathers.

The horrors of the Nazi camps and the heinous atrocities there committed upon the innocent Jewish and non–Jewish populations of Europe became a major world issue when Adolf Eichmann was tried for mass murder in Jerusalem in 1961.

Although the horrors of the Nazi camps had been described in great detail in the world's press immediately after the Second World War, and although the survivors had told their stories in numerous postwar war crimes trials, these killings were rarely associated with Christian theology at that time. In fact, until 1961, and sometimes beyond, Christians continued to separate the monstrous deeds of the anti–Semites from the anti–Judaism taught in churches throughout the world. In fact, numerous Christian sources quibbled over the legal aspect of that trial and seemed far more concerned with the rights of Eichmann than with the need to examine the Christian conscience with a view to revising Christian theology in this regard. Summarizing this episode succinctly was the work of Father Edward Flannery, who in his widely read book *The Anguish of the Jews* made this observation: "Historians can ask, moreover, whether the fact that the post war world has not grasped the magnitude of Nazi anti–Semitism—as the quibbling over the Eichmann trial has amply shown—may not itself point toward an unrecognized anti–Semitism."[28]

Nevertheless, such works as those of Flannery, the Sisters of Notre Dame de Sion, the Seeligsberg conference, and similar efforts made it almost imperative that both Catholic and non–Catholic Christians reconsider their relationship to Judaism and the Jewish people.

The Holocaust was however not the only motivation for this reconsideration. Several additional changes and pressures were also of importance here.

Surely one of these had to be the immense change in world relationships that came about as a result of the Second World War. After 1945 the world has shrunk. Television, jet planes and all other means of communication showed Christians that the Jews were certainly not the only non–Christian community in the world. It is of course true that the European Christian community knew as early as the seventh century that Islam had conquered a large segment of the then-known world. In Luther's day, Islam had been defeated in Spain but was advancing upon the gates of Vienna. The crusades had been fought to halt the threat of Islam, beginning at the end of the eleventh century. The response of Christian Europe to this threat was not only to fight the Moslem invaders but also to kill the Jews in Europe as equally guilty of unbelief.

However, after 1945, and in view of the great advances in science, technology and the social sciences for the preceding 400 years, such a response was no longer possible. Christianity was now confronted with the inescapable fact that it is itself a minority religion embraced by about 20 percent of the world's population, with little hope of converting the other four-fifths.

Thus, the belief that the conversion of the Jews, by force or otherwise, would save the world by giving it one religion became visibly impossible to the Christian world. It became obvious that even if all the Jews still surviving would promptly convert to Christianity, that religion would yet remain a minority religion.

This was well summarized by the Catholic Bishop Blomjous of Tanganyika in East Africa in these words: "We used to think that the church was sent into the world to gain the adherence of all men to Christ and her missionary effort was destined to convert all men to live in brotherhood in a single church.... Today, however, we are faced with the realization that pluralism, and specifically religious pluralism, is established in most parts of the world and that the forces of history will eventually make it a universal phenomenon.... It seems that religious pluralism is part of God's plan.... We are forced to ask ourselves the serious question ... what is God attempting to tell us through the multiplicity of religions?"[29]

Another impetus for the need to revise Christian theology concerning the Jews and Judaism was the establishment of modern Israel in 1948. As we have seen, it had been Christian dogma for at least 1,600 years that the Jews were driven out of the Holy Land and that Jerusalem was destroyed in 70 C.E. because of the Jewish rejection of Jesus. After 1948 this belief was hardly tenable. Not only had the Jews returned to the Holy Land and established there their own state, but they had also returned to Jerusalem and become the majority of the population. Their return was particularly dramatic because in 1948 and 1949 seven Arab armies attempted to wipe out the Jewish community, which at that time had only 600,000 persons, only to be defeated in a truly David versus Goliath struggle.

Moreover, the belief that Jews must live in misery everywhere was further weakened by the prosperity of the Jewish community in America. It was difficult to believe that Jews, punished by God for unbelief, must forever be second-class human beings when the very contrary was already then the case in the United States.

The influence of the American Christian community upon Christian belief was also felt after the Second World War. Some have claimed that the whole twentieth century can be seen as the American Century, and this certainly became the case after 1945 when American influence in the world rose to truly imposing proportions. This influence upon Christian thinking became profound from then on and thereby helped greatly in bringing the need for a new and more democratic approach to the Jewish minority to the attention of the Christian leadership.

In addition, the defeat of Nazism, and with it racial theories of all kinds, placed all bigotry in ill repute, making anti-Judaism and anti-Semitism as offensive as racism of other kinds.

Finally there were those Christians who saw Jewish survival despite the Nazi catastrophe as a miracle. Fundamentalist Christians particularly, but others as well, began to point out that all who had ever attacked the Jewish people were ruined thereafter, but that in the end Israel survived.

Thus, the stage was set, by these and other influences, to reconsider the "Jewish Question" in the light of Christian teaching and to seek once more to define the relationship between these two faiths, bound together inexorably, for better or for worse.

V

This unbreakable bond was recognized by the World Council of Churches when it met on August 22, 1948, in Amsterdam, The Netherlands, and remained until September 4.

The World Council of Churches represents almost all non–Catholic Christians, including Protestant, Eastern Orthodox and others. Together, they considered the position of the Jews at that historic meeting and acted favorably upon the report of the committee on "The Christian Approach to the Jews." This report made five statements concerning the Jews and then made two recommendations—one to the member churches of the World Council and the other to the council itself.[30]

The five statements were labeled "Christian Approach to the Jews" and began with an introduction that said in part: "We cannot forget that we meet in a land from which one hundred ten thousand Jews were taken to be murdered. Nor can we forget that we meet only five years after the extermination of six million Jews. To the Jews our God has bound us in a special solidarity linking our destinies together in His design."[31]

That document listed the following approaches:

1. To preach the gospel to Jews.
2. To teach Jews that "The Messiah for whom you wait has come."
3. To make these two efforts possible by showing Christian love to Jews, to fight anti–semitism and to hold that "anti–semitism is a sin against God and man."
4. To train special missionaries in approaching the Jews with a view to converting them and to make certain that the converts be treated as equals with other Christians and to remember that "the converted Jew calls for particular tenderness and full acceptance just because his coming into the Church carries with it often a deeply wounding break with family and friends."

The fifth statement of the committee dealt with the emergence of the state of Israel taking a neutral position concerning the claims of Jews and Arabs in that situation.

Remarkable in these five statements is that their principal thrust was still the conversion of the Jews to Christianity. The two recommendations of the committee were of a similar mold. The first sought to encourage member churches to train ministers in missionary work to the Jews by having such missionaries receive special training in Jewish concerns, and the second not only recommended an assault on anti–Semitism but also sought to cooperate with Jews in civic and social affairs.[32]

The effort to approach the Jewish community in a more positive manner was thus begun in Amsterdam but was doomed by the hope of bringing about conversion. Christians had yet to learn what Rabbi Abraham Heschel told the *Herald Tribune* in September of 1964: "I am ready to go to Auschwitz any time, if faced with the alternative of conversion or death."[33]

The Second Assembly of the World Council of Churches took place in Evanston, Illinois, August 15–31, 1954. Once more the issue of the Jews and Israel was placed on the agenda of the assembly. This time the hope for converting the Jews was coupled not only to recognition of the "guilt of Christian people toward the Jews," but was challenged by delegates from various Christian communities in Arab countries who saw in the statement of the Assembly entitled "The Hope of Israel" a threat to their position vis-a-vis the state of Israel.

Here is the final paragraph of "The Hope of Israel": "We cannot be one in Christ nor can we truly believe and witness to the promise of God if we do not recognize that it is still valid for the people of the promise made to Abraham. Therefore we invite all men to join in praising and magnifying God who 'concluded them all in unbelief that He might have mercy on them all'" (*Romans 11:32*).

Twenty-four delegates from ten European countries, the United States and Canada signed this declaration. However, the Anglican Bishop of Jerusalem, a representative of the Syrian Coptic Church, a Lebanese delegate and an Egyptian delegate all joined with Dr. Charles Taft of the United States in urging the avoidance of any mention of Israel whatever, as they considered such a mention a "disservice to the World Council of Churches."[34]

The Third Assembly of the World Council of Churches once more took up this issue while meeting in New Delhi, India, from November 19, 1961, to December 14 of that year. Upon the recommendation of the Policy Reference of the assembly, that group adopted this final resolution:

> We call upon all the churches we represent to denounce anti-semitism, no matter what its origin, as absolutely irreconcilable with the profession and practice of the Christian faith. Anti-semitism is sin against God and man. Only as we give convincing evidence to our Jewish neighbours that we seek for them the common rights and dignities which God wills for his children, can we come to such a meeting with them as would make it possible to share with them the best which God has given us in Christ.

The assembly augmented that statement by calling upon member churches "to do all in their power to resist every form of anti-Semitism" and made a special effort to disassociate the Jewish people from sole responsibility for the death of Jesus.[35]

Throughout the debate on these resolutions the issue of Israel was once more presented. Again delegates from Middle Eastern nations opposed the resolutions but were overruled mainly by European and American delegates. The assembly nevertheless summarized the position of Protestants concerning Israel by first recognizing how Christian support for the establishment of Israel came about and then expressing its concern for the plight of the Arabs living there.

The reasons for the initial Christian support of the state of Israel were listed as the horrors of the Nazi killings, the belief of many Christians throughout the centuries that Palestine belonged to the Jews, the belief of some Christians that Jesus would return if the Jews first returned to the Promised Land and the feeling among many Christians that they could pay their debt to the Jews by supporting Zionist aspirations.

The positions taken by the assembly in New Delhi became the foundations for Protestant–Jewish relations thereafter. While members of the council have never wavered in their opposition to anti–Semitism as they understood it, they came in time to be opponents of Israel and thereby were perceived by some in the Jewish community to have once more returned to the "Great Hatred."

VI

The ferment in Christian theology which led to these considerations by the World Council did not escape Catholic scrutiny. When on January 20, 1959, Pope John XXIII announced his intention of calling an Ecumenical (Greek: *oikumenikos* = "of the whole world") Council and followed this with a request for agenda items to the 2,800 members of the hierarchy in 134 countries, the issue of Catholic–Jewish relations was prominent among the requests of the members.

The "unique personality of Pope John XXIII" undoubtedly contributed greatly to the new attitude toward the Jewish people visible in that request. "When greeting a delegation of Jewish visitors to the Vatican in 1962 he opened his arms and said: 'I am Joseph, your brother.' In that one simple gesture, springing from his great heart, he proclaimed to the world the true meaning of the Christian spirit."[36]

In addition, the strong participation of the Americans gave this issue a prominent place in both the Protestant and Catholic considerations of Christian–Jewish relations. Coming from a country committed to democracy and ethnic diversity, and having just won the Second World War, which was largely fought over the issue of Nazi racism and injustice, the American delegations to both the Protestant and Catholic councils insisted on the passage of declarations distancing Christianity once and for all from religious hatred and persecution.

This is best illustrated by several quotations from American "interventions" made during sessions of Vatican II concerning the position of the Jews and others. Bishop Charles Helmsing of Kansas City-St. Joseph, Mo., said, "The proposal to include a statement on the Jews within the schema on ecumenism has already been made known to the world." He urged the council to adopt a schema including Jews in the ecumenical dialogue.

Father Thomas Stransky, "who had a key role in the final passage of the Declaration [on the Jews]," said during a speech in the United States, "If you study conciliar history of the Church, you will recognize that this is the first time a Council looked not only to the Jews, but the Hindus, Moslems, Buddhists and even to its enemies, recognizing and praising the work of God among these people."

In September of 1964, Richard Cardinal Cushing of Boston spoke to the Vatican Council before the Declaration on the Jews was passed. Said Cushing: "In this Declaration in clear and evident words we must deny that the Jews are guilty of the death of our Savior, except insofar as all men have sinned and on that account crucified Him, and, indeed, still crucify Him. And especially we must condemn any who would attempt to justify inequities, hatred, or even persecution of the Jews as Christian actions...."

Another American proponent of a strong Declaration on the Jews was Albert Cardinal Meyer of Chicago. "Justice demands," said Cardinal Meyer, "that we give explicit attention to the enormous impact of the wrongs done through centuries to the Jews." To which Joseph Cardinal Ritter of St. Louis added "Therefore all should be careful lest they represent the Jewish people as a rejected people, cursed, or in any way as deicides; lest they impute to the whole Jewish people then living, nor *a fortiori* to the Jews of our time, what was perpetrated in the passion of Christ...."[37]

The contribution of the American Catholic theologian Thomas Merton should not be overlooked in this connection. Before the Declaration on the Jews Merton corresponded extensively with Rabbi Abraham Heschel and Rabbi Zalman Schacter, both important Jewish theologians. In that correspondence he expressed the desire "to be a true Jew under my Catholic skin," and in *Conjectures of a Guilty Bystander* he says, "One has either got to be a Jew or stop reading the Bible. The Bible cannot make sense to anyone who is not 'spiritually a semite.'"[38]

Merton also thought of the Holocaust as the great eschatological sign of this century indicating that one cannot separate Israel from Christ. Merton commented extensively on the proposed declaration concerning the Jews and made considerable efforts to ensure its pasage.[39]

These and numerous other efforts by Americans indicated succinctly the immense influence the American delegation had on the final Declaration on the Jews at Vatican II. This is not to say that delegates from elsewhere were not also willing to make such a declaration both among Protestants and Catholics. It does indicate however, that the influence of democratic thinking could not be denied at either council and that this was then and still is due to the evident fact that American thinking dominates almost all international issues in the second half of the twentieth century.

Americans were of course not the only ones to seek a review of the Christian attitude toward the Jews. There were Europeans and others who sought such a revision as well. For example, there was the Pontifical Biblical Institute in a brief called *De Antisemitismo Vitando* (*On Avoiding Anti-Semitism*) as well as the Jewish-Catholic dialogue which formulated its position paper at a conference at Apeldoorn, Netherlands, in 1960.

The outcome of these preparations was the debate and the final passage of a Declaration on the Jews as part of the Declaration on Non–Christians as published by the Vatican on October 28, 1965.[40]

The worldwide discussion which this document engendered before it was adopted fills volumes and cannot be repeated here.

However, some of the comments made by influential and interested parties after this document was proposed and before it was passed in its final form are of interest.

Some Jews objected to the very idea of being excused from a "crime" they never recognized, while some Christians insisted that the "guilt" of the Jews concerning the death of Jesus should not be minimized.

The most prominent of these Christians were those living in Arab countries. To them, the effort to minimize religious antagonism against Jews was "a Zionist plot." They sent innumerable telegrams to the pope and others hoping to prevent the proposed Declaration on the Jews.[41]

There were also orthodox Jews who feared that a dialogue with Christians would lead to a weakening of the Jewish position in that it would produce further intermarriages, create confusion concerning the Jewish faith and lead to futile exchanges while resolving nothing.[42] There were also Jews who felt that "a straight line leads from the first act of oppression against the Jews and Judaism in the Fourth Century to the holocaust in the Twentieth . . . that this knowledge should determine our attitude."

Meanwhile, other Jews and many Christians were not only willing to engage in the proposed dialogue but were anxious that the final statement of Vatican II concerning the Jews go far enough. Many of these people were discouraged and angry because they believed that the document concerning the Jews would not be accepted at all or would be so "watered down" as to become meaningless. Editorials and articles in Christian journals dealt with these issues at length, some calling the document "absurdly defective."[43]

In 1965, *The Journal of Ecumenical Studies* was founded and from then on served as a major conduit for interfaith discussions in the United States.

In a series of editorials by prominent Christian theologians, that journal promoted a new theology concerning Jews and made every effort to influence the Church fathers, then assembled in Rome, to reject the charge of deicide and other ancient accusations against the Jewish people. Franklin Littell of Philadelphia wrote, "Removing the question of anti–Semitism to the purely theoretical level, it has been possible during the previous session of the Council for many to discuss the question whether the Jews should be 'absolved of the crime of deicide etc.'. . . It is not the Jews but the so-called Christians who need absolution. No crime in human history can equal the guilt which lies upon Christendom for abetting or permitting the Nazis' murder of six million Jews."[44]

These considerations, and many more, all influenced the delegates to the Vatican Council II when, on October 28, 1965, they voted on the Declaration on the Jews.

The final vote of the Council on the declaration as adopted was as follows:

1. On the introduction, Yes—2,071; No—110; Null—4.
2. On non–Christian religions in general, Yes—1,953; No—184; Null—6.
3. On the Islamic religion, Yes—1,910; No—189; Null—6.
4. On the first section dealing with the Jews, setting forth the spiritual relations between the peoples of the Old and New testaments, Yes—1937, No—153; Null—9.
5. On rejecting the collective guilt of the Jewish people for the death of Christ, Yes—1,875; No—188; Null—9.
6. Declaring that the Jews must not be represented as accursed or rejected by God, Yes—1,821; No—245; Null—14.
7. On rejecting anti–Semitism, persecutions against the Jewish people and the spreading of anti–Jewish sentiments through preaching or teaching, Yes—1,905; No—199; Null—14.
8. A summary on universal brotherhood excluding all discriminations, Yes—2,064; No—58; Null—6.[45]

Here follows the full statement of Vatican II concerning anti–Jewish conduct:

> The Church repudiates all perseuctions against any man. Moreover, mindful of her common patrimony with the Jews, and motivated by the Gospel's spiritual love and by no political considerations, she deplores the hatred, persecutions, and displays of anti–Semitism directed against Jews at any time and from any source. Besides, as the Church has always held and continues to hold, Christ in His boundless love freely underwent his passion and death because of the sins of all men, so that all might attain salvation. It is, therefore, the duty of the Church's preaching to proclaim the cross of Christ as the sign of God's all-embracing love and as the fountain from which every grace flows.

> We cannot in truth call upon that God who is the Father of all if we refuse to act in a brotherly way toward certain men, created though they be to God's image. A man's relationship with God the Father and his relationship with his brother men are so linked together that Scripture says; "He who does not love does not know God."
>
> The ground is therefore removed from every theory or practice which leads to a distinction between men or peoples in the matter of human dignity and the rights which flow from it.
>
> Accordingly, the Church rejects, as foreign to the mind of Christ, any discrimination against men or harassment of them because of their race, color, condition of life, or religion.[46]

Upon passage of this declaration, the Roman Catholic Church, which comprises four-fifths of all Christians, entered upon a new phase of relationship to the Jewish people which required and continues to require an explanation of all that came before this declaration and all that was then to come.

By changing course concerning the Jews from condemnation to acceptance, the Church was suddenly faced with a need to deal with "Auschwitz," if that one word may be used to encompass all the horror which the Nazi hate, the Nazi camps, tortures and gas ovens mean. It therefore became necessary to develop a theology of Auschwitz and to explain Auschwitz in those terms.

VII

There are innumerable books, learned discussions, personal recollections, sociological and psychological explanations for the Auschwitz phenomenon in all the languages of this world. There are those who try to explain this almost unexplainable horror by referring to psychiatric theories, to postmortem psychoanalyses of Hitler and to economic theories having to do with the Great Depression of the 1920s and 1930s etc. Yet, no adequate explanation of Auschwitz exists, and it seems that none may ever be developed. The Jewish theologian Emil Fackenheim argues that it is immoral even to search for meaning in the Holocaust.[47]

Then there are Jews who firmly believe that the nightmare that was Auschwitz is a Christian phenomenon. Such Jews make no distinction between the worst Nazi brutes and Christians generally and are firmly convinced that Christianity is a form of Nazi ideology and vice versa and that Christians are *ipso facto* Nazis.

Then there are Christians who hold that the Nazis were somehow invaders from another planet who had nothing to do with Christian civilization in Europe. Such thinkers totally separate the Nazi phenomenon from the Christian sphere and admit of no connection while others attribute the whole episode to insanity and irrationality. The Christian theologian John Pawlikowski, however, argues that the Holocaust was a rational "planned event with roots in philosophies developed by thinkers still recognized as giants of liberal Western thought."[48]

Furthermore, there is a Christian theology which has its own explanation for these events.

This means that some Christian theologians explain Auschwitz in terms of drawing an analogy to the life and death of Jesus. To Jews, and for that matter to non–Christian secularists, this may seem strange if not offensive. Strange because non–Christians seldom understand the centrality of the life and death of Jesus Christ in Christianity and offensive because to so many Jews Jesus was the founder and instigator of all their miseries.

This inability to understand the Christian point of view is largely the result of the difference in approach to the founders of the several major religions of this world. While Jews do not claim divinity for Moses, and Moslems and Buddhists make no such claim for either Mohammed or Siddhartha Gautama, Christians do claim that Jesus was God incarnate. This claim for the founder of Christianity makes a great deal of difference in the fashion in which Christians and others perceive the world and makes it understandable why Christians tend to review all events as abstracts of Christ's experience. Christian theology teaches that "Christ's sacrifice ... summarizes all agonies."[49]

Thus "the God who lives after Auschwitz is the God who participates in the suffering of men."[50]

Theology usually teaches that suffering is the result of sin. In the case of the European Jews, this doctrine was supported by claiming that the sin of the Jews was their refusal to accept Jesus. However, the case of Auschwitz is of such magnitude that it is hard to blame the victims, particularly since so many Christians were also murdered in the Nazi holocaust. What then was their "sin"?

Christian theology therefore tends to view the crimes of the Nazis as the outcome not of Christian doctrine, but of the opposite—that is, the refusal to accept Christian doctrine. Here this theology agrees with our view that anti–Judaism and anti–Semitism are not the same. While the contribution of Christian anti–Judaism to the Holocaust cannot be denied, and is not denied by the preponderance of Christian theologians, it is generally held that "liberal substitutes for traditional theodicy" are responsible for Auschwitz. Christianity always taught that man is not an end in himself but a subject of God and therefore subject to the law and command of God. Despite endless efforts to depict only Judaism as subject to that law, Christians lived by that law at all times, although clothed in somewhat different language. The Christian effort to be a religion of love always interfered with the anti-Jewish polemics and deeds of Christians, however cruel. Note, for example, that although the European Jews were expelled from their ancestral homes again and again over many years, and although murderous attacks on Jews were practiced throughout Europe at all times, no Christian government ordered the mass extermination of Jews even then. The theological argument then is that only the belief that "everything is permitted," a belief advanced by the secular opponents of Christianity, made Auschwitz possible.

Christian theology further holds that the Nazi view condemned not only the Jews but through them Christianity as well. "By slaying Israel ... the whole Jewish ideology would be killed." While few Christians recognized this during the 1930s and 1940s, it turned out that the assault on the Jews by the totalitarian Nazi machine was in fact an assault on the God of Jews and Christians.

Christian theology draws an analogy between the arrest, trial and execution of Jesus and the manner in which this also happened to the victims of the Nazi extermination policy. "The people destined for Auschwitz share with Jesus the immediacy of their destruction...."[51]

This is the meaning of the comments of the theologian Clemens Thoma, who writes,

> For a believing Christian the meaning of the victimization of the Jews under the Nazi terror ... is not too difficult to establish. The six million who were killed in Auschwitz and elsewhere direct their thoughts first of all to Christ, whom these Jewish masses in their suffering and death are like. Auschwitz is the most monumental modern sign for the most intimate bonding and unity of Jewish martyrs—representing all Judaism—with the crucified Christ, although this could not have been conscious for the Jews concerned. The Holocaust is for believing Christians, therefore, an important sign of the unbreakable unity, grounded in the crucified Christ, of Judaism and Christianity despite all divisions, individual paths, and misunderstandings.[52]

In the effort of the victims of the Nazi camps to maintain at least some order, decency and rationality the Christian theologian sees the continuation of the Spirit of God even going so far as to attribute to the victims the words "Weep not for us, weep for yourselves."[53]

This need of the prepetrators to weep for themselves stems from the theological view that "there is a sin against Man and Spirit which Christ declared to be unforgivable" and that sin is Auschwitz. From the Christian point of view, Christ died to save the world from paganism while the victims of Auschwitz died because the pagans sought to reverse that development.

This argument may well be supported by the effort on the part of the

Nazis to create their own "Salvation History" by claiming Hitler to be the new Messiah and the "Aryan Race" the Saved. This view challenged Christianity directly and was meant to do so.[54]

The reestablishment of Israel in the Holy Land after Auschwitz gives rise to further analogies between the events in the life and death of Christ and the Jewish people and also serves to bolster the view that God always keeps his promises. Thus that reestablishment is seen by some theologians as the Resurrection so that "the dead of Auschwitz have risen from the dust." Without the Jewish resurrection, the end of the Jews as well as Christianity would have arrived. The creation of modern Israel saved both from destruction. This means to some Christians that the threat of Auschwitz cannot be met by vindictive measures, but by resurrection. It is met "by rising with the Risen, by ascending with the Ascended."[55]

For example, the Rev. Jerry Falwell, a leader in the evangelical fundamentalist Christian movement, is typical of that group's attitude towards the State of Israel and its meaning for Christians. Said Falwell: "Now, concerning the State of Isreal, I am convinced that the miracle of statehood in 1948 was providential in every sense of the word. God promised repeatedly in the Old Testament that He would regather the Jewish people onto the land." He goes on to view this event as a form of resurrection analogous to that described in the New Testament.[56]

Likewise, the German theologian Rudolf Pfisterer also sees in the "rebirth of Israel" the fulfillment of God's promise and analogy to the resurrection of Jesus.[57]

One more lesson of Auschwitz from the Christian point of view is that "situation ethics" have produced the horror that was Auschwitz and have therefore failed. Situation ethics are believed to have arisen because man has asserted his freedom from God and has finally realized his co-creator role as promised in Genesis. This, however, has led men to abandon all humility and has led to hate and destruction and hence failure.[58]

Christians see in this failure the need to regulate conduct according to objective principles which are inviolate and unchanging and which Christians believe were taught them by that common heritage which Americans generally label the Judeo-Christian tradition.

Thus it came about that in the last half of the twentieth century there developed a worldwide effort on the part of Christians and Jews to seek reconciliation and to go forward, hand in hand, in the name of a common God and a common heritage. Many difficulties still obstruct this effort. For example, the importance of Israel and Zionism to the Jews and the attitude of Christians toward the Jewish state is at least one issue that needs yet to be resolved. Nevertheless, a great deal has already been done to bring about reconciliation between these two faiths. The nature of these deeds is the topic of our next chapter.

Notes

1. Preserved Smith and Charles M. Jacobs, *Luther's Correspondence and Other Contemporary Letters*, Vol. II (Philadelphia, The Lutheran Publication Society, 1918), pp. 185-187.
2. Solomon Grayzel, *A History of the Jews* (Philadelphia, The Jewish Publication Society of America, 1947), p. 492.
3. Jean-Paul Sartre, *Anti-Semite and Jew*, George J. Becker, trans. (New York, Grove Press, 1948); Sigmund Freud, *Moses and Monotheism* (New York, Alfred Knopf, 1939), p. 145.
4. Charlotte Klein, *Anti-Judaism in Christian Theology* (Philadelphia, Fortress, 1975), p. 7.
5. *Ibid.*, p. 4.
6. Jacques Maritain, *A Christian Looks at the Jewish Question* (New York, Longmans, Green, 1939); Rudolf Bultmann, *Jesus and the Word* (New York, Scribner's, 1934), pp. 16-23 and 64-75.
7. *Ibid.*, p. 23.
8. *Ibid.*, p. 30.
9. *Ibid.*, p. 36.
10. *Ibid.*, p. 42.
11. See Klein, *op. cit.*, p. 11.
12. See Klein, *op. cit.*, p. 13.
13. Rudolf Bultmann, *Jesus and the Word* (New York, Scribner's, 1934), pp. 17-23 and 65-75.
14. *Ibid.*, p. 66.
15. *Ibid.*, p. 67.
16. Klein, *op. cit.*, p. 29.
17. Max Weber, *The Theory of Social and Economic Organization* (1925), Talcott Parsons, ed. (New York, The Free Press, 1964).
18. Karl Barth, *Church Dogmatics*, Vol. IV, "The Doctrine of Reconciliation," Edinburgh, Clark, 1962, p. 878.
19. *Ibid.*, p. 878.
20. Karl Barth, "Die Judenfrage und ihre christliche Beantwortung," *Judaica*, Vol. 6, 1952, p. 72.
21. Dietrich Bonhoeffer, *No Rusty Swords: Letters, Lectures and Notes 1928-1936*, Vol. 1, Edwin H. Robertson and John Bowden, trans. (New York, Harper & Row, 1947).
22. Bonhoeffer, *Ibid.*, p. 227.
23. *Ibid.*, p. 229.
24. Klein, *op. cit.*, p. 30.
25. Arthur Gilbert, *The Vatican Council and the Jews* (New York, World, 1968), p. 34.
26. This statement was first published by the National Conference of Christians and Jews in 1947 but is also reprinted in Gilbert, *op. cit.*, pp. 27-28.
27. *Ibid.*, p. 33.
28. Edward Flannery, *The Anguish of the Jews* (New York, Macmillan, 1965), p. 45.
29. Gilbert, "Jewish Resistance to Dialogue," *The Journal of Ecumenical Studies*, Vol. 4, No. 2, Spring 1967, pp. 283-284.
30. David P. Gaines, *The World Council of Churches: A Study of Its Background and History* (New York, Smith, 1966), pp. 310-311.
31. *Ibid.*, p. 311.

32. *Ibid.*, p. 312.
33. *The New York Times*, September 4, 1964.
34. *Ibid.*, pp. 588–589.
35. Third Assembly of the World Council of Churches, *The New Delhi Report* (New York, Association Press, 1961), pp. 148–149.
36. Vincent A. Yzermans, ed., *American Participation in the Second Vatican Council* (New York, Sheed and Ward, 1967), p. 569.
37. *Ibid.*, pp. 586–593.
38. Thomas Merton, *Conjectures of a Guilty Bystander* (Garden City, New York, Doubleday, 1966), pp. 5–6.
39. William J. Shannon, "Thomas Merton and Judaism," *America*, Vol. 163, No. 9, October 6, 1990.
40. Walter M. Abbott, ed., *The Documents of Vatican II* (New York, Association Press, 1966), pp. 663–668.
41. Leonard Swidler, "Vatican II and the Jews—A New Hochhuth?", *The Journal of Ecumenical Studies*, Vol. 2, No. 1, Winter 1965, p. 470.
42. Gilbert, *op. cit.*, p. 281.
43. George A. Lindbeck, "The Jews, Renewal and Ecumenism," *The Journal of Ecumenical Studies*, Vol. 2, No. 1, Winter 1965, p. 473.
44. Franklin H. Littell, "Politics, Theology and the Jews," *The Journal of Ecumenical Studies*, Vol. 2, No. 1, Winter 1965, p. 477.
45. Floyd Anderson, ed., *Council Day Book, Vatican II, Sessions One and Two* (Washington, D.C., National Catholic Welfare Conference, 1965), pp. 6–7.
46. Abbott, *op. cit.*, p. 667.
47. Emil Fackenheim, *God's Presence in History* (New York, New York University Press, 1970), p. 37.
48. John T. Pawlikowski, *The Challenge of the Holocaust for Christian Theology* (New York, The Center for Studies on the Holocaust, 1978), p. 4.
49. Ulrich Simon, *A Theology of Auschwitz* (Atlanta, John Knox, 1979), p. 13.
50. Pawlikowski, *op. cit.*, p. 16.
51. *Ibid.*, pp. 36–52.
52. Clemens Thoma in Franz Mussner, *Tractate on the Jews* (Philadelphia, Fortress, 1984), p. 44.
53. Ulrich Simon, *op. cit.*, p. 56.
54. See Michael D. Ryan, "Hitler's Challenge to the Churches: A Theological-Political Analysis of *Mein Kampf*," in Franklin H. Littell and Hubert G. Locke, eds., *The German Church Struggle and the Holocaust* (Detroit, Wayne State University Press, 1973).
55. Simon, *op. cit.*, p. 110.
56. Merrill Simon, *Jerry Falwell and the Jews* (New York, Jonathan David, 1984), p. 43.
57. Rudolf Pfisterer, *Juden und Christen: Getrennt, Versöhnt* (Neukirchen-Vluyn, Aussaht und Schriftenmissions Verlag, 1973), p. 58.
58. Pawlikowski, *op. cit.*, p. 22.

6

After the Holocaust: A New Christian Theology

The reactions of Christian and Jewish theologians to the reformulations of Christian attitudes toward the Jews have determined the progress of the Christian-Jewish dialogue since the declaration by the World Council of Churches in 1961 and the Conciliar Declaration "Nostra Aetate" by the Catholic Church in 1965.[1]* Subsequently, many Protestant denominations issued their own declarations on the subject of the Jews.

As we shall see, there were and are of course exceptions to this new attitude. There still are Christian theologians who have steadfastly ignored these teachings and continue to view "the Jews," meaning all Jews, as reprobate enemies of Christ and deserving of hatred. Further, there are Jews who still view all Christians as potential persecutors and Christianity a form of irrational paganism not worthy of serious attention.

Principally, however, the Jewish attitudes toward these developments are best expressed by the statement of the American Rabbi Marc H. Tannenbaum concerning the Declaration of the Jews by the Catholic Church in 1965. This declaration received far more attention than the Protestant declaration of 1961, not only because the number of Roman Catholic Christians is so much greater than the number of non–Catholic Christians but also because Roman Catholic Christians can speak with one voice, having no denominations. The Jewish view concerning this has as much relevance to the Protestant as the Catholic efforts in this connection.

It is significant that the principal Jewish respondent to these declarations is an American. We have already seen that American Christians were important contributors to the discussions that led to these declarations in the first place. Now American Jews responded, and spoke for world Jewry.

*Notes to this chapter begin on page 149.

The reasons for this shift of influence from the European to the American scene after World War II lies mainly in the eradication by murder of a large segment of the European Jewish community. While nearly 3 million Jews did survive in the Soviet Union, these Jews had no influence on Jewish communal life because the Soviet dictatorship would not permit them to travel or have any religious life worthy of the name.

Meanwhile, Germany has had only 30,000 Jews after World War II, of whom no more than 5,000 were native survivors of the camps. The others were Jews from Eastern Europe who also survived the camps and then settled in Germany after their liberation.

There are about 500,000 Jews in France and an equal number in England. Nevertheless, these communities were not and are not comparable to the American Jewish community with nearly 6 million members, numerous theological schools, communal institutions and far greater economic strength than is available to European Jews.

In short, after World War II the center of Jewish life had moved from Europe to America and Israel. Israel however had its own problems. Forced to fight several wars of survival against overwhelming odds, it could not adequately participate in the world arena in the dialogue between Christians and Jews begun by the two declarations we have now discussed.

That task has fallen to Americans, whose chief spokesman Rabbi Marc Tannenbaum begins with the observation that the mass murder of Jews and the recognition that Christianity is a minority religion in the world "are compelling us to confront the deep realities of the relationships between Christians and Jews."[2]

Referring briefly to some of the positive statements concerning Jews made by Christian theologians over many years, Tannenbaum then makes the observation that the early Church fathers sought to gain autonomy for Christianity as a recognized religion in the Roman Empire by separating Christians from Jews, not only by instituting different Holy Days and different ceremonies, but also by maligning Jewish practices.

Writing in the early 1960s, Tannenbaum held that the consequences of these teachings permeated the Christian world to such an extent that the word "Jew" became in itself a pejorative in the conversation of Western man. For example, even the dictionary definition of the word Jew included the phrase "to jew-down" which is defined as "to induce a seller by haggling to lower his price" and the phrase "jewed" or "jewing" is defined as "cheating by sharp business practices." At last these definitions are somewhat ameliorated by the addition of the editorial comment "Usu. taken to be offensive."[3] Yet, in his *Theological Dictionary*, the German theologian Karl Rahner defines Jews in terms of the election of Israel, the covenant and the Jewishness of Jesus. There are no slurs or anti–Jewish interpretations concerning Jews and Judaism in that influential work.[4]

While anti–Semitism in its grossest forms had become no more than a social nuisance in the world of the 1960s, Tannenbaum showed that in some places this hatred was still very much alive as evidenced by the physical attacks upon Jews in Argentina and the conduct of the Polish population toward the remnants of the once-great Jewish community.[5]

Furthermore Tannenbaum demonstrated that the actions of the World Council of Churches and Vatican II in labeling religious hatred a sin were not immediately understood by everyone in the Jewish community nor accepted by one and all as the great step forward which these declarations turned out to be. In fact, there were Jews "who opposed the declaration and resented it."[6]

The reason for this was media treatment of the Vatican Declaration which included such headlines as "Vatican Council Exonerates Jews for Death of Christ" and "Catholic Church absolves Jews of Crucifixion." As Tannenbaum says: "No Jew ... ever felt guilty for the death of Jesus. Therefore, no Jew ever felt in need of absolution." Many Jews also felt, according to Tannenbaum, that the Church owed the Jews an apology for the millions persecuted and slaughtered in its name. Yet none was forthcoming. Other Jews considered the declarations too little and too late. They believed that the world of the twentieth century was so secular that the views of Christians did not matter anymore; the fate of the world in their estimation now lay in the hands of secular government, not religious establishments.

Nevertheless, during the 25 to 30 years since these declarations, their effect has been considerable. For these declarations became the catalyst for a number of important actions which since then have reduced interreligious conflict, opened new opportunities for Christians by more firmly attaching Christianity to its Jewish roots, helped Jews benefit from the Christian tradition without the overlay of antagonism and anxiety which for so long maintained a wall between the two faiths and finally made Christians and Jews allies in dealing with the world's most serious problems, such as poverty, illiteracy, war and misery.

Among the important actions these declarations provoked were the revision of several Christian practices in favor of more amiable relations with the Jewish community. For example, the organizers of the German passion play at Oberammergau were moved by Cardinal Döpfner of Munich to revise the play be removing all anti–Jewish phrases and references.

Extensive efforts have been made by both Protestant and Catholic textbook writers to remove unfavorable stereotypes concerning Jews from these books while clergy of all Christian denominations have made a great effort to present Judaism in a favorable light.

Christians have recently commemorated the Holocaust, chairs of Jewish studies have been established in Christian colleges and universities, and conferences are held regularly to discuss the concerns of both communities.

In order to make such discussions possible it is of course necessary to remove the immense ignorance of each community concerning the other. As Tannenbaum said in 1966, "At the heart of Christianity's problem of what to make of the Jew is the Christian's immense ignorance, if not illiteracy, regarding Judaism." Similarly, few Jews know anything about Christianity except that Jews had erstwhile been its victims.[7]

Therefore it became quite obvious to those who sincerely meant to bridge the gulf of 1,600 years of misunderstanding and hatred that education and dialogue had to go hand in glove in order to reach the level of mutual understanding and respect which the two declarations had promised and which the world expected of these two great faiths. It is both unnecessary and impossible to present here every speech, conference and meeting held between Christians and Jews during the quarter century since Vatican II. There are, however, some significant and representative statements and meetings which illustrate the direction these efforts have taken.

Robert McAfee Brown, a leading Protestant theologian, summarized these trends in 1967.[8] He begins with reciting "Why the Christian Needs the Jew" and prefaces his remarks by citing the great Jewish theologian Rabbi Abraham Joshuah Heschel, who said, "We are all involved with one another. Spiritual betrayal on the part of one of us affects the faith of all of us. Views adopted in one community have an impact on other communities. Today religious isolationism is a myth. For all the profound differences in perspective and substance, Judaism is sooner or later affected by the intellectual, moral and spiritual events within the Christian society, and vice versa."[9]

The benefits to Christians from an interfaith dialogue with Jews as seen by Brown are that Protestants and Catholics recognize their common heritage even before the first century; that Jews can give Christians greater depth of insight into the Old Testament, which both religions hold in common; that Christians can recover "many dimensons of their faith that have been distorted due to isolation from the leaven of the Judaic perspective"; that Christians and Jews can help one another in creating a new theology concerning the relationship of both to one another; that Christians, in solidarity with Jews, can tackle many civic problems together; and finally, that "Christians need the constant reminder that the mere presence of the Jew affords, of the scandalous treatment of Jews by the Christians of the past. If contrition is the presupposition of ecumenical encounter, nothing should be more calculated to keep the Christian humble than the presence of the Jew."[10]

Not all Jewish or Christian theologians have agreed with Heschel or with Brown. There are those on both sides who believe that a dialogue is neither needed nor possible because Jews cannot forget the Holocaust and all the anti–Jewish Christian conduct that preceded it and because Jews cannot agree to any Christological interpretation of the world, while anything in Christianity with which they can agree is Jewish in the first place. Among these is A. Roy Eckardt, a Christian theologian whose chief concern is Jewish-Christian relations.[11]

Nevertheless, a dialogue has occurred and has had distinctive consequences already. We shall therefore address these dialogues and consequences and see what they have meant for the rapprochement which is the hope of those who have so long engaged in them.

II

Robert McAfee Brown asks: "What are to be the subjects of the Jewish-Christian dialogue?"

Three topics were suggested from the Jewish side in the early days of the new ecumenism. These were "a. the need for critical commentaries on the New Testament that will remove the possibility of exploiting certain passages for anti–semitic purposes, b. historical studies that will set Jewish-Christian relations in clearer context and remind each of the episodes the other has forgotten and c. theological studies dealing with Jewish-Christian relations to dispel the ancient canards that the Jews are a deicide people."[12]

The utter ignorance of Jewish history in the Christian community is matched by Jewish knowledge of all the horror of persecutions long past but not forgotten. Said Edward Flannery: "The pages Jews have memorized have been torn from our histories of the Christian era."[13]

Every conversation between Christians and Jews is thus burdened by the past which Jews remember and bring along to all interfaith encounters even while Christians, utterly ignorant of that burden, assume that Jewish history never happened and never suspect that that history makes all contacts between Christians and Jews a triangle. The need to remember Jewish history is also visible in discussions concerning Israel. While non–Jews may be able to talk dispassionately about Israel or to make recommendations as to what that country's actions should or should not be, to Jews all arguments concerning Israel are overlaid by the Holocaust and are understood only in the light of those burning ovens.

Catholics are of course not the only Christians concerned with the condition of the Jews. As we have already seen, Protestants were the first to issue a declaration concerning the Jews during their councils in Amsterdam, Evanston and New Delhi. It is therefore not surprising that a number of Protestant denominations issued declarations regarding the Jews upon the recommendation of the World Council of Churches.

The Lutheran church, which has a large number of German members, has been particularly interested in making an effort to live with Jews and overcome ancient prejudices which were so strong and marked in its founder, Martin Luther (see appendix).

Writing in *The Lutheran Quarterly*, Robert Karsten lists three recognitions which Christians and particularly Lutherans had made in 1968 when his article was written.[14]

These three "recognitions" are that Jews and others can be as sincere in their religious outlook as Lutherans, that Jews have a very valuable tradition and that Christians insult Jews by telling them that they do not understand their own heritage and that Christians can "witness" for their religion, but that they cannot convert the Jews.

Karsten recommends that in addition to witnessing, Christians practice reconciliation with the Jewish community. It must be understood that he speaks here from American experience where no persecutions have ever taken place and where reconciliation is based on the hostilities of everyday life but not on the mass murders which need to be addressed in the European setting.

This reduction in hostility is to be achieved by dialogue, says Karsten. Returning to the theme of the Tetragrammaton which so occupied Luther, Karsten recommends that Christians attempt to see the concept of God in the light of the Jewish scriptures, adding that Christians need to recognize that Jews have added a large body of Talmudic literature to their scriptures since the 39 books of the Torah were written. This is almost unknown among Christians, who have a tendency to overlook that the Jews of Jesus's time were different from those of Moses's time and that the Jews at the end of the twentieth century are different yet again.[15]

Karsten concludes by reminding his Lutheran readers that "we Christians have as much or more to learn from Jews as they do from us."

In view of these admonitions by Karsten and a number of other theologians, the Lutheran World Federation's Department of World Mission held a "Consultation on the Church and the Jewish People" in Logumkloster, Denmark, in 1964.[16]

Significant is that this meeting was attended by representatives of the World Council of Churches and by Rabbi Arthur Gilbert of New York. So one Jewish viewpoint was heard and given some attention.

The outcome of this discussion was not only a strong stance against anti–Semitism but a determination, for the first time, not only to dissociate all Jews from those who rejected Jesus, but also to dissociate Christians from the "hate and persecution which were inflicted on the Jews by the official church and by nations claiming a Christian tradition." The Consultation acknowledged "the cruel and dangerous anti–Jewish attacks in some of the writings of the old Luther" and asserted "our Christian responsibility for their right to exist as Jews."[17]

The final affirmation of that Lutheran "Consultation" is grounded in theological positions which at one time were seen in exactly the opposite light. Lutheran theology now holds these concepts:
"We as Lutherans affirm our solidarity with the Jewish people.... Thus our solidarity with the Jewish people is to be affirmed not only despite the crucifixion of Jesus but because of it. ... The existence of the Jewish people in the world today cannot ... be seen ... as a problem ... but as a profound cause for wonder and hope ... as a reminder of our origin, as a partner in dialogue to understand our common history. ... The church, therefore, may never ... understand the Word which has been entrusted to it ... as possessions which give Christians superiority over Jews."[18]

Willis Erickson has summarized some of the principal theological issues facing Christians and Jews in relation to each other. Among these are the oft-repudiated anti–Semitism issue, the issue of ignored Jewish history, the inability of many Christians to understand the difference between the Jewish home-centered religion and the Christian church-centered religion and the belief that Jews are ipso facto unscrupulous in business.[19]

Baptists and others have also discussed the Christian-Jewish need for dialogue since the early 1960s when the various declarations on the Jews were first promulgated. In all of these discussions the Christian wish to proselytize Jews and to thereby fulfill the Christian conversion purpose has been emphasized. Nothing is more essential to Christianity than its missionary function, yet nothing is more resented by Jews than just that effort. Quoting Rabbi Samuel Sandmel, Baptist theologian Joseph R. Estes writes, "The fact is the missionary impulse is central in Christianity."[20]

Recognizing this impulse, Estes writes that "it must not be forgotten that the Christian missionary impetus may degenerate into all manner of religious imperialism and exploitation.... The possibility of genuine Christian-Jewish dialogue depends on the acknowledgment of legitimate Jewish resistance to all unworthy attempts by Christians to proselytize them."[21]

Estes too makes some recommendations concerning Christian attitudes toward Jews with particular emphasis on the missionary tendencies already mentioned. These recommendations are meant to influence all Christians, not only Baptists.

Citing such influential theologians as Karl Barth, who, as we have already seen, rejected Judaism as a "living faith," Estes argues that Christians need to recognize the present faith of the Jewish people and relinquish the view that Judaism is a "fossil." Further, Christians must renounce anti–Semitism or anti–Judaism and show that Christianity does not include an anti–Jewish element in the first place.

This is also the argument of Father Gregory Baum in his book *Is the New Testament Anti-Semitic?*[22]

Unfortunately, Baum makes no distinction between anti–Judaism and anti–Semitism, when in fact the distinction is a vital one with reference to the extent to which Christianity has a share in the persecutions which Jews have endured over the centuries.

There is of course also a Jewish dimension to anti–Judaism and anti-Semitism. That is the historical refusal of the Jewish community to become entirely absorbed by its surrounding culture. This does not mean that Jews should be blamed for the hatred or persecutions they have endured. Nothing is further from sociological evidence than the suggestion that the victim of a crime is ever at fault. Crimes are always the fault of the perpetrator, even when victims make a contribution to their own victimization.

The issue here is that Christians could and should learn from Jews that the refusal of Jews to assimilate entirely into the surrounding culture was both a source of pain and a strength. While this failure made Jews easily identifiable and hence easily targeted by haters of all kinds, it also made it possible for Jews to survive as a separate culture. It made it possible to hold on to Jewish values and attitudes in an otherwise hostile world.[23]

Here Christians could learn from Jews that they too need to hold back somewhat and maintain their own traditions and values apart from the secular world. Christianity has become so identified with the secular world that there are many who believe that anyone not Jewish must be a Christian, a belief far from reality. This overidentification has been to the detriment of Christians since the fourth century, for as we have seen, the mistakes and errors, including the persecution of the Jews, generally carried out by secular authorites were and are still blamed on Christians because of this overidentification of Christianity with governments and other non–Christian institutions.

Christians would do well to make a solid appraisal of Jewish theology with a view to learning how such a separation from the secular world can be achieved without relinquishing participation in the democracies in which most Jews and Christians now live.[24]

Joseph Estes argues that Jews need to make a scholarly appraisal of Christian theology as well with particular reference to the life and death of Jesus and the claim that he was the Messiah. Estes believes that this would lead to a reappraisal of the significance of Jesus in the Jewish community.

Estes also recommends the alteration of Christian missionary efforts so as to allow Jews who have become converts to maintain their Jewishness. Additionally, Estes, like so many other Christians, recommends that Jews learn at least something about Jesus since at present the synagogue treats history "as if Jesus never lived."[25]

III

A new theology toward Judaism has been the concern of almost all Christian theologians since World War II. The main shift in this theology away from the old has been the substitution of a dialogue relationship between Christians and Jews for a proselytizing one in which Christians sought incessantly to convert Jews to Christianity.[26]

This is not to say that all who conduct such dialogues have given up on possible conversion. Some have in fact sought to use the new attitude as yet another means of bringing about such conversion, this time by example and kindness. While such Christians agree that missions to the Jews are no longer possible, they nevertheless intend to tell Jews that they are wrong and misguided and need to enter the Church.

There are however those who see dialogue as having quite a different meaning. Such Christians recognize the need to abandon in all forms the unwarranted proselytism of Jews on the grounds that "faith must be a free act between God and the believer."[27]

These Christians begin by recognizing the significance of Judaism for Christianity without giving up their own view or confidence in their religious commitment. This significance of Judaism for Christianity as summed up by Stefan Schreiner lies in the Jewish concept of God, the Old Testament Jewish prophets, the futuristic eschatology of Judaism, the development of Jewish Torah ethics, the Jewish "wisdom" teaching and the contribution of Judaism to Christian traditions.[28]

Schreiner holds that an encounter with Judaism provides "first of all an indispensable help to an intellectual understanding of Christianity," that further it recalls forgotten dimensions of biblical and theological substance and third, that it forces recognition that Judaism and Christianity are indeed two different religions. Schreiner concludes that even though for him as a Christian there is only one path to God, "God's possibilities of self-revelation to human beings are multiple."[29]

The German theologian Jurgen Moltmann describes the crux of Jewish-Christian relationships to stem from the understanding of the messianic question by both confessions. The chief issue for Christian theology here is the Jewish "No," says Moltmann.[30]

The central question for Christians to consider therefore is, "Is the Jewish 'No' anti–Christian?" The issue from the Jewish point of view is that Jews are not able to believe that the Christ has come or that God has bestowed his redemption on mankind. "No" was of course the famous answer given by the great Jewish philosopher Martin Buber during his discussion of this issue with the New Testament scholar Karl Ludwig Schmidt in Stuttgart in 1933.[31]

The point here is not that Jews are obstinate or defiant as Luther would have it, but that Jews cannot—are utterly unable to—believe the Christian message. This inability, Moltmann teaches, must be accepted by Christians and must not be converted into cause for enmity. Christians need to understand Israel's "No" because it is "a provisional act on God's part. It is an act performed for a particular purpose, as the story of Moses and Pharaoh shows." According to Moltmann, the purpose of Israel's "No" is to lead the Church to convert gentiles "so that they are seized by faith in Christ directly, without becoming Jews first of all."

This teaching finally makes something positive out of the Jewish refusal to accept Jesus and, according to Moltmann, makes it possible to relinquish what he calls anti-Semitism but is better called anti-Judaism. From this theology Moltmann also derives the view that Israel has not been rejected by God for refusing Jesus because God planned this refusal all along but will yet see to it that the gospel comes to the Jews, for "The first shall be the last," and that "last" to Moltmann is Israel.[32]

Clemens Thoma has summarized "the basic Jewish statements of identity and experiences of faith," as he calls them, claiming that these statements can be evaluated in a Christian context and used in dealing with Judaism and its adherents the Jews.[33]

The statements which Thoma believes need definition for Christians are "Israel," which is not only a state in the Middle East but a state of "existential identity" beyond the religious community; "Judaism," which is a religious reality but also a social reality; and the inherence of history in Judaism, a religion which "lives in and by its history." Jews are seen by Thoma as a precursor people who run ahead, paving the way for other nations and communities and serving as a model. While Thoma, like other theologians of the new theology, rejects missionizing Jews, he too believes that Christians should "witness for Christ" in the presence of Jews without propagandizing Jews or causing unrest and anxiety.[34]

The German Roman Catholic theologian Franz Mussner has contributed an "Outline of a Christian Theology of Judaism" which has been very influential in the years since its publication because it summarizes almost all Christian thinking on the matter as of the late twentieth century.

It is significant that this new theology has been proposed by a German. Mussner recalled in 1984 that the German bishops gathered in Rome during the '60s for Vatican Council II made a special declaration at the beginning of the debate concerning the Jews. This declaration was as follows:

> We German bishops welcome the conciliar decree on the Jews. When the Church in council makes a statement about itself, it cannot remain silent concerning its connection with the people of God of the Old Testament. We are convinced that this conciliar Declaration provides the occasion for a renewed contact and a better relationship between the Church and the Jewish people.

We German bishops, therefore, especially welcome the decree because we are conscious of the grave injustice that has been perpetrated on the Jews in the name of our people.[35]

A similar statement was made in 1975 by the Joint Synod of the Dioceses of the Federal Republic of Germany. This statement pointed to the guilt of Christians in participating in, or keeping silent about, the Nazi persecution of the Jews and seeks to establish a new relationship with the Jews yet surviving in Germany. In Mussner's terms, a rethinking and new understanding of Judaism became necessary after Auschwitz and led to a new theology of Judaism in six categories: the Old Testament as the continuing source for the faith of Israel, Israel as the enduring "root" of the Church, the continuance of the covenant of God with Israel, the Jewishness of Jesus, specific statements of the New Testament and the special role of the land of Israel.

The first of these categories refers to the election of Israel. Agreeing with Karl Barth, Mussner holds that "Israel is the people chosen by God for his own possession.... With this election Israel is set apart from all other peoples." Quoting a number of biblical passages to that effect, Mussner makes a point of citing the New Testament in support of this position. In particular he looks to *Acts 13: 17–19*. Here Mussner finds that God is the one who chooses, the Fathers of Israel are the ones chosen, Israel is "the people of God," there are references to the Exodus, there are references to the taking of the land and the land is an inheritance. Further, Mussner finds that *Romans 9:11–13* predicts that all Israel will be saved and that Israel's election endures. "God does not reject Israel," says Mussner. "According to Paul, the election of Israel will never be revoked by God." This theology directly contradicts all those earlier polemics against the Jews with which the reader has become familiar and which post–Holocaust Christian theologians seek to remove.[36]

Mussner next argues that the Church "is *not* the people of God which has taken the place of Israel." Instead he sees the Church as "the participant in the root" and the extended people of God who together with Israel form the one people of God. This view is supported by numerous references to both the Old and the New testaments but especially *Acts 15:14; Amos 9:11; Jeremiah 12:15* and *Zechariah 2:15*. Mussner makes the point that the New Testament nowhere says that after Christ only the Church is the people of God.

Mussner's theology now deals with the continuing covenant of God with Israel. He demonstrates by citing *Acts 3:25* and *Romans 11:26* that "the apostle declares thereby once again that God has not rejected his people Israel." Further, Mussner shows that the law which the Jews call the Torah is essential, for "a world without Torah is a world without Jews." Rather than accusing Jews of being mere loveless ritualists, Mussner argues that for Paul "Christ is the end of the Law unto righteousness for everyone who believes" (*Romans 10:4*) but that this thesis of the apostle is *not* founded on the notion that the Law is something of lesser value which misleads people to a mere formal obedience.

The belief that Judaism no longer had any function after the arrival of Christianity has been extensively reviewed. Mussner argues that the Jews have not only a function, but indeed a salvific function *post Christum*. The argument here is one that Karl Barth advanced, namely that the existence of the Jewish people was the only proof of God to which he (Barth) granted validity. Mussner, and Barth before him, hold in this connection that the continuing existence of the Jewish people, despite its small number, despite the more than 2,000-year Diaspora (Exile) among the peoples of the world, despite the terrible catastrophes which in the last hundred years and even before have been visited upon Judaism, "probably cannot be otherwise explained except that God himself stands behind this people as its real advocate."[37]

Similarly Mussner promotes the view that the return to Zion "precedes the messianic kingdom. God himself will lead the scattered back home," says Mussner, meaning thereby the reestablishment of Israel, the lifting of the Exile and the restitution of the people as "the unconditional presupposition of the eschatological lordship of the Messiah, which is included in the lordship of God."

Mussner again cites the New Testament in support of this view. *Acts 7:33* and *Hebrews 11:9* and *Matthew 5:5* are mentioned together with innumerable references to this return in the Old Testament. Mussner teaches that without the will of God a return of Israel to the land of their fathers would never have been possible.

This then brings us to a consideration of Christian Zionism, an aspect of the new theology which has been clouded by controversy but cannot be ignored in view of the dramatic events associated with the Jewish return to Israel during the hundred years ending in 1990 and the recent arrival in Israel of the Russian Jews whose liberation in this century was not expected by anyone.

IV

The phrase "Zionism" derives from an ancient name for Jerusalem, Zion. Zion was probably a hill on which King David located a fortress for the city's defense. Since the first Zionist Congress was held in Basel, Switzerland, in 1898, the political movement designed to establish and then maintain a Jewish state on the land of ancient Israel has been called Zionism.

At first, Zionists were those Jews who actually went to that land and participated in its rebuilding. In more recent years however, a Zionist is also someone who advocates and promotes such a development and who favors such a Jewish state. Among these are many Christians, particularly since the new Christian theology of Judaism often includes the belief that the establishment of Israel has a special meaning in Christian theology.

Karl Barth viewed the reappearance of Israel as "a miracle for all that have eyes to see" and viewed Israel as an eschatological sign and the events succeeding the declaration of Israel's independence in 1948 as a repetition of the biblical account of Israel's entrance into the Promised Land.[38]

Christian theology concerning the Jews and Judaism has been profoundly affected by this return. Particularly evangelical Christians whose origins are in England and who see themselves as having a continuity with the Jewish people have been Zionist in their orientation.[39]

The evangelical movement was promoted by such men as the Methodist Wesley brothers, the Calvinist George Whitefield and Anglicans such as John Newton and William Wilberforce. We have already seen (Chapter 4) that at the height of that movement in the seventeenth century the Puritans under Cromwell permitted the Jews to return to England. This means that the Ecumenical movement has always identified itself with Israel and that therefore their interest is not one of a mere uninvolved bystander. This is not to say that Cromwell sought to rebuild Israel in its ancient land. However, Cromwell's spiritual descendants, the British people of the nineteenth century, did in fact aspire to do so as best seen in the "Balfour Declaration" of November 2, 1917.[40] That declaration, issued by Arthur Balfour, then prime minister of England, proclaimed the intent of the British government to establish the Jews in their ancient homeland. Although the declaration was issued in the twentieth century, its author and his supporters were surely nineteenth century men in education, opinion and heritage, as were all Europeans until the beginning of World War I.

Anthony Arthur Cooper, the seventh Earl of Shaftesbury, was undoubtedly another excellent example of an English Christian Zionist whose beliefs concerning the redemption of Israel on its own land reflected a long line of British politicians whose evangelical concerns were never viewed as inconsistent with practical politics.[41]

Evangelists and those who are willing to permit evangelical concerns to enter their political considerations have always believed that the conflict between Israel and its Arab neighbors cannot be judged solely in human terms but must take into consideration the influence of God upon the course of history. It is for this reason that such Christians were very much concerned with Israel's astounding victory over its Arab enemies in 1967 and with the attitude and conduct of a majority of Christians concerning Israel during and since the 1967 Six Day War.

To those who view the world in evangelical terms, Israel's ability to defeat so large an Arab enemy bent on the mass murder of the Jews appeared to have a divine origin. The refusal of others to support Israel then and since is regarded by evangelicals as unwillingness to accept not only Israel, but Jews.[42]

The evangelical view, based mainly on Arab pronouncements, is that the dispute between Israel and its neighbors "has nothing to do with border questions.... Israel could withdraw to a half-acre settlement along the Mediterranean sands and she would remain as 'guilty' as she is now or as she would be ... were she to occupy Cairo or Damascus.... It is the being of Israel that we see bound to the stake.... No other nation is told to aspire to universal sainthood, no other nation is subjected to a trial that is never permitted to end."[43]

The evangelical view concerning Christian attitudes toward Israel is that failure to support Israel during and since the Six Day War of 1967 is based on theological considerations which seek once more to annihilate the Jews in a manner reminiscent of the Holocaust.

In June 1967 Israel succeeded in defeating the combined armies of Egypt, Jordan and Syria, which backed by the Soviet Union and 18 other Arab countries, had surrounded Israel entirely and closed its access to the Red Sea, the Suez Canal and other waterways. Abandoned by the United States, whose President declared the country "netural in thought, word and deed," it appeared to all the world that the 2.6 million Israeli Jews would be slaughtered in Nazi-like fashion upon being overrun by so large and superior an Arab force.

But Israel, far smaller in manpower and resources, succeeded in defeating all of her enemies and in capturing Jerusalem and the entire Holy Land as well as parts of Egypt and Syria.[44]

The issue with which evangelical Christians are concerned here is that during the several weeks when the annihilation of Israel seemed imminent and a second Auschwitz a real possiblity, most Christians remained silent or sided with the Arab nations on the grounds that the Arabs, like the Nazis before them, were an instrument of God assigned to punish the Jews. "Just as in 1933–1945 unnumbered people in the churches were never quite convinced that the Nazis were not unwitting allies of God—since the Jews were no longer his people—so in 1967 a powerful ideological affinity is manifest between Christian predispositions and the annihilationist designs of the Arabs."[45]

Since 1967 those Christians who still cling to the old theology, namely that the Jews are the enemies of God, Christ killers etc., have found endless grounds for siding with the Arabs and against Israel. Thus, Christians still call on Israel to return the land captured in the 1967 war and label the Jews the aggressors despite the evidence that Israel barely escaped annihilation.

"Perhaps," writes Eckardt, "we will next be told that the death camps [of the Nazis] were actually protective measures created . . . to keep Germans from being exterminated by the Jews."[46]

When the former president of Egypt, Abdel Nasser, declared before the Six Day War that he meant to exterminate the 2.6 million Jews then in Israel, his statement sounded to all Jews and to evangelical Christians like another threat to conduct yet another Holocaust. Failure of the mainstream Christian churches to come to the aid of Israel was therefore reminiscent to both Jews and evangelical Christians of the same failure of most Christians to stand up to Nazi atrocities between 1933 and 1945.

That such an attitude toward the present state of Israel is frequently the outcome of theological considerations is best illustrated by the antagonism shown Jews and Israel by the historian Arnold Toynbee. Persistently anti–Jewish, Toynbee not only labels Judaism a "calcified" religion and exhibits considerable antipathy to Judaism but then transfers his hatred of Jews generally to Israel. Together with so many anti–Jews, Toynbee finds the very existence of Israel immoral in view of the Arab claim to the land, yet he ignores that attitudes like his caused Auschwitz, which consequently led to the creation of Israel.[47]

Another example of anti–Judaism clothed in anti–Zionism is the endless criticism of Israel, but never the Arabs, by the World Council of Churches and its most important theologians as expressed for many years in their leading journals *The Christian Century* and *Christianity and Crisis*. This theological bias against Jewish survival became visible at the time of the Holocaust when the major Protestant and Catholic organizations refused to believe the stories concerning Nazi atrocities and labeled all this propaganda. In this they were of course not alone. As we have seen, after the Second World War the World Council of Churches did designate anti–Semitism a sin and did encourage its member churches to resist this evil.

In face of the near annihilation of Israel in 1967 and the "potential massacre of 2,500,000 Jews," however, the churches again said and did nothing. Instead they ascribed this situation to the Jews themselves and once more blamed the victims.

"In face of what appeared to most Jews as the imminent prospect of another Auschwitz for the corporate Jewish body in Israel, this [Christian] rhetoric, with its echo of the earlier flight into pietism by Christian leaders in Nazi Germany, contributed to a pervading sense of gloom in American Jewry." So said an American Jewish spokesman.[48]

Henry van Dusen, erstwhile president of the Union Theological Seminary, called Israel's victory "the most violent, ruthless aggression since Hitler's blitzkrieg," a view which his former student A. Roy Eckardt described as another chapter in "the teaching of contempt" according to which Christians understand that "The only good Jew is a dead Jew."[49]

Since 1967 the anti–Israeli bias of *The Christian Century* and *Christianity and Crisis* has never ceased. Such contributors as Alan Geyer of the United Church of Christ, James L. Kelso of the United Presbyterian Church and Willard G. Oxtoby are typical of these anti–Israeli polemicists.

At present, Rosemary Radford Ruether, an American theologian, is undoubtedly at the forefront of the anti–Israeli writers in these journals. For example, in criticizing Paul van Buren's book *A Christian Theology of the People of Israel*, she seeks to distinguish between Jews and "Zionist Jews," casting the latter in the light of what Nazi propaganda called "culture destroyers." To Ruether "the God of Israel is said to be the author of ... victimization and injustice. God saves Israel," says Ruether, "by mandating the dispossession and slaughter of the former inhabitants of the land."[50]

The Wrath of Jonah is another contribution by Rosemary and Hermann Ruether to this strident anti–Israel polemic.[51]

Finding nothing legitimate whatever about the existence of Israel, the Ruethers have no sympathy for the Jewish survivors of the Holocaust who founded that state as the only home left for them. To the Ruethers Zionists are anathema.

Innumerable editorials and essays in a similar vein appear regularly in *The Christian Century* and similar journals.

All this led A. Roy Eckardt to find that "Christian anti–Zionism is the new Christian anti–Semitism.... The Christian death wish for Jews finds a new actualization" in the Arab-Israeli conflict.[52]

Recognizing this danger, the Pontifical Commission for Peace and Justice issued a document at the request of Pope John Paul II on February 9, 1990. This document once more attacked all forms of racism and anti–Semitism but also warned that "anti–Zionism serves at times as a screen for anti–semitism."[53]

Meanwhile, the Vatican has not yet extended diplomatic recognition to Israel on the grounds that the Vatican does not extend such recognition to any country whose borders are not established.

V

After both the World Council Declaration on the Jews and "Nostra Aestate" were promulgated, many questions concerning the relationship between Christians and Jews still remained. Undoubtedly the Christian attitude toward Israel was and is the most important of these questions since to Jews there can be no difference between an attitude expressed toward the Jewish people and Jewish believers. It is true that there are those who seek to make such a distinction, but Jews everywhere recognize that Israel is the focus of their existence and that the true test of acceptance of Jews is acceptance of Israel.

In view of this and other questions concerning the daily implementation of the declarations by both Protestants and Catholics concerning the Jews and Jewish-Christian concerns, numerous meetings have been held to discover how best to deal with these issues now and in the future.

To facilitate such meetings, the pope issued "Guidelines" concerning "Nostra Aetate" on December 1, 1974, and augmented these guidelines with "Notes" on June 24, 1985.[54]

These "Guidelines" once more mention the mass murder of 6 million Jews as the catalyst for the changes ordered by Vatican II and also mention the "mutual ignorance" between the Jewish and Christian communities.

The first recommendation, also promoted by Protestant Christians, is that dialogue be pursued between Christians and Jews. Catholics are admonished in the "Guidelines" "to maintain the strictest respect for the religious freedom of others while bearing witness to their own faith." Catholics are specifically instructed not to offend Jews and to keep the past in mind.

This same attitude is recommended with respect to Catholic liturgy in that a better understanding of the Old Testament is furthered and prejudicial or insulting phrases and passages are to be reinterpreted in order to avoid misunderstandings that give rise to hatred.

It is next recommended that textbooks and other written material be revised to exclude passages which give the impression that the Old Testament is invalid, that Judaism is a dead religion or that Jews of any time period are to be blamed for the death of Jesus. In addition, it is recommended that "chairs of Jewish studies should be created and collaboration with Jewish scholars encouraged."[55]

Finally the "Guidelines" ask that Christians and Jews undertake joint social actions for the good of humanity.

These "Guidelines" undoubtedly have been instrumental in promoting the worldwide meetings of Christians and Jews such as the National Workshop on Christian-Jewish Relations which began in 1979.

In June of 1985, "Notes on the Correct Way to Present the Jews and Judaism in Preaching and Catechesis" (Greek: *katechein* = to teach) was published in Italian and English at the Vatican.[56]

These notes were presented in six sections as follows:
1. *Religious Teaching and Judaism.* This segment affirms that the Church views itself as the only agent of salvation but that "the Jews have been chosen by God to prepare for the coming of Christ." This view is regarded by Jews as yet another affirmation of the old motto *Extra ecclesiam nulla salus* ("Outside of the church there is no salvation"). Furthermore, it assumes that Jews have no role to play other

than to serve as a vehicle for Christian aspirations. Yet, on several other occasions Pope John Paul II expressed the view that "We shall be able to go by diverse—but in the end convergent—paths and with the help of the Lord, who has never ceased loving His people, to reach true fraternity in reconciliation, respect, and full accomplishment of God's plan in history."

2. *Relations Between the Old and New Testaments.* Here it is emphasized that Christians and Jews read the "Old" Testament differently, inasmuch as Jews neither call the 39 books of the Torah the "Old" testament nor use the word testament at all. Christians, however, view the Old Testament as preparation for the coming of Christ. Nevertheless, it is held in the "Notes" that Christians can profit from the Jewish tradition in this regard.

3. *The Jewish Roots of Christianity.* This section emphasizes that Jesus was and remains a Jew. It also shows Jesus to be in agreement with the Pharisees (Aramaic Hebrew: *perishayya* = separated) in some doctrines and further indicates that the Pharisaic movement was diverse and complex and not altogether to be condemned.

4. *The Jews in the New Testament.* This deals principally with the history of the early Church and its rupture with Pharisaic Judaism. It acknowledges the role of both groups in the separation which followed and also deals with the responsibility of "authorities of the Jews and their followers" in the death of Christ. In addition it emphasizes that "the *Credo* of the Catholic Church has always mentioned Pontius Pilate and not the Jews."

5. Here brief mention is made of the Jewish roots of the Catholic liturgy.

6. This section deals with the attachment of the Jews to the land of Israel, the history of the Jews since 70 C.E., and the Holocaust.

While there are those who viewed this statement as insufficiently recognizing the *religious* significance of the state of Israel to both Jews and Christians, the statement underscores the right of Israel to exist and goes so far as to say, "It is the duty also of the Christians to confirm the sovereignty, freedom, even the mere existence of the country that has given its Jewish citizens a home and has strengthened a healthy self esteem of Jews everywhere." The history of Israel and its continuation after the rise of Christianity is discussed in terms of the anti–Judaism which Christanity promoted. It is explained in terms of the erstwhile Christian perception that both Judaism and Christianity cannot be true. This view has now been revised to the effect that both have a role to play and that these roles complement each other.

As to the Holocaust, there are those who believe the statement did not go far enough in recognizing Christian responsiblity for some Nazi actions although it sought to divorce Christian responsibility from them. Julius Streicher, the most malicious of all Nazi criminals, declared before the Nuremberg court in 1946 that in accusing him, Streicher, of crimes against humanity the court was also accusing Martin Luther. Streicher argued that he had only carried out what Luther had ordered every righteous and believing person to do.[57]

Finally, there are those Christian theologians whom one may well call "Judaizers," a term at one time an opprobrium but now a not uncommon view. An example is the recently published "Confessions of a 20th Century Christian Judaizer," by the Catholic theologian Matthias Neumann.[58]

Neumann recognizes that for centuries "Judaizers" were viewed as enemies of the Church but that in view of the new theology Christians would do well to find "permanent, authentic roots in this tradition."

Neumann, who is a professor of theology at a Catholic seminary, teaches a class in Jewish Studies. As late as November 1990 he found that most seminarians still associate the word "Jew" with a variety of stereotypes and that the decrees of Vatican II and subsequent efforts have hardly changed the attitude of the average parishioner.

Furthermore he found an almost total ignorance of things Jewish among his students and among Christian congregations generally.

The things Neumann would like his fellow Christians to accept from Judaism are first, the Jewish tradition of study and learning which in Judaism is ranked as equal to or even more important than public prayer. Secondly, Neumann would have Christians imitate the Jewish attitude of "public courage as a witness to one's faith."[59]

The theologian Paul van Buren writes in a similar vein but more extensively. In *A Christian Theology of the People of Israel*, van Buren promotes the view that God has made himself known to man in only one way, as the God of the People of Israel. To van Buren the covenant between God and Israel includes not only the giving of the Torah, the Jewish scriptures, but also the Land of Israel including all that which is still in dispute. To van Buren, Israel is a "light unto the gentiles" so that the essential meaning of Jesus Christ and the Church is to be a vehicle by which the God of Israel has chosen to carry the message of Israel to the world. Van Buren believes that Christians have a special obligation to resist all forms of anti–Judaism and that Jews have an obligation to live by the commandments of the Torah while Christians should encourage Jews to do so. To van Buren, those who fight the Jews fight against God for to him the Jews are God's elect.

In connection with the 25th anniversary of "Nostra Aetate" in 1990, Pope John Paul II met with a delegation of the International Jewish Committee for Interreligious Consultation. Calling that occasion "very important," the pope called the decree of 1965 "nothing other than the divine mercy which is guiding Christians and Jews to mutual awareness, respect, cooperation and solidarity. He further said that the Church views the Jews as "His own people" and proclaimed his belief in "the absolute singularity of God's choice of a particular people, Israel." Once more the pope referred to the Holocaust and affirmed that "no dialogue between Christians and Jews can overlook the painful and terrible experience of the *Shoah*" (*Shoah* is the Hebrew word for the Holocaust). Referring to the joint Jewish-Catholic statement made in Prague on September 6, 1990, the pope urged that its recommendations to fight anti–Judaism "be widely recognized and implemented wherever human and religious rights are violated." Calling for repentance for past Christian wrongs against Jews and labeling anti–Judaism and anti–Semitism as sin, the Church sought as of 1990 to put this teaching into concrete plans of action, particularly in the countries of Eastern Europe where it seems to be needed the most.[60]

Even the Polish clergy has readied a document concerning Christian-Jewish relations and begun a journal, *Masada*, designed to introduce Jewish culture to the Christian population of Poland.[61]

Poland has been devoid of Jews since the slaughter of 3 million Jews during the Nazi occupation from 1939 to 1945. These efforts may succeed, but they face a real challenge in the land of Auschwitz and Treblinka where surviving Jews were murdered even after the Second World War by Polish Christians inflamed by hate and all those myths which Christian theology had taught so long and abandoned so late.

Therefore the Polish Roman Catholic bishops issued the following statements on December 20, 1990: "We express our sincere regret over all cases of anti–Semitism which were committed at any time or by anyone on Polish soil. All cases of anti–Semitism are against the spirit of the Gospel ... and are contrary to the Christian vision of human dignity." The statement continues, "If there was only one Christian who could help but did not extend his hand to a Jew in danger or contributed to his death then it makes us ask our sister and brother Jews for forgiveness."[62]

Three months later this declaration was followed by the launching of and intensive education and dialogue campaign by the Polish episcopate designed to "teach the clergy and priests about the close relationship between Jews and Catholics."[63]

In order to make this form of education possible, the Polish clergy has asked American Jewish theologians to visit Poland and to participate in Catholic-Jewish dialogue there inasmuch as there are so few Jews in Poland that most Poles have never seen a Jew. Moreover, there are no Polish Jewish scholars among the 2,000 Jews now living there.

In an effort to improve Christian-Jewish relations, the Polish Episcopate appointed Bishop Henryk Muszinski to chair the Polish Episcopate Commission for Dialogue with Judaism. This commission has sponsored an increasing number of seminars and conferences to the subject of Jewish history in Poland and the present status of world Jewry, two topics about which Poles know almost nothing.

Finally, another example of the new Catholic sensitivity to Jewish concerns was the decision of the Pontifical Council for Christian Unity to recommend against the beatification of Queen Isabella of Spain because she was the driving force behind the expulsion and forced conversion of the Spanish Jews in 1492. That panel concluded that Isabella's actions contradicted "current church positions on the freedom of conscience."[64]

Christian theology at the end of the twentieth century has moved a long way from the diatribes of St. John Chrysostom and Martin Luther. Indeed a truly new Christian theology of Judaism already exists as both Christians and Jews seek now to evaluate positively many features of the other religion which they previously evaluated negatively. Yet it will no doubt take centuries for Christians to become truly cognizant of that change so that the messianic hope of mankind may yet be realized by whatever vehicle can be devised.

Notes

1. "Nostra aetate, in qua genus humanum in dies arctius et necessitudines inter varios populos augentur, Ecclesia attentius considerate quae sit sua habitudo ad religiones non–christianas," etc. ("In our age when humanity is coming closer together and the bonds between various peoples are being strengthened, the Church examines with more attention her relations with non–Christian religions, etc.)
2. Marc H. Tannenbaum, "A Jewish Viewpoint," in *Vatican II: An Interfaith Appraisal*, John H. Miller, ed. (New York, Association Press, 1966), p. 349.
3. *Webster's Third New International Dictionary*, 1981.
4. Karl Rahner, *Theological Dictionary*, Richard Strahan, trans. (New York, Herder and Herder, 1961), p. 243.
5. Konstanty Gebert, "Do the Jews have a Future in Poland?" *Moment*, Vol. 15, No. 4, pp. 28–35.
6. Tannenbaum, *op. cit.*, p. 362.
7. Tannenbaum, *op. cit.*, p. 366.
8. Robert McAfee Brown, "The Enlargement of the Dialogue: Ecumenism and the Jews," in *The Ecumenical Revolution* (Garden City, N.Y., Doubleday, 1967), pp. 247–275.
9. Abraham J. Heschel, "No Religion Is an Island," *The Union Seminary Quarterly Review*, Vol. XXI, No. 2, Part I, January 1966, p. 119.
10. *Ibid.*, p. 250.
11. A. Roy Eckardt, "Can there be a Jewish-Christian Relationship?" *The Journal of Bible and Religion*, April 1965, pp. 122–130.
12. Brown, *op. cit.*, p. 254.
13. Edward Flannery, *The Anguish of the Jews* (New York, Macmillan, 1964), p. xi.
14. Robert E. Karsten, "What Stance for Lutherans," *The Lutheran Quarterly*, Vol. XX, No. 3, August 1968, pp. 238–250.

15. Karsten, *op. cit.*, p. 243.
16. Heinrich Meyer, "The Church and the Jewish People: Report on a Consultation," *The Lutheran Quarterly*, Vol. 21, No. 4, November 1969, pp. 451–459.
17. *Ibid.*, p. 458.
18. *Ibid.*, p. 458–459.
19. Willis F. Erickson, "A Parish Pastor's Reflections on Christian-Jewish Relations," *The Lutheran Quarterly*, Vol. XX, No. 3, August 1968, pp. 229–235.
20. Joseph R. Estes, "Jewish-Christian Dialogue as Mission," *Review and Expositor*, Vol. LXVII, No. 1, Winter 1971, p. 5.
21. *Ibid.*, p. 9.
22. Gregory Baum, *Is the New Testament Anti-Semitic?* (Glen Rock, N.J., Deus Paulist, 1965).
23. Gerhard Falk and Vern Bullough, "Achievement Among German Jews Born During the Years 1785–1885," *The Mankind Quarterly*, Vol., 27, No. 3, Spring 1987, pp. 337–365.
24. For a good discussion of this issue see Robert E. Willis, "Why Christian Liturgy Needs an Enduring Jewish Presence," *The Journal of Ecumenical Studies*, Vol. XXV, No. 1, Winter 1988, pp. 23–37.
25. *Ibid.*, p. 16.
26. Plan T. Davies, *Anti–Semitism and the Christian Mind* (New York, Herder and Herder, 1969), p. 156.
27. Emerson S. Colaw, "Why Dialogue," in Jakob J. Petuchowski, ed., *When Jews and Christians Meet* (Albany, New York, The State University of New York Press, 1988), p. 179.
28. Stefan Schreiner, "Why the Dialogue with Judaism Is Indispensable for Christian Theology," in Leonard Swidler, ed., *Breaking Down the Wall* (Lanham, Md., The University Press, 1987), p. 115.
29. *Ibid.*, pp. 115–127.
30. Jurgen Moltmann, "Israel's No: Jews and Jesus in an Unredeemed World," *The Christian Century*, Vol. 107, No. 32, November 7, 1990, pp. 1021–1024.
31. *Ibid.*, p. 1021.
32. *Ibid.*, p. 1032.
33. Clemens Thoma, *A Christian Theology of Judaism*, Helga Croner, trans. (New York, Paulist, 1980), pp. 162–176.
34. *Ibid.*, p. 175.
35. Franz Mussner, "Outline of a Christian Theology of Judaism," in *Tractate on the Jews: The Significance of Judaism for Christian Faith* (Philadelphia, Fortress, 1984), p. 3.
36. *Ibid.*, p. 7.
37. *Ibid.*, p. 19–46.
38. Karl Barth, in Eva Fleischner, *Judaism in German Christian Theology* (Metuchen, New Jersey, Scarecrow, 1975), p. 28.
39. Carl Edwin Armerding, "The Meaning of Israel in Evangelical Thought," *Evangelicals and Jews in Conversation on Scripture, Theology and History*, Marc Tannenbaum, Marvin R. Wilson and A. James Rudin, eds. (Grand Rapids, Mich., Baker, 1978).
40. Solomon Grayzel, *A History of the Jews* (Philadelphia, The Jewish Publication Society, 1947), p. 718.
41. Amerding, *op. cit.*, p. 136.
42. A. Roy Eckardt, "The Affirmation of Israel," in *Your People, My People* (New York, Quadrangle, 1974), p. 171.

43. *Ibid.*, p. 175.
44. *Newsweek*, Vol. LXIX, No. 25, June 19, 1967.
45. A. Roy Eckardt and Alice Eckardt, "Again, Silence in the Churches," in *Elder Brother, Younger Brother* (New York, Scribner's, 1967), p. 171.
46. *Ibid.*, p. 172.
47. Arnold Toynbee, "Jewish Rights in Palestine," *The Jewish Quarterly Review*, Vol. LII, No. 1, 1962.
48. Hertzel Fishman, *American Protestantism and a Jewish State* (Detroit, Wayne State University Press, 1973), p. 168.
49. *Ibid.*, p. 171.
50. Rosemary Radford Ruether, "Listening to Palestinian Christians," *Christianity and Crisis*, Vol. 48, No. 5, April 4, 1988, p. 114.
51. Rosemary Radford Ruether and Hermann J. Ruether, *The Wrath of Jonah* (New York, Harper & Row, 1983).
52. *Ibid.*, p. 175.
53. *The New York Times*, February 11, 1990, p. 1.
54. Richard Neudecker, "The Catholic Church and the Jewish People," in *Vatican II: Assessment and Perspectives*, Vol. 3, Renee Latourelle, ed. (New York, Paulist, 1989), p. 289.
55. *Ibid.*, p. 291.
56. *Ibid.*, p. 293.
57. H.J. Gamm, *Judentumskunde*, Fourth Ed. (Frankfurt, 1962), p. 140.
58. Matthias Neumann, "Confessions of a 20th Century Christian Judaizer," *America*, Vol. 163, No. 13, November 3, 1990, pp. 323–26.
59. *Ibid.*, p. 325.
60. The Jewish Telegraph Agency, "Pope Meets with Jews: Calls it 'Very Important.'" *The Buffalo Jewish Review*, Vol. 83, No. 13, December 14, 1990, p. 11.
61. Michal Cjajkowski, personal communication to the author, September 18, 1990.
62. *The Daily News Bulletin*, The Jewish Telegraph Agency, December 21, 1990.
63. *Synagogue Council of America News*, March 15, 1991, pp. 1–2.
64. "Isabella Beatification Voted Down," *Weekly News Digest*, The Jewish Telegraph Agency, Vol. 56, No. 12, March 22, 1991.

7

Great Expectations: From Conflict to Unity

I

Competition is a form of opposition that can lead to conflict in the form of war or annihilation.

As has been seen, Judaism and Christianity competed for adherents in the Roman Empire until Christianity became the state religion and then tried by many means to eliminate the Jewish competition and annihilate it. Those efforts did not succeed. Accommodation therefore took the place of opposition, as it always must in the affairs of men.

Finally, accommodation has resulted in cooperation, the most basic of human social processes. It has taken 1,600 years, from the Council of Nicea to Vatican II, to arrive at this state of cooperation from which new expectations may now be derived. Let us see what these expectations are.

II

More than a quarter century has elapsed since Christians have made an effort to accept the Jews in their midst and to explore Judaism with a view to the contributions to Christian theology which such an exploration can make.

The advantages of that new attitude are already visibly giving Christianity a new dimension and pointing to a great future for both Christianity and Judaism.

For some years there have been those who claimed that "God is dead" and that Western Civilization is living in the post–Christian age. While there may have been cause to believe this in view of the moral failure which the Holocaust and the two world wars underscored, Christianity has recovered and will continue to recover from these defeats because of a new alliance with Judaism which can no longer be reversed but will move forward inexorably.

For centuries Christianity attempted to shake off its Jewish roots, remove itself from all Jewish associations and divorce itself from a theological entanglement which cannot be sorted out or separated. It is evident than it is no more possible for Christianity to divorce itself from Judaism than it is possible to divorce the American idiom from the English language.

Now that this close alliance with things Jewish has been recognized by Christian theologians it has also been recognized that the adversarial attitude heretofore in vogue regarding Judaism led to disaster not only for Jews, but also for Christians. By furnishing the hatemongers and killers with legitimacy through the promotion of anti–Jewish theological concepts such as the "Christ-killer" epithets, Christianity not only became associated with that entire anti–Jewish movement epitomized by the Nazi party, but also became in part responsible for the mass persecutions and murders committed upon Christians as well as Jews.

The root of the Christian problem has lain in the excessive secularization of Christianity. This came about because Christianity was for so many centuries the official religion of most European nations and thus became entangled in the power politics of each nation in which it was recognized. For years, this seemed to Christians to have a great advantage as it ensured them of a monopoly on religious adherence and income. The advantages of all this power appeared obvious to everyone; the disadvantages were seldom recognized. In fact, it seemed to Christians that the whole world agreed with them except the Jews. Alone among all Europeans, the Jews remained as the only obstacle to unity. At least it appeared that that was the case.

Since Christianity is in truth not a unified, self-contained system but rather a multifaceted, ever-changing theology, the Jews were in fact not the only dissenters even when Christianity was at the medieval height of its power. There were always dissenters, from the Arians to the Albigensians to the Protestant sects of the seventeenth century and beyond.

Ever seeking unity by using government to enforce one or another version of Christianity on various populations, Christianity weakened its message through these acts of force, persecution and tyranny. Judaism faced no such danger. Because of their small numbers, their extreme poverty and their endangered condition in Christian lands, Jews could not exercise any secular power in all of European history. While these conditions made Jewish life a frequent horror and finally led to the mass murders known as the Holocaust, they also made Judaism immune from the pitfalls of a religion which rests on secular power to enforce its edicts.

Judaism was always forced to rely on persuasion alone. Not only were there no Jews in Europe who were forced to belong to the synagogue against their will, but on the contrary, Jews who remained in that community were confronted with the great temptation to escape persecution by leaving Judaism. Therefore they must have had cause to be willing to remain. The first great advantage that Christianity can gain from its recent association with Judaism is to learn that Jewish secret—that is, how to capture the allegiance of millions of women, men and children even under the most trying circumstances.

This is an important lesson as Christians now face a world in which, despite their numbers, they are a distinct minority. There are about 1 billion people living in Christian countries. In a world of more than 5 billion inhabitants, that makes Christianity a minority religion. In addition many people who live in Christian countries are not Christians. It is an error to assume that anyone not Jewish or not an adherent of another religion and living in America or Europe is therefore a Christian. Christians already face a considerable challenge from secularists, a challenge that will increase ever more. How can Christianity deal with both of these challenges, that is, the competiton from other religions and the competition from disinterested non–Christians who constitute at least half of the European and North American population? Ask the Jews. Since Jews have never had political power in Europe, they learned to survive without it. This is a lesson that Christians must learn in order to survive.

Because Jews had no political power in Europe, Judaism needed to separate itself from the concerns of the secular world in both philosophy and action. Jews survived their long persecution because they knew how to lead an inner life focused on theology, on learning, on family life and on community responsibility.

Because for Christians that which was public was also Christian for so long, many forgot or never learned how to preserve their distinct Christian lifestyle in a world that seemed to be publicly Christian anyway.

That this Christian nature of the public world was really never true and is in any event no longer the case should be evident to anyone who observes the secularization of Christmas. Even the Japanese, who are almost entirely non–Christians, have learned to "celebrate" this season as a commercial American circus.

The second benefit which Christianity can derive from Judaism is therefore to learn how to survive in an otherwise un–Christian world.

A third benefit which close association of Christianity with Judaism can achieve is that of mutual action respecting common social concerns. Poverty and racism, war and persecution, illiteracy and disease and a myriad of other difficulties beset mankind. It may well have appeared to Christians that Jews were really not needed in dealing with any of these problems since there are only 18 million Jews in this world (including Jewish secularists). This is so small a number that the Jews are almost negligible as a percentage of the world's population. Yet numbers alone are not the issue. Jews have shown that devotion to a cause, enthusiasm for an idea, willingness to serve and belief in the human spirit are more powerful than mere numbers. In association with Jewish communities everywhere, the Christian and the Jewish agenda will both be better served. Whatever one may mean by the Messianic Age or the Second Coming, it is obvious that the problems of mankind need to be dealt with here and now and therefore a Christian-Jewish alliance will go a long way to deal with them.

The Jewish zeal for learning is a fourth advantage for Christians. The reasons for this zeal lie in the history of the Jews and the limited opportunities of their past. Whatever the reason, it has been a mighty force in making the world a better place to live. The evidence is everywhere: Jews have won prizes and succeeded in the arts, music, literature, science and medicine in immensely disproportionate numbers. It is worth learning why and how this became possible. If admiration can be substituted for envy, all will gain and all will learn. As observers of the Tenth Commandment, Christians will be the first to seek to emulate this intellectual trait.

A fifth advantage which association with Jews and Judaism has for Christians is a greater understanding of Christian history. Not only is the history of the early Church the history of a Jewish sect, but the entire history of the Jewish people, so long ignored in the Christian world, adds many a chapter to an understanding of Christianity as well. This is true with reference to Christian scriptures, Christian theology and Christian life generally. An understanding of Judaism is needed in order to understand the gospels. An understanding of the work of the great Jewish philosopher Rabbi Moses ben Maimon is a prerequisite for understanding St. Thomas Aquinas, and he who wants to understand the Protestant Reformation can do so only by studying the Hebrew roots of that great movement.

For centuries Jews have maintained an exemplary family life. So have Christians. Nevertheless, in proportion to their numbers, Jews have seldom exhibited alcoholism, delinquency, divorce, drug addiction or criminal conduct. Whatever the reasons, the Jewish religion has emphasized the family over the synagogue. The Jewish home has been the center of observances, and the celebrations of Judaism have taken place within the Jewish family. Such an emphasis is worthy of emulation so that association with Jews should give Christians additional strength in combating all the ills which the secular world impinges on everyone. That is the sixth advantage Christians can gain by initiating a dialogue with Jews.

Tolerance for the views of others is another and important advantage that comes from an interfaith dialogue with Jews. Judaism has never accepted a formal dogma. It is therefore not bound to a category of beliefs which must be accepted by all Jews. This gives Judaism a flexibility not always seen in Christian communities. Recognizing this, without relinquishing what is uniquely Christian, will allow Christians to accommodate those who think otherwise. For it is certain that Christians in the twenty-first century will meet many people who are not only not Christians but whose religion, philosophy, history and purpose is utterly foreign to the Judeo-Christian point of view. It is important to learn how others think. Learning to live with Jews can teach this lesson.

Finally, Christianity has gained from its new association with Judaism in that it has become a more mature religion, no longer dependent on defaming its mother religion to secure its position in the world. By giving up the contempt for Judaism which characterized it for 1,600 years, Christianity today can proclaim its message for its own sake and not as a message important only because it is deemed superior to the Jewish message. Thus Christianity has now reached its maturity and given up its adolescence. We can expect a stronger Christian voice in the twenty-first century.

III

John T. Pawlikowski, a Roman Catholic priest, has written extensively on Christian-Jewish relations. Recognizing that Jews may well know about Christian ritual such as Christmas than Christians' know about Jewish ritual, Pawlikowski nevertheless believes that Jews know even less about Christianity in general than Christians know about Judaism.[1]*

The reasons for this are in part the history of the two faiths. Christianity is an outgrowth of Judaism, so Christians are familiar with the Jewish Bible. Not so the other way around. Judaism does not include the New Testament, knowledge of it is not necessary to an understanding or practice of Judaism and therefore it is ignored by Jews. Moreover, says Pawlikowski, "the bitter history of Christian persecution of Jews throughout the centuries" has made it hard for Jews to read Christian theology or to give Christian beliefs and rituals much meaning.

Then there is the fear of Christian proselytism. While the zeal to convert Jews may be less among Christians than was once the case, and while the application of physical force to that end is now impossible, Jews are still worried that their children may become the object of such efforts by Christians if closer relationships to Christians are permitted. Fear of Christian missionaries has also kept the Christian tradition out of Jewish school curricula.

Pawlikowski favors the view of the German Jewish philosopher Franz

---

*Notes to this chapter are on page 160.

Rosenzweig, who thought that Christianity could be seen as Judaism for the gentiles, a view which Pawlikowski considers "far superior to Jewish indifference to Christianity."

In view of the efforts by Christians to include the Jewish people and the Jewish religion in their considerations, the issue raised by Pawlikowski is, "What can the Jewish community do to now include the Christian community in its theology and community life?"

Some predictions are in order.

First, it is inevitable, because it is already happening, that Jews in Europe and America will become more and more assimilated to Christians as the intermarriage rate rises past the 40 percent mark it attained in 1990. While these intermarriages do not by any means always result in the conversion of the Jewish spouse to Christianity, and while indeed a large number of these intermarriages result instead in the conversion of the non–Jewish spouse to Judaism, there can be no doubt that the influence of Christianity on Jewish belief and practice is therefore enhanced.

This phenomenon is not new. The German Jews who founded Reform Judaism in the early nineteenth century imitated the Protestant service so greatly that to this day the Reform liturgy resembles that of a Protestant church in its singing of hymns, sermonizing by the rabbi, organ music, and above all, the shortening of the Sabbath service to one hour. Some of these influences can be seen in Conservative synagogues as well.

At the same time, Christians have begun once more to observe Jewish customs long forgotten among them. Most important among these is the effort on the part of some Catholic and Protestant churches to participate in the Passover "Seder" (Hebrew: *seder* = order) the ordered and prescribed ritual meal taken by Jews on the first and second night of that eight-day festival.

This meal, together with its readings and rituals, is almost unchanged over the past 2,500 years and therefore dramatizes the Last Supper for Christians.[2]

While such a dramatization, surrounded by Christian rituals as well, does not conform entirely to the Jewish manner of observance, it nevertheless gives Christians some idea of how Jews observe this ritual today. Secondly, such a dramatization allows Christians to understand their own tradition better as the Last Supper can thereby be better envisioned.

Third, the link between Passover and Holy Communion is better shown by this demonstration, particularly if the congregants are encouraged to participate in the ritual.

This is generally done during Holy Week, a time when Jews also celebrate the Passover. Thus, the link is well established and reinforced.

There are today some Christians who call themselves the Church of the New Covenant. They use the Hebrew phrase *Brith Chadoshah*, meaning

"New Covenant," include a number of other Hebrew phrases in their services, celebrate the Jewish Sabbath on Friday evening, observe Chanukah, Passover and other Jewish customs and yet worship Jesus Christ and are included in the Christian community. Whether or not such enterprises will succeed in the long term cannot yet be discerned. It is remarkable in any case that these forms of "Judaizing" have a considerable following and appeal to many Christians. Evidently, the relationship between the two faiths finds its most prominent expression in these churches.

In addition, interfaith services are held on numerous occasions between Christians and Jews in Europe and in America. In the United States the Thanksgiving holiday, a particularly American institution, has for years lent itself to interfaith religious experiences.

There are also some houses of worship in the United States and Europe which serve both faiths on Saturday and Sunday.

Organizations of clergy such as the Metropolitan Ministries in various communities include rabbis as well as priests and ministers. Common political statements concerning racism, poverty and war have been made by various Jewish and Christian groups, and both groups have invited clergy of the other faith to speak to their congregations.

IV

Recently the German Catholic theologian Hans Kung published *Projekt Weltethos*,[3] which is devoted to "Liberation Theology." Kung's contention is that three requirements need to be fulfilled by all religions in order to bring about a "worldethos." These are the development of a "World Ethos" of the nations, peace among all religions and dialogue among all religions as a prerequisite for peace.

Kung tells us that every minute the nations of the world spend $1.8 million for military expenses, that every hour 1,500 children die of starvation, that every day a species of animal or plant dies out and that the '80s saw more arrests, tortures, murders and repression than any time in the history of mankind except for the Second World War. Numerous other horrors are listed by Kung, who then asks whether any possibility of rescue still exists for mankind. Demanding a coalition of believers and unbelievers, Kung makes his case for a world ethos. His example is the moral victory of the West over the East as best exemplified by the tearing down of the Berlin Wall. All of this, claims Kung, was achieved by spiritual power, not by armies or by force.

Kung therefore proposes ethics as a form of "crisis prophylaxis." Kung opposes the concept of "one holy and Catholic church." To him this is a form of exclusion which cannot succeed. Catholicism, teaches Kung, is one religion among many. Further he argues that the right to freedom of religion also includes the freedom *from* religion, that is, the freedom not to have any religion whatever.

Kung believes that the great religions of the world are predestined to found a "World Ethos for the World Religions in the Service of the World Community," without which Kung believes humanity cannot survive.

Calling on the various religious forces to cease their fighting, Kung reviews the Lebanese war of Christian against Christian and Moslem, the Jewish-Moslem fight in Israel, the Hindu-Moslem fighting in India and the intra-Christian war in Northern Ireland.

Kung makes the point that Christians and Jews developed atomic energy and used it to make the atom bomb. He appeals to all the world religions to cease their destructive activities and build a world ethos together.

Whether Kung will succeed in his appeal will not be known for many years to come. That his prescription is needed cannot be denied. It may well be that Kung, like other prophets preceding him, has come too soon for most and is yet to be heard even by those who regard him as anathema and have cut him off from his church.

V

The way is set and there is no returning. Ecumenism, at one time a word referring only to Christians, now includes Jews as well. While both faiths will and should maintain a core of beliefs and practices that will be specifically and peculiarly Christian or Jewish, much that these two great faiths have in common will be and is now available to both peoples. Thereby both will be strengthened in their common hope: "Peace on Earth and Good Will to Men."

Notes

1. John T. Pawlikowski, "A Challenge to Jewish Attitudes," *Moment*, Vol. 15, No. 4, August 1990, pp. 36–39.
2. Roland de Corneille, "The Purposes of Presenting the Dramatized Passover Seder Meal," *Christians and Jews: The Tragic Past and the Hopeful Future* (New York, Harper & Row, 1966), pp. 148–149.
3. Hans Kung, *Projekt Weltethos* (München, Germany, R. Piper, 1990).

APPENDICES

A

Vom Schem Hamphoras und vom Geschlecht Christi (Of the Unknowable Name and the Generations of Christ)

Introduction to the English Translation

Written in 1543, this book, now published in English for the first time, must seem difficult if not impossible to understand. Not only is the English usage confusing and ungrammatical, but the thoughts and views of the author, Martin Luther, seem so foreign to our thinking.

The original German is of course even more difficult. The reasons for this are not hard to find. In the first place it must be remembered that prior to Luther, literate Germans (indeed all literate Europeans) used Latin to write almost anything, especially something as serious as theology. Luther's failure to be grammatical and use a consistent style is explained by the fact that there was no German grammar in 1543, any more than there was an English grammar. Thus, anything went. Luther mixed tenses in the same sentence, jumped from one thought to another in the same paragraph, rushed from the singular to the plural and back, had no consistent punctuation and spelled any way at all.

In addition, the expressions and idioms used by Luther are antiquated. This is best understood by considering that Luther was a contemporary of William Dunbar in English literature, and wrote earlier than Spenser and before Shakespeare was born.

With these problems in mind, I first translated this long essay into modern German and then into English, although I have kept the English translation as Luther wrote German. I left all of the errors where they were. This gives the non-German reader at least some notion of Luther's style.

Luther alludes to many Hebrew and Latin words, uses Latin and Hebrew phrases without translating them into German and quotes biblical sources inaccurately.

Luther's Hebrew was weak, as he himself readily acknowledged. As a result, there are numerous mistranslations in the text. I have left these as they were written. In short, I made no effort to correct Luther's mistakes.

I did make many judgments concerning the English vocabulary best suited to reflect Luther's meaning. All translators must do that. I have no doubt that another translator may have chosen different interpretations in some instances.

It is nevertheless my contention that I have faithfully reflected the book *Vom Schem* Hamphoras* by this English rendition and have given the reader an opportunity to look at an aspect of Luther's work and thinking which needs to be understood in order to comprehend the spirit of his age and the consequent fate of the European Jews.

In making this translation I followed these principles. First, I tried to reflect the manner in which Luther wrote. Second, within these limits I tried to make the English version reasonably understandable to its reader. Third, I tried to remain flexible enough, using certain American idioms where necessary, to give the translation the meaning it deserves. This means that I did not translate verbatim if such translation would have led to a total distortion of the author's intent.

This translation is based on the German St. Louis edition published by the Concordia Press in 1890. I used this edition because the editor, Johann Georg Walch, succeeded in updating many of the antiquated phrases and words used by Luther. This made this edition much more understandable to me.

I also referred to another German edition begun at Weimar in 1883. This edition was published by the Herman Bohlaus Publishing Co., which issued over 60 volumes through 1983. None was published during World War II. The 53rd volume of this edition contains the *Vom Schem Hamphoras* and was published in 1920. However, the language is that of 1543. Consequently it is accurate to say that the St. Louis edition is now the most modern in the German language.

Nevertheless I referred extensively to the footnotes in the Bohlaus Edition.

The Collected Works of Martin Luther also exist in English and were published by Concordia Press in 1971. However, *Vom Schem Hamphoras* was not translated and was therefore omitted from that English edition. Therefore the present translation is the only English version of that book yet published.

The notes attached here are my own. They serve to explain some of the obscure references made by Luther to various authors whose names and works are seldom known today or to whom Luther refers so casually that they cannot be easily identified. This lack of precision is also true of Luther's references to historical names and places. I have tried therefore to explain these as well in the footnotes, particularly since Luther did not always know the dates of various events in the history of Israel or Christianity.

The Bohlaus Edition of *Vom Schem Hamphoras* published in 1920 contains several introductory remarks. The following is a translation of these remarks, which may be found on pages 573 and 574 of that edition. These remarks are not signed. No name is associated with them. However, the editors of Volume 53, in which this essay appears, are F. Cohrs and O. Brenner. Printed in Gothic German, they are

---

* *German spelling of the Hebrew word for "name." The usual English spelling is "shem."*

Vom Schem Hamphoras (English translation)

slightly longer than this translation. I have rendered into English only that part which makes the Luther text more understandable than it would otherwise be. The remainder of the introductory remarks in the Bohlaus edition concerns the fate of the original Weimar edition of this book and has nothing to do with the content.

In his publication *Concerning the Jews and Their Lies*, Luther already announced another publication concerning the Jews: in special notes he sought to exhibit what Porchetus had written about the power of the Shem Hamphoras. Directly after finishing that publication Luther fulfilled that promise. Our publication was already finished on the 7th of March 1543, so that the preparation must have succeeded directly the publication "Of the Jews etc." Luther announced the conclusion of "Of the Jews etc." to Justus Jonas who promptly translated it into Latin and who was therefore particularly interested in the development of the new work. [That is, *Vom Schem Hamphoras*.] He wrote this about it: "non is facile transferes in Latinum."[1]
Jonas did not risk the translation of this publication.

In "Of the Jews," Luther already used the work of Salvagus Porchetus de Salvaticis, a 14th century Cartesian monk, *Victoria adversus impios Hebraeos*.[2]

This time he exhibits in German translation the part from the 11th chapter of Part 1 which deals with the sacred incantation of the Schem Hamphoras and the legends concerning its origins. He (Luther) censures the superstition which is evidenced by the veneration of that incantation and ridicules the Jews who believe these silly tales.

But, as its entire heading indicates, the announced contents have yet a second part: "Of the Lineage of Christ." Luther says himself what motivated him to present this part. The publication which had been the inducement for Luther's work "Of the Jews" also claimed that it could not be proved that Jesus was of the tribe of Judah because the apostle Matthew directs the tribe of Juda toward Joseph and not toward Mary; that therefore he could not have been the Messiah because of the tribe of Juda and the House of David. Since Luther had not yet discussed this issue in "Of the Jews" he made up for it now and provides harmony between the divergent lines of descent in Matthew 1, 1–16 and Luke 3, 23–37. Thus he lets Jesus descend from David in one instance through his stepfather Joseph and in the other through his mother Mary. This second part is attached to the first without any other connection. They hang together only because they constitute a supplement to *Of the Jews and Their Lies*.

1. *"It is not easy to translate into Latin."*
2. *Victory over the impious Jews.*

The Lineage of Christ (Matth. 1)

March 1543

Doctor Martin Luther

1. In the last pamphlet [*Of the Jews and Their Lies*] I have announced that I will henceforth ignore what the ferocious, miserable Jews lie about their Shem Hamphoras[3] as described by Purchetus in his book called *Victoria*.[4]

This I have done herewith, in honor of our belief, and in opposition to the devilish lies of the Jews so that those who want to become Jews will see what kind of "fine" dogmas they must believe and keep among the damned Jews.

For as I plainly stipulated in that pamphlet, it is not my opinion that I can write against the Jews in the hope of converting them. That is why I did not call that pamphlet *Against the Jews*, but *Against the Jews and Their Lies*, so that we Germans may know from historical evidence what a Jew is so that we can warn our Christians against them as we warn against the Devil himself in order to strengthen and honor our belief; not to convert the Jews which is about as possible as converting the Devil.[5]

---

3. *As discussed in Chapter 3, this Hebrew phrase means "Hidden name" and reputedly refers to the true name of God.*

4. *Luther here refers to the Genoese monk Porchetus Salvaticus and his book,* Victoria adversus impios Hebraeos *or* Victory over the impious Jews, *published in 1315. A pamphlet of 94 pages, this tract by Porchetus was reprinted several times. A Parisian edition of 1520 came into Luther's possession. The book is now stored in the municipal library at Karlsruhe. In 1938 the Karlsruhe librarian Gerhard Katterman discovered seven German and Latin notes in the margins of that book written by Luther. See* D. Martin Luthers Werke, Weimar, Herman Bohlaus, Nachfolger, 1980.

5. Diabolos *comes from the Greek verb* diabolein *meaning "to calumniate or throw across." This is a close translation of the Hebrew word* Shoton *or* Satan. *The ancient Iranian word* daeva *or evil spirit is involved here and has a Sanskrit cognate* deva *meaning a benevolent deity of India. The reason for this apparent divergence in meaning between the two cultures is that the Hindu Indians and the Parsis of Iran fought many a battle over religion until the benevolent god of the Hindus became the malicious spirit of their enemies, the Parsis.*

The name Beelzebub is also used to signify the devil. This name is derived from the Hebrew Baal Zebub *meaning Lord of the Flies, an expression found in* Kings II 1:2 *and referring to the god of the Ekronites, hence a Phoenician deity. As the god of strangers he became the devil of the Israelites.*

There are of course innumberable other names for the devil in other cultures. All however indicate that men everywhere and at all times recognized that evil and natural calamities such as disease and death are inevitable. Consequently a large literature concerning the devil exists not only among religious writers but also in folklore, mythology and in art. Consider the role of the devil, called Mephistopheles, (From the Latin mefitis, *stench) in the story of Faust. See George V. Tomashevich, "Unbelief in the Concept of the Devil," in* the Encyclopedia of Unbelief, *Buffalo, N.Y., Prometheus Press, 1985, pp. 141–150.*

2. For just as we must teach and write concerning the Devil, Hell, Death and Sin; what they are and what they can be, so I also write about the Jews so that we can guard against all of these. Not that we can make an angel out of the Devil or a heaven out of Hell or Life from Death or Holiness from Sin. All that is impossible.

A Jew or a Jewish heart is as hard as stone and iron and cannot be moved by any means. Even if Moses and all the Prophets came and did all their wondrous works in front of their eyes as did Christ[6] and his apostles, so that they would quit their unreason, it would still be useless.

Even if they were punished in the most gruesome manner that the streets ran with blood, that their dead would be counted, not in the hundred thousands but in the millions, as happened under Vespasian in Jerusalem and for evil under Hadrian,[7] still they must insist on being right even if after these 1,500 years they were in misery another 1,500 years. Still God must be a liar and they must be correct.

In sum, they are the devil's children damned to hell; if however, something human still remains in them, for him this essay may be of use and come to some good. Some, so inclined, may still hope for that whole gang as they wish. I have no hope there anymore and know of no writings concerning such hope. We cannot even convert the majority of Christians and have to be satisfied with a small number; it is therefore even less possible to convert these children of the devil! Although there are many who derive the crazy notion from the 11th chapter of the Epistle to the Romans that all Jews must be converted, this is not so. St. Paul meant something quite different.

6. Christ is derived from the Greek word chriein *meaning "to anoint." This in turn is a direct translation of the Hebrew word* mo'shiach *which also means "to anoint." The kings of ancient Israel were anointed with oil. The word anoint is derived from the Latin* unguere, *"to smear."*

7. The emperor Vespasian had the full name of Titus Flavius Sabinus Vespasianus. It was he who commanded the Roman armies which put down the revolt of the Jews in Galilee, i.e., northern Israel. As a consequence of that victory he was elected emperor of Rome and left his son, Titus, in charge of the army. Titus destroyed Jerusalem in 70 and later became co-emperor with his father, assuming sole power on Vespasian's death in 79.

Publius Aelius Hadrianus was born in 76 C.E., became emperor of Rome in 117 and died in 138. Buried at Castel Sant Angelo in Rome, he was known in his lifetime as a great builder of public works and a man of many talents, interests and considerable education. He declared his intention to rebuild the Jewish temple and the city of Jerusalem which had lain in ruins since 70 when the first Judean revolt was put down with great ferocity. Hadrian, who visited Judea in 130, declared that the intended temple was to be dedicated to the Roman god Jupiter and that the city was to be called Aelia Capitolina.

This announcement led to the second Jewish revolt under Bar Kochba in the year 132, a revolt fueled by the additional rumor that Hardian intended to prohibit circumcision. Despite some initial successes, the Jewish armies were defeated again by the Romans and their allies.

This second defeat lead to the final exile of most Jews from their homeland and their dispersion throughout the Middle East and Europe. It was this dispersion and the failure of the Jews to have their temple rebuilt which Christians for many centuries viewed as divine punishment for the rejection of Jesus by the Jews.

FROM THE ELEVENTH CHAPTER IN THE FIRST PART OF PURCHETIS BOOK,
TRANSLATED INTO GERMAN BY D.M. LUTHER.

1. We will now see how the Jews were always such enemies of Christ's wonders that they attributed them to Beelzebub, the lord of the devils. For he (Christ) did do so many wondrous works as no one else has ever done as he himself says in John 15.

It has also never been claimed that anyone else in his Name made the blind see, the deaf hear, the lame walk, the dumb speak as Isaiah prophesied in verse 35, 4.5.: "God, the Rewarder, will come and help you. Then the eyes of the blind will be opened, the ears of the deaf will be opened, the lame will jump like a deer and the tongue of the dumb will say praises."

2. Over and above these many wondrous signs he did many more, woke up the dead, cleaned the leprous, and healed many others among the sick and did so many other signs that no one, except God, could have done them; yet, the meanness of the Jews, always associated with evil tricks, had the nerve to blaspheme and shame these miracles with lies. They have composed a book against Christians in which they write the following lies:

3. It happened at the time of Helen, the Queen, who reigned over the whole land of Israel,[8] that Jesus, the Nazarene, came to Jerusalem. In the Temple of the Lord he found the stone upon which in earlier times was set the Ark of the Lord; Shem Hamphoras was written upon this stone; whoever learned the names of these letters and understood them, could do whatever he pleased.

4. Our wise men worried, however, that if the Children of Israel were to learn this Name they would destroy the world by means of that power. Therefore they constructed two bronze dogs and set them on two pillars in front of the door of the sacred place. Now if someone entered and learned the letters of the aforementioned Name, and came out again, then the metal dogs barked at him so dreadfully that from fright he forgot the Name and the letters which he had learned.

5. Now Jesus, the Nazarene, came and learned the letters and wrote them on a parchment. Then he ripped up the flesh along his leg and placed the notes therein. And because he named the Name, nothing hurt him and the skin came together as it had been before; as he now left the Temple, the bronze dogs barked at him so that he forgot the Name promptly; as he came home, however, he ripped

---

8. *In the first century C.E. Monobaz I, king of Adiabene, "a district in the upper Tigris region," became a convert to Judaism. His sister, his wife Helena and her son Izates likewise converted to Judaism. On the death of Mondoaz, Izates became king and ruled from 36 to 60 C.E. Helena spent the rest of her life in Jerusalem, where she built herself a palace. Although she was known for charity and piety, she never ruled in Israel as claimed by Porchetus.*

Helena was buried in the Tomb of the Kings still found in the north of Jerusalem today. See Encyclopedia Judaica, *Jerusalem, Keter Publishing House, Vol. 2, p. 267, and Vol. 8, p. 288.*

open his leg with a knife and took the notes out upon which the letters of the Shem Hamphoras were written and learned them again.

6. Thereafter he gathered about him 310 young men of Israel and said to them: Look here, the wise men say I am the son of a whore, because they want to rule over Israel; you however know that all prophets prophesied concerning the Messiah; I am he, that is true. As Isaiah prophesied concerning me: "See, an Alma[9] is pregnant and will bear a son and his name will be Emanuel" (*Jes. 7, 14*). That is how my ancestor David prophesied and said: "You are my son, I begot you today" (*Psalm 2, 7*): Thus, my mother bore me without contribution from a man, alone from the power of God. Therefore, not I, but they themselves are children of a whore, as Hosea says: "I will not have mercy on their children for they are the children of whores" (*Hosea 2, 4*).

7. Then the youths from Israel answered him: If you are the Messiah, give us a sign. What kind of sign do you want from me? They said: Make a lame man stand, as we are. He said: Bring one here to me. Soon they brought a lame man who had never stood on his feet and he spoke the Shem Hamphoras over him; at that same hour he arose and stood on his feet. Then they all bowed before him and said: He is without any doubt Messiah. They also brought a leper to him. He spoke the Name over him and laid his hand on him and he recovered at once. Therefore a good number of worthless persons from our people associated with him.

8. However, the wise men, as they saw that Israel was beginning to believe in him, caught him and brought him to the Queen Halani who possessed the land of Israel at the time and said to her: Gracious Lady, this man makes magic and tricks the world. Jesus the Nazarene answered: Gracious Lady, the prophets prophesied years ago about me and one of them says the following: "A twig will grow from the clan of Jesse" (*Jess. 11, 1*). I am he, and of him David says: "Well being to him who does not wander in the advice of the Godless" (*Psalms 1, 1*).

9. She said: Is what this one says in your law? They answered: Yes, it says so in our law, but it does not refer to him, but this is written concerning him in 5 Moses, 13, 5: "The prophet should be killed for he taught injustice against God." But of the Messiah it is written (*Jer. 23, 6*): "In his time, Judah shall be helped." Thereupon this Godless one answered and spoke to the queen: I am the one, for I can wake the dead.

10. The queen sent with them her most trusted servants and the Godless one made a dead man live by means of the Shem Hamphoras; from then on the queen was astonished and said: Certainly, that is a great miracle. She held the wise men in contempt so that they had to leave her in shame which hurt them and those from Israel a great deal. And Jesus the Nazarene moved to upper Galilee.

9. The word alma *is Hebrew. Christians translate this word to mean "virgin"; Jews translate it to mean "young woman." Thus, the famous sentence in Isaiah 7:14 is rendered in the Jerusalem Bible, "Behold the young woman is with child."*

11. And the wise men returned to the queen and said to her: Gracious Lady, this fellow deals in magic and confuses all living things. She thereupon sent her mercenaries so as to catch him; but the people in Galilee did not like it but fought against her. However, he said: You should not fight for my sake; for the power of my father in heaven and the sign he has given me will defend me. And the people in Galilee made birds of clay before him, so he said Shem Hamphoras about them and the birds flew promptly; and they fell upon their face and prayed to him.

12. At that same hour he asked that a large millstone be brought and thrown into the sea; when that had been done, the Godless one pronounced the Shem Hamphoras, and caused the stone to lie still upon the sea and he sat on it and said to the mercenaries: go to your lady and tell her what you saw. Thereupon he got up in front of them and walked about on the sea.

13. The mercenaries went and told the queen Halani everything they had seen. She became exceedingly upset and called the wise men and said to them: You claimed that this man Jesus the Nazarene is a magician, but you should know that his signs prove that he is indeed the son of God. They however said: Gracious Lady, let him come here so we can expose his michief. Meanwhile, the elders of Israel went and admitted a fellow by name of Judas Iscariot into the most holy of the Temple. He learned the letters Shem Hamphoras in the same manner as Jesus of Nazarene had learned them and ripped open the flesh on his leg which the other one (Jesus) had done.

14. Then Jesus the Nazarene came with his following and the queen asked the wise men to appear as well. And he stepped before the queen and said: David prophesied about me: "Dogs surrounded me and an assembly of evil doers encircled me" (Ps. 22, 17). But this is also said by me, Jer. 1,8: "Be not afraid of them for I am with you, that I rescue you, says the Lord." But the wise men disputed this.

15. And he said to the queen: I shall rise to heaven, for thus said David of me: "Rise up, God, above the heavens." (Ps. 57, 12) and raised the hands like wings, through the name Shem Hamphoras, and flew between heaven and earth. Since the wise men saw this, they spoke to Judas Shariot, he should say Shem Hamphoras and go up after him. He rose up and wrestled with him so that both fell back down together; and the Godless one broke an arm: Christians weep about this every year before their Easter.

16. At that same hour, the Israelites seized him and hid him with cloths and beat him with whips of pomegranate trees. And said to the queen Halani: If he is the son of God, then let him say who beat him; but he could not say it. The queen spoke to the wise men: See, he is in your hands, do with him what pleases you.

17. Then they grabbed him and led him to the gallows; however, no matter what tree or beam they hung him on, it broke in two at once; for he had conjured all trees and woods by means of Shem Hamphoras so that they could not hold him. So they went and got a cabbage stem, which does not grow from a tree but from

a weed, and hung him on it. Such is no miracle. For in the Holiest there grows a stem every year as about 100 pounds of seed hang from it. *Haec ille.*[10]

18. Where are they now, the unfaithful Christians who became Jews or wish to become Jews? Come here for a kiss, the devil has thrown it in the N. and emptied the stomach again, that is truly a holy place that the Jews, and whoever wants to become Jew, must kiss, devour, booze and pray to and then the devil also boozes and devours which his disciples see and can throw out both from above and below.

Here the right guests and hosts have come together, cooked it right and prepared it. Oh, how it served both of them right!

The devil had been created a beautiful angel so that he could, together with the other holy angels, forever sing the eternal *Te Deum Laudamus* with his holy, angelic mouth. That he could not tolerate and became a devil who now devours with his angelic trunk and devours with joy what the Jews spit out and from above and below. That became his dainty morsel in which he grazes like a sow behind the fence on St. Margareth's Day[11]; right, right, that's how he wanted it.

19. The Jews too got what they deserved. They had been called and elected to be God's mouth as Jeremiah says: (*Jer. 15, 19* and *Ps. 81, 11*): Open your mouth wide and I will fit it; they however, kept tightly closed their muzzles, eyes, ears, nose, whole heart and all senses, so he polluted and squirted them so full that it oozes from them in all places and devil's filth comes from them.

Yes, that tastes good to them, into their hearts, they smack their lips like swine. That is how they want it. Call more: Crucify him, crucify him. Scream more: "His blood come upon us and our children" (*Matth. 27, 25*).[12] I mean it came and found you.

20. Now let us take a look, one at a time, at the "fine" dogmas of the Jewish belief as given in this essay, so that anyone who has the inclination to become a Jew will be relieved. If you want to become a true Jew then listen and learn the catechism of the holy Jewish belief, but not in the name of God.

21. First, you must believe that Helen had been queen in the land of Israel or Canaan, during the time that our Lord Jesus Christ lived, taught and did miracles. Not alone the Apostles and Evangelists oppose this, but also the Roman Empire as it then existed; in addition the testimony and exile of the Jews which began at the time of Vespasian, 250 years before Helen was born; you must not be fooled in this, but think: the rabbis (authors of such a book) cannot be wrong, heaven and earth

10. *What else. This is the end of the Porchetus quotation.*
11. *St. Margareth of Antioch was a 15-year-old martyr who jumped off a building to her death in order to preserve her virginity. Hers was one of the voices heard by Joan of Arc. See* The Catholic Encyclopedia, 1967.
12. *Numerous Christian writers have commented on this phrase from Matthew, using it as justification for the bloody persecutions which mark all of Jewish history. As late as this century, some Christian pastors used this phrase as a technique of neutralization for the Nazi atrocities they themselves witnessed.*

and all angels and creatures together with God must be wrong sooner than they. That you must believe if you wish to become a true Jew.

22. Thus, you must also believe everything that is written here concerning the queen Helen, as she dealt with and let others deal with Jesus the Nazarene 250 years before she was born; for that belongs to what is to be known as part of the catechism of whoever wants to become a Jew. If someone were to say: the Jews had not been in the land for 200 years at the time of Helen, but were dispersed in the whole world, and Jerusalem had neither a temple nor a government; against that you must smile sarcastically against the damnable *goyim*[13] and say: our Rabbis write it, therefore it must be so, even if God himself, using Scriptures and the work of creation says otherwise; he must do what the Rabbis want.

23. In addition you must believe, that two bronze dogs could at that time also have barked without Shem Hamphoras; before then, and now, no one can do it anymore; even with their bronze eyes could discern sharply who went in and who came out and in addition, who had copied the letters engraved into the stone: those must have been very sharp eyes, particularly since they were ore, and could see through such thick walls, doors, and a curtain. No doubt you would have difficulty with this since all living dogs in this world, who can of course bark naturally, and much less the bronze dogs, would not believe such a thing if they could hear and understand such a thing.

But don't let it worry you; whatever the Rabbis say, that is right, ask nothing further if you wish to be a pious Jew.

24. Now you must also believe that the wise men of Israel were no wiser than to protect the Shem Hamphoras with two bronze dogs instead of iron doors, fences and similar things, even though the damned *Goyim* could have found other wise men. Would it not occur to you here that the wise men of Israel had far less sense in this than the bronze dogs themselves. Yet, you must forget such thoughts and think rather: what those rabbis say is right and cannot be a lie.

25. In the third place you must believe that in the Sanctuary in Jerusalem there grew each year such large cabbage stems that they were stronger than any other gallows beam and that 100 pounds of grain had grown on it. In addition you must believe that 200 years after the destruction a temple stood in Jerusalem.

Not only that, but that it was simultaneously a cabbage patch and a sanctuary.

13. The Hebrew word goy *means nation. Thus, "Goy Israel" means the nation of Israel. However, in the Yiddish language, a form of medieval German mixed with Hebrew and Slavic phrases and used by Eastern European Jews, the word* goy *came to mean "non-Jew," that is, a nation other than Israel. Goyim is the masculine plural form of that word. In the Hebrew language, the ending* –im *refers to the masculine plural as in* Elohim *("Gods," derived from* El, *"God"). This is a remarkable matter because the third word in* Genesis *is* Elohim *thus leading to the exact translation of that first sentence in the Bible to mean: "In the Beginning* the Gods *created...."*

Even if all histories, Moses and all the prophets, even God with all the angels say otherwise, than that is a lie, for the belief of the Jews must be right. Remember that well if you want to become a Jew.

26. Finally, you must surrender to that which a rabbi says, no matter how peculiar it may be, you must believe it is right regardless if God himself ordered it otherwise and said: For so Moses ordered them *5 Mos., 17, 8.* "If they do not understand something, they should go up to the priests and the judges, who are at that place and whom God elected. They shall (says he) give you a verdict; according to the law that they teach you shall you do, and according to the judgment that they tell you, you shall conduct yourself so that you do not deviate from it, neither to the right or to the left." Here it is concluded (I almost said shit upon)[14] that everything the Rabbis say a Jew shall believe without deviating from it. Therefore they now say, they must believe their rabbis even if the same said the right hand is the left and the left the right, as Purchetus writes. Just as the two Jews who visited me did. When I urged them to regard the text they said they must believe their rabbis unsupported by any text; that is why, according to my own experience, I must believe Purcheto in this matter.

27. If you now wish to become a true, pious Jew, submit then as said, that you believe what the Rabbis say even if it is against God, reason, angels and all creation. For now you are told that a Jew is expected to believe that the right hand is not the right hand if a rabbi says so. God must have said, yes, he has created it according to his eternal Word, and specifically ordered that the right hand shall be called the right hand as all angels and creatures acknowledge. Now that may be the truth until a rabbi comes along and says, no, it is not so, but what I call the right hand, that is the right hand. What shall God's word and work together with that of all angels and creatures testify as against a rabbi who is so much higher and better than God and all creatures?

28. Now you must also believe that the queen Helen and her wise men and Jesus dealt with this matter 200 years before she was born; that cabbage stems grew annually in the sanctuary, as thick as no beam able to carry one hundred pounds of seeds; that bronze dogs can bark; that Jesus as well as Judas Sharioth[15] did miracles through Shem Hamphoras, as said above and again here.

Yes, if a rabbi put garbage before your very nose in a bowl and said: here you have a tasty almond broth, you would be expected to say you had not eaten a better

---

14. In German, Luther wrote: "Hie ist's beschlossen, (ich hatte schier gesagt beschissen)." Note the play on the two German words beschlossen, *meaning to conclude and* beschissen, *meaning to shit upon. Luther was by no means ashamed to use such language throughout his works.*

15. Reference is made to Judas, the betrayer of Jesus. Usually, Judas is referred to as Judas Iscariot as if Iscariot were his last name. It should be remembered however, that the use of last names was utterly unknown in the ancient world. The word should therefore be read "Ish Kariot," "A man from Kariot." The Hebrew word ish *means "Man" and Kariot was a town in ancient Israel.*

broth in all your life. Risk your life when you say otherwise. For whoever has the power to say left is right and right is left, never mind God and all his creatures, can certainly also say his behind is his mouth and his mouth his behind and his belly a brothpot and a brothpot his belly.

29. Whenever you have learned these things and can believe them, then run there quickly and let yourself be circumcised before the bronze dogs see this and come from Jerusalem and bark out of you again such high understanding of the all-holy Jewish beliefs, or before the seducer HaNozri (The Nazarene) enchants you into the Christian beliefs with his Shem Hamphoras. For now you are a righteous, fine, holy, clever Jew and yourself competent to call left, right and making the belly into a brothpot so that you have enough to devour with all the Jews all your life when you invite as guests all the devils. Thank also such high and heavenly rabbis from whom you are so highly learned and deeply hallowed that God himself and all his angels must be astonished at your holiness, the damned *Goyim* are not worth it to smell or hear anything about this.

30. Perhaps, one of the merciful Saints among us Christians may think I am behaving too crude and disdainfully against the poor, miserable Jews in that I deal with them so sarcastically and insultingly. But, good God, I am much too mild in insulting such devils; I would like to do it but they are much too superior in sarcasm, and even have a God who is a master at sarcasm and is called the actual devil and evil spirit. What I can do to insult him to his anger, that I should do cheaply for he had earned it. I want to show you a bit (for those who don't otherwise notice) what an unmentionable scoffer he is here.

31. The haughty, evil spirit plays with three types of derision in this book. First he derides God, the creator of heaven and earth, with his son Jesus Christ, as you can see yourself, so long as you believe as a Christian, that Christ is God's son.
Furthermore, he derides us, the whole of Christianity, because we believe in that son of God. Thirdly, he even derides his own Jews, ascribes to them such shameful, foolish, silly things concerning bronze dogs and cabbage stems that all dogs would bark themselves to death if they understood such a wild, raging, senseless, angry, ridiculous fool. Is that not a master of derision who can, with one and the same ridicule, accomplish three insults at once? The fourth derision is that he insulted himself with this, as we, God be praised, will see with joy in those days.

32. The Jews deride themselves the most in that they obey the devil, their God, in this derision and thereby become raging fools. For they don't do it in error, but because they know it full well and because natural reason given by God warns them, shows them and convinces them that this cannot be true; still they delude and flatter themselves that they learn from the devil and preach such obviously shameful lies and slander against us Christians and Jesus the Nazarene. Indeed, it is right, master and pupil have come together in the right school.

33. Further. Besides this derision they prove once and for all their mastery over

heaven as they say Jesus the Nazarene, (Jesus of Nazareth is meant)[16] has done his miracles through Shem Hamphoras which means "the interpreted name"; more later. Here they admit, as they must, that the miracles of Jesus the Nazarene were true, legitimate signs and they accuse and damn themselves just as their ancestors in the Gospels that he has woken up the dead, made the lame walk, cleaned lepers (*Matth. 11, 5*) which are such works which are possible for and pertain only to the singular, eternal, divine power; men and angels are not capable of doing them any more than that creatures can create something from nothing. All reason must say this.

34. Now let's take a look at the delicate fruits, the circumcised[17] holy men. They attribute such divine works and miracles to the Shem Hamphoras, that is the empty dead, miserable letters, written in a book with ink, or hovering on the tongue or in the heart so that even the godless are carried along. Let the Shem Hamphoras be what it may; they are, and cannot be anything but, single, dead, powerless letters, although the Jews act as though it were the same as God's Holy Scriptures of which they prattle a lot although they don't know what they are talking about. What can letters accomplish as letters from their own power if nothing else is added? What do they, those letters, help the devils, Turks, Jews and all the godless who misuse God's name incessantly and violate the commandment. After all, Satan and all godless names and works are also cast in holy letters.

35. But the mad Jews give the Shem Hamphoras the divine power, as the only, sole letter, without any promise or commandment from God. For they all say that even the godless and seducers can do many miracles and divine works through these letters. Where are they now, the circumcised holy men who pride themselves as against us Christians, that they alone are the ones who honor the single right God since the damned Nazarenes pray to three gods?[17]

Here they give divine power and honor the bare, single, dead letters in the Shem Hamphoras to such an extent that even the godless and the deceivers of God's majesty can do works of their own against God's will and prohibition (in the Ten Commandments).

> 16. *Nazareth is a town in northern Israel (Galilee) where Jesus spent his youth.*
> 17. *Circumcision is an ancient practice widespread in many human societies. Among Jews it has been viewed as a divine commandment and is regarded as evidence of a covenant between Israel and God. Genesis 17:11 reads, "And you shall circumcise the flesh of your foreskin; and this shall serve as the token of the covenant between me and you." This practice is regarded as so important in the Jewish community that Spinoza in* Tractatus Theologico-Polititicus *(1670) "declared that the practice of this rite was alone sufficient to ensure the survival of the Jewish people." See* Encyclopedia Judaica, *1971.*
> *Frazier in* The Golden Bough *mentions numerous societies which practice circumcision as a signal of initiation into adult life, as a substitute for castration and, among modern Americans, as a health measure. In Europe, this practice was regarded as Jewish. Christians did not circumcise until about the middle of the twentieth century. Thus, circumcision was viewed with disgust by European Christians and became so firmly associated with Jews that a few Europen Jews escaped death at the hands of the Nazi murderers during the Holocaust because they had, for one reason or another, not been circumcised.*

Indeed those are holy children of God who placed so many gods over their own God as there are letters in the Shem Hamphoras. It is said that there are 216 of them as will follow; that is, they pray to 216 thousand devils and not the right God whom they insult so and whose divine honor they steal with the Shem Hamphoras; they are the same ones who appropriate the miserable letter.

36. Oh, how the mad Jews had it coming! they did not want to accept Jesus of Nazareth as savior and son of God so that they could have remained with the only righteous God as we Christians have remained. For it is impossible that he who accepts the right belief and Jesus Christ as Messiah should or could accept more than the one, right and unified God for he must, as the devil wants, accept strange and several more Gods even if it is only naked, dead, worthless letters or Shem Hamphoras, that is, big bags full of piled-up devils. Yes, such Gods the Jews wanted to have instead of the right God, Jesus of Nazareth.

37. Here they might say: you Christians do the same thing. You speak words over the water and calling it baptism wash away all sins and make a newborn person. You make bread and wine into body and blood with words; you place the hands on the head of a sinner and with words free him of his sins. This is what your Luther writes: Whoever picks up even a straw in God's word does a better act than all monks, nuns, bishops, pope etc. Now words are no more than solitary, bare, poor letters: you just as well give them the tasks, which are in the nature of Gods majesty, as forgiving sins, new birth and resurrection.

38. We Christians are sufficiently and well instructed and informed concerning this, that it can be settled in a few words; Christians say therefore that water is nothing but water, words no more than mere letters which cannot do or help beyond their nature and even less so capable of producing divine tasks in us; for water and letters do not make a baptism.[18] I have often seen a horse or an ox slurp up a bucket of water. Now if you were to immediately pronounce the words of baptism over that then the horse surely would not be slurping up baptism nor be born again; more is demanded. The baptism is the sort of thing from which all devils may not swallow one drop for it would become a poisonous weed for them, burning like hellfire; instead they flee as far as they can for they may not witness the baptism nor remain present. Why is that? They certainly do not pay regard to water and letters.

39. However, because God has ordered and commanded that we should employ our hand and tongue and pour water over the one to be baptized with the words and letters he has commanded, promised us and assured us in all certainty that he himself will be present with his divine grace and power and will do this task himself.

Here you understand that we Christians do not give the water and letter any divine power nor claim it is our deed, but admit that it is alone God who wants this in this fashion as he likes it, that is to prove and show it on us through water, letters and the word.

18. Baptisma *(Greek) = dipping.*

That doesn't mean vacant letters and just water such as a cow slurps, but that through which God joins Himself to us so that he can exercise his grace and his power through us and upon us as his tool. Therefore, both water and letters are in baptism (not otherwise) full and rich in God's grace and power, because he has promised and revealed it, he himself will do it. "Go and baptize" (he says) not in your name, but "in the Name" so that it be a work of the Father, the Son and the Holy Ghost.

40. Therefore we reject the Pope together with his whole church, for he filled the whole world with similar tricks, magic, idol worship, for he too has his particular Shem Hamphoras; he comes along and conjures the water with empty, simple, vacant letters, pretends it is holy water which washes away sin, drives the devil away and has a number of other powers; seeks to imitate God like a monkey. Then he conjures wax the same way with void and empty letters, sells it to emperors and kings as holy Agnus Dei[19] which has a great deal of virtue, sustains himself with that, in fact, becomes rich in the world, just like any arch trickster, magician and idol worshiper. So he conjured caps and plates and all the world with mere words or letters, so that they become monks, nuns, priests, who hold mass and sell, call upon and celebrate saints, cash in indulgences, pray to corpses, serve the Devil, and earn heaven through their own works, that is, that heaven in which the Devil is bishop and pope [Hell].

41. That he needs good words from the scriptures and God's name is even more digusting since God not only did not command him to do so, but has specifically prohibited this. It is written: "You shall not misuse God's name"; that is why his power is not there, but there are only empty, void powerless letters. If, however, something does occur because of it, it is not the work of God but of the Devil, so as to strengthen his lies and tricks (through God's permission) to confuse the unbelievers, and to tempt the believers and to warn them; as we can see, witches and other magicians often do great harm. The Turks also conduct such swindle among each other, in wartime they bring with them beautifully written Arabic letters, (I have seen many of them) so that these vain letters, or as they claim, good and holy words, ensure their safety in face of weapons and danger.

19. This prayer, said in almost all Christian denominations consists of the words: "Agnus Dei, qui tolles peccata mundi, miserere; dona nobis pacem," or "Lamb of God, who takes away the sins of the world, have mercy; give us peace."

"Lamb of God" is a designation derived from John 1:29. In modern English the sentence is: "On the following day, John saw Jesus coming toward him and said, "Look, there is the Lamb of God who will take away the sin of the world." An earlier use of the designation "lamb" can be found in Isaiah 53:7. "He was oppressed, but he humbled himself and opened not his mouth; as a lamb which is brought to the slaughter...." This is given a Christological interpretation by Christian theologians.

Felecien Challaye (Petite Histoire de Grandes Religiones Paris, Presses Universitaires de France, 1947, p. 138) shows that the archeologist Masson Oursel translated the following sentence from ancient Assyrian-Babylonian cuneiform script: "He delivered the head of a lamb for the head of a man" and that this refers to the belief of the Assyrian-Babylonians that the sins of the community could be alleviated by substituting a "scape goat" for punishment earned by one and all.

Thus, the devil fills the whole world with swindle, idol worship, deception as if he had nothing better to do than to instigate special Shem Hamphoras in every community.

42. Now I am concerned that it is time to know, and the reader ought to be astounded to discover, what the Jews' Shem Hamphoras is. As I have said, I know and am certain, that it is not nor can be anything but ordinary, common, poor letters. However, to uncover and exhibit and advertise their foolishness and to uncover the devils' maliciousness, I want to advertise it here as much as I can do it and know it: let those who don't have it any other way read Antonius Margarit.[20] There is in 2 Mos. 14, 19, 20, 21, a text as follows:

43. "And the angel of God, who traveled before the army of Israel, arose and moved behind them, and the pillar of clouds also moved away from before them and moved behind them and came between the army of the Egyptians and the army of Israel. However, it was a dark cloud, and lit up the whole night, so that they could come together the whole night, this night and no other. And Moses stretched his hand out over the seas and the Lord let it move away through a strong east wind all night, and made the sea dry and the water divided from one another."[21]

44. This text has 216 letters in the Hebrew which are divisible into three lines or paragraphs so that each verse receives seventy-two letters. One could make six good verses from this, but the rabbis won't have it. Here note now the high art of Shem Hamphoras. If you write the three rows under one another, so that one letter is positioned exactly under another one, then do this: Take the first letter in the first row and the last one in the other row, and the first one in the third row, place them together you will have a word of three letters; do it in the same manner with all letters in the three lines or rows, you will find seventy two letters since each one has three letters.

45. They can easily do this in the Hebrew alphabet since all letters also serve as digits or numbers; for they count with letters as do the Greeks. We, however, have no more than seven numerical letters, i.e., C D I L M V X.[22] Nevertheless, I want to try and show it to us, the Germans, although it is only a rough example. So I align three rows of twelve letters so that the text is this:

20. *Antonius Margarit was a contemporary of Luther. He had converted from Judaism to Christianity and thereupon became Professor of Hebrew at the University of Vienna. He published* Der Ganze Judische Glaub *(All the Jewish Beliefs). This anti-Jewish book became one of the sources for Luther's* Vom Schem Hamphoras. *See D. Martin Luthers Werke, Kritische Gesamtausgabe 53, Band, Weimar, Herman Bohlaus, Nachfolger, 1920, p. 413. (Dr. Martin Luther's Works, Annotated Complete Edition, 53rd Volume, Weimar, Herman Bohlaus, Successors, 1920, p. 413.*
21. *This refers to* Exodus 14:19–21. *The author continued the number of letters in these three Hebrew verses and found them to be indeed 216 as asserted by Luther.*
22. *In Latin, not German.*

L	V	C	I	M	I	L	X	D	I	C	V
L	V	X	L	I	C	V	M	D	V	M	I
I	V	D	I	C	V	D	I	C	L	I	I

46. Now I take the foremost letter L in the first row and the last one, I in the other row and the foremost letter I in the third row, constituting the word LII. If thereafter you also do the same with the other letters this will produce the word VMV; and if you do the same with the third letters, then the word CVD will occur. Now do the same with the fourth letters then you will have the word IDI and so forth as the Jews do with the three verses of Moses. They make seventy-two words, each of three letters, from this. These words of three letters each, made from this art, have no meaning, are not expected to mean anything just as you can see from the four examples which give us Germans the four words, LII, VMV, CVD, IDI. Instead, the text of Moses remains in its natural meaning as it is read.

47. I would have been glad to make the example more plain, however, the numeral letters cannot be used that easily. However, help them with a bit of contemplation; for it should say about this:

Lucy milks the cow.
Luxli, you come to me.
Jew, chew the swill[23]

48. However, since k.a.e.n.x. are not numerical letters, I had to omit them or speak that awful wendish or danish German.

49. Now you ask: What have the seventy-two three-letter words from the text of Moses done? So listen to the other piece of great art. They are expected to be only number letters but no longer reading letters; not grammatical as they are read in school, but arithmetic as they are read in an arithmetic school. Now you must not read my example LII as in school, but as in a financial office where one would not read LII, but fifty two. The other word is not read VMV, but one thousand and ten. The third word is not read CVD, but six hundred and five. The fourth word is not read IDI, but five hundred and two and so forth. Therefore all letters in the Mosaic text must become arithmetic, for grammatically, they contribute nothing to the Shem Hamphoras.

50. Furthermore, and in the third place, you must learn that those seventy-two three-lettered words, made from the Mosaic text, are the names of seventy-two angels (I almost used the word devils) just as if in my example I had spoken the four words, LII, VMV, CVD, IDI, so that four angels have been named. One is called fifty-two, arithmetically; the next one one thousand and ten, the third one six

---

23. Luther uses the antiquated middle-high German word Klien, which is Kleie in modern German. This word occurs in the popular German proverb, "Who mixes among the pig's swill, will be eaten by the sows." (Wer sich mischt in die Kleie, den fressen die Säue.")

hundred and five and the fourth one five hundred and two. Therefore the seventy-two angels are called by numerical names, one called seventeen, the other one twenty-two, another seventy-nine and so forth.

51. What good are now those seventy-two names of angels from the arithmetic point of view? Clear your throat, now we get to the target, now we get to the true main issue. You have heard that the entire text *Moses 2 Mos. 14, 19, 20, 21* has become numericals divided into 73 names of angels. Now you must recognize that these selfsame numerical letters will again become grammatical or reading letters but remain numerical as well; namely thus: the first angel, LII, is called fifty-two arithmetically. Now you must go and seek one or two other words which also mean fifty-two, but it must be a word that names God or says something about God's power or works. Thus, I follow my example: "God's love is absolute."

Here you hear a well understood saying, that God's love can do and accomplish everything. The letters are all grammatical or reading letters. Nevertheless you can find the angel's LII name arithmetically; that is, an L and two I are fifty-two. You can look for more such examples yourself, as in: "God helps a lot" or "God gives salvation" etc. Here you can recognize an understandable sentence following grammar and reading letters, and yet you have here at the same time the arithmetic or numerical letters LII which constitute the name of the first angel. This you must now do with the other names of the seventy-two angels, that is, with the whole text of Moses, *2 Mos. 14* which is divided into these seventy-two names of angels as you have heard earlier.

52. Now here you can see how God's name, or whatever one may say about his deeds, is mixed into the names of the seventy-two angels. And it is thus a name adopted throughout the whole text of Moses, that is, through all of the seventy-two names of angels, that is Shem Hamphoras, the well interpreted name. Such tomfoolery is easily committed in Hebrew because they can convert all letters arithmetically, and LII, that is fifty-two, can be given in other words which we cannot do with our A B C as we have few, that is only seven, arithmetic letters, C D I L M V X. Therefore, although I can write LII as well with these letters xxxxxii or xl and xij, I certainly cannot make a grammatical word or speech from that, as they can do in the Hebrew. Surely, "x" is seldom used, particulary among us Germans, so that we would probably not miss it at all in the German language. That is why in the sentence "God's love is absolute" we must borrow additional grammatical letters, so that the angel's LII name can be written grammatically and arithmetically.

53. Now you can object and say that in this fashion one could as well make something else of these numerical letters, in Hebrew in Latin or in German. For example: "Satan helps a lot," "Satan saves."

In that case LII is still the name of the first angel, that is, fifty-two; or "Hans helps a lot," etc. Here, Shem Hamphoras would also become the adopted name of the devil or humans and anything I might want. But, dear Goy, you have heard before that you must believe and do whatever the Rabbis say and want; otherwise the bronze dogs of Jerusalem will come and bark you to death, and, what is even more dangerous, the cabbage stems from the Sanctuary with the 100 pounds of grain will fall on you and beat you to death.

54. Finally, so that the Shem Hamphoras may be complete, they add a benediction or prayer to it, put alongside each of the names of the seventy-two angels a verse from the psalms so that it becomes seventy-two verses. With this pious devotion, (pay attention to it) the great name of God, Jehovah, called Tetragrammaton,[24] is found in each verse; be sure, however, not to name the letters but say Adonai[25] (the Lord) instead; for he is unpronounceable—more of that later. Now you have the Shem Hamphoras entirely and complete, now you are not merely a circumcised true Jew, but you can also accomplish all kinds of miracles and signs as the deceiver, Jesus the Nazarene had done through it. Now hurry to Jerusalem and order the bronze dogs that they bear 100,000 bronze dogs, since each one barks ten times louder than the old ones so that they bark the world's *goyim* deaf, blind, stupid, and to death, so that they leave the world to the holy children of Israel even before their Messiah Kochab arrives.[26]

55. How is it possible, that during fifteen hundred years[27] of misery they did not use the art and power of the Shem Hamphoras, but, oddly, as they were destroyed by the Romans through Vespasian (for then it was time to do wonders) and later when they were slaughtered and dispersed with their Messiah Kochab?

The answer of the rabbis is that they were not pious enough, that they are homeless and in God's disfavor, and that after such a long time the power of the seventy-two angels has been forgotten. But how is that possible? Are they not forever the noble blood and circumcised saints, God's personal people before all the world, the dearest children of Israel who do not pray to more than one God? Such as these

---

24. *Tetragrammaton means "Four letters" in Greek and refers to the four Hebrew letters which traditionally make up the name of God.*

These are the four letters also known as the "Shem Hamphoras," the "Unpronounced (or Hidden) Name." They are Yud, Hay, Vov, Hay. This is of course a transliteration of the Hebrew into the English and hence only approximate.

25. *Since the Jews believed that the name of God was too sacred to be pronounced, the original pronounciation of Yud, Hay, Vov, Hay has been forgotten. Jews have for centuries pronounced Adonai, meaning "My Lord," when in fact the scriptures exhibited the tetragrammaton.*

26. *Luther refers to Simeon Bar Kochba who led the second Judean revolt against the Romans in 130. Kochab is the Hebrew word for star. As Bar Kochba was initially successful in his fight against the Roman legions, some Jews viewed him as the expected Messia. However, the revolt was crushed by the Roman forces in the same year in which it began and Bar Kochba was killed in the fighting.*

See A History of the Jews *by Solomon Grayzel or any other of the many volumes on Jewish history.*

27. *Luther was evidently of the opinion that Jerusalem was destroyed earlier than was in fact the case. This is not surprising. Many writers, prior to the nineteenth century, were not certain concerning the exact dates of past events. History, before Ranke (1795–1886), was often more conjecture than fact. For example, the great English historian Edward Gibbon (1737–1794) mixed legend and myth with facts in his famous* Decline and Fall of the Roman Empire.

cannot be in disfavor (unless scripture is wrong) as the damnable *goyim* who pray to more than one God and consider Jesus the Nazarene as the messiah. They ought to be in disfavor so that no Shem Hamphoras can help them.

56. Furthermore, how could the wise men become so foolish that they would forget the power of the angels in the Shem Hamphoras, as they had been so clever that they preserved this treasure with two bronze dogs and were so powerful that they could permit Judas Shariot to enter? They themselves wanted badly to enter there whenever they desired and became like Judas Shariot with all his doing, which they still are, now. That is why the great treasures of art must still be with them, inherited from Judas Shariot and his ancestors, and cannot be altogether lost. How could they otherwise write and talk so certainly about them?

57. The damnable *Goyim*, who are stupid louts, will not and cannot learn anything. Haven't you heard earlier that if a rabbi says the right hand is left, then she is left. If he says the left hand is right, she is right. Therefore, also, when a rabbi says the art of the Shem Hamphoras is lost, then she is lost; but if he says they still have it, then they still have it. If he says they are in disfavor, then they are in disfavor; and if he says they are the only dear chosen people of God then they certainly are that.

58. Here you will probably ask me: whence do the Jews have this high wisdom so that the text of Moses, the holy, innocent letters, divided in three parts be divided into three verses, and make arithmetic or counting letters from them and name 72 angels and at once, the whole Shem Hamphoras becomes restored? You must leave me alone with that but ask the rabbis about it, they will no doubt tell you. — Yes, but I want to hear your opinion in advance, before I become a Jew; thereafter I will know that I must believe what the rabbis say; you have promised me the Jewish catechism. Keep that promise.

59. Well, now, I don't know in detail where they got it from, but I can guess approximately. Here at Wittenberg, in our parish church, there is a sow carved into the stone under which lie young pigs and Jews who are sucking; behind the sow stands a rabbi who is lifting up the right leg of the sow, raises the behind of the sow, bows down and looks with great effort into the Talmud[28] under the sow, as if he

---

28. The word Talmud *is Hebrew and means "Instructions." It is derived from the Hebrew word* Limad *to instruct. The Talmud consists of 34 large volumes in its English translation.* (The Babylonian Talmud, *I. Epstein, ed., London, Soncino, 1935–1948.) It took several centuries and numerous authors to write this vast literature which may be compared to the publication of all the lectures ever given at Harvard University on all subjects ever taught there during the 350 years of the existence of that institution. Thus, the Talmud deals with a vast body of knowledge affecting every phase of Jewish life. During the Middle Ages copies of the Talmud were repeatedly burnt by the Christian authorities who believed that the Talmud contained anti–Christian messages or that the Jews would convert to Christianity if only the Talmud were no longer available to them.*

Today, the Talmud is still studied by a small group of interested scholars. It has now been published in English in several editions and can be seen in most university libraries.

wanted to read and see something most difficult and exceptional; no doubt they gained their Shem Hamphoras from that place. For in earlier years there were many Jews in this area, as proved by the Hebrew names of country towns, villages, as well as citizens and farmers which exist even today, so that even a learned and honest man who was an enemy of the nasty lies of the Jews would have torn down such a picture. For among the Germans it is said of someone who pretends to great wisdom without good cause: "Where did he read that? On the behind of the sow [crudely expressed]."[29]

60. One might easily want to use the word "Shem Hamphoras" in this connection; however, it turns out to be Peres Shema or, as they do, have the gall to make it Shem Ha Peres so that it sounds close together. The same as if a German while listening or reading understood *narren* for *nahren* [fooling for feeding]; or he has improved [*gebessert*] my property rather than [*gewassert*] watered. Thus the evil spirit ridicules his imprisoned Jews, lets them say Shem Hamphoras while believing and hoping for great things; he however means Sham Haperes which means "here is filth," not the kind that lies in the street but the kind that comes out of the belly. Sham means "here" or "there"; *Peres*, which is in the intestines of the sow and all animals, as used by Moses in the third book (*Cap. 8, 17*) as he promised to burn the sin offering with skin and hair and with its *Peres*, i.e., its filth.[30]

61. For the devil has possessed and caught the Jews, so that they must act according to his will, (as St. Paul said) to fool around, to lie, to blaspheme and to curse God and everything that belongs to God. As wages for that he gives them his ridicule, Sham Haperes, and helps them believe that this and all their lies are a valuable thing. They do not complain or cry out about such a dreadful prison, nor do they seek to get out of there with even the least sight, but instead are glad to be inside, consider it as a particularly great freedom and would love to have us Christians in there too. However, they do scream about the Roman prison, as they are not imprisoned by us, but we, our money and our possession, by them in our country; for they feel too good and therefore deal with us as the devil with them, scorn us to our detriment just as the devil scorns them for their eternal damnation.

62. As a concrete example of how the mad Jews deal with foolishness, they let the above text remain, because God promised and predicted that Moses shall split the sea with his rod in order to lead the children of Israel through it etc. Yes, that is the correct main text which does it, because God promised and predicted that it shall happen. But the senseless Jews don't act accordingly, confront the story, seek

29. Many European churches, built in the Middle Ages, i.e., between the fall of Rome in the third century and the fall of Constantinople in 1453, depicted anti-Jewish stone carvings in their edifices. This can be easily seen in the great cathedrals of Europe and also in many of the lesser church statues such as the statue of the synagogue in the Cathedral at Trier which appears blindfolded and carrying a crown about to fall off its head.

30. Shom does indeed mean "there." Thus, Shom Haperes ("there is dirt") sounds similar to "Shem Hamphoras," the phrase which so excited Luther.

like the monkeys to deal only with dead letters, that God added to it at one time through his word and law, make no difference between God's law and word, make no difference between God's power and word, and their void, senseless foolishness.

63. They even say that whoever knows the strength and virtue of the seventy-two angels can force them through Shom Haperes to prove their power. First, and in that they are right, whoever knows the source of the power of the seventy-two angels can do all miracles through that; true as that may be, whoever has a jackass which brings forth gold can have Gulden[31] but where is there such a jackass? In cuckoo land. Therefore the seventy-two angels of the Jews are also in cuckoo land, were never created, will never be created; that is why they rightly say that whoever knows the power of these angels will do miracles, as many and wherever he wants. We will therefore see that by means of such angels' power they will cajole God for their Messiah whether he wants it or not and win Jerusalem; how can it fail?

64. On the other hand, we see how the mad, senseless fools wanted to cast spells on the angels and to enslave them with mere letters, and set themselves above God, so that the angels would have to do what they want. That's them, the holiest of the holy, who pray alone to one God. For praying to one God means among them to name one God with their big mouth, to exhibit oneself before one God by kneeling and bowing down, but to pray with their hearts to thousands of lies and devils for that upon which one's heart can rely and confide, that is, one's God; as we, the Christians, the mad, damnable *Goyim* say, that when the mouth keeps quiet, and the knees do not bend, nevertheless, because the heart bends without cessation, that is, his trust, comfort and reliance rests on the unified God, that is how truly and justly we pray to the unified God.

65. But that is nothing but foolishness among these circumcised holy ones who can sometimes name one God (that suffices) while at the same time making gods and angels from letters as they please, and in whom they do not trust alone (which we the mad *Goyim* call worship) but also bewitch for any purpose they want.

A *goy* ought to want to become a Jew, since they have such power[32] that one can make Gods and angels according to our own desires, while we damnable *goyim* can do nothing more than believe that the only God has made us all, and that the angels govern us, and not we the angels. In sum, a Jew is so full of superstition and magic as nine cows have hair, that is, untold and infinite, like the devil their God, full of lies.

31. A Gulden is a medieval German coin. The word is no longer used in German but the Dutch call their money a Gulden, pronouncing the G like a German "Ch."
32. The myth of Jewish power was and continues to be widely believed. Such forgeries as The Protocols of the Elders of Zion, *concocted by Russian monks at the end of the nineteenth century, claimed that an international Jewish world government exists and that this hidden conspiracy controls all finance and all politics on earth. Similar beliefs concerning the power of the pope have been circulated among non–Catholic Christians.*

66. If they nevertheless need such witchcraft with letters, just as one teaches children in school to know the letters because they must recite the ABC forward and backward, move the letters here and there, so that they learn to make syllables, and practice reading, or make pictures and forms with the letters, as many boys used to be capable of doing; so it would be tolerable, as an enjoyable childsplay, to see how one can do this much better with Hebrew letters than with others; however, to give power to bare, solitary, worthless letters; power that can do miracles, even through the godless and the enemies of God, that is not only shame and Shem Haperes, but the unbearable, slandering devil himself, escaped from hell with all his evil. For in that manner the Jews pray to so many devils, so many thousands of devils as they invent angels with their Shem Haperes as said above. For they build on that and believe it as if the truth although it is a lie. That is what the prophets called idol worship, *confidere in mendacio*,[33] to rely on lies, to which honor only God is entitled.

67. Now look what fine holy people the Jews are; they damn us cursed *Goyim* that we pray to more than one God but they, the blessed fruit of noble blood and circumcised holiness, alone pray to the only God. That is true if the seventy-two invented angels, that is, twenty-seven thousand devils, can be called a sole God, then they do indeed pray to one God. So you can see what a big, new, miracle-making holy man you become, if you deny Christianity and become a Jew instead. For through Shem Hamperes you can achieve that all devils are a singular God, something that God himself cannot do. Therefore, think and be grateful to the rabbis for their almighty filth, that is, I meant to say Shem Hampheres. Yes, so it goes if one does not want to hear God's word, but wants to slander incessantly, then one must listen to all the devils and pray to them, as our Lord Christ says, *Joh. 5, 43*: "I came in the name of my father, but you have not accepted me, another will come in his name and you will accept him."

68. Even if they permitted such foolishness and stupidity to be bad lies, and lie like the tricksters, and admitted that they are not true signs, what should have happened through the Shem Hamphoras: one could still hope they would in time become tired of the tomfoolery and on their own accord desist from it. Now, however, they cling to this bad error and rely on it as if it were the truth of God himself, create a worship service and idol worship from it, refuse to see what happens through Shem Hamphoras as false magic; it is viewed as serious and true divine power is expected to operate in it, as they say above in the text, that Jesus, the godless, has awakened a dead man among the servants of the queen Helen; just as their ancestors admitted that Jesus could exorcise the devils which was no trick but in the name of Beelzebub (*Luc. 11, 15*).

For their Shem Hamphoras can do everything and anything in a natural manner.

69. Finally, it is an unheard of slander, that they attribute such divine power in the Shem Hamphoras, to do miracles, also to the godless, such as Judas Sharioth

33. To rely on lies.

and the deceiver (as they slander) Jesus the Nazarene and deliberately teach such things. This also moves Lyra and Burgensis[34] and many others although they do not become sufficiently incensed by it. I don't know how I should speak or write about this. If I say that the Jews are mad, blind and crazy (as Moses said of them) and are full of devils, then it would all be too little to say about those who wish to pray to the only God and are permitted to spit out such slander and teach such things as a right. May whoever can understand what may be meant by that, that the divine, eternal majesty our loving creator, may he be praised in eternity, should be scolded by these damned devil's children so that he is a witness, through his miracles which he alone does and can do, *Psalm 72, 18*.[35] A witness, defender, supporter of all lies, seducer, error, idol worship, blasphemy, slander and all abomination which they blame on our Lord Jesus Christ; or it is claimed cannot and will not defend himself against a false prophet Sham Haperes.

70. I cannot understand this in any other manner than that they make God himself into a devil, in fact into a servant of all devils, who helps, strengthens, achieves all the evil which the Devil wants and has the wish and the enjoyment to seduce poor souls, to curse himself with his own wondrous works and rage against himself—in sum, to be more malicious than all Jews, in fact, than all devils. Oh, my God, my dear creator and father, you will credit me graciously that I must speak of your eternal majesty in so shameful a manner with distaste against your damnable enemies, devils and Jews. You know that I do it from the passion of my belief and in honor of your divine majesty, for it seizes me body and soul.

71. However, your judgment is right, *justus es, Dominie*. Yes, so shall Jews but no one else be punished, who held your word and miracles in contempt and ridiculed, insulted and damned it for such a long time without interruption, so that they will not fall, like other humans, heathens and all the others, into sin and death, not up in Hell, nor in the middle in Hell but in the pit of Hell, as one cannot fall deeper. For that too is their sin, which cannot be worse, for they do not only have contempt for you, the righteous and eternal God, by insubordination and disdain for your word, but seek to make you into the Devil and servant of all the devils, that you, with your magnificent divine power should be witness and serve the Devil in his lies, insults and murder, and whatever else is the Devil's work; just, just are your courts, heavenly father, they want to blaspheme, and they have done that sufficiently.

34. Nicolaus de Lyra was the provincial for the Franciscan order in Burgundy beginning in 1325. He studied Hebrew in Paris in the interest of writing polemics against Judaism. He wrote three books against the Jews and 50 books of commentary on the Bible transcribing the great Jewish scholar "Rashi," whose actual name was Rabbi Shlomo ben Yitz'hak (1040–1105). Luther consulted Nicolaus Lyra in his translation of Genesis and owed his knowledge of rabbinics almost entirely to Lyra.

Paul of Burgensis was the author of another anti–Jewish text entitled Scrutinium Scipturarum *(A Search for the Intended Meaning). See the Bolhaus edition of Luther's* Works, *vol. 53, pp. 10–11.*

35. This verse is translated, "Blessed be the Lord God, God of Yisrael, who does wondrous things alone."

72. Moses writes, *5 Mos. 18, 20*, ff.[36] that God does not want miracles and signs to occur on the word of a false prophet, and says: "This you shall remember, if that which a false prophet says does not happen, then it is certain that the Lord did not say that word." But these devils say that Jesus the Nazarene is a deceiver and false prophet; that real miraculous signs, such as wakening the dead, making the lame walk, cleaning the lepers, (which no one other than God is able to do) came about through such a deceiver. It would not be astonishing, that we Christians who permit such God damned open slanderers to live among us would long ago have been sunk by hellfire into the pit of Hell with the Jews by God's anger, except that it helped us that we did not know it and therefore are innocent of their gruesome conduct. Therefore, better be careful nobles and lords, who protect and tolerate Jews among them, for I want to be excused for what you do. Here it is not only Christ who is our Lord, and the father in Christ, but God, the father himself in himself, that in his divine majesty is insulted even more than Christ, having been made not only into the Devil but also made into the servant of the Devil and all devils. Scream more, Jew, scream now: Crucify him, his blood be on us and our children; that which you wanted has happened.[37]

73. Enough has been said of this, a Christian heart and ears no doubt would wish that it had heard nothing of this, nor think of it for it is too horrible, frightful and immoderate.

74. Against the misery it is a bit less as to what they claim foolishly and drivel concerning the name Tetragrammaton, thereby exhibiting their stupidity to us Germans. In the holy scriptures, God has many names; however, they amount primarily to ten, among which is one which they call the big one and Tetragrammaton, the most holy. The others are sometimes also attributed to the angels, but this one to God alone. Here they are so holy and spiritual that they will not name that same name, but rather in its stead place another or the four letters of the same name, Yud, He Vov, He for it is reputedly unpronounceable. Therefore St. Hieronymous says: The Greeks, because they did not know these letters, read PJPJ, believing the Hay to be a Pay.[38]

36. *The* Jerusalem Bible *published in 1988 translates this reference as follows: "But the prophet, who shall presume to speak a word in my name, which I have not commanded him to speak, or that shall speak in the name of other gods, that prophet shall die. Know that when a prophet speaks in the name of the Lord, if the thing follow not, nor come to pass, that is the thing which the Lord has not spoken...." It is evident that the believer cannot lose here. If the prophecy comes true, the believer is right. If the prophecy does not come true, then the believer is still right since this means that the prophet is a liar.*

37. *Numerous Christian clergy, both Catholic and Protestant used this phrase for years as an "explanation" for the Nazi persecutions and the Holocaust occurring in Europe between 1933 and 1945. This "explanation" for Jewish misfortunes was used for centuries to blame the victim.*

38. *Luther means Hieronymous Sophronius Eusibius, also known as St. Jerome (340–420). He is not to be confused with the historian Hieronymous who accompanied Alexander the Great on his campaigns in 323 B.C.E. St. Jerome was a prolific writer who learned Hebrew in order to translate the Pentateuch into Latin. He moved to Bethlehem in Israel in his middle age and founded a monastery there.*

75. First of all, I'll let the matter of the ten names go, as it is not new, for it is already mentioned in St. Hieronymus' *In epistola ad Mercellam [Letter to Marcel]* where he counts them as follows: El, Elohim, Elohe, Zebaoth, Eljon, Ehje, Adonai, Jah, Jehovah, Schadai. Others do it otherwise; I care nothing for that. There are no doubt more names of God in the scriptures than these, such as Ab, Bore, Or, Chai, etc. Father, Creator, Light, Life, Salvation and others similar. And what can be called good or be good that must not be attributed to God before all others as he has it in himself, as Christ says: "God alone is good; we have received from him, everything we are and have." But now we want to deal with the only name, Jehovah, a name with which the Devil and Jews commit all kinds of magic, misuse and idolatry.

76. This name, Jehova, according to grammar, is derived from the word Haja, or Hava, which means in Latin: *fuit in preterito, esse*; in German: *wesen* or *sein*, "to be"; and the "J" could be *nota nominis verbalis*,[39] as in Josaphat, Jesaias, Jeremias and many other names, and amounts to the same as the Latin *ens* or the Greek *on*. We Germans must pronounce: *er ist's* ["he is it"]; and so it becomes Trigrammaton in Latin, Dygrammaton in Greek, Hexagrammaton in German, or if we simply take *ist* ["is"] then it is also Trigrammaton. In that they now pretend that the name Jehovah is unpronounceable, they don't know what they are babbling; if they mean the letters, then it cannot be true for his name is Jehovah. And so he can be written with pens and ink so why should he not be called with the mouth which is much better than pen and ink? Then why don't they also call him unwritable, unreadable, unthinkable? In sum, it is a negligible matter. If, however, they do it for the sake of honor, then they should do it also with all the other names, and leave them unspoken as well. For it says: "You shall not misuse the name of God"; therefore that is rotten. Nowhere in scripture does it say that any one of God's names shall be unpronounceable, for then all those who misuse God's name would be innocent, for they would say, they could not name his name, let alone misuse it.

77. This really means that God's being, power, wisdom, goodness and whatever else one can say about God is unpronounceable, immeasurable, unending, incomprehensible, etc., so that it is not the letters or syllables, but that which is signified by them which is unpronounceable. Yes, that is how one ought to speak of the unpronounceable name of God. For he has his being from nobody, has no beginning and no end, but is eternal, in and of himself, so that his being cannot be called "was" or "will be" for he never began, cannot become, has never ceased, cannot end being; for it is written that with him it is useless "to be" or "to have been" Jehovah (*2 Mos. 3, 14*).[40] Since creatures are created his being is already there, and what is yet to come is already in his being. In this fashion Christ speaks of his divinity, *Joh. 8, 58*: "Before Abraham existed, I am"; do not say: There I was, as if he wasn't it later; but, "I am" that is, my being is eternal, has not been, will not become, but is an eternal Is.

39. a. *"has been in the past" or "is"*; b. *"a noteworthy verbal sign."*
40. Luther refers here to the famous sentence from Exodus 3:14 *in which Moses asks God what his name is and God answers, in Hebrew:* Eheye Asher Eheye, *"I will ever be what I now am." For the Hebrew original see the* Jerusalem Bible, *p. 65.*

78. Therefore, as his Is, Being, or Nature are incomprehensible, so it is also unpronounceable, for no creature can comprehend that which is eternal. Since the angels are eternally blissful, for they cannot satiate their desire to see and enjoy and comprehend the eternal Being; for it could be comprehended it could not be eternal, for then it would itself have a beginning and an end, and could not give anyone a Being nor maintain one, because it would be uncertain of its own existence. Further, his wisdom, power, goodness etc. are also incomprehensible, for it cannot be anything other than his divine Being. Third, and this is higher, that in the divine Being, God is Father, Son, Holy Ghost, three persons in one, eternal, incomprehensible being. Yes, to say all that of God would require an incomprehensible, unpronounceable name. Who will name, think of the ultimate, speak about, write about such a wondrous Being? In this fashion, the ancestors have perhaps pronounced the name Jehovah, because God's being, (although as already mentioned cannot be known), according to grammar means "of eternity" and names three persons.

79. Therefore one ought to concern oneself with this, and learn to recognize Jehovah—that is, the divine Being—and search the scriptures where he revealed himself through his word in this life and how he will reveal himself in the next life without the Word.

But that is too high for the Jews; indeed, it is nothing to them, for this is how the Holy ones behave: with the mouth they honor the letters of the name Jehovah, which shall and must be unpronounceable, but the divine Being which is indicated through the letters they comprehend and measure it with yards, pounds and bushels, how it must be, how big, long, wide, deep, heavy and full as they wish. Remember now, that God had promised them the Messiah, whom he did indeed send according to his divine, wonderful, incomprehensible wisdom; so they come along and paint a picture or form of him, limit his wisdom and understanding, as he is expected to send the Messiah, in the same manner as Kochab did, not as Jesus of Nazareth; for their Messiah shall not allow himself to be crucified, but kill the heathens and make the Jews masters of the world.

80. The eternal, divine Being and his eternal incomprehensible wisdom shall be found or met in this prescribed manner but in this manner imagined by humans who force themselves to limit and compress it; if not, then he shall not be their God. For they are the ones whom God can target, a measure, weight, manner and form, not only in his works but also in his eternal divine being that he must not be three persons in his own being. For there they stand with their compass and angle-iron, with yards and lead weights, they will not tolerate that God, ought to be such an unknowable Being, and they are not much smarter, wiser, and insightful than God is himself. What is it that the Jews will not name nor pronounce the literal name with the mouth, but in their hearts not only name his divine being, the righteous Jehovah, but express it, judge it, and even compel it and force it into their standards. Therefore they must do, because it is their way (as Isaiah foretold in 29, 13[41]) to

41. *The Hebrew prophet Yesha'Yahu is called Isaiah in English. In* Isaiah 29:13 *he writes, "And the Lord said, since this people draw near and with their mouth and with their lips do honor me, but have removed their hearts from me...."*

honor the letters with their mouths while shaming and slandering in their hearts; and still God should always permit himself to be fooled, that they swallow the pits and spit the shells under his eyes.

81. They have devoted themselves not to do, live or say anything righteous but are instead of a nature that must be vain, false, blind, mad, and senseless as Moses says. They believe they are doing something unusual when they do not name the name of Jehovah. Do they not meanwhile see that they carry this same name in the shameful misuse in their Shem Haperes, that their seventy-two invented angels, i.e., seventy-two lies and devils, are enhanced, honored and strengthened with the same holy name of God adding all kinds of miracles, illusions and idol worship. I would want, and they are worth it, that they not only do not name the name Jehovah, but not name, read, write, hear or have one letter in the entire scriptures, for they use it to dishonor God, dishonor the scriptures and bring on their own damnation.

82. And how can it be otherwise, dear brother! If God's word does not illuminate us and shows us the way, *Ps. 119, 105*,[42] and his light does not shine in a dark place, *2 Petr. 1, 19*,[43] then nothing else but darkness, error, lies can be there all of which we invented for ourselves. Look at our experiences, when we lost His divine word under the Papacy and seized human teachings instead. What kind of thick darkness, lies and misery we adored with masses, hellfire, holy orders, monkishness and our own works etc. Now the Jews have no word from God, therefore only darkness can be there, for circumcision and Moses' law are no longer in force than the Messiah, who should teach them something else, *5 Mos. 18, 15*[44] as he has done; they did not want to accept that, but must act in such a way that they do not do what God wants, for God should do what they want. At the time that the law of Moses was incumbent on them, they did not want to do it, killed all prophets because of it; now, that it is not obligatory anymore, they want to do it, and murdered the Messiah and all his Christians because of it[45]; in earlier times with the deed, now with full intent, enthusiasm and wish in their hearts. The anger of God has come over them as they deserved it.

The Other Part

83. From the beginning of the gospel, as St. Luke and St. Mark wrote it, the question has arisen: why the two apostles have told the story of the origins of the

---

42. *"The word is a lamp to my feet and a light to my path."*
43. *"You should give that word your closest attention, for it shines like a lamp amidst all the dirt and darkness of the world."* See The New Testament in Modern English, J.B. Phillips, trans., New York, Macmillan, 1958, p. 512.
44. *Here is a good example of the Christian point of view which holds that this sentence predicts the coming of Jesus the Messiah. The sentence is: "The Lord your God will raise up to you a prophet from the midst of you, of your brethren like me; you shall listen to him."*
45. *For centuries, including our own, "Christ killer" and "Jew" were synonymous in Christian communities. It is hard to estimate how much bloodshed was justified by this analogy. However, there can be no doubt that it contributed greatly to much murder.*

family of our Lord Jesus Christ so differently (or, as many have explained it, so contradicted by one another?) and it is peculiar that both agree upon the lineage or origins of these persons and end with Joseph and not with Mary and Christ; from this the wise sought to conclude it is not proved with that that Christ is of the family of David, because he does not come from Joseph, whom the apostles trace as coming directly from the line of David, and then suddenly abandon the same Joseph and substitute Mary.

84. Here everyone is involved, particularly the Jews, and thereafter the emperor Julian and his heathens.[46] In fact, many of the old teachers and not a few of the new; they need to better understand this and other wonders as to whether our Christian belief is wrong here, or uncertain or totally in the dark. That is why we want to talk about this a bit but with permission, if I may, that we are happy to let anyone do it better.

85. First, to answer the Jews, if anyone even wants to get into an argument with them. Since the Jew moved me the last time to write about the Jews and touched upon this point: it cannot be proved that Jesus is of the tribe of Judah, because the apostle Matthew traces the tribe of Judah to Joseph and not to Mary; therefore he could not be Messiah as proved by the tribe of Judah and David. Prickly and poisonous are the snakes and make every effort to make our books appear wrong. For they do not ask because they wish to learn from us and know the truth, but to bother and heckle us with such questions—with scorn and derision of our beliefs as if we could not prove it.

86. Therefore one should step on the heads of these poisonous snakes and answer in the coarsest and rawest manner, defying the Devil, that Mary, the mother of Jesus, is of the tribe of Judah and the house of David says not only the apostle Matthew, (about whom they laugh) but even Moses, the first to say it after whom all the prophets agreed together. And if we Christians otherwise had nothing of the Old Testament, other than Moses, then we would have enough, easily enough, to prove that Mary must be of the tribe of Judah and the House of David so that all devils and the whole world cannot overthrow. (Keep quiet the miserable, screaming Jews.)

87. Moses however says (*1 Mos. 49, 10*): "the scepter shall not be removed from Judah until the Silo comes." Here it is certain that the Silo or the Messiah shall come from the tribe of Judah, as there is also no doubt about it among the snakes,

---

46. *This refers to Flavius Claudius Julianus (331–363). He was called the Apostate (from a Greek word meaning "rebel"), a label he earned in Christian history because he deserted the Christian religion and sought to reestablish the pagan Roman religion. He also promised the Jews that he would rebuild their temple in Jerusalem. When he died suddenly at the age of 32, Christians viewed this as a sign that God did not wish the temple rebuilt because, according to Christian theology, it had been destroyed as punishment for the crime of deicide.*

no matter how poisonous they are.⁴⁷ Moses 5, 18, 15, says this: "God will arouse a prophet from among your brethren just like myself and you shall hear him." Verse 18 follows: I will, says God, raise a prophet for them from among their brethren, just like you, and will place my words in his mouth so that he may say everything that I command him to say and I will myself revenge myself against those who will not hear him."⁴⁸

88. Here it is written that Mary is of the tribe of Judah and David, and therefore needs no more proof; the Jews owe it this Shilo and Prophet to obey him as Moses commanded and God himself warned. Now this Shilo and Prophet has said, his mother Mary is of the tribe of Judah and David and commanded his apostle Matthew to write it. With this, the prickly Jews have their answer: If they will not believe Moses, that he said this concerning Mary, then it is not necessary and they aren't worth it, that they should listen to Matthew or a few Christians or believe in the truth, but Shem Hamphoras, yes, Shom Haperes⁴⁹ they shall believe. Such a belief belongs to such Saints.

89. We Christians know (and no devil or Jew can deny it) that the Messiah or Silo must come from the house of David. As he does not have a father, but only a mother, the mother must of course be David's daughter. Therefore, whoever believes that Jesus, born of the virgin Mary, is the true Messiah has already acknowledged, sealed and proved that his mother Mary must be of the house of David, as certain or more certain as her bridegroom Joseph.

90. Yes, here one encounters resistance from the Jews: they don't want to have Jesus as the Messiah, therefore they bother us with their poisonous, slanderous goads about Joseph, Mary; for they are hardly concerned as to whether Mary is of the house of David or not. And even if they had seen it themselves, that she was born of David, like Solomon and his other children, still they would not believe that Jesus, her son, was the Messiah. They are concerned with the son, whom they do not want; they know, the knaves and lying mouths, that if Jesus is the Messiah, then there is no question that Maria is of the house of David.

47. Luther views this passage as final proof of the Christian message because Luther and other Christian commentators chose to translate the Hebrew word Shiloh to mean "The Messiah."

However, "Shiloh was the location of the Jewish sanctuary in the days of the Prophet Samuel before Jerusalem became the center of Jewish worship." See Genesis, additional notes, in The Pentateuch, *J.H. Hertz, ed., London, Soncino, 1961, p. 202. Hence, Jewish authorities claim that this passage means only that Judah will be established in Shiloh.*

There are also numerous other interpretations of this sentence based on various possible spellings of the word Shiloh in the Hebrew.

48. Luther uses the German word rächen, *derived from* sich rächen, *which means to avenge oneself. However, the Hebrew word* Edroshe, *which Luther translates "revenge," can also be translated "to require."*

49. There is dirt.

91. It is precisely the son who is our Christian concern. For if he is not considered Messiah, then we care nothing as to what the origin of his mother is, in fact, as little as what the origins of Sara, Isaac's mother, or where other unknown women came from. If, however, he is Messiah then God speaks to the Jews through Moses: "You shall listen to him." And if we Christians believe the evangelists and apostles the one main contention that Jesus is Christos or Messiah, why then should we not also believe all other lesser assertions? For whoever does not believe or want to believe that Jesus is the Messiah, does not need to know who or where his mother is; in fact he would have been better off if he had never heard one word of the entire scriptures and would also have been better off if he had never been born. For God gambled everything on this man, has shown and changed, and judged everything and put everything into his hands; whoever has him shall have everything, whoever does not have him shall have nothing; so it says.

92. And what would we do if St. Matthew and St. Luke had not described the lineage of the birth? How many things are not described, as St. John says at the end. And as proof of the truth he writes a good deal that was omitted by Matthew, Mark and Luke. What Christian would not love to know what the Lord did during the thirty years before his baptism. St. Paul described Jesus far more glorious and in more detail as the Messiah than all the others; nevertheless, he deals with the mother and touches her in passing so briefly, that he mentions her only once even then without a name, *Gal. 4.4*: "He was," says he, "born of a woman,"[50] and, *Rom. 3, 1* "who was born from the seed of David according to the flesh." He knows, the dear apostle, that if this main issue is presented, that it makes the Messiah believable, so that everything which is the truth must be discovered, or it must not be necessary to find it: "For in him, [he says] all treasures of wisdom and revelation are hidden"[51] (*Col. 2, 3*) since the Holy Spirit does not let anything false be taught or believed.

93. But the Jews, the circumcised saints, carry themselves with a proud courage, brag and hold their heads high against us damnable, miserable heathens, and consider it certain that not we, but they alone have the holy scriptures; therefore it is ridiculous to them what we teach concerning baptism, sacraments, keys and other articles of the New Testament, because they don't find it in their book. They believe that everything must be only in their book or it cannot be right. And also because they do not find in their book the words: Mary is David's daughter, or from the house of David, so they argue and rebel against this as if they were certain that it may no be so.

94. Very well, I will pay them in their own coin and say that they are not Jews; for there is not one letter in the Holy Scripture about these Jews and are unable to prove it from their book that they are Jews or the seed of Israel; I surely believe that they would deny this. Further, I say in a serious mood and on my conscience: If

---

50. *"Born of a human mother," Phillips, p. 405.*
51. *The modern English translation is, "For it is in him and in him alone, that men will find all the treasures of wisdom and knowledge." See Phillips, p. 431.*

nothing more existed than the Old Testament, I would close down, and no man should try to talk me out of it, than that the present day Jews must be the worst; the most vicious and malicious fellows from the whole world who come together here and again scatter here and there like the Tartars or the Gypsies and their ilk, to make life hard for people with their usury, to spy out and betray all countries, to poison water, steal children, and to do all sorts of other dastardly damage; as brother Richards writes in the edition of the Alkoran concerning the assassins who were sent into all the world by the Saracenes to rob the rulers of all the world with stealth and to murder whoever they can, in order to seize countries deprived of masters. They are called Ismaelites. This can be read in the tenth chapter of the work called Al-Koran.[52]

95. History supports such views of mine, as it is written of the Jews and learns more and more each day how in all the world into which they have been driven, burnt and killed as is mentioned in that book.[53] Now one can also see how they love to encroach upon lords and nobles using the physician's skill as a pretext. They trade skill with magic and letters with which they have satiated Christendom for all kinds of weapons and irons. For even the village pastors and sextons have been fooled by these tricks in which we found many of the books with names such as Tetragrammaton, Ananisapta,[54] and rarely prayers, signs, names of angels and devils which are undoubtedly Hebrew. That is how we found out how they often helped noble ladies to get from illness to the graveyard, meanwhile and without doubt laughing up their sleeves.

96. About thirty years ago I heard it told, how a Jew ingratiated himself with Count Albrecht of Saxony, and taught him magic against all weapons so that he could not be punctured, beaten, shot, etc. Oh, those are fine arts by which our masters are misled so that they are murdered by stealth. But Count Albrecht was clever and wanted to be sure of that magic in advance. So he rode out to the field

---

52. a.) *The word "Koran" is Arabic, meaning "The Writings." It refers to the revelations received from Allah by Mohammed, who was his prophet. Mohammed lived from 570 to 632 according to the Gregorian calendar. In the tenth chapter of the Koran, called Jonah, there is indeed a suggestion that unbelievers (in the Koran) will be punished. However, Luther's interpretation of this chapter is enormously exaggerated.*

It should be kept in mind, however, that Luther and Christians generally were frightened by the swift Turkish Moslem advances in the Balkans which they witnessed in their lifetime. Thus, Christian Serbia was overrun in 1459, one year after Athens was taken by the Turks. In 1529, five years before Luther wrote Vom Schem Hamphoras *the Turks besieged Vienna.*

b.) In 874 C.E., an Iraqi peasant, Hamdan ibn al-Ashrath, also known as Quarmat, became the leader of the Ismaeli sect of Islam. He inspired the Ismaelis of Northern Iran to wage a campaign of murder against all opponents at the end of the eleventh century. Seeking to give themselves courage and to disregard the emotional consequences of their murderous conduct, the killers used a hemp derivative called hashish. Hence they were called "hashishin," from which the English word "assassin" is derived.

53. Of the Jews and Their Lies.
54. *A medieval book of magic.*

with that Jew and said: "Jew, I must try this magic on you," drew and stuck the Jew through and through that he lay dead so that neither his Shem Hamphoras nor his Tetragrammaton and any of his tricks could help him. "You lout," said the count, "how you led me around by the nose risking my life!" Yes, he may even have softly laughed up his sleeve. Now it was better that the count tried it on the Jews than that the Jew tried it on the count. I still have a crystal ball which once belonged to Count Frederick of Saxony, which my present gracious lord, Count John Frederick, gave me. It is covered with gilded Hebrew letters and symbols and is without doubt finished in this manner. But that same count was far too clever for such tricks. Nevertheless, the louts tried it.

97. Yes, I say, I would consider these Jews to be evil vagabonds and no true Israelites, if there were nothing else available than the Old Testament. For that same [book] tells us about Jews who were in the land of Canaan, and should still be there, and if they were led away because of their sins, then they should have come home long ago, according to the promise in Moses *5 Mos. 4, 31, 3 Mos. 26, 44.*[55] However, since that did not take place, one cannot think otherwise than that they will be dried up with time and disappear entirely (like Moab, Ammon and several other peoples) or even change into another people and nothing [more] be left of them than a bad remainder of meandering foreign louts or gypsies, who circumcise themselves and pretend as if they were Jews, for they keep nothing in Moses or the Prophets. Since they praise the Old Testament, however, we are better off than they. That they circumcise themselves, that the Turks do also, and is no more a true sign of Jewish kind or blood, but a real den of cutthroats, full of all kinds of meanness and loutishness, to damage country and citizens and to make life hard for them. This is also found in the "Beggarbook" that the same people talk a dialect including a lot of Hebrew as a sign that they are with or of the Jews.[56]

98. Since however, the New Testament asserts that the Jews shall be dispersed among all the heathens, and Jerusalem trampled out by the heathens, until the time of the heathens is fulfilled, (that is until the end of the world) as our Lord says, *Luc. 21, 24*[57] for Christ will remain for ever and no other Messiah will come: that is why

---

55. *"He will not forsake you, nor will he destroy you, nor forget the covenant of your fathers which he swore to them."* 3 Moses 26: 44: *"I will not cast them away, nor will I abhor them, to destroy them utterly, and to break my covenant with them."*

56. *The dialect Luther mentions here refers to the Yiddish language.*
This German-Hebrew mixture of words and phrases was first used by the German Jews at the end of the eleventh century and came to be known as "Jüdisch" or "Yiddish." The language was spoken by millions of Jews in all of Eastern Europe until the Nazi annihilations of the 1930s and 1940s. Today the language is hardly used by anyone so that in Israel, where Hebrew is spoken, Yiddish is regarded as a foreign language and is listed as such in university catalogues. In the U.S. the language has nearly disappeared as evidenced by the fact that erstwile Yiddish newspapers have either ceased publication or are now published in English. Nevertheless, the Yiddish writer Isaac Bashevis Singer won the Nobel Prize in literature in 1978.

57. *This passage predicts that "Jerusalem will be trampled under foot by the heathen until the heathen's day is over." See Phillips, p. 173.*

I must believe that a few remnants of Jews will remain in the world without ever having their own sovereignty, but be always in a precarious condition as is predicted by *Psalm 59*, verse 11, 12, in the spirit and in the person of Christ and his people: "By my enemies, God lets me see my joy, he does not kill them so that my people not forget; disperse them with your might, Lord, our shield, and knock them down."[58] And it should happen to them as to Cain the fraticide, *1 Mos. 4, 14*: You shall be Nogvonod uncertain and flighty, with no home of your own, to sit on the swing and on the scales, and have not certain roots nor place.[59]

99. At the same time, because they are so greedy to attract to themselves and collect the loose, wayward, depraved Christians, although they collect nothing good there, having done this for many years, the Israelite blood is being mixed, unclean, watery and brutalized who have soon learned from them to hate Christians and to murder them. Again, the Jews have learned nothing good from them, so that masters and students have practice on each other, sharpened and improved, until they became a den of cutthroats and devil's dregs for a renegade Christian will be a bitter enemy of Christians.

100. This is said in reference to the pride with which the miserable Jews brag about their holy scriptures, as if no one else had the holy writ; they ought to make use of our New Testament, where they ought to be known as Jews who have nothing otherwise, so that they prove it. Furthermore, there is nobody who has the Holy Scriptures less than the Jews; that we shall see.

101. If the Jews had ears or eyes, so that they could hear and see, then it would be easy to tell them and show them, that more than one Book constitutes the Holy Scriptures, and that the Old Testament cannot be alone, although they concern themselves thoroughly and interpret with Moses and the Prophets and yet do not understand them. For they must admit that the Messiah has been promised in the Holy Writ. Therefore, when he comes he will not be dumb and lame, but will talk and do better than Moses, David, Solomon, and all prophets talked and did. A book will develop from such talk and deeds. For he will let it be written just as Moses recorded his sermons and deeds, Isaiah his, and so forth. The book about the Messiah will be much better, holier, and gorgeous than Moses and the entire Old

---

58. The Jerusalem Bible *of 1988 renders these sentences as:* "God who loves me shall come to meet me: God shall let me gaze upon my enemies. Slay them not, lest my people forget: scatter them by thy power; and bring them down."

59. *The German transliteration of the Hebrew is mistaken. The words should be "Na Vanad" which means "perpetual wanderer." This refers to Cain, who, according to Genesis, was to be a "navanad baaretz," i.e., a perpetual wanderer on the earth. The current translation of this sentence as presented in the* Jerusalem Bible *of 1988 is* "Behold thou has driven me out this day from the face of the earth; and from thy face I shall be hid; and I shall be a fugitive and a vagabond in the earth; and it shall come to pass that anyone that finds me shall slay me."

Some Christian theologians view this passage as justification for the expulsions of the Jews from numerous communities over many centuries and further see in the last section of that sentence justification for the mass murders committed against the Jews.

Testament, for the Messia is not alone holy, as Moses and the Prophets, but the most holy of all the prophets as the prophet of all the prophets must be. Therefore his book must be the most sacred of all the holy books in the Bible.

102. We damned *Goyim* did not invent this, for Moses clearly and distinctly declared this to his people, namely that another book of the Holy Scriptures was yet to come and which they were to accept. For this is what he said *Deut.* at 18, 15. (as mentioned): "God will send you a prophet from among you brethern, like myself, listen to him."[60] I hope the Jews, however poisonous mean worms they are, can certainly not say that we invented this passage. Now let us hear the words, we do not want to add anything from our own mind, as they are to drag into Scriptures their mad, crazy comments.

103. Moses does not speak of his person in that place, how he was born of his father, but speaks of his position, how he was called and awakened by God to be a prophet; he wants to say: as God has wakened me from among your brethren to be a prophet, so he will again awaken another prophet from among your brethren. This other prophet cannot be Samuel, David, Elia, Elijah, Jesaiah or any other who occurred in the Old Testament; for they were all under Moses, taught what Moses (a prophet of God) ordered and promised or announced, that is, circumcision, the Ten Commandments, the laws of the priesthood, nobility, of the services to God, the temple and whatever was to be taught the people from the substance and parts of the Old Testament, outside of that which Moses had ordered and predicted.

104. If this other prophet is expected to do with his prophecy what Moses did, then he must establish other commandments, laws, and rights, a different priesthood, nobility, divine service, temple and rules. Should he, however, teach nothing other than what Moses taught, then it would be Moses himself or one of the old prophets who were under Moses and would not be like him. What did Moses do that he promises with useless words, "God will arouse another prophet like himself and they shall listen to him"? Even better he said then: when that prophet comes then you shall listen to me, that is, my prophecy. But now he lets go of his mastery, position and prophecy and transfers them to that other prophet and says: "You shall listen to him." For that they should listen to Moses and his prophets drove him earlier, and later drove all prophets, to disgust.

105. This also is proven by the fact that he introduced God himself, who says in *5 Mos. 18, 18*: "I will place my words in his mouth, so that he will preach what I shall tell him."[61]

These words and sermons must be words and sermons differing from Moses' word and sermon; for they shall be future and not yet existing expressions while the

---

60. The Jerusalem Bible *translates as follows: "The Lord thy God will raise up to you a prophet from the midst of thee of they brethern like me; to him you shall hearken...."*

61. Jerusalem Bible: *"I will raise them up a prophet from among their brethren like thee, and will put my words in his mouth; and he shall speak to them all that I shall command him."*

words of Moses, placed into the mouth of Moses about forty years earlier at Mt. Sinai, were also written by Moses. That is why Moses defended himself against the disagreeable Jews and let it be known that he plainly enough announced to them that another book, holier than his, will come through another prophet and that another priesthood, divine service, people and law will be founded.

106. Accordingly, all prophets together with Moses announced in agreement with one another, that the Messiah shall be a Prophet and Priest, who will institute another sermon, as Moses proclaimed here. *Jes. 2, 3, Mich. 4, 2.* Many heathens will say: "Let us go up to the House of the Lord, that he teach us his ways; for a law will go forth from Zion, and the Word of the Lord from Jerusalem."[62] Do you realize from this that it did not arise like the Law and the Word of Moses, but that it is to arise in the future and will be a new and different word? *Jes. 61, 1:* "The spirit of the Lord in upon me, therefore he has anointed me (made me Messiah of the Anointed One), for I am to preach the gospel to the wretched, to heal the sorrowful hearts." *Ps. 110, 4:* "You are forever a priest, according to the manner of Melchizedek." *Zach. 9, 10:* "He will preach peace from one sea to another, until the end of the world." *Jes. 9, 6:* "He will be a prince of peace." That is what Zachariah also says in 9, 10, "Put away horse and wagon," and *Jesiah 11, 4,* "rule without the sword."

107. If he should rule without the sword, and still maintain peace and keep it, then he will not be a king like David and all other kings (who cannot rule without a sword), nor teach their wordly laws, so that his kingdom must be an entirely different kingdom than a worldly kingdom, which is nothing without the sword and his law is nothing, and can have no peace. Even where he should be a priest, preacher and prophet, who shall reign in peace, how can he wait for such a rule, which has no peace, and must have such far-fetched law, but no eternal peace, as the prophets say of him? Israel had peace under Solomon, but only partially so, so that they themselves let it be known that he despoiled and impoverished them; nevertheless, it was no eternal peace. Therefore, it must be different with these other prophets, than with Moses, all prophets, and kings in this world and still remains; or Moses must be a liar with all his prophets. He should not be like other prophets or kings, that is what the Holy Scriptures of the Old Testament assert; that is why his book, the New Testament, must be a different and a higher testament than the Old Testament.

108. No one is so stupid and senseless as to confirm all of this from Moses and the prophets as in *Jeremiah 31, 31,* for he has too much contempt for these learned, full of shit, (circumcised) saints, and may without permission dismiss all Talmudists and Rabbis (oh that the worst shall be their lot) and say: "See the time will come, says the Lord, that I shall make a new covenant with the house of

---

62. *Here is at least one Biblical passage which Zionists like to quote as evidence for their claim that Jews have a right to establish themselves in Israel and in Jerusalem. Luther, however, views such claims as unjustified and ascribes them to "heathens." The quotation used by Luther occurs in both Isaiah and Micah.*

Israel."⁶³ Oh, Jeremiah, keep going, where will you end? You do not know how the Rabbis, after 2,000 years are so clever with their comments, which are better than your clear text. Shall a new covenant and testament come? What will become of the old? What will become of the circumcised saints, who do not want to know or tolerate more, not even from Christians, the damned *Goyim*, than the old? Should you be so courageous as to throw away Moses with the entire holy old scriptures and with it the Talmudists, and the high and super scholarly saints, so that you can prophecy in front of them about a new book and testament?

109. And, what is even worse, you impudent heretic, allow yourself to say: "Not as the covenant was, which I had made with their fathers, as I led them out of Egypt." Oh, Lord, God! Mercy on you, God, you poor Jeremiah, how could you become so mad, that you abolish the old covenant, which was surely made by God himself, as you admit yourself and say: "which I made with their fathers"; mentions the time with it, as if you were not mad, "as I took them by the hand and led them out of Egypt." Well, you are beyond help, you want to be damned by the circumcised saints; so I do not want to beg for you, nor interpret your words otherwise (which I couldn't do anyway), for the circumcised saints cannot tolerate it, it would bring things from bad to worse.

110. But here the super-learned Jews hand us damned *goyim* a most painful defeat as they write, our Jesus said himself, *Matth. 5, 17*: "He did not come to abolish the law and the prophets, but to fulfill it, for not a single letter nor particle shall be lost, for heaven and earth shall be lost before this would happen etc."⁶⁴ There you have it you damned *Goyim*. Well, now, who would have ever believed that the Jews are so learned that they could even teach us Christians the New Testament? No doubt a bronze dog in Jerusalem made them so smart with his barking, or a fresh Shom Haperes (vulture) with a lot of smoke, (I meant to say spirit) fulfilled them so that they understand so excellently what it means to fulfill the law.

111. Oh, dear God! the miserable Jews have not known all their lives what the least law even is, let alone what the fulfillment of the law is, and cannot (as long as they are such Jews) ever understand it. Other kinds of folks belong here, such as St. Paul, *Romans, 3, 21*: "God's justice is revealed, and witnessed through the law and the prophets," and *Joh. 1, 17*: "The law was given through Moses; but grace and truth came through Jesus Christ"; St. Peter, *Apost. 15, 10, 11*: "That is the

---

63. *There are some Christians who associate in a New Covenant Church basing their beliefs in part on this sentence. Nevertheless, this passage is given a wholly different interpretation in Judaism.*

64. *Mathew 5:17: "You must not think that I have come to abolish the Law or the Prophets: I have not come to abolish them but to complete them." In this verse lies one of the most important claims of Christianity concerning the succession of Christianity to the divine privileges earlier accorded Judaism. Some Christians today, and almost all Christians in Luther's day, claimed the Tora, (the Jewish law) claimed that the Jews who convert to Christianity are really not giving up the Tora because belief in Jesus as the Christ or Messiah fulfills the law far better than any effort by any man to meet the requirements of the 613 commandments which the Tora imposes.*

burden, which neither we nor our fathers could have born, instead we believe we will be saved through the grace of the Lord Jesus Christ, just as they were." Better tell me how it is possible that the scamps (I meant to say Rabbis) and Sow Jews in their Sow school should understand such great words, when all their lives they did nothing more than to burrow in the Shom Haperes (vultures) with their tusks.

112. I want to say less, for how can a Jew understand what has been said in *Matth.* at 7, 12: "What you want people to do to you, do it also to them; that is the law and the prophets." Here almost all of Moses' laws go to ruin. *Matth. 22, 37*: "Love your neighbor as yourself; that commandment is as the first: you shall love God with all your heart. In these two commandments are wrapped up the whole law and the prophets."[65] Moses evidently understood it as he said *2 Mos. 34, 6*: "Lord, lord, compassionate God, who forgives sin and no one is innocent before you," and David, *Ps. 130, 3*: "Lord, where you look upon sin, who can remain before you?" *Ps. 51, 8*: "See, you love the truth in the hidden, and teach me the hidden wisdom." Here, Jeremiah also says: he does not want to write the new covenant in stone tablets, like the other covenant which never entered the mortal heart of a Jew, and which he never understood, and kept even less; as Jeremiah says (*Cap. 31, 32*): "They did not keep that covenant," instead he wanted to write the new covenant in living tablets, upon the hearts so that it would be with living burning letters, so that God's will be done.

113. Now, one must of course speak of and write a book about such a living scripture, written on the heart, just as Moses had to write a book concerning the scriptures on the stone tablets; for less and less will occur in secret as the New Testament has its effect on the hearts upon which it is written, as compared to that testament that is written in stone tablets but not on the hearts. Of course those of us who are true Christians know all about this; for even the Pope with his church knows nothing of this and gives it no heed. The Jews know about as much about this as a sow knows of the Book of Psalms.

114. From this it is certainly proved that a New Testament was destined to supersede the old one, so that the pride and fame of the Jews is nothing but a crying shame, as they will not permit any testament nor holy scripture to supersede the old one. But it won't help them; their own Old Testament is against them, damns them with their reputation, because its prophecy is so weak, for the old covenant won't do it, the reign of Moses is finished, and the Messiah will not govern

---

65. *Matthew quotes* Leviticus 19:18. *The entire sentence reads:* "*You shall not take vengeance, nor bear any grudge against the children of your people, but you shall love your neighbor as yourself.*" *This so-called Golden Rule is also repeated in* Romans 13:10, *the Teachings of the Twelve Apostles and in the Apostolic Constitution.*

It is remarkable that for centuries Christians and Jews argued vehemently over which of the faiths should receive credit for this teaching. Since Judaism is older than Christianity, Christians would sometimes argue that Judaism states the Golden Rule only in the negative form but Christianity states it in a positive form and is therefore entitled to more credit.

according to it, for the New Testament will do it. That is why Moses relinquishes his office and leaves room for the new prophet. That is why the Jews must accept the New Testament, baptism and our belief or they are lost forever. The Old Testament, Moses himself and all the prophets cannot help them but are opposed to them and relegate them to Hell.

115. Here the question arises again as to whether the Messiah did come. If he came, then Jews, heathens and all the world are obliged to accept the New Testament, not only as a sacred scripture, but the most holy writ superseding the old holy writ.

Now it has been sufficiently proved that the Messiah came about 1,500 years ago; so we Christians, and first several thousand children of Israel, thereafter many heathens, accepted the New Testament 1,500 years ago and will continue to accept it until the end of the world; but the dregs, the other Israelites, they won't accept it, they hold such a negligible thing in contempt. They have despised the food and disputed all joy, all because of great arrogance and stubbornness; then they wanted to be insulted and grunt because they found nothing in their hunger. Is it tolerable that they should brag and pride themselves that they alone, in all the world, have the holy Scripture, when in fact they do not have one page, not one letter of it, as far as the understanding is concerned, for use and good of the soul; we are not concerned with the physical body or its uses. For what they look for in the scriptures, that they will never find; it is not there, nor was it ever in there, as little as in the most worthless book made on this earth. The Messiah is predicted in it, but not the Messiah they want and about whom they dream.

116. We Christians, however, have both books of the Holy Scriptures, the old and sacred, and in addition, the new and most sacred. The old predicts the Messiah and says: he shall surely come and will be given. The new calls and says: he certainly has come and was given. If the Jews could now accept the new Book, the most holy scriptures, as so many did 1,400 years ago, then they would surely understand that circumcision and all old holiness must yield to baptism and the new holiness which is greater than all other holiness. For at the time that the Messiah and his book were still stuck in the old book, that is, in the promise, there was evidently no other holy scripture than the old book, in whose promise all saints who hoped for such a promised Messiah were saved. For he is the one and the only Messiah, who was promised to them but came and appeared to us, so that no other can be expected nor come.

117. After, however, the Messiah published this book and gave it to us, there is no need to wait for any further promises. Just as the old book is now a form of witness for God, that the Messiah was to have come, so the new book is so much more a witness of God, now that the Messiah has come. Thus, the two Cherubim[66] facing each other in the Chair of Grace, that is, the Old and New Testament, say

---

66. *The word* cherub(im) *is Hebrew for "attendant(s). " It is sometimes translated as "angels," although the Greek word* angelos *means messenger.* Angelos *was introduced into the Greek version of the Bible as a direct translation of the Hebrew* malach, *which means "messenger."*

that Jesus Christ, the son of Mary, is the Savior of the world and the right Chair of Grace before God, against our sin, death, Devil and Hell. Therefore it is fulfilled as it has been said: "Israel shall live in safety," when the last Jews seek to interpret as the end of time.

118. Since, however, the Jews refuse to accept this, they have neither the old nor the new book, neither God the provider not Messiah the deliverer, are suspended between heaven and earth, touch down nowhere, do not meet either the old or the new book, as *Zachariah 5, 1*[67] showed the flying letter which he called *maledictio*, curse; for their lessons are boastful cursing; otherwise they truly know nothing about the scriptures. In the first place, it is sure that they do not know the promises of the Messiah. Furthermore, they do not understand the Ten Commandments, because, without Messiah, they cannot be understood. In the third place, they cannot understand what the ceremonies mean. In addition, because the priesthood has disappeared, they also do not well understand the origin of the ceremonies. In the fourth place, no Jew understands the noble, precious examples of the lives of the fathers, Adam, Noah, Abraham, Isaac, Jacob, Joseph, David, all told, the whole people of Israel. For they do not know what true belief, true good works, are. This is proved by their blind, mad, miserable Talmud companions, their commentaries and finally their grammar. That is why they have nothing more from the Old Testament. It says: "I am the light," (says Messiah, *Joh. 8, 12*) where that is not so, what else can there be there except only darkness?[68]

119. This should be said in answering in a dull and crude fashion the stiff-necked Jews and their prickly, poisonous question, namely that *1 Mos. 49, 10* and *5 Mos. 18, 15* powerfully prove, and with him all prophets together and sufficiently, that Mary was and must be the mother of Messiah from the tribe of Judah and the house of David. If they will not believe Moses, then they'll believe the apostles less. Furthermore, such an answer is certain and good enough for us Christians, as said, the son Messiah must come from David, and we believe in addition that his mother was virgin, in which case she must be David's flesh and blood and natural daughter: otherwise, her son Messiah could not be David but of a different breed, because his mother would be of a different blood, although it is curious that she, Mary, had to bear (a child) without any man's blood and flesh.

120. Through this evidence in the Old Testament we shall now see the New Testament and how richly and powerfully it proves the same thing, i.e., that Mary must be David's daughter. First, St. Matthew, 1.1 begins his book, "This is the book about the birth of Jesus Christ, the son of David, the son of Abraham." Here you

67. Zachariah 5: 1: *"Then I turned and lifted up my eyes, and looked, and behold, a flying scroll...." Zachariah lived in the sixth century B.C.E. He is regarded as one of the "minor" prophets. His prophecy consisted of visions which needed interpretation. He was one of those who urged the rebuilding of the temple after its first destruction by Nebuchadnezzar in 597 B.C.E.*

68. John 8:12: *"I am the light of the world; The man who follows me will never walk in the dark but will live his life in the light."*

are told that Jesus Christ or the Messiah is the son of David and the son of Abraham; therefore, his mother must be the daughter of David and Abraham, because she is a virgin who bore without a man as is proved by the apostle. And if St. Matthew had not written another word about this, except this opening of his book, then that would have been enough proof that Mary must be of the House of David. For the son, Messiah, proves where the mother comes from, not the mother (as the mad Jews seek) where the son comes from, or that he is of the tribe of Judah. Now the apostle carries this to the extreme, and counts three times fourteen generations since Abraham, those are two hundred and forty generations, so that one could say for each generation: his daughter is Mary and Jesus is his son, as he is David's and Abraham's son; so that Matthew acknowledges forty-two times in the course of the generations that Mary is of the tribe of Judah and the flower of David. And, to sum it up, as often as Jesus is called the Messiah in the Old and the New Testament, that is how often Mary, his mother, is proved to be the daughter of David.

121. However, since many are concerned why the apostle turns to those words in the last paragraphs, he derives Joseph, places Miriam, whom he cannot derive in a straight line from David as he derives Joseph: here we ought (if we know nothing else) honor the Holy Ghost and think that Matthew knew the relatives of Mary very well at Nazareth, because he knows Joseph, her husband so well and considered him a friend, and it is unbelievable that he should testify forty-two times that Christ is David's son in a straight line of the generations, and that still the mother came from a foreign tribe, as if he had become mad and dullminded in the extreme.

122. Nevertheless, we want to take a look at the words of the apostle, and see if he too can derive Miriam from David as well as Joseph. It is certain that St. Matthew derives the line through Solomon and St. Luke through his brother Nathan: those are two lines, through one relationship as two brothers, from David; for in King Joas they come together, and must come together in one line because *2 Chron. 22, 9, 10* says that Athalja killed all royal seed except for Joas, and as the text states: "There was no one of the house of Ahasja who would become king." Here ends the line of Solomon so that Christ could come of his blood, according to the line of the brothers and fathers, but not from the posterity of his body, but, as Luke says, from Nathan, his brother.

123. Whether the two apostles separate these lines from one another later, I will not explain now; it is certain that they remain in the House of David; but when it comes to the grandfather of Joseph they agree, for both agree upon Matthan or, as Luke calls him, Mathes. I noticed that he was called Matthan according to the *Grammar* but Matthes according to ordinary laymen's language, just as we Germans derive from Johannan, Hans, Hansel, and Henno; or Nicolaus, Nickel, Claus, etc. We Germans pronounce the name Matthes plain and right, as it is written in Hebrew, Matthath, *Thaf raphato* [the weak letter Thaf][69] *et A puro vel Italico*

---

69. *In the Hebrew language the last letter of the alphabet in the Ashkenazi tradition may be pronounced either "saf" or "taf" depending on the meaning of the word in which*

(that is with a--- that has been augmented with Raphe and with a clear and Italian A).⁷⁰

124. Let us note this Matthes, everything depends on him, for there is where the blood of Abraham and David comes close to the Messiah, almost in the last house. For up to the house of this Matthes, Messiah came from up above, and we certainly have him in this house; for he must come from this house alone, it is insignificant and whatever comes from the houses of brothers or cousins is placed in the rear, they do not concern us, he is in the house of Matthew. Even if we had nothing more than this Matthew, then we would still have more than enough to answer those who are concerned how Mary and Joseph could have been from one tribe and one House. Because the Messiah is in the House of Matthes, and must come from the House of Matthes, the apostle has thereby clearly and obviously proved that both Mary and Joseph must not only come from the tribe of Judah and the House of David but also from one house of Matthew, the grandfather of Joseph; because the Messiah must come from the house of Matthes. If the Messiah is in the House of Matthes, then his mother must certainly also be of it, as the one who, a virgin, and of the House of Matthes, David and Abraham, shall bear the Messiah. For in whatever house the Messiah may be, his mother Mary must certainly be there before, (as was said above) which shows that she is a virgin and has no husband; it is achieved by the virginity which leads the Messiah with his mother from all fathers to himself.

125. What was the shortcoming which prevented St. Matthew from proving to us that Mary and Joseph are of one tribe and one house and father? The shortcoming lay in the fact that we did not notice from which father the Messia came, and that his mother must be in the same one, because she shall be a virgin, and cannot acknowledge that her child stems from any human other than herself and her father. That Hieronymus, Lyra and others write that it will have to be proved that Mary and Joseph are of the same origin and that he took her in marriage according to the Law of Moses, *4 Mos. 36, 6, 7*,⁷¹ so that the possessions would not be separated into strange tribes, that is far too indifferent and too unimportant and also too far in the past and looking to supersede David and yet does not help at all; just as Burgensis justly and correctly rejects this. Why did we not investigate this Matthes? then we would have gotten a lot closer to this, so close that it could not have been closer.

(note 69 continued) *the letter occurs. In the Sephardic tradition, the letter is always pronounced "taf." Luther refers to the Ashkenazi pronunciation inasmuch as the German Jews whom he knew used the Ashkenazi pronunciation. In fact, the word "Ashkenaz" was used for centuries to denote Germany while the word "Sefarad" was used to denote Spain, another center of Jewish culture in the Middle Ages. Modern Hebrew as spoken in Israel is pronounced according to the Sephardic or Spanish pronunciation.*

70. *This Latin phrase means "and moreover with a clear Italian 'A.'"*

71. *The laws of inheritance among the ancient Hebrews are mentioned here as follows: "Only within the family of the tribe of their father shall they marry. So the inheritance of the children of Yisra'el shall not remove from tribe to tribe."*

126. Because the Messiah must come from the House of Matthes and from nowhere else, let us see what comes from that House. First, his son Jacob comes from there, as Matthew writes. The Messiah does not come from the house of this Jacob, hasn't been included either, for his son, Joseph, comes from it.

Mary cannot as yet come from it, nor be his daughter, although she is in it with her son the Messiah; otherwise Joseph would have taken his father's sister or his grandfather's natural daughter, which God, through Moses, prohibited. *3 Mos. 18, 12.*[72] It could even less be another daughter of Matthes, who became the mother of the Messiah, so it must be alone Mary. For the daughters leave the houses of the fathers for other houses, that is why the scripture does not regard the female line. Therefore, Matthes must at least have one son, from whom the Messiah comes and he is Eli, as Luke writes. He begot a daughter, Maria Jacobi, and she is not the one; and thereafter a younger daughter, Maria, she is the one. If he had more sons and daughters, it would make no difference; for the Messiah must come from a virgin, the daughter of Eli.

127. Here we now have the mother of the Messiah, she is a sibling of Joseph, and both are grandchildren of one grandfather, Matthes. Therefore, it has been sufficiently proven that Mary and Joseph are of the same tribe and lineage, while she is a grandfather's grandchild, the children of two brothers, and could not be closer unless they were physical brothers and sister.

Through Moses it was permitted in this people, that siblings could marry one another, that is, a grandfather could associate his two grandchildren or two brothers could do this with their children among this people, so that the apostle calls Joseph Mary's husband and Mary the bride of Joseph; as if he meant to say: because you have heard that Joseph is Mary's husband, you knew her well enough to know that according to common usage those of one lineage are siblings.

128. Thus, the apostle brought the Messiah, his mother with him, from the beginning through all the houses of the patriarchs to Matthes' house then to Eli's house and from there to Joseph's house, where he was born and educated; not of his body, but of the body of his wedded wife, or in his married state, and Messiah is his legal son, and Joseph his legal father, but only from the virgin Mary. Since we are aware that Joseph and Mary are the grandchildren of the great patriarch Matthes, we have enough evidence and are certain that Mary is with Joseph of the House of David. Whoever wants to quibble about the two brothers Jacob and Eli, as to whether Jacob took his brother's daughter Mary and gave her to his son Joseph, or whether Eli took his brother's son, Joseph, and gave him to his daughter Mary, he may do so; it is enough for us that they, the two fathers of Joseph and Mary, were the sons of Matthes.

129. That Hieronymous writes that according to the lineage of St. Matthew Jacob is the natural father of Joseph while according to Luke's lineage, it is Eli whom he also calls Eliakin and Joakim (for all three are regarded as one name as Nicolaus,

---

72. *"Thou shalt not uncover the nakedness of thy father's sister: she is your kinswoman."*

Nickel, Claus), who is his father, that is, his father-in-law or cousin, in the sense that the daughter's husband is called son, and the son's wife is called daughter, and according to the law that a brother must permit the children of his deceased brother [to] call him father and be one.[73] That pleases me a good deal, and better than Eusebius with Lyra, who believes Jacob took his brother Eli's widow and begot Joseph with her. In that event, Mary and Joseph, (Joakim or Eli's daughter) would be mother, children and natural siblings, which Moses would not tolerate, *3 Mos. 18, 6*.

130. Here the old question arises: Which one of the apostles among the two, Matthew and Luke, describes the paternal line, since it is obvious that Matthew, as is proved above, followed the fraternal line from Salomon down to Ochosias. First, one must let go of Lyram and his part in this, with their opinion, for they go too far afield, for he holds that Nathan was not the natural son of David, but of the prophet (who would have been as old as David himself) and came from Uria and Bethsaba together with the other brothers, Simea and Sobab, *1 Chron. 3, 5*, whom David late elected to be adoptive children and only Salomon was the son of Bethsaba; that is the meaning of the saying in *Proverbs 4, 3*: "I was the only son of my mother," etc. That is nothing; in that manner, Christ would be Uriah's son, he was a Hittite, a heathen, although more pious than a thousand Israelites.

131. Furthermore, it suffices for a Christian, that both apostles introduce David's children, be that father's or brother's line, and both remain in the house of David, do not count adoptive children or alien blood. From when Christ comes, he comes from David. I hold with those like Luke who derive it from the paternal line, until Eli; since the line of Metthes splits in two, one part on Jacob and the other on Eli, he must place Joseph, the son of Eli, that is Edom, on the grounds, as he himself says, that Joseph is the putative father of Christ, but not the natural father as the line would have demanded it if Mary, his bride, had not been a virgin mother, and in the manner of scripture will not tolerate to follow the line of women; nevertheless he is still putative. One body with his bride Mary as he is putative father of Christ. In sum, as said before, the father Matthes makes it clear that Mary and Jesus are the children of one house and one father.

132. It worries some that Matthew says again and again, *genuit, genuit*, he begat or bore; they therefore believe that Matthew talks about the natural line which

---

73. *This is called the "Levirate" in anthropological usage. From Latin* levir, *the husband's brother. This was important in Jewish law and is mentioned repeatedly in several sections of the Bible. Thus, Genesis 38: 8–10 concerns Onan, who "spilled his seed upon the ground" rather than impregnate his sister-in-law with whom he was duty bound to have children. The children would, however, carry on the family of his brother and would be attributed to his brother. The eldest son of such a union inherited the property and the name of the deceased. Deuteronomy 25:5 states, "If brethren dwell together, and one of them die, and have no child, the wife of the dead shall not be married abroad unto one not of his kin; her husband's brother shall go in unto her, and take her to him to wife, and perform the duty of a husband's brother unto her."*

follows birth, from father to son, on and on; Luke, however, talks about the fraternal or paternal line, which they call *legalem*, not *adoptivam*, as Lyra believes but, because a brother, according to the Law, he must concern himself with the children of his deceased brother, as if he were their father. This, I do not believe, St. Matthew does not believe it himself and cares nothing for it. For he lets only three members outside, among the kings and says: Joram begat Usia; which is impossible because Usia was born four generations, i.e., one hundred years, after the death of Joram, in addition descends in the fraternal line from Nathan, not Solomon, from where Joram came. The same thing was done among the nobility after the Babylonian captivity, for he leaves a lot out, counts only fourteen, where Luke counts twenty-two, and could not name anything: Asar begat Zadok, where perhaps two or three are left out; that is why the *genuit* adds nothing here to the belief that Matthew ought to be the paternal line.

133. His manner of speaking is to say *genuit*, or he begat him etc. With that he means only: he is from him or born of his blood, as we say in German; Carolus comes from or is born of Maximilian. He shows this also in the title with these words: "This is the book concerning the birth of Jesus Christ, the son of David, the son of Abraham." Christ was of course not born of nor begotten by David; nor is he his son, because he comes from him according to the blood. Therefore birth in this case cannot mean the personal birth of the Savior, where he lists forty births of his ancestors. Luke, however, uses the paternal line. For he praises himself at the beginning, that he researched it all carefully and wants to write about it. We must believe him because we believe far greater and different things. For such registers were known among the Jews, wrote down everything, (as was their fashion) as two examples show, i.e., Chronicles (and) Esra; also Moses, who diligently describes the generations of Jacob and Esau.

134. Matthew admits freely that he wanted nothing more than to count in an orderly fashion, for he says, he wants to calculate three *Tessaradecadas*, three times fourteen, from Abraham to Christ. And because he found fourteen partriarchs, he did not want to name more than fourteen kings and fourteen nobles. Because the writers, through no fault of the apostle, a king, Joakim, the father of Jechonja, was left out, so that only thirteen kings are mentioned, a shortcoming which Hieronymus also shows in the Greek books. Luke, however, lists four times fourteen, takes all of them, even those who were not kings, as also Nathan and his offspring. Added to this same Luke by the scribes is the fourth generation after Noah, i.e., Kenan, which cannot be. Therefore I consider it a useless effort, to compare all names with one another, because we do not have the registers. And it is not written in the first place for us heathens (but for the Jews) who no doubt knew it. It suffices that we compare as much as we can; you can ask Josephus and Philo about that.

135. I am willing to risk any friendship on my opinion or understanding; whoever can do it better, shall be right.

Levi.*			Abraham.**	
Aaron.			David.	
Zadok.			Joas.	
Jojada.			Zerubabel.	
A*			Matthes.	
Zacharias Elisabeth Anna		Eli		Jacob.
John the Baptist				
Maria Cleophae	Maria		Joseph	Salome Zebedaus
1. Jacob 2. Simon		JESUS	1. Jacobus major	
3. Joses.** 4. Juda			2. John Evang.	

* Refers to the priestly line   ** Refers to the royal line

136. This Mary, the mother = sister of our Lord or his aunt, is called Maria Jacobi of the son, in the Gospels; is also called Maria Cleophae by the other man who was still alive on Christ's Easter Day, *Luke 24, 18*. Therefore, Juda is also called Jacobi, perhaps because he is the brother of Jacobi, Alphao, the first husband of Maria Jacobi. These are called the brothers of our Lord, because they are the children of his Mother's sister.

137. Furthermore, the angel Gabriel says, *Luc. 1, 36*, that Elizabeth is the older female relative or aunt of Mary; that cannot be otherwise, for Mary's mother was Elizabeth's sister, we will let her be Anna as she is called everywhere. Because Elizabeth is of the tribe of the priests, as the angel says, from the daughters of Aaron, that is why I place the two sisters, Anna and Elizabeth, into the line of Aaron, so Joachim or Eli of the tribe of David takes the one sister, Anna, and Zacharias of the tribe of the priests the other one, Elizabeth. Therefore, Mary becomes Aaron's daughter of the tribe of the priests, on her mother's side and David's daughter of the royal house on her father's side; therefore, Christ is both of the priestly and the royal blood. And Elizabeth is her aunt and the great aunt of the Lord; thus, Mary would be a sibling of John the Baptist, and he a near cousin in the third degree of our Lord Jesus Christ.

138. Now Salome wants to be something special, expects an advantage with the Lord, because she asks him to place her two sons, one at the right (*Matth. 20, 21*) the other on the left, in his kingdom, which I interpret to mean that they must have listened to him carefully. That is why I consider her Joseph's sister; she thought Maria Jacobi the sister of the mother, I am, however, the father's sister; that is why I am entitled to precedence with my children before the mother's sister with her children. Although Joseph no longer has a child, my sons are Jesus' closest friends, and she thinks, Jesus is the son of Joseph, as everyone held the same view at the same time (*Luc. 3, 23*). The others grumbled against this, no doubt the children of the mother=sister, and perhaps untold more with them who also sought to be the greatest, as we read in the Gospels. Herewith, Jacobus the Great and John the Baptist also become cousins of the Lord, with the name so close as Jacobus and Simon, Juda and Joseph, but one generation further, according to the blood. For Joseph is

not the natural father of the Lord, only his mother Mary and Salome are the daughters of two brothers, etc.

139. From this one can see, how the Lord's closest relatives forced themselves on him according to the human manner, and still he conducts himself in a friendly and brotherly way. No gleam of majesty glows here, but the outward servile form.

140. Many, such as Bonaventura,[74] believe, with conviction and a clear conscience, that John the Baptist and Mary Magdalene were groom and bride at the wedding at Cana, according to the sequence in John the Baptist. Someone else may have a different (but free) conviction it may be Simon or Juda the bridegroom, and the bride also a near aunt in the next or third degree; for the apostles call Simon of Cana and Juda zealots, that is, of Cana. It ought to be considered, that bride and groom must have been the close relatives of Mary, since she is present herself and helps to run it [the wedding]. For she would not frivolously mix into a strange or distant friend's wedding, as there were other women, closer.

141. However, the final opinion of the apostles, particularly Matthes, with such a line of the family, is this, that he wants to instruct and strengthen the ignorant, weak Jews, but stuff the mouth of the stubborn with these two statements: Jesus is Messiah and Mary is a virgin. For these two statements were the most difficult for the pious to believe, and utterly impossible to believe for the stubborn; the cause was, he was well known in Nazareth with his father, mother and many friends, for he was raised there and had lived there for thirty years, and like any apprentice, worked as a carpenter with his father Joseph, did not go to school, learned nothing, the same after his father's death when he supported himself with his poor mother, did not let anyone notice anything special but kept himself simply quiet like any other young man of his kind, that she was used to him and could not in her heart accept that this unschooled, gross and poor carpenter was to be learned and in addition a preacher all his life.

142. Suddenly, when the thirty years are over, he leaves his trade, runs away, lets himself be baptized by St. John with others, begins to preach, to interpret and teach scripture and do wonders, so that the whole world is aghast, so that all priests and teachers appear as useless, meaningless gossips compared to him. That was a strange, incomprehensible thing in their eyes and ears. It was even stranger that he was not only a prophet but the Messiah himself. Oh, what strange, contemptuous speeches were made about that! Dear one, keep quiet, should Jesus preach, do you think I don't know him? I have lived with him for thirty years, and know well who he is and what he can do.

143. Take yourself as an example: If you had lived, worked, eaten, drunk etc.

---

74. *Giovanni de Fidanza, also known as St. Bonaventura (1221–1274), was a famous medieval writer. A bishop and a cardinal, he was canonized in 1482 and immortalized in Dante's* Inferno *as a saint.*

with Hans N., the son of a poor citizen for thirty years, and you knew him as well as yourself, that he never knew one letter, and that he wandered into another country that same year, and you now heard that he is preaching and is learned, and that all scholars consider this a miracle; you would say to the reporter: Are you silly or are you joking? Do you think I don't know Hans N. with whom I broke bread for thirty years? And if a great noise came about to the effect that he had become king or Roman emperor you would say: Well, he has gone crazy and the world has gone mad and wants to be mad, but don't tell it to me, I know him too well. That is how it appeared to the Nazarenes with regard to Jesus.

144. Since he came home again a bit over one-half year later, he went to school, gets up, takes the book *Isaiah* in hand, reads from it, sits down, and holds a beautiful sermon so that all are astonished; now they all see him themselves, cannot deny it is Jesus, whom they know very well, begin and say, *Matth. 13, 54ff*: "From where does so much wisdom and power come to him? Is he not the son of a carpenter? Is not his mother called Maria? And his brothers Jacob and Joses, Simon and Juda? And are not his sisters all with us? From where does all that come to him? And they were angered by him." Why were they angry? They could not believe that what they heard and saw was from God. This person they knew too well and he was too unimportant; that is why they thought he had submitted to the Devil, who sought to commit this unheard of thing through him. And since he attacked them with one word, they took him at that same hour, led him outside of town, meant to break his neck by driving him down from the mountain as a malicious person.

145. For in his lecture on Isaiah he allowed them to notice that he is the Messiah, for he said, the same word is fulfilled in him *Jesiah* at 61, 1: "The spirit of the Lord is upon me, therefore the Lord anointed me," that is, made into the Messiah, although he was a beggar as they knew him. Thereupon he rebuked them, as if they were not worthy of his miraculous deeds, as Luke mentions at 4, verse 16. Then they became angry and thought: Get rid of such a Messiah, he will cause trouble; we know he is a beggar, but wants to be Messiah. Away with that lout who only recently helped to erect a house and picked up shavings with us, and suddenly became Messiah, that is, king of all kings, and holds us holy people of Israel in contempt as he will not do what pleases us, etc.

146. Now, however, they become even more angry because he rose from the dead and rose to heaven (but they thought he was dead now as he deserved as a deceiver), and they should now not only view this Jesus, who had dealt with them as he pleased as the Messiah but accept him even after death as a Lord of Heaven and earth; that was a repugnant and unbearable sermon for them, they found it offensive and the greatest number of them fell to this day; for their thoughts must have been right, God must have lied and been wrong, as they do even now, and have lied and murmured against Jesus, so that it is unspeakable and can also not be put in writing.

147. Yes, that is (as I began) the foremost and final task of the apostle, that he was anxious to convince the Jews of Jesus so that they would accept him as the

Messiah, and forget about all difficulties and not be hindered by the fact that he lived among them so contemptuously for thirty years and that he was crucified so shamefully. For this is the son of Abraham, David and all the patriarchs, counted out according to the line, up to the mother Mary who was identified as a virgin by both Isaiah and the Holy Ghost; not a common son of David and the patriarchs, as several others, such as Joseph, Simon, Juda and Jacob; but the singular, exceptional, wonderful son, in whom the prophecy and promise of Abraham and David and all the prophets happened and was fulfilled. If they were to accept this son, that is, the prophecy and the promise, then they would have seized upon the right Messiah, then they would let go of the Old Testament, including circumcision, priesthood, nobility, the temple, Jerusalem and all laws, which come from this and belong to it: for they would not need it anymore. Instead they would gladly accept the New Testament, including Baptism, sacraments and everything the Messiah taught and ordered and keep much more holy than the Old Testament has ever been and would not insist that no further Holy Book or scriptures can be except the Old Testament of which they dream.

148. The evangelist did not work for nothing and in vain, among other evangelists and apostles. Many were converted, and accepted Jesus with great joy, could not wonder enough, before they could understand it that God had fulfilled his promises in so lovely and so friendly a manner. The others held on and still hold on to the word of *Jes. 53, 2, 3*: "We saw him, but there was no body, that we could have desired him. He was the most contemptible and worthless, full of pain and illness, he was so contemptible that one would cover the face before him: that is why we did not pay attention to him" etc. However, he who wants to be the Kochab or Messiah to the Jews, he need not be well formed or good to look at, for they certainly hold him in contempt, says Isaiah.

149. Let us then conclude, the Jews, as mentioned, will easily believe that the line as proposed by Matthew correctly reaches from Abraham to Jesus; that long they stand still and listen. For at that time all men and women of the tribe of Judah, many thousands, came as well from Judah and the greater part of the house of David as Joseph, Mary and their son Jesus although they never looked at them. But as the apostle insists: "of whom is born Jesus, who is called Messiah," they recoil as if thunder had struck them down, they no longer hear anything, even though the apostle inserted so many links into the line of which he may have wanted to use far fewer; even though he leaves out many of them, in order to show that it is not necessary to name them all (for they were glad to hear their descent praised) so that this holy matter would conclude in a friendly and nice manner.

150. To this, St. Matthew wants to say, not only from his own spirit (although he has power, right and command), that Mary, a virgin, has given birth, but also introduces the prophet Isaiah, so as to coax them in a friendly way through their own scriptures. But what good is it among the stubborn, gnarled, stiff necked, damned Jews? They have made a great effort to explain their views as they have with all the others, but cannot achieve anything any way for they are always seeking excuses and seek to make true one lie with seven more lies. However, as said earlier, one should

leave the Jews alone and ignore how the devil riots in them. If there is a human heart among them, God will find it; with the others, the proverb applies: Lost like the Soul of a Jew. Therefore, to strengthen and ornament our belief, how hilarious (but poisonous) that the devil treats them with this proverb and against St. Matthew.

Concerning the Word *Alma*, and the Virginity of Mary

151. First, "See, (says Isaiah), the virgin is pregnant." Here the word *Alma* is used, as many, including myself have written, hold that it means a virgin or maid, who is still walking with her hair in a wreath[75] and in innocence, and is not yet a woman. Now, if a Jew or Hebraist can prove to me that *Alma* means a woman anywhere in the scriptures, I will give him 100 Gulden, God help me to find them.

The word *Alma* appears four times and no more in the Holy Scriptures. First, *1 Mos. 24, 16* concerning Rebecca, who is described by Moses with many words to the effect that she had not transgressed with any man. In addition, *2 Mos. 2, 8* concerning the sister of Moses, Miriam: "The *Alma* went and called her mother" etc. Miriam could not have been ten years old at the time as the Jews themselves must admit. In the third place, *Isaiah 7, 14*: "See, the *Alma* is pregnant." In these three places is an article which means *singulariter unam*,[76] and none else. In the fourth place, *Proverbs, 30, 18ff*: "Three things are too wonderful for me and the fourth one I do not know: the way of the eagle in the sky, the ship in the sea, the way of the snake on the boulder, and the way of a man with a maid. Thus is the way of an adulteress, who acts as if nothing has happened and says: I have not done evil."

152. Here, here *Alma* is used with a man (so they say). I do not ask whether *Alma* is used in connection with a man; for I see it for myself, praise God, and do not need a Jew to show it to me. I say, prove to me that here *Alma* means a woman and not a virgin; I would be glad to hear that master and contribute 100 Gulden to him. How, when Solomon at that place (as the damned *Goy*, Doctor Luther, understands, and it won't be easy to take it from him, if it oughtn't to be worth 100 Gulden) spoke of the discouraging misfortunes in the world? since a *Gever* [Hebr.], that is, a husband, cannot land in a woman's bed in the name of God but sneaks after a virgin in the name of the devil. On the other hand, *Gevirah* [Hebr.] the woman cannot find the man's bed, in the name of God, and crawls to a servant or other lout in the name of the devil, has a spacious conscience, swallows the adultery like a wolf a moth, acts as if nothing has happened and nobody can cuss her out as a whore. Who will prove it?

153. Because such things must be played out in the dark and must be plotted secretly, there belong to this tricky ways, stratagems and intrigues which no Solomon

---

75. *A custom denoting unmarried virginity. Today some Orthodox Jewish married women shave their hair or cut it short and cover their head with a wig. Some keep their hair but always wear a cloth to hide it. This custom is also known in all Moslem countries although everyone does not observe it.*

76. *"Absolutely one."*

nor ruler can every think of or prevent with prohibitions, or convince, nor more than he could dictate the path of a bird in the air, because the whole heavens are his path, and the whole ocean is the path of the ship, and goes wherever the wind wishes, and the snake on the boulder, having neither a line nor a direction, can do nothing but writhe too much.

It is one of the sorrows of this life, that it is not possible to prevent secret adultery, and that a maid (unfortunately) will often please a husband more than his wife, and a wife will love a servant better than the master; as the poet says: *Quod licet, ingratum est. Nitimur in vetitum. Lex occasio peccati [est]*.[77] That is what the whore of Potiphar wanted to do to the pious Joseph, *1 Mos. 39, 7*.[78]

154. Nevertheless, *Alma* means in this case a maid or virgin whom a man will pursue; if he brings her down, she is no longer a maid; if she stands firm, she remains an *Alma*, as I have well undersood some such stories, that the pious virgins brought the lustful men to them with stealth and in their name. Therefore, the Jews cannot prove that *Alma* here at *Isaiah 7* means a woman, because the word *Alma* means a virgin or maid in the entire scriptures; even *in plurali numero*, Alamoth, they cannot prove, that it means anything but virgins or maids. Prove otherwise, but do a good job, so that I will not lose my one hundred Gulden in so shameful a manner. And in advance, so that St. Matthew does not become a liar; otherwise the Holy Ghost himself will have to let himself be circumcised; it would be a shame for the beautiful relatives if they had to become Jewish.

155. In addition, Isaiah says that the *Alma* should be pregnant, and that that is a miracle and a sign; she did not say, she will become pregnant as all the ravens (rabbis) would like to interpret: they ought to be ashamed for their own "grammatica," that *Hara* means *concepit es praegnans*, she is pregnant, she has received. But nevertheless, they want to worm out of it that the prophet took a young maid in his old age and made her pregnant; thereupon he begins and says: See, the *Alma* is pregnant and will bear a son, so that opinion shall be: that is not the sign that the *Alma* is pregnant, the prophet caused this himself, he is her man; but that she bears a son and not a little girl.

156. Whom shall we believe then? God says: That the *Alma* is pregnant shall be a sign. The Jew says: Oh, no, God lies, that is not a sign, for the prophet impregnated the *Alma*. Thus, we have two texts here; the text of Isaiah is obvious and clear: God will give you a sign, see the *Alma* is pregnant etc. But the text of the Jews is this one: See the *Alma* has a man and is pregnant by the prophet, that is how God will give you a sign that she will bear a son, and not a daughter. Would you like to ask where the Jews got the great art that they can play dice with the text and God's word as if they were engaged in a phony game, and that the least becomes the foremost; and give a man to the *Alma* of which Isaiah writes nothing, but says, that the *Alma* is pregnant does not mean that the prophet did it.

77. *What is allowed, is not pleasing. We struggle within our prohibitions. Law is an opportunity to sin.*
78. *And it came to pass after these things, that his master's wife cast her eyes upon Joseph; and she said: "Lie with me."*

157. Damned *goy* that I am, I cannot understand where they got such great ability, unless, I must believe, that when Judas Sharioth hanged himself, his intestines burst, and, as happens to the hanged, his bladder burst: perhaps the Jews had their servants there with gold and silver jugs and basins which caught the Judaspiss (as it is called) together with the rest of the holy things, thereafter they mixed it into the excrement and ate it among each other and drank it so that they developed such sharp eyes, so that they see such comments in the scripture, which neither Matthew nor Isaiah himself, nor all the angels, let alone we damned *Goyim* can see. Or they looked up the behind of their God, Shed,[79] and found this written in that impossible place. It is not in the scripture, that is certain; therefore it cannot be taken from there.

158. Therefore we damned *Goyim* must leave the all holy Jews their heavenly wisdom, which they found outside of scripture in the piss of Judas and in their Jewish sweat, so they alone will remain smart, and we continue to be fools with Isaiah and Matthew so that we remain with the poor, meager and thin texts which include no such ingenuity when the piss of Judas and the Jewsweat is removed, namely that this *Alma* is pregnant without the contribution of a man, and bear a son without the loss of her virginity. In the entire scriptures, no woman is promised a child unless the man or the father of the child is named; no matter how one looks at it, the child must have a father, except this *Alma*, in whose case there isn't any mention of a man, and still she is promised a son.

159. One ought to prevent the evil and dangerous example, that the widows and virgins could brag that they had children without men, and that they had done it as did the woman in scripture, who also had no men. For it would become a peculiar creature if our daughters, virgins and widows meant to set a lot of children into our houses, and said they had produced it from the snow, and had no father otherwise. Oh, no, one does not produce children from the snow. Moses says, *1 Mos. 1, 27*, a male and female belong there; God did not want to give the blessing for the fruit of the body until he had created them both and gave them together.

160. However, this unique Maria is the only one who had no man to whom she could ascribe the child, but must stand there alone and without a man and hear that she is pregnant and will bear a son; but it shall be extraordinary, a sign and a miracle (says God), not the usual way; yes, it shall be my sign, I will give it and do it, I will be father and husband, she shall be the mother. Now all know, (even a cow ought to know it) that it is not a sign if a young married woman becomes pregnant; what else should the young women do with their husbands, than that they become pregnant? For what else are they created? No one considers it a sign or a miracle but a common condition and example which is seldom missing.

161. Therefore, it is neither a sign nor a miracle that a pregnant woman carries a son and bears him, because it is the common manner, ordered by God, that they

---

79. The Hebrew word "Shadai" means Almighty. The Hebrew word "Shade" means ghost or spirit.

shall not carry vain daughters; only that the Jews want to make God into a careless fool, that he should call that a sign, that, according to their Judas piss they invent a sign, since the women can give their own advice and the physicians can easily do so, whether it is a son or a daughter. But, if this sign remains, showing that the *Alma* could become pregnant without a man, then the Jewish interpretation is not more than jew-piss and jew-sweat; no doubt they feel this themselves and that is why they fight against the first part about the pregnancy of the *Alma*. For it depends on that that the mother is a virgin.

162. If Isaiah were no prophet and Matthew no apostle, which one is obliged to believe on divine grounds, but they were poor history writers, one ought to then easily believe them, as one does concerning Joseph and Philo,[80] and more than the lying, blaspheming and stubborn Jews, who had practiced, with every possible effort, upon the whole scripture for 2000 years how to pile one lie upon the other so that one ought not easily believe one word of theirs. For one does not believe anything said by a lying mouth, even if he speaks the truth (as proverb says) if God presents him with one word of truth, then no one will believe it. *Et illiud: Si mentiris etiam, quod verum dicis, mentiris.*[81] Christ, Our Lord, would not let the devils speak either, even if they spoke the truth; therefore one should in advance prevent the Jews, bad and mendacious as the devils, when two pious honest men or historians say otherwise; how much more when a prophet and an apostle say otherwise. For it is unseemly to elevate the piss of Judas and the sweat of Jews over the salve of the Holy Ghost.

163. Further, it is not Isaiah alone who proclaims the mother of Christ a virgin; God proclaimed it at the beginning of the world after the fall of Adam when he gave the first promise of the New Testament or gospel when he said: "I will bring about enmity between you and a woman, between your seed and her seed, the same shall trample down your head and you will sting him in the heel" (*1 Mos. 3, 15*). God the Lord could of course say so much more and may have wished to say: the seed of a man shall trample down your head, or name the man whose wife it was; but now he is silent about the man and gives the child or the seed alone to the woman; that can be no other than Mary, the mother of Christ; otherwise all children and seed would be attributed to the men.

164. Whether all saints come from Adam, and we Christians until the end are also of that seed, who trample the head of the devil, we are surely not that of ourselves, but from the seed of the woman, of whom we believe just as we, following

---

80. *Flavius Josephus was the "Benedict Arnold" of the Jewish revolt against Rome. Commander of Jewish forces in Galilee, he surrendered to the Romans without a fight, and speaking their language, became attached to their high command. He followed the Roman armies and wrote, among other books, a history of the Jewish revolt 66–70.*

Philo of Alexandria, Egypt, lived from 30 B.C.E. to 45 C.E. A Jewish philosopher, he is credited with introducing rational analysis to Judaism and laying some of the foundation of Christian philosophy by his promotion of the idea of "the Logos" which views the word of God as the will of God.

81. *"And this: If you lie, even when you speak the truth, you will lie."*

him are called and are Christians and the children of God, because we remain in him, that is, in Christ and in the Son of God; we must become like him. Through that belief in the promise of the seed Adam, Eve, Abel recovered from the power of the snake and became his head crushers. Whatever the many fathers meant with this statement couched in allegories we will let go. For some parts of it are worth nothing; for example that Adam should be *portio superior rationes*; Eve *inferior portio*.[82] Such philosophy does not belong here. On the one hand, the church, i.e. Christians see their seed coming from Eve. But that is of a piece with right reasoning, namely, as said before, that all saints are also of such seed through the belief in the one seed of the one woman. And if anyone wanted to pretend that with that there is still no proof that that woman must be a virgin, could however be a widow; very well, God did not want to proclaim it all at once, but proclaim it in time clearer and clearer; it is now sufficient that Christ should be the seed of a woman without the seed of a man; here the virginity is shown. Everything depends on the seed. Thereafter, Isaiah should express that it is an *Alma*, that is, a virgin. The New Testament shall clearly and freely express her name is the virgin Mary of Nazareth, the bride of Joseph and the mother of Christ.

165. The patriarch Jacob assumes (as the Grammatici of the Hebraists warn us) by using the word Silo, 1 *Mos. 49, 10*: "The scepter of Judah shall not be removed, until Silo comes." For it is well to assume that the patriarchs, since Adam's day, daily practiced the promise concerning the woman's seed, which had been her life and her salvation after the sorrow and fall of Adam. Silo is derived from *Silva* or *Siljah* (as they say) and ought to mean secundinam[83] since the child lies in the mother's body, or newly born infants, *continens pro contento*,[84] as the *5 Mos.* at 28, V. 53[85] appears, that he threatens the Jews with such misery that a woman will eat her own Silo (afterbirth), which come from her own body, that is, her infant, newly born by way of *Synecdochen*,[86] which expression is meant in all languages. As if we say, he can empty a barrel, devour a whole pot, although one does not drink nor devour barrels and pots but what is inside of them. "Jerusalem, Jerusalem you beat the prophets to death" *(Matth. 23, 37)*[87] since the stones and the wood did not do that, but people, who are inside. That is an evil house in which there are evil people.

166. Therefore Jacob now wants to say: until the Silo comes, that is (the woman's, not the man's) child comes, that she alone received carried and bore in her body, of whom it was said to our father Adam: the seed of a woman etc. in German, until the son of the virgin comes. For he was not to be received or born in sin as

---

82. a. A higher part of reasoning; b. the lesser part.
83. Here Luther refers to the afterbirth, secundae partus.
84. "Self-control is for the satisfied."
85. "And thou shall eat the fruit of thine own body...."
86. This Greek word passed into Latin and into English and refers to the use of comprehensive terms to stand for specific terms within a larger category or vice versa as Luther explains.
87. "Jerusalem, Jerusalem! you murder the prophet and stone the messengers that are sent to you."

other children of Adam; that is why his mother had to be a virgin, whom no man had touched, nor a widow, who had had a man previously, and who had increased and helped in the original sin. *Psalm 51, 7.*[88]

167. And if the Devil had been willing to have this cause, that Mary were a widow, he should have made us so many Christs, as a widow might have borne children, so that we would not have known which one it is, and therefore had lost the right and only one among so many sons. It otherwise would have been difficult to have kept even this one in view of his anger. For he already began through his manipulations to create another Christ, not the natural son of Mary, but an apparition that had come from her. That is how Helvidius,[89] the fool, sought to give Mary more sons after Christ, according to these words of the apostle: "and Joseph did not recognize his bride Maria until she bore her first son"; such as this he wanted to understand, as if she had had more sons after the first son; the ignorant fool. St. Hyronymus gave him the right answer. In sum, he is the enemy of the seed of the woman, would like to have it annihilated or at least insecure. Since the apostles (as we heard) describe the line of descent so ambitiously that the Jews should not become confused and think it must be a different Jesus, of whom such great things are being said, this one (whom they knew well) the son of Mary could not be it. Oh yes, (they say) he is the same, the single Jesus the son of Mary the son of David, Abraham, and all ancestors.

168. That is why it was necessary that his mother was a virgin, a young virgin, a holy virgin, who freed of original sin and cleansed by the Holy Ghost, no longer bore an only son, a Jesus, who could certainly be her *Siljah*, fruit of the seed from her body, without father, an only Christ. But there is no time here to feature this extensively for I would have to preach how from the seed of the woman there must be a blessing, promised to Abraham, that is, God would have to be like him. I have written and spoken about this elsewhere, that is why I let it be enough now.

169. That the Rabbis make an issue concerning the Hay and the Cholem[90] in Silo does not bother me, they can remove the Cholem; if right away Silo is not to be read as Silah *femenino genere* still the fruit of the woman would be alone, because no man is there, and would be called the son of the Virgin from Judah or of Judah. But, *5 Mos. 28, 53*[91] the man stands by the woman who devours her children; here alone is the fruit of the woman Silo, without a man. Many of his sermons will take place here, and books written, which are forgotten and lost in time; as we see now, as a good book or good sermon lasts hardly a year, and as one says, one sings a new

88. *"I was shaped in iniquity and in sin did my mother conceive me."*
89. *Helvidius was a fourth-century Christian writer whose views were refuted by St. Jerome, also known as St. Hieronymous. Helvidius held that the virgin mother of Jesus had subsequent children and also argued that virginity ranked below matrimony. These views were condemned as heresies by the Church. See William Smith and Henry Wace, A Dictionary of Christian Biography, New York, AMS, 1967, p. 892.*
90. *Hebrew letters.*
91. *"And thou shalt eat the fruit of they own womb, the flesh of thy sons."*

song one year, with the exception of a few people who hold on to this for their descendants. The crowd lets it pass and waits all the time for something new; that is why the Devil holds the whole world more and more as a mistake and remains with that which he received *(Joh. 8, 31)*.

So it happened, and so it goes, from the beginning to the end of the world, that great events shall happen and yet few pay attention to it; the others let it go and forget it.

170. Accordingly, Isaiah would be a fine interpreter, who, as a master, interpreted the word Silo and the woman's seed, as if he meant to say: Do you want to know what Silo and what the woman's seed means? I will tell you: It is the magic sign that the Messiah shall be the son of a virgin, his mother shall be an *Alma* who receives in her virginal body without the contribution of a man.

St. Elizabeth also comes right out with this in that she received Mary happily and said: "Blessed is the fruit of your body" *(Luc. 1, 42)*[92] that is Silo, the fruit *matricis tue*[93] your Siljah, or alone from your body, and without a man; for the child of my body has a father called Zachariah.

171. David sings so as well in *Psalm 22, 10*[94] in the person of Christ: "You have pulled me out of the body of my mother." Here he calls himself Silo, who has come out of his mother's body (not of his father's thighs like all other children). V. 11: "I depend on you since the day of my mother's body, you are my God from the time of my mother's body." No child of Adam can say that, all of whom are born in anger and sin and without God, *Ps. 51, 7*. Alone this one is God's child in grace, at the moment that he is taken from his mother's body, and yet must suffer great martyrdom worthy of grace etc.

172. David's *Psalm, 110, 3*, says further: "From the mother, from the dawn comes the throne of your birth." No matter how the dew falls from the dawn, so your birth comes from the mother (mother does not mean here the whole person of the woman, as in the Fourth Commandment, but refers to what women call the womb in their bodies, *matricem* or *Siljah*.) Now the dew falls from the heavens without any contribution by men, *Mich. 5, 6*,[95] yes, even without clouds, even when the heavens are bright and the dawn the most beautiful, then it falls at its most lovely; no one can say from where or how it began to fall. Thus, Christ came from the other, which is in the body of the virgin Mary, that no father knows of it, yes, not a human being, nor she herself can say or know how it came about that this beautiful dew, Christ, was caught and born in her mother or body. He is called: received from the Holy Ghost, from above.

92. *"Blessed are you among women and blessed is your child."*
93. *Luther meant* Matricis tuae, *"your womb." He carelessly left out the "a" in* tuae, *as was common in the vernacular Latin of the late Middle Ages.*
94. *"You are he who took me out of the womb...."*
95. *"And the remnants of Jacob shall be in the midst of many peoples like the dew from the Lord...."*

173. Accordingly, all Christians may be called, "born like the dew in the heavens," *Mich. 5, 6*. For, because we believe in Him we are equal to Him and are respected. *Joh. 1, 2*: "He gave them the power to become God's children, who are not born of the blood but from God." For no one can say or know where a Christian comes from; "for he is born of spirit and water," *Joh. 3, 5*.[96] The water can be seen just as dew can be felt, but birth is seen by no one. Therefore we too are children received and born of the Holy Ghost, Christlike except that we receive it from grace for His sake; he, however, has it because of His person, because He, God's son, was not permitted to be born again is not entangled in the old birth of sin and death like we the lost children of Adam.

174. In addition we cite as evidence the saying of *Jeremiah* at 31, 22: "The Lord will create something new on earth, a woman will encircle a man." That was read in all of Christendom and understood by Christ and his mother Mary as is only fair. "It shall be something new," he says, that has never been on earth before. From the beginning children were born, there has been regularity, evil and good people have lived, bettered or worsened, as is still the case, and will continue until the end of the world: but here the new miracle shall take place, that has never occurred before, namely a *Nekefa*,[97] a woman who is not a man, shall surround a man, that is, Mary shall receive and bear the son of God.

175. For this must be, if our belief is to be right, that Christ, our Lord, was at the same time God and perfect man in one Person, as the moment that Mary gave her assent to the angel Gabriel and said, "it shall happen to me according to your word, as the dear fathers maintained it against Nestor at the council of Ephesus.[98]

For if that were not the case, she would not be *theotocos*, called the Mother of God, nor would Christ be called her son; of that I have disputed elsewhere, it is too long to discuss now. Let me have only that one unique man, who is God and Human, a child in his mother's womb, no matter how small. He must have been small as the doctors Damacenes and others thereafter calculated it. Accordingly, Elizabeth, full of the spirit, calls Mary the mother of the Lord even though Mary was hardly pregnant for fourteen days, a time that would not permit any other child to live in a woman; as all know.

176. In the end, I cannot let it be, I must proclaim what fine thoughts St. Bernard develops from *3 Mos. 12, 2*, as he says: "When a woman is impregnated, and

---

96. *"I assure you," said Jesus, "that unless a man is born from water and from spirit he cannot enter the kingdom of God."*

97. *The Hebrew word* nekeva *means woman and is derived from the masculine word* nekev *meaning a cavity as in the uterus. However in the Yiddish language the word means whore.*

98. *Nestor was a fifth-century Syrian Christian theologian who taught what is known as "The Nestorian Heresy" to the effect that Jesus had two separate natures as both son of Mary and son of God. This teaching was condemned at the Council of Ephesus in 431 C.E.*

bears a little boy, she shall be unclean for seven days." Here St. Bernard wonders why Moses permits himself to waste his words: when a woman is impregnated, why doesn't he say briefly as follows: any woman, who bears a little boy, shall be unclean for seven days? For all know that all women must be impregnated if they are to bear children, and none bears a child who is not impregnated. From this he concludes that Moses wanted to guard his mother and not express an error concerning the mother of the Lord whom he wanted to exempt from his law, so that she would not be unclean like the other women; thereby announced that some day the mother will come who will bear a little boy although she is not impregnated, who will carry the Silo, a mother's child without father.

177. All of this I had wanted to write at that time, in honor of our dear Lord, Praise and Thanks, to strengthen our belief, in scorn and annoyance for the Devil and his circumcised saints. For I know full well how they insult and desecrate the verses that I cited so that no one should say that I don't know their business, damned them unmistakably although I would not sin against them if I knew their state of mind. No, (praise God) I know full well what their knowledge of the scriptures is. I have proved it in those pamphlets,[99] in the saying of *Jacob 1, Mos. 49, Haggai 2, Daniel 9* and in the article concerning circumcision and the nobility of lineage; in the Schom Hapares part of this small book, *Isaiah 9* and such. I did not want to deal with something I did not know.

178. I do want to show their competence by citing the sentence in *Jeremiah 31, 22* where they say: "A woman will surround a man" should mean: the people of Israel are the woman, God the man. Now Israel was a whore in idolatry; thereafter she was converted and repented and surrounded the man, that is God, and reconciled. If now the words could produce what cannot be true, how can that be called something new on earth? Was the people of Israel never such a whore but was converted later? Ask the Book of Judges. This ought to establish that whatever a rabbi calls new is new and whatever he calls old is old similar to the rule indicated above concerning the left and right hand.

179. But that is yet higher and greater art; at this point they say that the woman is to be understood as the whore Israel; but when they have a wedding, they lead the bride three times around the bridegroom so that they satisfy the saying of Jeremiah, a wife surrounds the husband. Here, *Nekefa*, the woman must mean a virgin, there a whore. Why? Because, that way the rabbis cannot fail when they say, a whore is a virgin, and a virgin is a whore, according to the rule that the left hand is right, if a raven (rabbi) calls her right. And no such new event need have occurred before, when a wife or bride is led around the man three times, for Jeremiah says: "something new shall be on earth, created by the Lord." But here a rabbi found a way out and said what he calls new that is new but what he calls old, that is old, *ut supra.*[100]

99. *Luther refers to his pamphlet* Of the Jews and their Lies.
100. *Literally, this Latin phrase means "that above." Luther means to say that he discussed this matter earlier in this essay.*

180. In sum, the desperate Devil's falsifiers mean nothing but that the holy writ is their own, like a paper of which they carve our little men, little birds, little houses and little children's toys as they want; what they say should be taken for right by both their Jews and us Christians.

181. That is why I want to sit in judgment on the damned rabbis once more. First, then: the Holy Scriptures are not the property of the Jews, of the heathens, nor the angels even less the devil, but God's alone, he alone has spoken and written them, he alone shall explain and interpret them where necessary; devil's and humans shall be students and listeners.

182. Furthermore, it is prohibited for us Christians to believe or view as right the interpretation and commentaries of the Rabbis concerning the scriptures on pain of losing the grace of God and eternal life. We may read it in order to see what kind of devil's work they promote among themselves and protect ourselves from it. For thus says Moses, *5 Mos, 28, 28*: "God will strike you with madness, blindness and a delirious heart." This Moses did not say of the damned *Goyim*, but about his circumcised saints, the noble blood, nobility of heaven and earth, who call themselves Israel. Hereby however, God damns their understanding, explanations and interpretations through their own action as utter madness, blindness, delirium, all that which they belabored in scripture these fifteen hundred years God not only calls and judges false and lies but also deliberate blindness, delirious, mad thing. And how such a sentence reads, so it is also found in the work and in the deed, as you saw above in the saying of Jacob, *1 Mos. 49, 10, Hagg. 2, 7*,[101] about the *Alma*; *Jer. 31, 22* about the *Nekefa*. In sum, they do the same in all pronouncements, as they talk of the Messiah and the right belief. A delirious person must rave.

183. This decision is confirmed, *Jes. 29, 13-14*: "Because this people is too close to me with its mouth, and honors me with their lips, but their heart is far from me, and fear me according to the law of men, which they teach, so I will deal with this people in a wondrous way, most miraculously and most peculiarly that the wisdom of their wise shall be swallowed up and the understanding of their cunning shall hide itself." That was not said of us *Goyim*, but of the people of Israel, which did have excellent, wise, cunning people and prophets and have their book still; but because they became a false, hypocritical nation of liars, who praise God with the mouth but go to Hell with their hearts, they shall also lose and not have the wisdom and understanding of the prophets, but, as they pay back God with their mouth, (that is, with the husks) and serve the Devil with their hearts, (that is, with the kernel) so that they shall have the letters (the empty shells) of the scripture, but the kernel, the true meaning, they shall not even suspect.

184. Just before that, in the same Chapter, V. 11, he says: " All prophets shall be promises for you like the words of a sealed book or letter, which one gives to read

---

101. 1 Mos. 49:10, *"The staff shall not depart from Judah, nor the scepter from between his feet until Shilo comes and the obedience of the people be his."* Haggay 2:7, *"And I will shake all the nations and the costliest things of all the nations shall come."*

(someone) who is literate or not; (he) must say I cannot read what is from him, for it is sealed" etc. Such, the Work (scripture) also gives to the blind, mad Jews; for although they have the book, there is no understanding, either for the Messiah or the Law of Moses for the heathens and the poets, in well done verses, teach better things than the Jews, for they are still worth the most. There are many more statements in the prophets, particularly *Psalm 69, 23f.*, which is introduced by St. Paul, *Rom. 11, 9*: "Their table could become a rope and a trap before them in vengeance. Their face must become dark so that they cannot see," etc.

185. But *2 Cor. 3, 14, 15, 16*, St. Paul paints them correctly as he speaks of the Jews since the time of Christ (for it cannot be understood by anybody else): "To this very day, when Moses is read, the cover remains on their hearts; for their senses are calloused. If however, they converted to the Lord, the cover would fall away." Thus, the Lord himself proclaimed to them, *Matth. 8, 12*: "The children of the land will be thrown into the darkness"; and *Joh. 8, 21*: "I leave forever and you will seek me and die in your sins; for where I go you cannot come." And what drives St. Paul in all his letters, but that he curses the Jew dogs, and circumcision as totally blinded and calloused, of whom one must be on guard?

186. If a Christian seeks understanding in the scriptures from Jews despite such damnation and judgment, what else does he do but that he seeks the face of a blind man, cleverness from a madman, death from life, and grace and truth from the Devil? It is right that he is damned by God, although he is crazy, blind and mad just as are his masters. It is well done that one learns the language and the grammar from them, just as they do as they learn the German language from us, the Welch from Welchmen, and learn the language of the country wherever they are; but our belief and understanding of the scriptures they do not learn. Therefore we too should learn the language from them; but avoid their beliefs and understanding, damned by God.

187. That is why our Hebraists (I have therefore pleaded with them about this for the sake of God) if this work is recommended or important to them should cleanse the holy old Bible of the filth and piss of Judas as they could have altered the points, distinctions, conjugations, construction, significance and whatever else the grammar has and deviate from the interpretation of the Jews so that it agrees with the New Testament, that they be sure to do this with joy as is taught by St. Paul, *Rom. 12, 7*, that the *prophetia* shall be *analogia* and shall be similar to these beliefs. For that is how they did to us, the Bible, these 1,500 years. Wherever they could change the Bible with dots, distinctions, conjugations so as to deviate from our Messiah and belief and dispute the New Testament, they did it with great and mad ambition, as can be seen from the above examples and similar things, *1 Mos. 49, 10, Haggai 2, 7, Daniel 9, 24, Isaiah 7, 14*.

188. Thus *Isaiah 9, 5*, as they made the text, Vajikra, Schemo, Pele etc.[102]

102. Vayikra *is the first word in the Third Book of Moses;* Shemose *is the first word in the Second Book of Moses. In Hebrew usage, these first words are also the names of these books.*

Wonderful, counselor, God, Hero, eternal father call the Messiah prince of peace. Here one can see their arbitrariness, and therefore disregard their points and interpretations, and read it as we read it because it results without difficulties and from the letters, so that one would read Vajikare for Vajikra and all names could be in the nominative. The Hebraists will find more of the same so that one will be able to take it from the thieves in honor what they have stolen shamefully these 1,500 years and perhaps longer. For the main point must be true, that the Holy Scriptures points to and witnesses for the Messiah and our beliefs; who does not understand it that way cannot have it.

189. That is why I said, that Moses and the scriptures are not known by the present-day Jews, nor is it the old righteous Moses, for they have befouled him with their Judas piss. For Moses wants to be the witness of the Messiah, that is certain. But because they deal so shamefully with the Messiah it is impossible for them to understand Moses in a *Pasuk*.[103] This task I would like to have undertaken by my dear lord and friend, M. Bernhard Ziegler in Leipzig, Professor of Hebrew, that he too promote himself for once, like the other Hebraists (Thank God) who have become visible but without much result; for he is an exceptional enemy of the Jewish Judas piss, and is capable and would bring the other Hebraists to him and would cleanse the Hebrew Bible for us. For if she should again be clean and in good Hebrew, then Christians must do it as they have the sense of the Messiah as Paul says, *1 Cor. 1, 24*, "We have the sense of the Messiah," and *Luc. 24, 45*: "He gave them the sense to understand the scriptures;" and *Matth. 13, 11*: "Understanding the secret of the realm of heaven has been given you."

190. Whether one should attack and denounce me, as I failed sometimes in translation, I will accept it with thanks. For how often did Hieronymus fail! And I see how two fine men, Sanctes and Munster, have translated the Bible *studio incredibili et diligentia inimitabili* and have done much good with it. But the Rabbis are too powerful for them, so that they failed also in the analogy of belief, in that they clung too much to the interpretations of the Rabbis. Even I followed their translation too much, so that I have to recall, particularly *2 Sam. 23*,[104] *in verbis novissimis David*, as I will do soon.

191. In this fashion one could weaken the understanding the Jews have of the Bible, and the advantage is that Moses and the prophets did not write with dots,

---

(note 102 continued) *The word* Pele *occurs in the Hebrew sentence frequently cited by Christian theologians as evidence for their views concerning the authenticity of their belief that Jesus is the Messiah. The sentence from* Isaiah 9:5 *is, "For to us a child is born, to us a son is given: and the government is upon his shoulder: and his name is called 'Pele,' [wonderful] yoez el gibbor [Counselor of the mighty God], avi ad [of the everlasting father] sar shalom [the prince of peace]."*

103. *Pasuik is the Hebrew word for paragraph.*

104. *Luther here refers to his last statement on the Jews called "The Last Words of David."*

which is a new human invention[105] after their time; therefore it is not necessary to hold to them as the Jews prefer, particularly wherever they are used to the detriment of the New Testament. One should do the same with the *aequivocatio* and *distinctio*[106] wherever they are used against the New Testament. The Jews enjoy making everything doubtful and uncertain. Therefore, where the *aequivocatio* resorts to a *vocabulo*, one should take the *significatio* which agrees with the New Testament, there one can be certain; and the right *significatio* has a strong witness and assistant in the New Testament; that leaves the other *significatio* for the Jews, the bare hull and *Peres* without witness or assistance.

192. That shall be commanded the Hebraists. Here I will let it go and have nothing more to do with the Jews, or write further or again against them; they have enough on what I already wrote. God give his grace to those who will convert, that they (many) recognize and praise God the father, with us, our creator, together with our Lord Jesus Christ, and the Holy Ghost in eternity, Amen.[107]

---

105. Hebrew has no vowels. However, the German Jews and others who do not live in Israel have invented a series of dots and dashes designed to provide vowels for those whose Hebrew is insufficient to understand the words otherwise.

106. Double meaning

107. Almost the entire literature concerning Vom Schem Hamphoras *is in German, not in English. This is of course understandable, considering that the book was not heretofore available in the English language.*

Nevertheless, mention is made of Luther's writings against the Jews in some English articles and books concerning Luther. One of the more recent of such discussions may be found in a book by Mark U. Edwards entitled Luther's Last Battles. *Quoting the German writer Wilhelm Maurer, Edwards holds that four basic theological principles held concerning the Jews throughout Luther's life. These were 1) that the Jews were suffering under the wrath of God, 2) that the Jews could not be converted by human effort alone but only by divine intervention, 3) that Judaism is always hostile to Christianity and blasphemes God and 4) that there exists a "solidarity of guilt" between Christians and Jews.*

Since Luther, as we have seen, recommended a number of severe anti–Jewish actions which he hoped Christians would take, some modern theologians attempt to divorce Luther's theology from these recommended actions. Edwards rejects this effort to "embrace Luther's theology without also having to embrace his anti–Semitic practices." Edwards argues that because Luther lived in the sixteenth century, and not in ours, he tied his theological description of the Jews closely to his recommendations as to what should be done to the "God forsaken" Jews.

It may well be true that Luther feared Jewish exegesis of the Bible particularly since some early Protestant Bible translators were in fact accepting Jewish interpretations of the Old Testament.

Furthermore, Edwards cites Oberman's view that Luther believed that the Last Judgment was at hand and that therefore he was called upon to defend the Truth against Jews, "papists," Turks and "fanatics," i.e., Protestant Christians whose views differed from his own.

B

Vom Schem Hamphoras und vom Geschlecht Christi (Original German Version)

1. Im nächsten Büchlein habe ich verheissen, ich wollte hinnach lassen laufen, was die rasenden, elenden Juden von ihrem Schem Hamphoras lügen und lästern, wie davon schreibt Purchetus in seinem Buch *Victoria* gennannt. Das will ich hiemit also gethan haben, unserem Glauben zu Ehren, und den Teufelslügen der Juden zuwider, daß auch die, so Juden werden wollen, sehen mögen, was sie für schöne Artikel bei den verdammten Juden glauben und halten müssen. Denn wie ich in jenem Büchlein bedingt, ist meine Meinung nicht, wider die Juden zu schreiben, als hoffte ich sie zu bekehren, habe darum dasselbe Buch nicht wollen nennen "wider die Juden," sondern, "von den Juden und ihren Lügen," daß wir Deutschen historienweise auch wissen möchten, was ein Jude sei, unsere Christen vor ihnen, als vor den Teufeln selbst, zu warnen, unseren Glauben zu stärken und zu ehren; nicht die Juden zu bekehren, welches ebenso möglich ist, als den Teufel zu bekehren.

2. Denn gleichwie wir müssen lehren und schreiben vom Teufel, Hölle, Tod und Sünde, was sie sind und thun, nicht daß wir aus dem Teufel einen Engel, aus der Hölle einen Himmel, aus dem Tod ein Leben, aus der Sünde Heiligkeit wollten machen, welches unmöglich ist; sondern daß wir uns davor hüten: also schreibe ich auch von den Juden. Denn ein Jude oder jüdisch Hertz ist so stock-stein-eisen-teufel-hart, daß es mit keiner Weise zu bewegen ist. Wenn Mose käme mit allen Propheten, und thäten alle Wunderwerke vor ihren Augen, daß sie sollten ihren harten Sinn lassen, wie Christus und die Apostel vor ihnen getan haben, so wäre es doch umsonst. Wenn sie auch so greulich gestraft würden, daß die Gassen voll Bluts rännen, daß man ihre Todten nicht mit hunderttausend, sondern mit zehnhunderttausend rechnen und zählen müsste, wie zu Jerusalem unter Vespasiano und zu Bitter unter Adriano geschehen ist, dennoch müssen sie recht haben, wenn sie auch über diese 1500 Jahr noch 1500 Jahr sollten im Elende sein, dennoch muß GOtt ein Lügner sein, sie aber wahrhaftig sein.

Summa, es sind junge Teufel, zur Hölle verdammt; ist aber doch etwas Menschliches in ihnen, dem mag solch Schreiben zu Nutz und Gut kommen: vom ganzen Haufen mag hoffen, wer da will, ich habe da keine Hoffnung, weiß auch davon keine Schrift. Können wir doch unsere Christen, den großen Haufen nicht bekehren, müssen uns am kleinen Häuflein genügen lassen; wie viel weniger ist's möglich, diese Teufelskinder alle zu bekehren! Denn das etliche aus der Epistel zun Römern am 11. Capitel solchen Wahn schöpfen, als sollten alle Juden bekehrt werden am Ende der Welt, ist nichts; St. Paulus meint gar viel ein anderes.

Aus dem elften Capitel im ersten Theil des Buchs Purcheti, verdeutscht durch D.M. Luther

1. Wir wollen fürder sehen, wie die Juden den Wundersthaten Christi immer so feind gewest sind, daß sie dieselbigen dem Beelzebub, der Teufel Fürsten zuschreiben.

Denn er so viel und große Wunderwerrke, als sonst niemand jemals, gethan hat, wie er selbst spricht Joh. 15. Es ist auch nie erhört, das jemand anders in seinem Namen die Blinden sehend, die Tauben hörend die Lahmen gehend, die Stummen redent gemacht hätte, wie Jesaias zuvor geweissagt hat am 35. v.4 5.: "GOtt, der Vergelter, wird kommen und euch helfen. Alsdann werden der Blinden Augen aufhgethan, und der Tauben Ohren geöffnet werden alsdann werden die Lahmen löcken, wie ein Hirsch und der stummen Zunge wird Lob sagen."

2. Ueber diese vielerlei Wunderzeichen that er noch viel andere mehr, weckte Todte auf, reinigte die Aussätzigen, und machte viel andere Kranke gesund, und that solche Zeichen, die niemand, denn allein GOtt, zu thun möglich waren; noch hat sich der Juden Bosheit, die all Zeit mit bösen Tücken umgangen, sich unterstanden dieselbigen mit Lügen zu lästern und zu schänden, haben ein Buch erdichtet wider Christum, darin sie diese Lügen schreiben:

3. Es ist geschehen zur Zeit Halani, der Königin, die über das ganze Land Israel herrschte, da kam Jesus HaNozri gen Jerusalem, und fand im Tempel des HErrn den Stein, darauf vor Zeiten die Lade der HErrn gesetzt war; auf demselbigen Stein war geschrieben Schem Hamphoras; war desselben Namen Buchstaben lernte und verstand, der konnte thun, was er wollte.

4. Es besorgten sich aber unsere Weisen, wo die Kinder Israel solche Namen lernen würden, möchten sie durch desselben Kraft die Welt umkehren. Darum machten sie zween Hunde von Erz, und setzten sie auf zwo Säulen vor die Thür des Heiligthums. Wenn nun jemand hinein ging und lernte die Buchstaben des vorbesagten Namens, und wider herausging, so bollen die ehernen Hunde ihn so greulich an, daß er vor großem Schrecken vergaß des Namens und der Buchstaben, die er gelernt hatte.

5. Also kam Jesus HaNozri und ging in den Tempel, und lernte die Buchstaben, und schrieb sie auf ein Pergamen. Danach riß er das Fleisch auf an seinem Bein und legte die Zettel drein. Und weil er den Namen nannte, that im nichts wehe, und ging die Haut zusammen, wie sie vorhin gewest war; als er nun aus dem Tempel ging, bollen die ehernen Hunde ihn an, daß der sobald des Namens vergaß da er aber heim kam, riß er mit einem Messer das Bein auf und nahm heraus die Zettel, darauf die Buchstaben standen des Schem Hamphoras, und lernte sie wiederum.

6. Danach sammelte er zu sich 310 Jünglinge aus Israel und sprach zu ihnen: Sehet da, die Weisen sagen, ich sei ein Hurenkind, darum, daß sie wollen über Israel herrschen; ihr wisset aber, daß alle Propheten weissagen von Messia; derselbe bin ich, das ist wahr. Und Jesaias hat von mir geweissagt: "Siehe, eine Alma ist schwanger und wird einen Sohn gebähren, und seinen Namen Emanuel heißen" (Jes. 7, 14.). So hat auch mein Großvater David von mir geweissagt und gesagt: "Der Herr hat zumir gesagt: Du bist mein Sohn, heute hab ich dich gezeuget" (Ps. 2,7.). Also hat mich meine Mutter geboren ohne Zuthun eines Mannes, allein aus GOttesKraft. Darum ich nicht, sondern sie selbst, sind Hurenkinder, wie Hosea sagt: "Ich will mich über ihre Kinder nicht erbarmen, denn es sind Hurenkinder" (Hos. 2,4.).

7. Da antworteten ihm die Jünglinge aus Israel: Bist du Messia, so gib uns ein Zeichen. Was wollt ihr für ein Zeichen von mihr haben? Sie sprachen: Mache einen Lahmen stehend, wie wir sind. Er sprach: Bringet einen her zu mir. Sobald brachten sie zu ihm einen Lahmen, der noch nie auf seine Füß getreten hatte, und er sprach über ihn Schem Hamphoras; zur selbigen Stunde fuhr der auf und stand auf seinen Füßen. Da bückten sie sich alle vor ihm und sprachen: Der ist ohne allen Zweifel Messia. Auch brachten sie zu ihm einen Aussätzigen, über den sprach er den Namen und legte die Hand auf ihn, und er ward sobald gesund. Daher fielen zu ihm viel loser Leute aus unserem Volk.

8. Aber die Weisen, da sie sahen, daß Israel begann an ihn zu glauben, fingen sie ihn, und brachten ihn zu der Königin Halani, die zu der Zeit das Land Israel inne hatte, und sprachen zu ihr: Gnädige Frau, dieser Mensch treibt Zauberei und verführt die Welt. Jesus HaNozri antwortete: Gnädige Frau, es haben die Propheten vor Zeiten von mir geweissagt, der selbigen einer spricht also: "Es wird ein Zweig auswachsen aus dem Stamm Jesse" (Jess. 11:1), derselbe bin ich, von diesem aber spricht David: "Wohl dem der nicht wandelt im Rath der Gottlosen" (Ps. 1,1).

9. Sie sprach: Steht solches in eurem Gesetze, das dieser sagt? Sie antworten: Ja, es steht in unserem Gesetze, aber es ist nicht von ihm gesagt, sondern also ist von ihm geschrieben 5 Mos. 13,5.: "Der Prophet soll getödtet werden, denn er hat unrecht wider Gott gelehrt," aber vom Messiah steht also geschrieben (Jer. 23,6.): "Zu seiner Zeit soll Juda geholfen werden." Darauf antwortete dieser Gottlose und sprach zur Königin: Ich bin derselbige, denn ich kann Todte auferwecken.

10. Die Königin schickte mit ihnen hin ihre allergetreuesten Diener, und der Gottlose machte einen Todten lebendig durch Schem Hamphoras; von Stund an endsatzte sich die Königin und sprach: Wahrlich, das ist ein groß Wunderzeichen, und that den Weisen damit einen großen Hohn, daß sie mit Schanden mußten von ihr weggehen; das that ihnen und den von Israel sehr wehe. Und Jesus Nozri zog hin ins obere Galiläa.

11. Und die Weisen gingen wieder zu der Königin und sprachen zu ihr: Gnädige Frau, dieser Mensch geht mit Zauberei um und verkehrt die Creaturen. Sie aber schickte hin ihre Kriegsknechte, daß sie ihn sollten fangen; aber die Leute in Galiläa wollten's nicht leiden, sondern wieder sie streiten. Er aber sprach: Ihr sollt nicht für mich streiten; denn die Gewalt meines Vaters vom Himmel, und die Zeichen, die er mir gegeben hat, werden mich wohl vertheidigen. Und die Leute von Galiläa machten Vögel aus Thon vor ihm, so sprach er drüber Schem Hamphoras, da flogen die Vögel alsobald; und sie fielen auf ihr Angesicht und beteten ihn an.

12. Auch hieß er zur selbigen Stunde einen großen Mühlstein herbringen und ins Meer werfen; da das geschehen war, sprach der Gottlose das Schem Hamphoras, dadurch machte er, daß der Stein still lag auf dem Meer, und er satzte sich darauf und sprach zu den Kriegsknechten: Gehet hin zu eurer Frau und verkündiget ihr, was ihr gesehen habt. Danach stand er auf vor ihren Augen und wandelte auf dem Meer.

13. Die Kriegsknechte gingen hin und sagten der Königin Halani alles, was sie gesehen hatten. Die entsatzte sich über die Maße sehr und ließ die Weisen rufen, und sprach zu ihnen: Ihr sprecht, dieser Mensch Jesus Nozri sei ein Zauberer, aber ihr sollt wissen, daß die Zeichen, so er thut, beweisen, daß er der wahrhaftige GOtess Sohn sei. Sie aber sprachen: Gnädige Frau, laßt ihn herkommen, so wollen wir seine Schalkheit aufdecken. Indeß gingen die Ältesten Israels hin, und ließen einen mit Namen Judas Scharioth hinein in den Tempel in das Allerheiligste gehen, der lernte die Buchstaben Schem Hamphoras, eben auf die Weise, wie sie Jesus Nozri gelernt hatte, und riß das Fleisch am Bein auf, und alles, was jener gethan hatte.

14. Also kam Jesus Nozri mit seiner Gesellschaft, und die Königin hieß die Weisen auch kommen. Und er trat vor die Königin und sprach: David hat von mir geweissagt: "Es haben mich Hunde umgeben, und die Versamlung der Bösen haben mich umringet" (Ps. 22,17.). Aber das ist dagegen auch von mir gesagt, Jer. 1,8.: "Fürcht dich nicht vor ihnen, denn ich bin mit dir, daß ich dich errette, spricht der HErr." Aber die Weisen widersprachen ihm das.

15. Und er sprach zur Königin: Ich will gen Himmel fahren; denn so hat David von mir gesagt: "Erhebe dich, GOtt, über die Himmel" (Ps. 57,12.), und hub die Hände auf, wie Flügel, durch den Namen Schem Hamphoras, und flog zwischen Himmel und Erde. Da das die Weisen sahen, sprachen sie zu Judas Scharioth, er sollte Schem Hamphoras sagen, und ihm nach hinauf fahren. Der fuhr

hinauf und rang mit ihm, daß sie beide miteinander herunter fielen; und der Gottlose zerbrach einen Arm: das beweinen die Christen jährlich vor ihren Ostern.

16. Zur selbigen Stunde griffen ihn die Israeliten, und verhüllten ihn mit Tüchern, und schlugen ihn mit Ruthen von Granatenbäumen. Und sprachen zur Königin Halani: Ist er GOttes Sohn, so laßt ihn sagen, wer ihn geschlagen hat; aber er konnte es nicht sagen. Die Königin sprach zu den Weisen: Siehe, er ist in euren Händen, thut ihm, was euch gefällt.

17. Da griffen sie ihn, und führten ihn zum Galgen; aber an welchen Baum oder Balken sie ihn hingen, der zerbrach sobald entzwei; denn er hatte durch Schem Hamphoras alle Bäume und Hölzer beschworen, daß ihn nicht konnten annehmen. Da gingen sie hin und holten einen Kohlstengel, der nicht am Baum, sondern am Kraut wächst, daran hängten sie ihn. Solches ist nicht Wunder. Denn im Heiligthum wächst all Jahr ein Stengel, da wohl hundert Pfund Samens dran hängen. *Haec ille.*

18. Wo sind sie nun, die losen Christen, so Juden worden sind, oder werden wollen? Hierher zum Kuß der Teufel hat in die N. geschmissen, und den Bauch abermal geleert, das ist ein recht Heiligthum, das die Juden, und was Jude sein will, küssen, fressen, saufen und anbeten sollen, und wiederum der Teufel auch fressen und saufen, was solche seine Jünger speien, oben und unten auswerfen können. Hie sind die rechten Wirte und Gäste zusammenkommen, haben's recht gekocht und angerichtet. O wie recht ist ihnen beiden geschehen! Der Teufel ward ein schöner Engel geschaffen, daß er mit seinem heiligen engelischen Munde sollte sammt der andern heiligen Engeln das ewige *Te deum laudamus* singen. Das konnte er nicht leiden, und ist ein Teufel worden, der nun mit seinem engelischen Rüssel frißt und mit Lust frißt, was der Juden Unter-und Ober-Maul speiet und sprützet, ja, das ist seine Galrede worden, darin er sich weidet, wie eine Sau hinter dem Zaun um St. Margarethentag; recht, recht, so wollte er's haben.

19. Also ist den Juden auch recht, o recht geschehen. Sie waren berufen, und dazu erwählt, daß sie sollten GOttes Mund sein, wie Jeremias spricht (Jer. 15,19.) und Ps. 81,11.: Thue deinen Mund weit auf, so will ich ihn füllen; sie aber hielten fest zu Maul, Augen, Ohren, Nase, ganzes Herz, und alle Kräfte. Da kam der Teufel, dem sperrten sie auf Augen, Rachen, Ohren, Herz und all Sinne, schiß und sprßutze er sie auch so voll, daß es an allen Orten von ihnen ausschwadert und schwemmt eitel Teufelsdreck; ja, der schmeckt ihnen ins Herz, da schmatzen sie, wie die Säue. So wollen sie es haben. Rufe nun mehr, kreuzige ihn, kreuzige ihn! Schreie mehr: "Sein Blut komme über uns und über unsere Kinder" (Matth. 27,25.) Ich meine, es sei kommen und habe dich funden.

20. Wollen gleichwohl die schönen Artikel des jüdischen Glaubens, in diesem Texte gegeben, nach einander ansehen, damit dem die Lust (Jude zu werden) gebüßt werde, wer sie hat. Willst du nun ein rechter Jude werden, so höre hie zu und lerne den Catechismum des heiligen jüdischen Glaubens, nicht in GOttes Namen.

21. Erstlich mußt du glauben, daß Helena sei Königin gwest im Lande Israel oder Cannan, da unser HErr JEsus Christus gelebt, gelehrt und Wunder gethan hat. Ob hie widerstehen nicht allein die Evangelisten und Apostel, sondern auch das ganze Römische Reich, so dazu mal gestanden; dazu der Juden selbst Zeugniß und Elende, das zur Zeit Vespaniani angefangen, bei 250 Jahren ehe die Helena geboren ist; das mußt du dich nicht irren lassen, sondern also denken: Die Rabbinen (solches Buchs Meister) können nicht irren, Himmel und Erde müßten viel ehe mit GOtt und allen Engeln und Creaturen irren. Das mußt du glauben, willst du ein rechter Jude werden.

22. Also mußt du auch glauben alles, was hie geschrieben steht von der Königin Helena, wie sie mit Jesu HaNozri hat gehandelt und handeln lassen 250 Jahre ehe sie geboren ist; denn solches gehört zu wissen im Catechismo, wer ein Jude werden will. Wo jemand dawider wollte sagen: Die Juden sind zur Zeit der Helene, bei 200 Jahren, nicht im Lande gewest, sondern in alle Welt zerstreut, und Jerusalem weder Tempel noch Regiment gehabt; dagegen mußt du höhnisch lächeln wider die verfluchten Gojim, und also sagen: Unsere Rabbinen schreiben's, darum muß es also sein, wenn gleich GOtt selbst mit aller Schrift und Creatur anders sagt; er muß wohl, was die Rabbinen wollen.

23. Zum anderen mußt du glauben, daß zween eherne Hunde zu der Zeit haben, auch ohne Schem Hamphoras, bellen können; vorhin und jetzt kann's keiner mehr; auch mit ihren eherenen Augen so scharf gesehen, wer aus- und eingangen dazu wer die Buchstaben, auf den Stein gegraben, abgeschrieben habe: das müssen sehr scharfe Augen gewest sein, sonderlich weil sie Erz sind, und durch so dicke Mauern, Thüren und Vorhang haben sehen können. Hie möchte dich vielleicht anfechten, daß alle lebendigen Hunde von der Welt an, die doch natürlich bellen können, solches nicht glaubem würden, wenn sie solches hören und verstehen möchten, viel weniger die ehernen Hunde selbst etc. Aber laß dich's nicht anfechten; was die Rabbine sagen, das ist Recht, frage nicht weiter, willst du ein frommer Jude sein.

24. Hiebei mußt du glauben, daß die Weisen in Israel zu der Zeit nicht klüger gewest sind, denn daß sie den Schem Hamphoras haben mit zween ehenden bellenden Hunden verwahrt, so die verfluchten Gojim wohl andere Weise hätten funden, als mit eisernen Thüren, Gittern und desgleichen. Ob dir hie einfiele, daß die Weisen Israel viel weniger Vernunft hierin gehabt hätten, denn die ehernen Hunde selbst, mußt du solche Gedanken ausschlagen, und denken: Lieber was die Rabbinen sagen, das ist recht, und kann nicht erlogen sein.

25. Zum dritten mußt du glauben daß im Heiligthum zu Jerusalem gewachsen sind jährlich so große Kohlstengel, daß sie stärker weder kein Balken am Galgen gewest sind, und bei 100 Pfund Samen dran gewachsen. Hiebei muß du glauben, daß zu Jerusalem 200 Jahr nach der Verstörung ein Heiligthum gestanden, nicht allein das, sondern daß es sei zugleich ein Kohlgarten und Heiligthum gewest. Wenn nun hiewider alle Historien, Mose und alle Propheten, auch GOtt mit allen

Engeln anders sagen, so ist's erlogen, sondern der Juden Glaube muß recht sein; das merke wohl, willst du ein Jude werden.

26. Zuletzt mußt du dich deß ergeben, was ein Rabbin sagt, es sei wie seltsam es möge sein, so mußt du glauben, es sei recht, unangesehen, ob GOtt selbst anders geböte und sagte. Denn so hat ihnen Moses geboten 5 Mos. 17,8. ff.: "Wenn sie eine Sache nicht verstehen, sollen sie hinauf gehen zu den Priestern und Richtern, so an dem Ort sind, den GOtt erwählt hat etc. Die sollen dir (spricht er) ein Urtheil sprechen; nach dem Gesetze, das sie dich lehren, sollst du thun, und nach dem Recht, das sie dir sagen, sollst du dich halten, daß du von demselben nicht abweichest, weder zur Rechten noch zur Linken." Hie ist's beschlossen (ich hätte schier gesagt, beschissen), da alles was die Rabbinen sagen, soll ein Jude glauben, und nicht davon weichen. Daher sagen sie nun, sie müssen ihren Rabbinen glauben, wenn dieselben gleich sagten, die rechte Hand wäre die linke, und die linke wäre die rechte, wie Purchetus schreibt. Auch thaten mir selbst die drei Juden, so bei mir waren, eben also: wo ich sie zum Text dringen wollte, sprachen sie, sie müßten ihren Rabbinen glauben, wollten mir keines Texts gestehen; derhalben ich hierin Purcheto desto mehr Glauben muß nach eigener Erfahrung.

27. Willst du nun ein frommer treuer Jude werden, so ergib dich, wie gesagt, daß du glaubest, was die Rabbinen sagen, es wider GOtt, Vernunft, Engel oder alle Creaturen. Denn die hörst du, daß ein Jude soll glauben, es sei die rechte Hand nicht die rechte Hand, wenn's ein Rabbi sagt. GOtt hat wohl gesagt, ja er hat's durch sein ewiges Wort geschaffen, geordnet und genannt, daß die rechte Hand solle sein und heißen die rechte Hand, wie es alle Engel und Creaturen bekennen. Aber solches mag wohl die Wahrheit sein, bis ein Rabbi dazu kommt und spricht, nein, es sei nicht also, sondern was ich die rechte Hand heiße das ist die rechte Hand. Was sollte GOttes Wort und Werk sammt aller Engel und Creatur Zeugniß sein wider einen Rabbi, der so weit höher und besser ist, weder GOtt und alle Creatur?

28. Eben also mußt du glauben hie, daß die Königin Helena habe mit ihren Weisen und Jesu diese Geschichte gehandelt 200 Jahre ehe sie ist geboren; item, daß Kohlstengel im Heiligthum jährlich wachsen, so dick als kein Balken, die hundert Pfund Samen tragen; item, daß eherne Hunde bellen; item, daß JEsus durch Schem Hamphoras habe Wunder gethan, Judas Scharioth auch; wie droben gesagt ist hievon. Ja, wenn ein Rabbi dir in die Schüssel vor deiner Nase thäte Dick und Dünn und spräche: Da hast du einen köstlichen Mandelbrei, so müßtest du sagen, du hättest dein Lebenlang keinen besseren Brei gessen. Trotz deinem Halse, und sage anders. Denn, wer die Macht hat, daß er kann sagen, es sei link, was recht, und recht, was link ist, GOtt und aller seiner Creaturen ungeachtet, der kann auch wohl sagen, daß sein Hintermaul das Vordermaul, und sein Bauch ein Breitopf, und ein Breitopf sein Bauch sei.

29. Wenn du nun solches gelernt hast und glauben kannst, so lauf flugs so hin, und laß dich eilend beschneiden, ehe die ehernen Hunde solches sehen, und von Jerusalem kommen, die dir solchen hohen Verstand des allerheiligsten jüdischen

Glaubens wieder ausbellen, oder ehe der Verführer HaNozri mit seinem Schem Hamphoras dich zum Christenglauben bezaubert. Denn nun bist du ein rechtschaffener, feiner, heiliger, kluger Jude, wirst nun selber können link recht heißen, und den Bauch zum Breitopf machen, daran du mit allen Juden zu fressen genug hast dein Lebenlang, wenn ihr schon alle Teufel zu Gast ladet. Danke auch solchen hohen himmlischen Rabbinen, von welchen du so hoch gelehrt und tief geheiligt bist, daß sich GOtt selbst und alle Engel deiner Heiligkeit verwundern müssen, die verfluchten Gojim sind's nicht werth, etwas davon zu richten noch zu hören.

30. Wohlan, es möchte vielleicht der barmherzigen Heiligen einer unter uns Christen denken, ich machte es ja zu grob und unesse wider die armen elenden Juden, daß ich so spöttisch und höhnisch mit ihnen handele. Ach, HErr GOtt, ich bin viel zu geringe dazu, solcher Teufel zu spotten; ich wollt's wohl gerne thun, aber sie sind mir zu weit überlegen mit Spotten, haben auch einen Gott, der ist Meister mit Spotten, und heißt der leidige Teufel und böse Geist. Was ich demselben zu Verdrieß spotten könnte, das sollte ich billig thun, er hätte es auch wohl verdient. Ich will dir ein wenig zeigen (wer's sonst nicht merkete), welch ein unaussprechlicher Spötter er hie ist.

31. Dreierlei Spötterei treibt der hochmüthige böse Geist in diesem Buch. Erstlich spottet er GOtt, den Schöpfer Himmels und der Erden, mit seinem Sohn JEsu Christo, wie du selbst siehst, so du glaubest als ein Christ, daß Christus GOttes Sohn ist. Zum anderen spottet er unser, der ganzen Christenheit, daß wir an solchen Sohn GOttes glauben. Zum dritten spottet er auch seiner eigenen Juden, gibt ihnen solche schändliche, närrichte, tölpische Dinge ein, von ehernden Hunden und Kohlstengeln, etc., daß sich alle Hunde möchten wohl zu Tode bellen, wenn sie verständen, an solchen rasenden, tobenden, unsinnigen, wüthenden, tollen Narren. Ist das nicht ein Meister mit Spotten, der mit einerlei Gespött solche große Spöttereien kann ausrichten? Die vierte Spötterei ist, daß er sich selbst hiemit soll gespottet haben, wie wir, GOtt Lob, an jenem Tage mit Freuden sehen werden.

32. Also spotten die Juden hiemit auch sich selbst am höchsten, daß sie dem Teufel, ihrem Gott, in solcher Spötterei gehorchen und werden zu solchen rasenden Narren. Denn sie thun's nicht irrender Weise, sondern weil sie es wohl wissen, und auch natürliche Vernunft, von GOtt gegeben, sie warnt, weist und überzeugt, daß solches nicht könne wahr sein; noch kitzeln sie sich damit, thut ihnen sanft, und thun's mit Lust, daß sie solche greiflichen schändlichen Lügen und Lästerungen mögen wider uns Christen und Jesum HaNozri vom Teufel hören, lernen und predigen. O recht, recht, Meister und Schüler sind in die rechte Schule zusammen kommen.

33. Weiter. Über solche Spötterei beweisen sie allererst recht ihr überhimmlische Meisterschaft, da sie sagen, Jesus HaNozri (daß soll Jesus von Nazareth heißen) habe sein Wunderzeichen gethan durch Schem Hamphoras, welches soll heißen "der ausgelegte Name"; davon hernach. Hie bekennen sie (wie sie wohl

müssen), daß die Wunderzeichen Jesu HaNozri seien rechte Wahrhaftige Zeichen gewest, und sie zeugen und verdammen sich hiemit selbst, gleichwie ihre Vorfahren in Evangelio, daß er habe Todte auferweckt, Lahme gehend gemacht, Aussätzige gereinigt etc. (Matth. 11,5.) welches sind solche Werke, die allein der einigen, ewigen göttlichen Gewalt zustehen und möglich sind; Menschen, auch Engel vermögen sie nicht zu thun, so wenig als Creaturen aus Nichts schaffen. Solches muß alle Vernunft sagen.

34. Nun siehe mir die zarten Früchtlein an, die beschnittenen Heiligen; solche göttlichen Werke und Wunderthaten schreiben sie zu dem Schem Hamphoras, das ist, den ledigen, todten, elenden Buchstaben, so im Buch mit Tinte geschrieben, oder auf der Zunge schweben, oder im Herzen, auch des Gottlosen, getragen werden. Denn der Schem Hamphoras sei was er wolle; so sind's und können nichts anders sein, denn ledige, todte, ohnmächtige Buschstaben, wenn's gleich GOttes heilige Schrift selbst (das desto ärger ist) wäre, davon die Juden viel plaudern und nicht wissen, was sie plaudern. Was sollten Buchstaben vermögen, als Buchstaben, aus eigener Kraft, wo nichts mehr dazu käme? Was helfen sie den Teufel, Türken, Juden und alle Gottlosen, so solcher Buchstaben, auch GOttes Namens ohn Unterlaß mißbrauchen wider das andere Gebot? Ist doch Satan und aller Gottlosen Namen und Werk auch in heilige Buchstaben gefaßt.

35. Aber die rasenden Juden geben dem Schem Hamphoras die göttliche Kraft, als den bloßen ledigen Buchstaben, ohne alle Verheißung oder Gebote GOttes. Denn sie sprechen allhie, daß auch die Gottlosen und Verführer durch diese Buchstaben viel Wunder und göttliche Werke thun können. Wo sind sie nun, die beschnittenen Heiligen, die sich rühmen wider uns Christen, daß sie allein die sind, so den einigen rechten GOtt ehren, da die verfluchten HaNozri drei Götter anbeten? Hie geben sie die göttliche Macht und Ehre den bloßen, ledigen, todten Buchstaben im Schem Hamphoras so völlig, daß auch die Gottlosen und Verführer, wider GOttes willen und Verbot (in den zehn Geboten), göttlicher Majestät eigene Werke thun können. Oh, das sind Heilige GOttes Kinder, die über den einigen Gott so viel Götter machen, als in dem Schem Hamphoras Buchstaben sind; der sollen 216 sein, wie hernach folgt;.das ist, sie beten an 216 tausend Teufel und nicht den rechten GOtt welchen sie mit dem Schem Hamphoras so schändlich lästern und ihm seine göttliche Ehre stehlen, dieselbige den elenden Buchstaben zugeeinigt.

36. Ach wie recht ist den rasenden Juden geschehen! sie wollten JEsum von Nazareth nicht annehmen für Messiam und GOttes Sohn, damit sie blieben wären bei dem einigen, rechten GOtt, wie wir Christen blieben sind. Denn unmöglich ist's, daß der sollte oder könnte mehr denn einen, den rechten einigen GOtt, annehmen, wer Jesum Christum für den Messiam mit rechtem Glauben annimmt; wiederum, unmöglich ist's daß der sollte bleiben bei dem einigen rechten GOtt, der JEsum Christum nicht für Messiam annimmt mit rechtem Glauben, sondern er muß (wie der Teufel will) fremde und andere mehr Götter annehmen, und sollten's gleich eitel blo(sz)e, todte, nichtige Buchstaben, oder Schem Hamphoras, das ist, gro(sz)e Säcke voll gehäufter Teufel sein. Ja, solche Götter wollten die Juden haben für den rechten GOtt in JEsu Nazareno.

37. Hie möchten sie sagen: Thut ihr Christen doch selbst auch also, sprecht Wörter über das Wasser, so muß es Taufe sein, die alle Sünde wasche und neugeborene Menschen mache. Item, Brod und Wein macht ihr zu Leib und Blut mit Worten; item, ihr legt die Hand dem Sünder aufs Haupt und macht ihn mit Worten von Sünden los. So schreibt euer Luther: Wer in GOttes Wort einen Strohhalm aufhöbe, thäte ein besser Werk, weder alle Mönche, Nonnen, Bischöfe, Pabst etc. Nun sind ja die Worte nichts anders denn ledige, bloße arme Buchstaben: denen gibt ihr gleichwohl die Werke, so göttlicher Majestät eigen sind, als Sünde vergeben, neue Geburt und Erlösung vom Tod.

38. Hievon sind nun wir Christen wohl und genugsam gelehrt und berichtet, daß nicht hie Not ist zu handeln; doch kürzlich zu überlaufen, sagen wir Christen also, daß Wasser freilich nichts denn Wasser ist, daß Worte nichts denn ledige bloße Buchstaben sind, thun und helfen über ihre Natur nichts, viel weniger wirken sie göttliche Werke in uns; denn Wasser und Buchstaben machen keine Taufe. Ich habe oft gesehen, daß ein Pferd oder Ochse einen Eimer voll Wassers ausgesoffen hat, und wenn du gleich die Worte der Taufe drüber sprächest, söffe das Pferd doch keine Taufe, würde auch nicht davon neugeboren; es gehört mehr dazu. Die Taufe aber ist ein solch Ding, daß alle Teufel nicht dürfen einen Tropfen davon schlingen, es sollte ihnen ein Kellerhals werden der wie höllisch Feuer sie brennen würde; sondern sie fliehen, wofern sie können, wo sie die Taufe sehen, dürfen nicht herzu, noch dabei bleiben. Warum das? Wasser und Buchstaben achten sie gewißlich nichts.

39. Aber, weil Gott geboten und befohlen hat, daß wir sollen unsere Hand und Zunge hiezu thun, und das Wasser über den Täufling gießen mit den Worten oder Buchstaben, die er befohlem hat, dazu verheißen und uns versichert aufs allergewisseste, daß er selbst mit seiner göttlichen Gnade und Kraft dabei sein will und solches Werk selbst thun. Hie greifst du, daß wir Christen dem Wasser und Buchstaben keine göttliche Kraft geben, auch nicht sagen, daß (es) unser Thun sei, sondern bekennen, daß es GOttes allein sei und bleibe, der solches will solcher Weise, die ihm gefallen hat, nämlich durchs Wasser und Wort oder Buchstaben, erzeigen und an uns beweisen. Das heißen nicht ledige Buchstaben oder bloß Wasser, das die Kuh säuft, sondern darin GOtt sich verbindet, daß er an uns und durch uns, als sein Werkzeug, seine Gnade und Kraft wolle üben. Und sind also beide, Wasser und Buchstaben in der Taufe (sonst nicht) voll und reich von GOttes Gnaden und Kraft, darum daß er's so verheißen hat und offenbart, er selbst wolle es thun. "Gehet hin, tauft" (spricht er), nicht in eurem Namen, sondern "im Namen" etc. daß es sei ein Werk des Vaters, Sohns und Heiligen Geists.

40. Daher verwerfen wir auch den Pabst samt seiner ganzen Kirche, der hat alle Welt erfüllt mit gleicher Gauklerei, Zauberei, Abgötterei, denn er hat auch sein sonderlich Schem Hamphoras; da fährt er zu, bezaubert das Wasser mit losen, bloßen ledigen Buchstaben, gibt vor, es sei Weihwasser, das die Sünde abwasche, der Teufel verjage, und andere viel Tugend habe; will's GOtt nachthun, wie ein Affe. Item, bezaubert des gleichen das liebe Wachs mit nightigen ledigen Buchstaben, verkauft's Kaisern und Königen für heilige Agnus Dei, das viel, viel

Tugend soll haben, nährt sich also hiemit, ja, ward reich in der Welt, recht wie ein erzlästerlicher Gaukler, Zauberer und Abgötter. Also bezaubert er auch Kappen und Platten und alle Welt mit bloßen Worten oder Buchstaben, daß sie Mönch, Nonne, Pfaffen werden, Messe halten und verkaufen, Heilige anrufen und feiern, Ablaß lösen, Todtenbeine anbeten, dem Teufel dienen, nämlich den Himmel, da der Teufel Abt und Pabst innen ist.

41. Daß er hiezu braucht gute Worte der Schrift, und GOttes Namen, ist desto ärger; GOtt hat's ihm nicht befohlen, sondern vielmehr hart verboten. Es heißt: "Du sollst GOttes Namen nicht mißbrauchen"; darum ist seine Kraft nicht dabei, sonder sind ledige, bloße ohnmächtige Buchstaben. Geschieht aber zuweilen etwas dadurch, so ist's nicht GOttes, sondern des Teufels Werk, damit seine Lügen und Zauberei (durch GOttes Verhängen) zu stärken und die Ungläubigen zu verführen, aber die Gläubigen damit zu versuchen und zu warnen; wie wir sehen das die Milchdiebe und andere Zauberinnen oft großen Schaden thun. Haben doch die Türken auch solche Gäucherei unter sich, führen bei sich im Kriege Briefe, arabisch, sehr schöhn geschrieben (der ich etliche gesehen), daß sie durch solche ledige, bloße Buchstaben oder, wie sie es nennen, gute heilige Worte wollen vor Waffen und Fährlichkeit sicher sein. Also füllt der Teufel alle Welt mit Zauberei, Abgötterei, Gäucherei, als hätte er nichts mehr zu thun, denn am jedem Ort sonderliche Schem Hamphoras zu stiften.

42. Hie, achte ich, wäre es wohl Zeit, und sollte den Leser schier die Lust rühren, zu wissen, was doch Juden Schem Hamphoras sei. Ich zwar, wie jetzt gesagt, weiß und bin's gewiß, daß es nichts anders sei noch sein möge, denn eitel ledige, bloße arme Buchstaben. Doch ihre Narrheit und des Teufels Bosheit aufzudecken, will ich's hie anzeigen, so viel ich's vermag und weiß: mag, wer's nicht anders hat, lesen Antonium Margaritam. Es steht 2 Mos. am 14, 19. 20. 21. ein Text, der lautet also:

43. "Und der Engel GOttes, der vor dem Heer Israel her zog, erhub sich, und machte sich hinter sie, und die Wolkensäule machte sich auch von ihrem Angesicht und trat hinter sie, und kam zwischen das Heer der Egypter und das Heer Israel. Es war aber eine finstere Wolke, und erleuchtete die ganze Nacht, daß sie die ganze Nacht, diese und jene nicht, zusammen kommen konnten. Und Mose reckte sein Hand aus über das Meer, und der HErr ließ es hinweg fahren durch einen starken Ostwind die ganze Nacht, und machte das Meer trocken, und die Wasser theilten sich von einander."

44. Dieser Text hat im Hebräischen 216 Buchstaben, die theilen sie in drei Riegen oder Verse, so kriegt ein jeglicher Vers zweiundsiebzig Buchstaben. Man könnte wohl sechs guter Verse draus machen, aber die Rabbinen wollen's nicht so haben. Hie merke nun die hohe Kunst Schem Hamphoras. Wenn du die drei Riegen unter einander schreibst, daß gerade ein Buchstabe unter dem anderen steht, so thue also: Nimm den vordersten Buchstaben in der ersten Riege, und den hintersten in der anderen Riege, und den vordersten in der dritten Riege,

setze sie zusammen, so hast du ein Wort von drei Buchstaben; solcher Weise nach thu mit allen Buchstaben in den drei Zeilen oder Riegen, so findest du zweiundsiebzig Worte, da ein jegliches drei Buchstaben hat.

45. Sie können's fein thun im hebräischen Alphabet, da alle Buchstaben Ziffern oder Zahlbuchstaben sind; denn sie zählen mit Buchstaben wie die Griechen. Wir haben aber nicht mehr denn sieben Zahlbuchstaben, C.D.I.L.M.V.X. Doch will ich's zum groben Exempel, uns Deutschen zu zeigen, versuchen, und setze drei Riegen von zwölf Buchstaben, daß der Text sei dieser:

```
L  V  C  I  M  I  L  X  D  I  C  V
L  V  X  L  I  C  V  M  D  V  M  I
I  V  D  I  C  V  D  I  C  L  I  I
```

46. Hie nehme ich den vordersten Buchstaben L in der ersten Riege, und den hintersten I in der ander Riege, und den vordersten I in der dritten Riege, da wird aus das Wort LII. Thust du mit den andern Buchstaben hernach auch also, so wird das Wort VMV daraus; thust du mit den dritten Buchstaben also, so wird das Wort CVD daraus. Thue mit den vierten Buchstaben auch also, so hast du das Wort IDI und so fortan, wie die Juden thun mit den drei Versen Mosis, und zweiundsiebzig Wörter draus machen, ein jegliches mit drei Buchstaben. Diese drei buchstabischen Wörter, so aus solcher Kunst gemacht werden, bedeuten nichts, sollen auch nichts bedeuten, gleichwie du hie ein Exempel siehst, daß uns Deutschen die vier Worte LII, VMV, CVD, IDI nichts bedeuten. Indeß steht der Text Mosis für sich selbst in seiner natürlichen Deutung, wie er gelesen wird.

47. Ich hätte mein Exempel auch gern deutlicher gemacht, aber die Zahlbuchstaben können's nicht so rein geben, aber hilf du ihm mit einem kleinen Nachdenken; denn es soll so viel gesagt sein:

Luci milks die Ku
Luxli kum zu mir
Jude kau du die Klien.

48. Aber weil k.a.e.n. etc. nicht Zahlbuchstaben sind, habe ich sie müssen heraußen lassen, und so böse wendisch oder dänisch Deutsch reden.

49. Nun fragst du: was sollen denn die zweiundsiebzig dreibuchstabischen Worte, aus dem Text Mosis gemacht? Da höre zu das andre Stück großer Kunst. Sie sollen Ziphra oder Zahlbuchstaben, nicht mit Lesebuchstaben sein; nicht grammatisch, wie man sie in der Schule liest, sondern arithmetisch, wie man sie in der Rechenschule liest. Als, in meinem Exempel must du nicht lesen LII, wie in der Schule, sondern wie in der Renterei oder Rechenstube, daselbst liest man nicht LII, sondern zweiundfünzig. Das andere Wort lieset man nicht VMV, sondern tausend und zehn. Das dritte Wort liest man nicht CVD, sondern sechshundert und fünf. Das vierte Wort liest man nicht IDI, sondern fünfhundert und zwei, und so fortan.

Also müssen alle Buchstaben im Text arithmethisch werden, denn grammatisch dienen sie nicht zum Schem Hamphoras.

50. Weiter und zum dritten mußt du lernen, daß solche dreißuchstabischen zweiundsiebzig Wörter, aus dem Text Mosis gemacht, sind Namen zweiundsiebzig Engel (wie schier wäre mir das Wort Teufel entfahren), gleich als wenn ich mich in meinem Exempel die vier Wörter, LII, VMV, CVD, IDI spräche, daß vier Engel also genannt sind, daß einer heißt arithmethisch zweiundfünfzig, der andere tausend und zehn, der dritte sechshundert und fünf, der vierte fünfhundert und zwei. Also heißen dort die zweiundsiebzig Engel auch mit eitel Zahlnahmen, der eine siebzehn, der andere zweiundzwanzig; item neunundsiebzig und so fortan.

51. Was sollen nun did zweiundsiebzig Engelnamen, arithmetisch verstanden? Räuspere dich, hie will's werden, hie kommen wir an das rechte Hauptstück. Du hast nun gehört, daß der ganze Text Mosis 2 Mos. 14,19. 20. 21. sei eitel arithmetisch oder Zahlbuchstaben worden, in dreimal zweiundsiebzig Engelnamen getheilt. Nun mußt du lernen, daß die selbigen aritmethischen Buchstaben wiederum grammatisch oder Lesebuchstaben werden doch gleichwohl aritmethisch bleiben; nämlich also: der erste Engel LII heißt arithmetisch zweiundfünfzig. Nun mußt du hingehen und suchen etwa ein ander Wort oder zwei, das auch zweiundfünfzig begreife, doch also, daß es GOtt nenne, oder etwas von GOttes Kräften oder Werken sage. Als, daß ich meinem Exemplar folge: "Gottes Liebe ist's gar." Hie hörst du eine verständliche Rede, das die Liebe GOttes thue und vermag alles, und sind die Buchstaben alle grammatisch oder Lesebuchstaben; dennoch findest du drinnen des Engels LII Namen arithmetisch, das ist ein L und zwei I die sind zweiundfünfzig. Solcher Exempel magst du für dich selbst mehr suchen, als: "GOtt hilft fein," "GOtt gibt heil" etc. Da hörst du eine verständliche Rede nach der Grammatica oder Lesebuchstaben, und hast doch zugleich drinnen die arithmetischen oder Zahlbuchstaben LII, die des ersten Engels Namen geben. Also mußt du thun mit den andern Namen der zweiundsiebzig Engel, das ist, mit dem ganzen Text Mosis 2 Mos. am 14., der in diese zweiundsiebzig Engelnamen getheilt ist, wie du droben gehört hast.

52. Hie siehst du nun, wie GOttes Name, oder was man von seinem Thun redet, gemengt ist in der zweiundsiebzig Engel Namen. Und ist also ein ausgelegter oder ausgebreiteter Name durch den ganzen Text Mosis, das ist, durch aller zweiundsiebzig Engel Namen, das heißt Schem Hamphoras, der ausgelegte Name. Solche Alfänzerei thut sich fein im Hebräischen, da sie alle Buchstaben können arithmetisch machen, und LII, das ist zweiundfünfzig, mit andern und andern Worten geben, das wir in unserem ABC nicht vermögen, die wir wenig, das ist, allein sieben arithmetische Buchstaben haben, C.D.I.L.M.V.X. Darum ob ich wohl kann LII auch mit diesen Buchstaben xxxxxii, oder, xl und xij schreiben, so ich doch kein grammatisch Wort oder Rede draus machen, wie sie im Hebräischen thun können. Denn x ist, sonderlich uns Deutschen, seltsam im Brauch, könnten sein wohl entbehren in der deutschen Sprache. Darum müssen wir in dieser Rede:

"Gottes Liebe ist's gar," auch mehr grammatische Buchstaben borgen, damit des Engels LII Name, die zweiundfünfzig, arithmetisch und doch auch grammatisch geschrieben werden.

53. Ob du hier wolltest einreden, man könnte der Weise nach auch wohl ein anderes aus den Zahlbuchstaben machen, beide im Hebräischen und Lateinischen oder Deutschen, nämlich also: "Satan hilft fein," "Satan gibt Heil." Da ist auch LII, des ersten Engels Name, das ist, zweiundfünfzig; oder also: "Hans hilft fein" etc. Hie würde Schem Hamphoras auch des Teufels und Menschen ausgelegter Name werden, und alles, was ich wollte. Aber lieber Goj, du hast droben gehört, du müssest glauben und thun, was die Rabbinen sagen und wollen; wo nicht, so möchten die ehernen Hunde von Jerusalem kommen, und dich zu Tode bellen, und, das noch wohl fährlicher ist, der Kohlstengel einer im Heiligthum mit den 100 Pfunden Samens auf dich fallen, und dich zu Tode schlagen.

54. Endlich, damit das Schem Hamphoras ganz vollkommen werde, thun sie das Benedicte oder Gebet dazu, legen zu einem jeglichen Namen der zweiundsiebenzig Engel einen Vers aus dem Psalter, daß es zweiundsiebenzig Verse werden. Mit dieser hohen Andacht (da hab) ja Acht auf, daß in einem jeglichen Vers stehe der große Name GOttes Jehova, genannt Tetragrammaton; doch, daß du die Buchstaben ja nicht nennest, sondern dafür Adonai sprechest; denn er ist unaussprechlich, davon hernach weiter. Nun has du den Schem Hamphoras ganz und vollkommen, nun bist du nicht allein ein beschnittener, rechter Jude, kannst nun thun allerlei Wunderzeichen, wie der Verführer, Jesus Nozri, dadurch gethan hat. Nun flugs hingelaufen gen Jerusalem, und durchs Schem Hamphoras den ehernen Hunden geboten, daß sie hunderttausend junge eherene Hunde zeugen, da ein jeglicher zehnmal heller belle denn die zween alten, auf daß sie die verfluchten Gojim in aller Welt taub, blind, thöricht, und stracks zu Tode bellen, und also den heiligen Kindern Israel die Welt einräumen, auch ehe denn ihr Messias Kochab kommt.

55. Wie geht's aber zu, daß sie nun 1500 Jahre im Elende solcher Kunst und Gewalt des Schem Hamphoras nicht gebraucht haben, sonderlich, da sie von den Römern durch Vespasianum zerstört (denn da war es Zeit Wunder zu thun), und hernach, da sie mit ihrem Messia Kochab unter Adriano erschlagen und zerstreut wurden? Ist der Rabbiner Antwort, daß sie jetzt nicht fromm genug, dazu im Elende und Ungnaden GOttes sind, auch in so langer Zeit vergessen sei, was der zweiundsiebenzig Engel Kraft sei. Aber wie ist das möglich? Sind sie doch ewig das edle Blut und beschnittene Heilige, das eigene Volk GOttes vor aller Welt, die liebsten Kinder Israel, die nicht mehr denn einen GOtt anbeten. Solche können nicht in Ungnaden sein (die Schrift möchte denn falsch sein) wie die verfluchten Goijim, die mehr denn einen GOtt anbeten und Jesum HaNozri für Messiam halten dieselben müssen in Ungnaden sein, daß ihnen kein Schem Hamphoras helfen kann.

56. Auch wie könnten die Weisen so töricht worden sein, daß sie die Kraft der Engel im Schem Hamphoras vergessen haben sollten, die so klug gewest sind, daß

sie solchen Schatz mit zween ehernen Hunden verwahrt haben, auch desselben so ganz mächtig gewest, daß sie Judas Scharioth haben hinein lassen kommen? Vielmehr haben sie selbst mögen hineingehen, wann sie gelüstet und gleich Judas Scharioth worden sein mit allem Thun, wie sie noch jetzt sind. Darum muß der große Schatz solcher Kunst gewißlich noch bei ihnen sein, von Judas Scharioth und ihren Vorfahren auf sie geerbt, und kann nicht so verloren sein. Wie könnten sie sonst so gewiß davon noch jetzt schreiben und reden?

57. Du verfluchter Gojim bist zumal ein grober Gesell, willst und kannst nichts lernen. Hast du nicht droben gehört, wenn ein Rabbin sagt, die rechte Hand ist link, so ist sie link; sagt er, die linke Hand ist recht, so ist sie recht? Also auch, wenn hie ein Rabbin sagt, die Kunst Schem Hamphoras ist verloren, so ist sie verloren; sagt er aber, sie haben sie noch, so haben sie dieselbe noch; sagt er, sie sind in Ungnaden, so sind sie in Ungnaden; sagt er sie sind das liebe auserwählte Volk GOttes allein, so sind sie es gewiß.

58. Hie wirst du mich vielleicht fragen: Woher haben die Juden diese hohe Weisheit, daß man Mosis Text, die heiligen unschuldigen Buchstaßen, so soll theilen in drei Verse und arithmetische oder Zahlbuchstaben draus machen, auch zweiundsiebenzig Engel nennen, und Summa, das ganze Schem Hamphoras dergestalt stellen? Da laß mich mit zufrieden, frage die Rabbinnen drum, die werden dir's wohl sagen. - Ja, ich will zuvor von dir hören deine Meinung, ehe ich ein Jude werde; denn darnach weiß ich wohl, daß ich den Rabbinen glauben muß aber du hast mir der Juden Cathechismum verheißen, das halt auch.

59. Wohlan, ich weiß nicht sonderlich, wo sie es her haben aber nahe hinzu will ich wohl raten. Es ist hie zu Wittenberg an unser Pfarrkirche eine Sau in Stein gehauen, da liegen junge Ferkel und Juden unter, die saugen; hinter der Sau steht ein Rabbin, der hebt der Sau das recht Bein empor, und mit seiner linken Hand zeucht er den Pirzel über sich, bückt und kuckt mit großem Fleiß der Sau unter dem Pirzel in den Talmud hinein, als wollte er etwas Scharfes und Sonderliches lesen und ersehen; daselbst her haben sie gewißlich ihr Schem Hamphoras. Denn es sind vorzeiten sehr viel Juden in diesen Landen gewest, das beweisen die Namen der Flecken, Dörfer, auch Bürger und Bauern, die hebräisch sind, noch heutiges Tages, daß etwa ein gelehrter ehrlicher Mann solch Bild hat angeben und abreißen lassen, der den unfläthigen Lügen der Juden feind gewest ist. Denn also redet man bei den Deutschen von einem, der große Klugheit ohne Grund vorgibt: Wo hat er's gelesen? Der Sau im (grob heraus) Hintern.

60. Hiezu möchte men leicht das Wort Schem Hamphoras ziehen und kehren, nämlich Peres schama, oder, wie sie thun, kühnlich meistern und machen Scham HaPeres, so lautet's nahe zusammen. Gleich als wenn ein Deutscher im Hören oder lesen verstände närren für nähren; item, er hat mir mein Gütlein fein gebessert, ja, gewässert. Also spottet der leidige böse Geist seiner gefangenen Juden, läßt sie sagen Schem Hamphoras, und große Dinge drinnen glauben und hoffen; er aber meint Scham Haperes, das heißt: "hie Dreck," nicht der auf der Gasse liegt,

sondern aus dem Bauch kommt. Scham heißt "hie oder da," Peres, das der Sau und allen Thieren in den Därmen ist, wie Moses deß im dritten Buch (Cap. 8, 17) braucht, da er gebeut, das Sündopfer zu verbrennen, mit Haut und Haar, und mit seinem Peres, Mist etc.

61. Denn der Teufel hat die Juden besessen und gefangen, daß sie müssen seines Willens sein (wie St. Paulus redet), zu narren, zu lügen, lästern, auch fluchen GOtt und alles, was GOttes ist. Dafür gibt er ihnen zu Lohn sein Gespötte, Scham Hapere, und hilft ihnen glauben, daß dies und alle ihre Lügen und Narrenwerk sei köstlich Ding. Ueber solch schrecklich Gefängniß klagen und schreien sie nicht, sie begehren auch nicht mit dem geringsten Seufzen daraus zu kommen, sondern sind gern drinnen, halten's für sonderlich große Freiheit, wollten uns Christen auch gerne hinein haben. Aber über das römische Gefängniß schreien sie, da sie nicht von uns, sondern wir von ihnen gefangen sind in unserm Lande, Geld und Gut; denn ihnen ist zu wohl, gehen gleich mit uns um, wie der Teufel mit ihnen umgeht, spotten unser zu unserem Schaden, wie der Teufel ihrer spottet, zu ihrem ewigen Verdammniß.

62. Damit aber greiflich sei, wie die tollen Juden mit Gäucherei umgehen, lassen sie den vorhergehenden Text stehen, da GOtt Mosi gebeut und verheißt, er solle das Meer theilen mit dem Stecken, und die Kinder Israel hindurch führen etc. Ja, das ist der rechte Haupttext, der's thut, da GOtt verheißt und gebeut, daß es geschehen solle. Aber die unsinnigen Juden fragen hienach nichts, nehmen die Geschichte vor sich, wollen's wie die Affen mit bloßen Buchstaben nachthun, das GOtt dazumal durch sein Wort und Gebot gethan hat, machen keinen Unterschied zwischen GOttes Macht und Wort, und zwischen ihrer nightigen, unsinnigen Gäucherei.

63. Auch da sie sagen, wer der zweiundsiebenzig Engel Kraft und Tugend wisse, der könne sie durch Scham Haperes zwingen, daß sie ihre Kraft beweisen müssen. Erstlich, in dem reden sie zwar recht, daß wer solcher zweiundsiebenzig Engel Kraft wisse, der kann gewißlich alle Wunder dadurch thun; gleich als das gewißlich wahr ist, wer einen Esel hat der Gold auswirft, der kann wohl Gulden haben; wo ist aber solcher Esel? Im Schlaraffenlande. Also sind diese zweiundsiebenzig Engel der Juden auch nirgend denn im Schlaraffenlande, sind nie geschaffen, werden auch nimmermehr geschaffen; darum sagen sie recht, daß wer dieser Engel Kraft weiß der thut auch Wunder, wiviel und warum er will. Wir werden's auch also sehen, daß sie durch solcher Engel Kraft werden ihren Messiam GOtt abzwingen ohne seinen Dank, und Jerusalem gewinnen; wie kann's fehlen?

64. Zum anderen sehen wir, wie gerne die rasenden, unsinnigen Narren wollten die Engel bezaubern und unter sich zwingen mit losen bloßen Buchstaben, und über GOtt sich selbst setzen, daß die Engel thun müßten, was sie wollen. Das sind sie, die Heiligen aller Heiligen, welche allein einen GOtt anbeten. Denn anbeten einen GOtt heißt bei ihnen, mit dem Maul einen GOtt nennen, und mit Knieen oder Bücken sich als gegen einen GOtt erzeigen, aber mit dem Herzen auch

bloße Buchstaben, das ist, viel tausend Lügen und Teufel anbeten; denn worauf sich ein Herz verläßt und vertraut, das ist sein GOtt: wie wir Christen, die tollen verfluchten Gojim, sagen, daß wenn der Mund gleich schweigt, und die Kniee sich nicht beugen, dennoch, weil das Herz ohne Unterlaß sich beugt, das ist, seine Zuversicht, Trost und Vertrauen setzt auf den einigen GOtt, so heißt's ohn Unterlaß recht und fein den einigen GOtt angebetet.

65. Aber das ist lauter Narrheit bei diesen beschnittenen Heiligen, die können zuweilen mit dem Maul Einen GOtt nennen (das ist genug) indeß aus Buchstaben Engel und Götter machen, wie viel sie wollen, auf welche sie nicht allein vertrauen (das wir tollen Goijim anbeten heißen), sondern auch bezaubern, wozu sie wollen. Sollte nicht billig ein Goj gerne Jude werden, da solche große Macht funden wird, daß man kann Götter und Engel machen unsers Gefallen, so wir verfluchten Gojim nichts mehr können denn glauben, daß uns der einige GOtt alle gemacht hat, und die Engel uns, nicht wir sie regieren. Summa, ein Jude steckt so voll Abgötterei und Zauberei, als neun Kühe Haar haben, das ist, unzählig und unendlich, wie der Teufel, ihr Gott, voller Lügen ist.

66. Wenn sie doch solcher Gäucherei mit Buchstaben dazu brauchten, wie man die Kinder in der Schule lehrt die Buchstaben kennen, daß sie müssen das Abc vor sich und hinter sich sagen, die Buchstaben so und so versetzen, damit sie lernen Silben machen, und sich zum Lesen üben, oder machten Bilder und Figuren mit den Buchstaben, wie etlich Knaben geschickt sind, und vorzeiten thaten; so wäre es zu leiden, als ein lustig Kinderspiel, wie man solches mit Hebräischen Buchstaben besser, denn mit anderen Buchstaben, thun könnte; aber den bloßen, ledigen, armen Buchstaben Kraft zueignen, und solche Kraft, die Wunder thun könne, auch durch die Gottlosen und Feinde GOttes, das ist nicht allein "Pfui dich an" und Scham Haperes, sondern der leidige, lästerliche Teufel selbst mit aller seiner Bosheit aus der Hölle heraus. Denn mit der Weise beten die Juden so viel Teufel, ja, so viel tausend Teufel an, so viel sie Engel erlügen in ihrem Sham Haperes (wie droben gesagt). Denn sie bauen hierauf und glauben's für die Wahrheit, das doch eitel Lüge ist. Das heißen die Propheten Abgötterei, *confidere in medacio*, auf Lügen trauen, welche Ehre allein GOtt gebührt.

67. Nun siehe, wie feine Heiligen die Juden sind; sie verdammen uns verfluchte Gojim, daß wir mehr wie einen GOtt anbeten, aber sie, die gebenedeite Frucht des edlen Bluts und beschnittenen Heiligen, beten allein den einzigen GOtt an. Das ist wahr, wenn die zweiundsiebenzig erlogenen Engel, das ist, zweiundsiebenzig tausend Teufel ein einiger GOtt heißt, so beten sie gewißlich einen GOtt an. Da siehe auch, was du für ein großer neuer wunderthätiger Heiliger worden bist, wenn du Christum verleugnet hast und ein Jude worden bist. Denn du kannst durch Scham Haperes machen, daß alle Teufel ein einiger GOtt sind, welches GOtt selbst nicht vermag. Darum denke und sei den Rabbinen dankbar für ihren allmächtigen Schmeißdreck, ah, Scham Haperes wollte ich sagen. Ja so geht's wenn man GOttes Wort nicht hören, sondern ohne aufhören lästern will, so muß man alle Teufel hören und anbeten, unser HErr Christus spricht, Joh. 5, 43.: "Ich

bin kommen in meins Vaters Namen, und ihr habt mich nicht angenommen; ein anderer wird kommen in seinem Namen, den werdet ihr annehmen."

68. Auch wenn sie doch solche Gäucherei und Narrenspiel ließen schlechte Lügen sein, wie die Stocknarren oder Gaukler lügen, und bekennten, daß es nicht rechte Wunderzeichen wären, was durch den Schem Haperes geschehen sollte: so könnte man noch hoffen, sie möchten mit der Zeit des Narrenspiels müde werden und von sich selbst einmal davon abstehen. Nun aber hängen sie dran den leidigen bösen Klick, daß drauf vertrauen, als auf die Wahrheit GOttes selbst, machen damit einen Gottesdienst und Abgötterei draus, wollen's nicht für falsche Wunderzeichen halten, was durch Schem Hamphoras geschehe; es soll Ernst sein, und rechte göttliche Kraft drinnen wirken, wie sie droben im Text sagen, daß JEsus, der Gottlose, habe einen Todten auferweckt, vor den Dienern der Königin Helena; wie ihre Vorfahren auch bekannten, daß JEsus die Teufel recht austriebe, und keine Gaukelei wäre, doch in Beelzebubs Namen (Luc. 11.15). Denn ihr Schem Hamphoras soll alles und alles vermögen, rechtschaffener Weise.

69. Zuletzt, ist das eine übermachte Lästerung, daß sie solche göttliche Kraft in dem Schem Hamphoras, Wundezeichen zu thun, auch den Gottlosen, als Judas Scharioth und dem Verführer (wie sie lästern) Jesu HaNozri zulegen, lehren solches wissentlich. Dies Stück bewegt auch Lyra, Burgensis und viel andere, ohne daß sie nicht heftig genug drum zürnen. Ich weiß nicht, wie ich hievon reden oder schreiben soll. Sage ich, daß die Juden hierin rasend, blind, wahnsinnig (wie Moses von ihnen sagt), voller Teufel sind, so ist's alles zu gering gesagt von denen, die den einigen GOtt abeten wollen, und solche Lästerung ausspeien dürfen, solches, dazu auch lehren als ein Recht. Begreif's wer da kann, was das sei gesagt, daß die göttliche, ewige Majestät, unser aller lieber Schöpfer, gelobt und zu loben in Ewigkeit, soll gescholten werden von diesen verdammten jungen Teufeln, daß er durch seine Wunderwerke, die er allein thut und thun kann, Psalm 72, 18., ein Zeuge, Bestätiger, Ueberhelfer, alle der Lügen, der Verführung, Irrthum Abgötterei, Lästerung, und aller Greuel, die sie unserm HErrn JEsu Christo auflegen; oder könne und wolle sich nicht wehren wider eines falschen Propheten Scham Haperes.

70. Ich kann solches nicht anders verstehen, denn daß sie hiemit GOtt selbst zum Teufel, ja, zum Knecht aller Teufel machen, der alles Uebel, was der Teufel will, helfe thun, stärken, vollbringen, Lust und Liebe habe, arme Seelen zu verführen, sich selbst mit seinen eigenen Wunderweken zu schänden, und wider sich selbst tobe, Summa, ärger sei denn alle Juden, ja, denn alle Teufel. Ach mein GOtt, mein lieber Schöpfer und Vater, du wirst mir gnädiglich zu gut halten, daß ich (gar ungern) von deiner göttlichen ewigen Majestät so schändlich muß reden wider deine verfluchten Feinde, Teufel und Juden. Du weißt, daß ich's thue aus Brunst meines Glaubens und zu Ehren deiner göttlichen Majestät, denn es geht mir durch Leib und Leben.

71. Aber recht ist dein Gericht, *justus es, Domine*. Ja, so sollen Juden und sonst niemand gestraft werden, die dein Wort und Wunderwerk so lange Zeit ohn

Unterlaß verachtet, verspottet, gelästert und verdammt haben, daß sie nicht fallen müssen, wie andere Menschenkinder, Heiden und wer sie sind, in Sünde und Tod, nicht, oben in die Hölle, da man nicht tiefer fallen kann. Denn das ist auch ihre Sünde, die nicht ärger geschehen kann, da sie dich, den rechten ewigen GOtt, nicht allein verachten mit Ungehorsam und Lästerung deines Wortes, sondern dich selbst zum Teufel und Knecht unter alle Teufel machen wollen, daß du mit deiner herrlichen göttlichen Kraft sollst Zeuge sein und dienen dem Teufel in seinen Lügen, Lästerungen, Mord, und was mehr Teufelswerk sind; recht, recht sind deine Gerichte, himmlischer Vater, lästern wollten sie, deß haben sie genug bekommen.

72. Moses schreibt, 5 Mos. 18, 20. ff. daß GOtt nicht wolle lassen Wunder oder Zeichen geschehen auf eines falschen Propheten Wort, und spricht: "Das sollst du merken, wenn das nicht kommt, das der falsche Prophet sagt, so sei gewiß daß solch Wort der HErr nicht geredet hat." Aber diese Teufel sagen, daß Jesus HaNozri sei ein Verführer und falscher Prophet; gleichwohl sind rechte Wunderzeichen, als, Todte aufwerwecken, Lahme gehend, Aussätzige rein machen (welches niemand denn allein GOtt vermag zu thun) durch solchen Verführer geschehen. Es wäre nicht Wunder, daß uns Christen, so solche GOttes verfluchte, offenbarliche Lästerer bei uns leiden, längst GOttes Zorn mit höllischem Feuer in Abgrund der Hölle mit den Juden versänkt hätte, ohne daß uns geholfen hat, daß wir's nicht gewußt und derhalben unschuldig sind an ihrem greulichen Thun. Aber nun hinfort sehet zu, lieben Fürsten und Herren, so Juden unter sich schützen und leiden, was ihr thut, ich will entschuldigt sein. Hie ist nicht allein Christus, unser HErr, und der Vater in Christo, sondern GOtt der Vater selbst in sich selbst, das ist, in seiner göttlichen Majestät ärger denn Christus geschmäht, und zum Teufel und aller Teufel Knecht gemachet. Schreie nun mehr, Jude, schreie nun: Kreuzige ihn, sein Blut sei auf uns und unsern Kindern; es ist geschehen, das du haben wolltest.

73. Es ist genug hievon gesagt, es muß ein Christenherz und Ohren wohl gern wollen, daß es nichts davon hören noch gedenken müßte, denn es ist zu greulich, schrecklich und unmäßlich.

74. Gegen diesen Greuel ist's etwas geringer, was sie von dem Namen Tetragrammaton narren und geifern, davon ich auch ein wenig sagen muß ihre Thorheit zu offenbaren uns Deutschen. In der heiligen Schrift hat GOtt viel Namen, aber vornehmlich zählen sie zehn, unter welchen ist einer, den sie den großen und Tetragrammaton, den allerheiligsten halten, darum, daß die anderen zuweilen auch den Engeln und anderen Creaturen werden mitgetheilt, dieser aber allzeit GOtt allein. Hie sind sie so heilig und geistlich, daß sie denselbigen Namen mit dem Munde nicht nennen, sondern an seiner Statt einen andern, oder die vier Buchstaben desselben Namens, Jod, He, Vof, He denn er soll unaussprechlich sein. Daher spricht St. Hieronymous: Die Griechen, weil sie diese Buchstaben nicht gekannt, haben sie PJPJ gelesen, das He für ein P angesehen.

75. Erstlich laß ich das fahren von den zehn Namen, als das nicht neu, sondern auch St. Hieronymous *"in epistola ad Marcellum"* anzeucht, da er sie zählt also: El, Elohim, Elohe, Zebaoth, Eljon, Ejhe, Adonai, Jah, Jehovah, Schadai. Andere machen's anders; ich halte nichts davon. Es sind wohl mehr GOttes Namen in der Schrift, denn diese, als, Ab, Bore, Or, Chai etc., Vater, Schöpfer, Licht, Leben, Heil, und dergleichen. Und was kann gutes heißen oder sein, das nicht GOtt zuvoraus zugeeignet werden muß als der's in ihm selber hat, wie Christus spricht: GOtt ist allein gut; wir aber von ihm alles empfangen, was wir sind und haben. Aber jetzt wollen wir den einen Namen, Jehovah genannt, handeln, mit welchen der Teufel und Juden viel Zauberei und allerlei Mißbrauch und Abgötterei treiben.

76. Dieser Name Jehovah, nach der Grammatica, kommt her von dem Wort Haja, oder Hava, das heißt Lateinische *fuit, in praeterito, esse,* Deutsch: wesen, oder sein; und das J kann sein *nota nominis verbalis*, wie Josaphat, Jesias, Jeremias und viele andere Namen, und ist so viel, als im Lateinischen *ens*, im Griechischen *on*. Wir Deutschen müssen sprechen: "er ist's"; und wird also *Trigrammaton* im Latein, Dygrammaton im Griechischen, Hexagrammaton im Deutschen, oder wollen wir schlecht "ist" nehmen, so ist's auch Trigrammaton. Daß sie nun vorgeben, der Name Jehovah solle unaussprechlich sein, wissen sie nicht was sie lallen; meinen sie die Buchstaben, so kann's nicht wahr sein, den er heißt JEhovah. Und so er kann mit Federn und Tinte geschrieben werden, warum sollte er nicht auch mit dem Munde der viel besser als Federn und Tinte ist, genannt werden? Oder warum heißen sie ihn nicht auch unschreiblich, unleserlich, undenkerlich? Summa, es ist faul Ding. Thun sie es aber von Ehren wegen, so sollten sie es auch in allen anderen Namen thun, und dieselben auch unaussprechlich sein lassen. Denn es heißt: "Du sollst GOttes Namen nicht mißbrauchen," darum ist das auch faul. So sagt's die Schrift nirgend, daß einiger GOttes Name soll unaussprechlich sein, sonst wären die alle unschuldig so Gottes Namen mißbrauchen, weil sie sagen möchten, sie hätten seinen Namen nicht können nennen, schweige denn mißbrauchen.

77. Da sagt sie wohl, GOttes Wesen, Gewalt, Weisheit, Güte, und was man mehr von GOtt sagen kann, sei unaussprechlich, unmeßlich, unendlich, unbegreiflich etc., daß nicht die Buchstaben oder Silben, sondern dasjenige, so damit bedeutet wird, unaussprechlich sei. Ja, so müßte man vom unaussprechlichen Namen GOttes reden. Denn er hat sein Wesen von niemand, hat auch keinen Anfang noch Ende, sondern ist von Ewigkeit her, in und von sich selbst, daß also sein Wesen nicht kann heißen "gewest" oder "werden," denn er hat nie angefangen, kann auch nicht anfahen zu werden, hat auch nie aufgehört, kann auch nicht aufhören zu sein; sondern es heißt mit ihm eitel ist oder "wesen," da ist, Jehovah (2 Mos. 3, 14). Da die Creatur geschaffen ward, da ist schon sein Wesen, und was noch werden soll, da ist er bereitan mit seinem Wesen. Auf diese Weise redet Christus von seiner Gottheit, Joh. 8,58.: "Ehe denn Abraham ward, bin ich"; spricht nicht: Da war ich, als wäre er's hernach nicht mehr; sondern: "ich bin," das ist, mein Wesen ist ewig, ist nicht gewest, wird nicht werden, sondern ist ein eitel Ist.

78. Darum, wie sein Ist, Bin, oder Wesen unbegreiflich ist, so ist's auch unaussprechlich, denn keine Creatur kann begreifen das, so ewig ist. Daher die Engel ewig selig sind, denn sie können sich des ewigen Wesens GOttes nich satt sehen und freuen, noch begreifen; und wo es zu begreifen wäre, so könnte es nicht ewig sein, müßte selbst auch ein Ende oder Anfang haben, und könnte niemand ein Wesen geben noch erhalten, weil es selbst ungewiß seines Wesens wäre. Weiter, ist seine Weisheit, Macht, Güte, etc. auch ewig und unbegreiflich, weil es nichts anders denn sein göttliches Wesen selbst sein muß. Zum dritten, das wohl höher ist, daß im göttlichen Wesen ist GOtt Vater, Sohn, Heilige Geist, drei Personen im einigem, ewigem, unbegreiflichem Wesen. Ja, solches alles von GOtt sagen, das möcht ein unbegreiflicher, unaussprechlicher Name heißen. Wer will ein solch wunderlich Wesen nennen, ausdenken, aussprechen, ausschreiben? Auf die Weise werden vielleicht die Alten den Namen Jehovah unaussprechlich genannt haben, weil er GOttes Wesen, nach der Grammatica, bedeutet, welches (wie gehört) ein eitel Ist, von Ewigkeit, und drei Personen gennant wird.

79. Hiemit sollte man sich bekümmern, und solch Jehovah, das ist, göttliches Wesen lernen erkennen und suchen in der Schrift, wie er sich selbst hat offenbart, durch sein Wort, in diesem Leben, und dort offenbaren wird, ohne Wort, in jenem Leben. Aber das ist den Juden zu hoch, ja, gar nichts, sondern so thun die zarten Heiligen: mit dem Munde ehren sie die Buchstaben des Namens Jehovah, der soll und muß unaussprechlich sein, aber das göttliche Wesen, welches durch die Buchstaben bedeutet wird, begreifen sie und messen's mit Ellen, Pfunden und Scheffeln, daß es muß sein, wie groß lang, breit, tief, schwer und voll sie wollen. Das merke dabei, GOtt hatte ihnen den Messiam verheißen welchen er auch gesand hat, nach seiner göttlichen, wunderlichen, unbegreiflichen, Weisheit; so fahren sie zu und malen ihm ein Bild oder Form vor, stellen seiner Weisheit ein Maß und Begriff, wie er solle Messiam senden, nämlich wie der Kochab eine Weise vornahm, nicht wie Jesus von Nazareth; denn ihr Messia soll sich nicht kreuzigen lassen, sondern die Heiden todtschlagen und die Juden zu Herren in der Welt machen.

80. Keine andere Weise soll das ewige göttliche Wesen und seine ewige unbegreifliche Weisheit finden oder treffen, sondern in dieser vorgestellten Weise von Menschen sich zwingen, begreifen und umfangen lassen; wo nicht, so soll er nicht ihr GOtt sein. Denn sie sind's, die GOtt können Ziel, Maß, Gewicht, Weise und Gestalt geben, nicht allein in seinen Werken, sondern auch in seinem ewigen göttlichen Wesen, daß er nicht müsse drei Personen sein in einigem Wesen. Denn da stehen sie mit ihrem Zirkel und Winkeleisen, mit Ellen und Bleischnur, die werden's nicht leiden von GOtt, daß er sollt so ein unbegreiflich Wesen sein, und die nicht viel klüger, weiser und verständiger sein lassen, denn GOtt selbst ist. Was ist's nun, daß die Juden mit dem Munde den buchstabischen Namen nicht nennen noch aussprechen, aber mit dem Herzen sein göttliches Wesen, das rechte Jehovah, nicht allein nennen, aussprechen, urtheilen, sondern auch eintreiben und zwingen in ihren Scheffel? Also müssen sie thun, ist ihre Weise (wie Jesias am 29,13. weissagt), mit dem Munde die Buchstaben ehren, und mit dem Herzen schänden und lästern; noch soll GOtt sich lassen immer narren, daß sie also die Kerne verschlingen, und speien ihm die Hülsen unter die Augen.

81. Sie sind dahingegeben, daß sie nichts Rechtaschaffenes thun, leben noch reden, sondern eitel verkehrt, blind, rasend, unsinnig Wesen führen müssen, wie Mose sagt. Es muß köstlich Ding sein, daß sie den Namen Jehovah nicht nennen, sehen dieweil nicht, daß sie denselben führen in dem schändlichen Mißbrauch zu ihrem Scham Haperes, daß sie ihre zweiundsiebenzig erdichteten Engel, das ist, zweiundsiebenzig Lügen und Teufel, mit demselben heiligen Namen GOttes zieren, ehren und stärken, dazu allerlei Zauberei, Gäucherei und Abgötterei damit treiben. Ich wollte und sie wären's auch wohl werth, daß sie nicht allein den Namen Jehovah nicht nennen, sondern auch keinen Buchstaben in der ganzen Schrift nennen, lesen, schreiben, hören, noch haben müßten, denn sie brauchen's doch GOtt zu Schanden, der Schrift zu Unehren, und ihnen selbst zum Verdammiß.

82. Und wie kann's auch anders sein, lieber Bruder! wenn GOttes Wort uns nicht leuchtet, und den Weg weist, Ps. 119, 105. und sein Licht uns nicht scheinet im finstern Ort, 2 Petr. 1, 19., so kann ja nichts anders da sein, denn Finsterniß, Irrthum, Lügen, die wir uns selbst erdichten. Siehe unsere Erfahrung an, da wir unter dem Pabstthum sein göttlich Wort aus den Augen gethan hatten und Menschenlehre dafür ergriffen, welche dicke Finsterniß, Lügen und Greuel wir da angebetet haben mit Messen, Fegfeuer, Heiligendienst, Möncherei und eigenen Werken etc.

Nun haben die Juden kein Wort GOttes, darum muß eitel Finsterniß da sein, weil die Beschneidung und Mosis Gesetz nicht länger gilt denn bis auf Messiam, der sollte sie ein anderes lehren, 5 Mos. 18,15., wie er gethan hat; das wollten sie nicht annehmen, müssen's ja also machen, daß sie nicht thun, was sie wollen. Zu der Zeit, da Mosis Gesetz ihnen geboten war, wollten sie es nicht thun, schlugen alle Propheten drüber todt; jetzt, nun es nicht mehr geboten ist, wollen sie es thun, und schlagen drüber todt Messiam, und alle seine Christen; vorzeiten mit der That, jetzt mit vollem Willen, Begierde und Wunsch ihres Herzens. Es ist der Zorn GOttes über sie kommen, wie sie verdient haben.

Der Andere Theil

83. Von Anfang des Evangelii, so St. Matthäus und St. Lucas beschrieben haben, hat sich geregt die Frage: Warum die beiden Evangelisten so ungleich (oder, wie es viel gedeutet haben, so wieder einander) die Personen oder Glieder des Geschlechts unsers HErrn Jesu Christi, und sonderlich, daß sie alle beide einträchtiglich die Schnur oder Riege der Personen im Geschlecht führen und enden auf Joseph, und nicht auf Mariam und Christum; daraus die Klugen gerne wollten schließen, es sei nicht beweist, daß Christus vom Stamm David sei, weil er nicht von Joseph komme, welchen die Evangelisten wohl fein führen, nach der Schnur des Geschlechts von David, und plötzlich denselben Joseph lassen, dafür Mariam setzten.

84. Hie haben sie alle zu thun, sonderlich die Juden, darnach Julianus der Kaiser mit seinen Heiden; item, viel der alten Lehrer, auch der neuen nicht wenig; jene

haben die zu meistern, diese sich zu verwundern, als wäre unser christlicher Glaube hierin falsch, ungewiß oder ganz finster.

85. Erstlich, den Juden zu antworten, so jemand mit ihnen wollt reden. Nachdem der Jude, so mich bewegt hat, nähestmal von den Juden zu schreiben, auch dies Stück anstach; es könnte nicht beweist werden, daß Jesus vom Stamm Juda wäre, weil der Evangelist Matthäus den Stamm Juda auf Joseph, und nicht auf Maria führte; darum könnte er nicht Messia sein, vom Stamm Juda und David beweiset. Stachlig und giftig sind die Schlangen, und suchen's genau, ob sie unsere Bücher könnten falsch machen. Denn sie fragen nicht darum, daß sie von uns wollten lernen und die Wahrheit wissen, sondern stackern und stacheln uns mit solchen Fragen zu Hohn und Spott unsers Glaubens, als den wir nicht beweisen können.

86. Darum soll man den giftigen, stachligen Schlangen auf den Kopf treten und also antworten, aufs allerstumpfste und rauheste, dem Teufel zu Trotz; Daß Maria, die Mutter Jesu sei vom Stamm Juda und Hause Davids, sagt nicht allein der Evangelist Matthäus (deß sie lachen), sondern auch Mose, der allererste, darnach alle Propheten einträchtiglich. Und wenn wir Christen sonst nichts hätten vom Alten Testament, denn allein Mosen, so hätten wir genug und reichlich genug, zu beweisen, daß MAria müsse vom Stamm Juda und Hause Davids sein, also, daß solches auch alle Teufel und alle Welt (schweige die elendenden rasenden Juden) nicht sollen umstoßen.

87. Also spricht aber Mose, 1 Mos. 49, 10.: "Es soll der Scepter von Juda nicht weggethan werden bis das Silo komme." Hie ist's beschlossen, daß Silo oder Messia soll vom Stamm Juda kommen, wie das auch bei den Schlangen, wie giftig sie sind, keinen Zweifel hat. Item, 5 Mos. am 18, 15., spricht er also: GOtt wird dir einen Propheten erwecken aus deinen Brüdern, gleich wie mich, den sollst du hören." Folgt (V. 18 f.): "Ich will (spricht GOtt) ihnen einen Propheten erwecken aus ihren Brüdern, gleich wie dich, und will meine Worte in seinen Mund legen, daß er mit ihnen rede alles, was ich ihm gebieten werde, und welcher Mensch ihn nicht hören wird, das will ich selbst rächen."

88. Hie steht's geschrieben, daß Maria sei vom Stamm Juda und David, darf keiner Beweisung mehr; diesem Schilo und Propheten sind die Juden vor andern schuldig zu gehorchen, wie Moses hier gebeut und GOtt selbst dräuet. Nun hat dieser Schilo und Prophet gesagt, seine Mutter Maria sei vom Stamm Juda und David, hat's also seinem Evangelisten Matthäus befohlen zu schreiben. Darum haben die stachligen Juden hiemit ihre Antwort: Glauben sie Mosi nicht, daß er solches von Maria rede, so it's nicht vonnöthen, sind's auch nicht werth, daß sie Matthäum sollen oder einigen Christen hören noch einige Wahrheit glauben, sondern Schem Hamphoras, ja, Scham Haperes sollen sie glauben. Solcher Glaube gehört solchen Heiligen.

89. Wir Christen wissen (und kann kein Teufel noch Jude leugnen), Daß Messia oder Silo müsse vom Stamm Juda und Hause Davids kommen. Hat er nun

keinen Vater, sondern allein eine Mutter, so muß die Mutter gewißlich auch Davids Tochter sein. Das kann keinen Zweifel haben, weil ihr Sohn, der Messia, muß vom Hause Davids sein. Summa, wer da glaubt, daß Jesus von der Jungfrau Maria geboren, sei der rechte Messia, der hat schon bekannt, versiegelt und beweist, daß seine Mutter Maria muß vom Hause Davids sein, so wohl und gewiß als Joseph, ihr Bräutigam, und viel gewisser.

90. Ja, hie stößt sich's mit den Juden: sie wollen den JEsum nicht zum Messia haben, darum stackern sie uns also mit ihren giftigen, lästerlichen Stachelworten von Joseph und Maria; denn da liegt ihnen nicht viel an, ob Maria sei vom Hause David oder nicht. Und wenn sie es selbst gesehen hätten, daß sie von David geboren wäre, wie Salomo und andere seine Kinder, dennoch würden sie nicht glauben, daß Jesus, ihr Sohn, Messia wäre. Um den Sohn ist's ihnen zu thun, deß wollen sie nicht; wissen wohl, die Schälke und falschen Mäuler, wenn JEsus Messiah ist, daß nicht mehr zu fragen ist, ob Maria vom Hause David sei.

91. Eben um denselbigen Sohn ist's uns Christen auch zu thun. Denn so er nicht Messia soll sein, so fragen wir nichts danach, wo seine Mutter Maria herkommt, ja, so wenig, als wo Sara (Isaaks Mutter) oder andere unbekannte Frauen herkommen. Ist er aber Messia, so spricht GOtt durch Mosen zu den Juden: "Den sollst du hören." Und glauben wir Christen den Evangelisten und Aposteln das hohe, einige, große Hauptstück, das JEsus sei Christus oder Messia, warum sollten wir nicht auch glauben alle anderen geringeren Stücke? Denn wer nicht glaubt noch glauben will, daß JEsus Messia sei, dem ist nicht noth, daß er wisse, wer oder wo seine Mutter sei; ja, es wäre ihm gut, daß er nie kein Wort aus der ganzen Schrift gehört hätte, auch wohl besser, daß er nie geboren wäre. Denn GOtt hat's auf den Mann alles gesetzt, alles geweist, alles gewandt, alles gerichtet, ihm alles in die Hand gegeben; wer den hat, der soll's alles haben; wer den nicht hat, der soll nichts haben; so heißt's.

92. Und wie wollten wir thun, wenn Sanct Matthäus und Lucas solche Schnur der Geburt nicht beschrieben hätten? Wie viel Dinges ist unbeschrieben, wie St. Johannes am letzten spricht. Und zu Wahrzeichen schreibt er selbst viel, das Matthäus, Marcus, Lucas ausgelassen haben. Welcher Christ wollte nicht gar gerne wissen, was der HErr die dreißig Jahr gethan habe vor seiner Taufe? St. Paulus allein hat JEsum viel herrlicher und reichlicher beschrieben, wie er Messia sei, denn alle anderen; noch geht er mit seiner Mutter und Geschlecht so kurz hindurch, daß er sie nur einmal, dennoch ohne Namen, anzeigt, Gal. 4.4.: "Er ist (spricht er) von einem Weibe geboren" and Röm. 1,3.: "Der geboren ist aus dem Samen David, nach dem Fleisch." Er weiß, der liebe Apostel, wenn dies Hauptstück da ist, daß JEsus Messia geglaubt wird, so muß sich alles finden, was die Wahrheit ist, oder muß nicht von nöthen sein zu finden: "Denn in ihm (spricht er) sind verborgen alle Schätze der Weisheit und Erkenntniß" (Col. 2, 3.) daß der Heilige Geist alsdann nichts Falsches läst lehren noch glauben.

93. Aber die Juden, die beschnittenen Heiligen, tragen einen stolzen Muth, brüsten sich und starren mit ihrem Hals steif wider uns verfluchten, elenden Heiden,

und halten gewiß, daß nicht wir, sondern sie allein die heilige Schrift haben; darum ist's ihnen lächerlich, was wir von der Taufe, Sacrament, Schlüsseln und anderen Artikeln des Neuen Testaments lehren, weil sie es nich finden in ihrem Buch. Sie meinen, es müsse alles in ihrem Buch allein stehen, oder könnte nicht Recht sein. Also auch, weil sie in ihrem Buch nicht finden diese Worte: Maria ist Davids Tochter, oder vom Hause David, so mäulen und rüsseln sie sich dagegen, als wären sie gewiß daß es müsse nichts sein.

94. Wohlan, ich will sie mit ihrer eignen Münze bezahlen und sagen, daß sie auch nicht Juden sind: denn es steht nicht ein Buchstabe in der heiligen Schrift von diesen Juden, und sie vermögen's nicht zu beweisen aus ihrem Buch, daß sie Juden oder Israels Same sind; das getraue ich ihnen wohl zu wehren. Weiter sage ich ihnen mit rechtem Ernst und auf mein Gewissen: Wenn nicht mehr da währe, denn das Alte Testament, so wollte ich schließen, und sollt mich deß kein Mensch anders bereden, daß diese jetzigen Juden müßten sein etwa eine Grundsuppe aller losen bösen Buben, aus aller Welt zusammen geflossen, die sich gerottet, und in die Länder hin und her zerstreuet hätten, wie die Tattern oder Ziegeuner und dergleichen, die Leute zu beschweren mit Wucher, die Länder zu verkundschaften und zu verrathen, Wasser zu vergiften, zu brennen, Kinder zu stehlen, und andre allerlei Meuchelschaden zu thun; gleich wie Bruder Richardus schreibt in der Verlegung des Alkorans, von den Assissinen, die von den Saracenen in alle Welt geschickt werden, die weltlichen Herren listiglich zu erwürgen und, was sie können, zu ermorden, ob sie also die ledigen Länder, und ohne Herren, einnehmen könnten, und heißen Ismaeliten. Davon magst du lesen das 10. Capitel in der Verlegung des Alkorans.

95. Solche Meinung sollten mir stärken die Historien, so man von den Juden schreibt, und täglich mehr und mehr erfährt in aller Welt, darüber sie oft vertrieben, verbrannt und erschlagen sind, wie in jenem Buch gemeldet ist. So sieht man auch, wie gern sie sich bei den Herren und Edelleuten eindringen, geben Arznei vor; item, Kunst und Zeichen und Buchstaben wider allerlei Waffen und Eisen, damit sie die Christenheit erfüllt haben. Denn auch die Dorfpfarrherren und Küster mit solcher Gäucherei umgangen, bei welchen wir in der Visitation viel der Bücher funden vom dem Namen Tetragrammaton, Anaisapta, und viel seltsamer Gebete, Zeichen, Namen der Engel und Teufel, die gewißlich hebräisch sind. So haben wir auch erfahren, wie sie den Edelfrauen weidlich von den Krankheiten zum Kirchhof geholfen, deß sie ohne Zweifel in die Faust gelacht haben.

96. Ich hörte etwa vor dreißig Jahren sagen, wie sich ein Jude Bei Herzog Albrecht zu Sachesen hatte eingedrungen, der ihn auch solche Kunst lehrte wider allerlei Waffen, daß er nicht sollte können gestochen, gehauen, schossen etc. werden. O es sind feine Künste, die Herren so hinan zu führen, daß sie listiglich umkommen sollen. Aber Herzog Albrecht war klug, wollte der Kunst zuvor gewiß sein, ritt mit dem Juden hinaus ins Feld und sprach: Jude, ich muß die Kunst an dir versuchen, zeucht aus und sticht durch den Juden, daß er da lag todt, und konnte ihm selbst sein Schem Hamphoras, Tetragrammaton, und andere seine Gäucherei nicht helfen. Daß dich (sprach der Herzog), du Bube, wie solltest du mich um mein

Leben hinangeführt haben! Ja, er hätte vielleicht gar sanft in die Faust gelacht. Nun war es besser, daß der Herzog am Juden versucht denn daß der Jude am Herzog versucht sollte haben. Ich habe auch noch einen Krystall bei mir, der Herzog Friedrichs zu Sachsen gewest, den mir mein jetziger gnädigster Herr, Herzog Johannes Friedrich, geben hat, der ist mit güldenen hebräischen Buchstaben und Zeichen, ohne Zweifel auch auf den Schlag zugerichtet. Aber der selbig Fürst war viel zu klug zu solcher Gäucherei. Aber gleichwohl versuchten's die Buben.

97. Ja, so sage ich, für solche losen bösen Buben, und für keine rechten Israeliten, wollt ich diese Juden halten, wenn nicht mehr da wäre denn das Alte Testament. Denn dasselbig sagt uns von Juden, die im Lande Canaan gewest, und noch sein sollten, und ob sie weggeführt würden um ihre Sünde willen, sollten sie doch ja längst wieder heimkommen sein, nach der Verheißung Mosis 5 Mos. 4.31. 3 Mos. 26, 44. Weil aber das nicht geschehen ist, kann man nicht anders denken, denn daß sie mit der Zeit versiegen und ganz untergangen (wie Moab, Ammon und andere mehr Völker), oder gar in ein ander Volk verändert sind, und nichts davon blieben denn eine faule Neige von zugelaufenen fremden Buben oder Zigeunern, die sich beschneiden und stellen, als wären sie Juden, denn sie auch kein Stück in Mose oder Propheten halten. Daß sie aber rühmen das alte Testament, das haben wir besser weder sie. Daß sie sich beschneiden, das thun die Türken auch, und ist nichts mehr Wahrzeichens da jüdischer Art oder Bluts, sondern eine rechte Mördergrube, vor allerlei Bosheit und Büberei, Land und Leute zu beschädigen und zu beschweren. So findet man auch in dem "Bettelbuch" daß die selbigen Rothwelsch reden, da viel Hebräisch unter ist, zum Zeichen daß sie bei oder von den Juden sind.

98. Aber weil das neue Testament zeugt, daß die Juden sollen unter alle Heiden zerstreut, und Jerusalem von den Heiden zertreten werden, bis die Zeit der Heiden erfüllt sind (das ist, bis an der Welt Ende), wie unser HErr spricht, Luc. 21,24., denn Christus wird ewige sitzen bleiben, und kein anderer Messia kommen: darum muß ich glauben, daß noch etliche und gar wenig Hefen von den Juden übrig bleiben müssen in der Welt, aber sollen doch keine eigene Herrschaft kriegen, sondern auf ungewissem Fuße sitzen, wie der 59. Psalm V.11.12. weissagt, im Geist und in der Person Christi und seines Volks: "GOtt läßt mich meine Lust sehen an meinen Feinden. Er würge sie nicht, daß mein Volk nicht vergesse; zerstreue sie aber mit deiner Macht, HErr, unser Schild, und stoße sie hinunter."

Und muß ihnen gehen, wie Kain, dem Brudermörder, 1 Mos. 4.14: "Du sollst Nogvonod sein auf Erden, unstät und flüchtig, das heißen wir nirgend heim, auf der Schuckel und Wage sitzen, keinen gewissen Fuß noch Raum haben.

99. Fleichwohl aber, weil sie so begierig sind, aufzuraffen und einzusammeln die losen abtrünnigen, abgefeimten Christen, an welchen sie freilich nichts gutes sammeln, und haben solches nun viel Jahre getrieben, wird das israelische Blut gar vermischt, unrein, wässerig und wilde worden sein, welche gar bald von ihnen gelernt haben, die Christen zu hassen und zu morden. Wiederum, haben die Juden von jenen auch nichts Gutes gelernt, haben also Meister und Schüler sich unter einander geübt, gewetzt und gebessert, bis sie solche Mordgrube und Teufels

Grundsuppe worden sind; denn ein abtrünniger Christ wird gar ein bitterer Feind der Christen.

100. Das sei auf den Stolz gesagt, da sich die elenden Juden brüsten mit ihrer heiligen Schrift, also habe sonst niemand die heilige Schrift; so sie doch müssen unsers Neuen Testaments genießen, wo man sie soll für Juden halten, und sonst nichts haben, damit sie es beweisen. Auch ist niemand, der weniger die heilige Schrift hat, denn die Juden; das wollen wir sehen.

101. Wenn die Juden Ohren oder Augen hätten, daß die hören oder sehen könnten, so wäre ihnen leichtlich gesagt und gezeigt, daß mehr denn ein Buch der heiligen Schrift sein müßte, und nicht könnte allein das alte Testament sein, da sie Mosen und die Propheten inne heben und legen, und doch nicht verstehen.

Denn sie müssen ja bekennen, daß in der heiligen Schrift der Messias verheißen ist. Nun wenn derselbige kommt, so wird er nicht stumm und lahm sein, sondern wird reden und thun, und besser weder Moses, David, Solomon noch alle Propheten geredet und gethan haben. Aus solcher Rede und thun wird ein Buch werden. Denn er wird's schreiben lassen, gleichwie Moses seine Predigt und Thun geschrieben hat, Jesaias seine, und so fortan. Dies Buch Messiä muß nun viel besser, heiliger und herrlicher sein, denn Moses und das ganze Alte Testament, sintemal Messia nicht allein heilig, wie Mose und Prophet über alle Propheten sein muß. Demnach muß sein Buch auch das allerheiligste, über alle heiligen Bücher in der Bibel sein.

102. Solches erdichten wir verfluchen Gojim ja nicht, sondern Moses hat solches seinem Volk klar und deutlich verkündigt, nämlich, daß noch ein Buch der heiligen Schrfit kommen sollte, welches sie sollten annehmen. Denn so spricht er 5 Mos. am 18, 15. (wie gesagt): "Einen Propheten aus deinen Brüdern wird dir GOtt erwecken, wie mich, den sollst du hören." Ich hoffe, die Juden, wie giftige böse Würme sie sind, werden sie ja nicht sagen können, daß wir diesen Spruch erdichtet haben. Nun laßt uns die Worte hören, wir wollen nichts aus eigenem Kopf hineintragen, wie sie in die Schrift ihre rasenden, wahnsinnigen Glossen zu tragen pflegen.

103. Moses redet an dem Ort nicht von seiner Person, wie er geboren ist von seinem Vater, sondern von seinem Amt, wie er berufen oder erweckt ist von GOtt zum Propheten; will sagen: Wie mich GOtt erweckt hat aus deinen Brüdern zum Propheten, so wird er auch einen anderen Propheten erwecken aus deinen Brüdern. Dieser andere Prophet kann nicht sein Samuel, David, Elia, Eliseus, Jesaias, oder der einer, so im alten Testament gewest sind; denn sie sind alle unter Mose gewest, haben gelehrt was Mose (als ein Prophet GOttes) geboten und verheißen oder verkündigt hat, nämlich die Beschneidung, die zehn Gebote, die Gesetze vom Priesterthum, Fürstenthum, von GOttesdienst, Tempel und was im ganzen Stand und Regiment und dem Volk und alten Testament zu lehren gewest ist, hat keiner dürfen etwas anderes lehren noch verheißen, ohne was Mose geboten und verheißen hat.

104. Soll nun dieser andere Prophet thun mit seiner Prophetia, wie Mose gethan hat, so muß er andere Gebote, Gesetze und Rechte, ander Priesterthum, Fürstenthum, Gottesdienst, Tempel und Regiment stiften. Sollte er aber nichts Anderes lehren denn was Mose gelehrt hat, so wäre es eben der Mose selbst, oder der alten Propheten einer, die unter Mose sind gewest, und wäre nicht wie Mose ist. Was macht denn Mose, daß er verheißt mit unnützen Worten, "GOtt werde einen anderen Propheten erwecken, wie er ist, den sollen sie hören?" So mehr hätte er also gesagt: Wenn jener Prophet kommt, so sollst du mich (das ist meine Prophetia) hören. Aber nun gibt er seine Meisterschaft, Amt und Prophetia auf, und weist sie zu jenem Propheten, und spricht: "Den sollst du hören." Denn, daß sie Mose und seine Propheten hören sollten, hatte er zuvor, haben's auch hernach alle Propheten, bis zum großen Ueberdruß genug getrieben.

105. Eben dasselbige zeugt auch, da er daselbst drauf einführt GOtt selbst, der spricht 5 Mos. 18,18.: Ich will ihnen einen Propheten erwecken aus ihren Brüdern, wie dich, und will meine Worte in seinen Mund legen, saß der soll predigen, was ich ihn heißen werde" etc. Diese Worte und Predigt des anderen Propheten müssen andere Worte und Predigt sein weder Mosis Wort und Predigt; des es sollen künftige und noch nicht gegebene Worte sein, weil Mosis Wort, wohl vierzig Jahre zuvor, auf dem Berge Sinai in den Mund Mosis gelegt, und dazumal auch durch Mosen geschrieben worden sind. Darum hat sich Mose wohl verwahrt wider die unartigen Juden, daß er ihnen hiemit hell genug verkündigt hat, es müßte ein ander Buch, das heiliger denn seins ist, kommen durch den anderen Propheten, und also viel ein ander Pristerthum, Gottesdienst, Volk und Recht gestiftet werden.

106. Demnach schreien nun alle Propheten mit Mose einträchtiglich, daß Messia solle ein Prophet und Priester sein, der eine andere und neue Predigt führen solle, wie Mose hie verkundigt. Jes. 2,3. Mich. 4.2. Viel Heiden werden sagen: "Laßt uns hinauf gehen zum Hause des HErrn, daß er uns lehre seine Wege; denn von Zion wird ein Gesetz ausgehen, und von Jerusalem des HErrn Wort." Hörst du hie, daß es nicht ausgegangen ist, wie Mosis Gesetz und Wort, sondern es soll künftig ausgehen, und ein neu ander Wort sein. Jes. 61, 1.: "Der Geist des Herrn ist auf mir, darum hat er mich gesalbet (zum Messia oder Gesalbten gemacht), daß ich soll den Elenden das Evangelium predigen, zu heile.: die betrübten Herzen.etc. Ps. 110, 4.: "Du bist ein Priester ewiglich, nach der Weise Melchizedek,.Zach. 9, 10.: "Er wird ein Fridefürst sein," das ist, wie auch Zacharias um 9,10 sagt, "Roß und Wagen wegthun," und, Jesaiä 11,4., "ohne Schwert regieren."

107. Soll er ohne Schwert regieren, und doch Frieden lehren und halten, so wird er nicht müssen sein ein König, wie David und alle anderen Könige (die nicht können ohne Schwert regieren), noch von ihrem weltlichen Recht lehren, und muß also sein Königreich weit ein ander Königreich sein weder ein weltlich Königreich, welches ohne Schwert und sein Recht ein lauter Nichts ist, und keinen Frieden haben kann. Auch wo er ein Priester, Prediger und Prophet sein soll, der im Frieden regieren soll, wie kann er solches Regiments warten, das keinen Frieden, und so

weitläufig Recht haben muß, sonderlich keinen ewigen Frieden, wie doch die Propheten von ihm sagen? Israel hatte Frieden unter Salomo, doch so hin, daß sie auch selbst über ihn schrieen, er habe sie überschätzt und ausgesogen; dennoch war es kein ewiger Friede. Summa, es muß mit diesem andern Propheten ein ander Ding sein, denn mit Mose, allen Propheten, Königen und aller Welt gewest, und noch ist; oder Mose muß mit allen seinen Propheten ein Lügner sein. Er soll nicht sein wie andere Propheten oder Könige, das will die heilige Schrift des Alten Testaments; darum muß sein Buch das Neue Testament, auch ein anderes und höheres sein denn das Alte Testament.

108. Aber keiner ist so gar grob und unsinnig, solches alles in Mose und den Propheten zu bestätigen, als Jeremias 31,31., der verachtet doch ja zu sehr diese hochgelehrten, beschissenen (beschnittenen) Heiligen, und darf ohne Urlaub aller Talmudisten und Rabbinen (oh, daß ihn dies und das bestehe!) herausfahren und sagen: "Siehe, es kommt die Zeit, spricht der Herr, da will ich mit dem Hause Israel und Juda einen neuen Bund machen." O, Jeremia, fahr schön, wo willst du hinaus? Du weißest nicht, wie die Rabbinen nach 2000 Jahren dir die Nase drehen werden mit ihren Glossen, die besser sind denn dein heller Text. Soll ein neuer Bund und Testament kommen? Wo will denn das alte bleiben? Wo wollen die beschnittenen Heiligen bleiben, die nichts mehr noch anderes wollen wissen noch leiden, auch bei den Christen, den verfluchten Gojim, denn allein das alte? Sollst du so kühne sein und Mosen mit der ganzen heiligen alten Schrift, dazu mit den Talmudisten, und so hoch und tiefgelehrten Heiligen, wegwerfen, daß du darfst vor ihrer Nase weissagen von einem neuen Buch und Testament?

109. Und, das noch viel ärger ist, du unverschämter Ketzer darfst sagen also: "Nicht wie der Bund gewesen ist, den ich mit ihren Vätern machte, da ich sie aus Egyptenland führete" etc. Ach, HErr GOtt! Gnade dir GOtt, du armer Jeremiah, wie bist du so gar toll worden, daß du den alten Bund so rein aufhebst, der doch gewißlich von Gott selbst gemacht ist, wie du selbst bekennst und sprichst: "den ich mit ihren Vätern gemacht habe"; nennst dazu die Zeit, als wärest du nicht toll, da ich sie bei der Hand nahm, und aus Egypten führte." Wohlan, dir ist nicht zu helfen, du willst von den beschnittenen Heiligen verdammt sein; so will ich auch nicht für dich bitten, noch deine Worte anders deuten (kann auch nicht), denn die beschnittenen Heiligen könnten es doch nicht leiden, möcht übel ärger machen.

110. Aber hie geben die hochgelehrten Juden uns verfluchten Gojim recht Haarab, da sie schreiben, unser Jesus hab selbst gesagt, Matth. 5, 17.: "er sei nicht kommen, das Gessetz und Propheten aufzuheben, sondern zu erfüllen, und solle nicht ein Buchstabe noch Tüttel vergehen, es müsse alles geschehen, müßte ehe Himmel und Erde vergehen etc. Da hast du's, du verfluchter Gojim. Wohlan, welcher Mensch hätte sich immermehr versehen können, daß die Juden so hochgelehrt worden wären, uns Christen auch das Neue Testament zu lehren? Es wird sie gewißlich ein eherner Hund zu Jerusalem mit bellen so klug gemacht, oder ein frischer Scham Haperes mit großem Rauch (Geist wollt ich sagen) erfüllt haben, daß sie so gewaltiglich verstehen, was Gesetz erfüllen heißt.

111. Ah, du lieber GOtt! die elenden Juden haben ihr Lebenlang nie gewußt, was das geringste Gesetz sei, viel weniger, was Erfüllung des Gesetzes sei, können's auch (so lange sie solche Juden sind) nimmermehr verstehen. Hie gehören andere Leute zu, als St. Paulus, Röm. 3,21.: "GOttes Gerechtigkeit ist offenbaret, durch das Gesetz und Propheten bezeuget," und Joh. 1, 17.: "Das Gesetz ist durch Mosen gegeben; aber Gnade und Wahrheit durch JEsum Christum geschehen"; St. Petrus, Apost. 15, 10,11.: "Das ist die Last, so weder wir noch unsere Väter haben können tragen, sondern wir glauben, durch die Gnade des HErrn Jesu Christi, selig zu werden, gleichwie sie worden sind..." Lieber, sage mir, wie es möglich sei, daß die Rangen (Rabbinen wolt ich sagen) und Säujuden in ihrer Säuschule solche hohen Worte verstehen sollten, welche ihr Lebenlang nichts gethan, und noch nicht anders thun, denn mit ihrem Rüssel im Scham Haperes wühlen?

112. Ich will wohl Geringeres sagen, wie kann ein Jude verstehen, was da gesagt sei, Matth. am 7,12.: "Was ihr wollt, daß euch die Leute thun, das thut ihr auch ihnen; daß ist das Gesetz und die Propheten." Hie gehen fast alle Mosis Gesetze unter. Item, Matth. 22, 37. ff.: "Liebe deinen Nächsten als dich selbst; das Gebot ist gleich dem ersten: Du sollst GOtt lieben aus ganzem Herzen. In diesen zweien Geboten hanget das ganze Gesetz und die Propheten." Moses hat's wohl verstanden, da er sagt 2 Mos. 34,6.: "HErr, HErr, barmherziger GOtt, der du Sünde vergibst und niemand vor dier unschuldig ist" und David, Ps. 130,3.: HErr, wo du willst Sünde ansehen, wer kann vor dir bleiben?" Item, Ps.51,8.: "Siehe, du liebest die Wahrheit im verborgenen, und lehrest mich die heimliche Weisheit." Also auch hie Jeremias spricht: er wolle den neuen Bund nicht schreiben in steinerne Tafeln, wie jenen Bund, der nie in keines fleischlichen Juden Herz kommen ist, denselben auch nie verstanden, viel weniger gehalten hat; wie Jeremia spricht (Cap.31,32): "Sie haben jenen Bund nicht gehalten" sondern er wolle den neuen Bund schreiben in lebendige Tafeln, in die Herzen, daß es lebendige, brennende Buchstaben sein sollen, und also GOttes Wille geschehe.

113. Nun, von solcher lebendigen Schrift, in das Herz geschrieben, wird man freilich müssen äußerlich reden und ein Buch schreiben, wie Moses von der Schrift in den steinernen Tafeln hat müssen ein Buch schreiben; denn es wird so wenig, und viel weniger, heimlich zugehen, was dies neue Testament oder Schrift in den Herzen thun würde, weder jenes Testament, das in steinerne Tafeln und nicht ins Herz geschrieben ist. Aber hievon reden und wissen wir, so rechte Christen sind; denn auch der Pabst mit seiner Kirche hievon nichts weiss, achtet sein auch nicht. Die Juden wissen eben so viel davon, als eine Sau vom Psalter.

114. Hieraus ist's gewiß beweist, daß ein Neu Testament hat sollen kommen über das Alte, daß also der Juden Stolz und Ruhm nichts ist denn ein Peres und Pfui dich an, da sie kein Testament noch heilige Schrift wollen sein lassen, ohne das Alte. Aber es hilft sie nicht; ihr eigen Alt Testament ist wider sie, verdammt sie mit ihrem Ruhm, weil es so dürre heraus weissagt, daß der alte Bund solle es nicht thun, Mosis Regiment solle aus sein, Messia solle nicht darnach regieren, sondern das Neue Testament müsse es thun. Wie auch Mose sein Amt übergibt, und dem neuen

Propheten weicht und Raum gibt. Darum müssen die Juden das Neue Testament, Taufe und unsern Glauben annehmen, oder sie sind ewig verloren. Das alte Testament, Mose selbst und alle Propheten werden sie nichts helfen, sondern stehen wider sie, und verurtheilen sie zur Hölle.

115. Hie kommt's aber wieder auf die Frage: ob Messia kommen sei? Ist er kommen, so sind Juden, Heiden, und alle Welt schuldig, das Neue Testament anzunehmen, nicht allein als eine heilige Schrift, sondern als die allerheiligste Schrift über die alte heilige Schrift. Nun ist genugsam beweiset, daß Messia vor 1500 Jahren kommen ist; da haben wir Christen, erstlich viel tausend Kinder Israel, darnach wir Heiden solch Neu Testament angenommen, auch bei 1500 Jahren her, und werden's annehmen bis an der Welt Ende; aber die Hefen, die anderen Israeliten, die wollten's nicht annehmen, verschmähet ihnen solch gering Ding. Haben also das Essen verzürnet und die Freude vermäulet, aus großem Hochmuth und Steifsinnigkeit; darnach wollten sie schmollen und grunzen, da sie nichts funden in ihrem Hunger. Also geht's denn, daß die sich stölziglich brüsten und rühmen, sie haben allein vor aller Welt die heilige Schrift, die haben nicht ein Blatt noch Buchstaben davon, so fern es den Verstand betrifft, der Seele zu Nutze und Gut; von Leib und Leibs Nutz reden wir nicht. Denn das sie in der Schrift suchen, das finden sie nimmermehr; es ist nicht drinnen, und noch nie drinnen gewest, also wenig als in dem schnödensten Buch, so auf Erden gemacht ist. Messia ist drinnen vrheißen, aber nicht der Messia, den sie wollen und erträumen.

116. Wir Christen aber haben alle beiden Bücher der heiligen Schrift, das alte und heilige, dazu das neue und allerheiligste. Das alte verheißt den Messiam und spricht: er solle gewißlich kommen und gegeben werden. Das neue ruft und spricht: er sei gewißlich kommen und gegeben. Wenn nun die Juden das neue Buch, die allerheiligste Schrift, könnten annehmen, wie etliche viel for 1400 Jahren gethan, so würden sie wohl verstehen, daß die Beschneidung und alle alte Heiligkeit sollten weichen der Taufe und der neuen Heiligkeit, die über jene Heiligkeit ist. Denn zu der Zeit, da der Messia mit seinem Buch noch steckte im alten Buch, das ist, in der Verheißung da war freilich keine heilige Schrift mehr denn das alte Buch, in welcher Verheißung alle Heiligen sind selig worden, die solches verheißenen Messia hoften. Denn er ist eben derselbige und der einige Messias der jenen Verheißen, uns aber kommen und erschienen ist, daß keiner mehr, oder ein anderer zu hoffen sei, noch kommen kann.

117. Nachdem aber der Messia mit seinem Buch heraus kommen und uns gegeben ist, so ist keiner Verheißung mehr zu harren. Und ist uns nunmehr das alte Buch ein gewisser Zeuge GOttes, daß uns der Messia hat sollen kommen, so ist das neue Buch noch viel ein gewisserer Zeuge Gottes, daß der Messiah kommen sei. Also sehen die zween Cherubim mit ihren Angesichten gegen einander in den Gnadenstuhl, das ist, Alt und Neu Testament, sagen JEsus Christus, Marien Sohn, sei der Welt Heiland und der rechte Gnadenstuhl vor GOtt, wider unsere Sünde, Tod, Teufel und Hölle. Also ist erfüllt, das gesagt ist: "Israel soll sicher wohnen," welches die Hefenjuden wollen von den Hefen dieses Lebens verstanden haben.

118. Nun aber die Juden solches nicht annehmen, so haben sie weder alt noch neu Buch, weder GOtt den Verheißer, noch Messia den Gesandten, schweben zwischen Himmel und Erde, und rühren nirgend an, treffen weder alt noch neu Buch, wie Sacharja, 5,1. den fliegenden Brief zeigt, welchen er nennt *maledictio*, Fluch; denn ihr lehren ist eitel Fluchen; sonst wissen sie doch wahrlich nichts in der Schrift. Denn erstlich ist ja das gewiß daß sie nicht verstehen die Verheißungen von Messia. Zum anderen verstehen sie nicht die zehn Gebote, weil ohne Messia die nicht können verstanden werden. Zum dritten können sie nicht verstehen, was die Ceremonien meinen. Dazu, weil nun das Priesterthum gefallen, verstehen sie auch nicht wohl die Weise oder Larve der Ceremonien. Zum vierten versteht kein Jude die edlen köstlichen Exempel oder Leben der Väter, Adam, Noah, Abraham, Isaak, Jakob, Joseph, David, Summa, des ganzen Volks Israel.

Denn sie wissen nicht, was rechter Glaube, rechte, gute Werke sind. Solches beweisen ihre blinden, tollen elenden Talmudgenossen, Comment, zuletzt auch ihre *Grammatica*. Darum haben sie nichts mehr am alten Testament. Es heißt: "Ich bin das Licht" (spricht Messia [Joh.8, 12.]), wo das nicht ist, was kann da anders sein denn eitel Finsterniß?

119. Solches sei gesagt von der stumpfen und rauhen Antwort, so man soll den halsstarrigen Juden geben auf ihre stachlichte giftige Frage, nämlich daß Mose 1, Mos. 49, 10. und 5 Mos. 18,15. gewaltiglich zeugt, und mit ihm alle Propheten einträchtiglich und reichlich, daß Maria Messia's Mutter sei, und müsse sein von dem Stamm Juda und Hause Davids. Glauben sie Mosi nicht, so glauben sie viel weniger den Evangelisten. Auch ist uns Christen selbst solche Antwort gut und gewiß genug, wie gesagt, weil der Sohn Messia muß von David kommen, und wir dazu glauben. Daß seine Mutter eine Jungfrau ist, so muß sie freilich auch Davids Fleisch und Blut und natürliche Tochter sein: sonst müßte ihr Sohn Messia nicht Davids, sondern eines andern Geblüts sein, weil seine Mutter eines andern Bluts wäre, sonderlich so sie, eine Jungfrau', ohne Manns Blut und Fleisch gebären sollte.

120. Ueber solch des Alten Testaments Zeugniß wollen wir nun sehen das Neue Testament, wie reichlich und gewaltiglich dasselbe zeugt, daß Maria muß Davids Tochter sein. Erstlich fähet St. Matthäus sein Buch an, Matth. 1.1.: "Dies ist das Buch von der Geburt JEsu Christi, des Sohns Davids, des Sohns Abrahams." Hie hörst du, daß JEsus Christus oder Messia sei Davids Sohn und Abrahams Sohn; so muß zuvoraus seine Mutter Davids und Abrahams Tochter sein, weil sie eine Jungfrau ist, die ohne einen Mann geboren hat, wie der Evangelist hernach beweist. Und wenn St. Matthäus kein Wort mehr hievon geschrieben hätte, denn diesen Anfang seines Buchs, so wäre damit genug beweist, daß Maria müßt vom Hause Davids sein. Denn der Sohn Messia beweist, wo die Mutter her ist, nicht die Mutter (wie die tollen Juden suchen), wo der Sohn her sei, oder daß er vom Stamm Juda sei. Nun thut der Evangelist zum Ueberfluß, und zählt wohl dreimal vierzehn Glied von Abraham, das sind zweiundvierzig, Glied, da mag man bei einem jeglichen Glied sagen: Deß Tochter ist Maria und JEsus ist sein Sohn, wie er Davids und Abrahams Sohn ist; daß also wohl zweiundvierzigmal Matthäus allein in der Schnur des Geschlechts bekennt, daß Maria vom Stamm Juda und Geblüt

Davids sei. Und Summa, so oft JEsus im Alten und Neuen Testament Christus oder Messia genannt wird, so oft wird daselbst Maria, seine Mutter, beweiset Davids Tochter.

121. Daß aber sich etliche bekümmern, warum der Evangelist in den letzten Gliedern die Worte so wendet, läßt Joseph fahren, setzt Mariam, die er doch nicht in der Schnur herab führt von David, wie er Joseph führt: hie sollten wir (wenn wir schon nichts anders wüßten) dem Heiligen Geiste die Ehre geben und denken, daß Matthäus die Freundschaft Mariä sehr wohl gekannt habe zu Nazareth, weil er Joseph, ihren Mann, so wohl kennt mit seiner Freundschaft, und nicht zu glauben ist, daß er sollte wohl zweiundvierzigmal zeugen allein in der Schnur des Geschlechts, daß Christus Davids Sohn sei, und doch die Mutter aus fremdem Stamm daher führen, als wäre er toll und thöricht worden im letzten Glied.

122. Doch wollen wir die Worte des Evangelisten ansehen, ob er Mariam auch könne führen von David, so wohl als Joseph. Das ist gewiß, daß St. Matthäus die Schnur führt durch Salomo, und St. Lucas durch seinen Bruder Nathan: das sind zwo Schnur, doch einerlei Gebluts als zweier Brüder, von David; aber in dem König Joas kommen sie zusammen, und müssen zusammen kommen in eine Schnur, weil 2 Chron. 22,9,10. steht, daß Athalja allen königlichen Samen tödtete, bis allein auf Joas, und wie der Text spricht; "Es war niemand mehr aus dem Hause Ahasja, der König würde." Hie geht Salomonis Schnur unter, daß Christus wohl kommt von seinem Blut, als nach der Brüder und Väter Schnur, aber nicht von seines Leibes Nachkommen, sondern, wie Lucas sagt, von Nathan, seinem Bruder.

123. Ob nun die beiden Evangelisten hernach mit der Schnur wieder von einander gehen, laß ich jetzt anstehen zu handeln; sie bleiben doch im Hause Davids, das ist gewiß; aber in dem großvater Josephs sind sie ja eins, treffen beide zugleich ein auf den Matthan oder, wie ihn Lucas nennt, Matthes. Ich achte, daß er Matthan nach der *Grammatica*, und Mathes nach gemeiner Laien Sprache genannt, sei, wie wir Deutschen Johannes, Hans, Hänsel, Henno Einen Namen machen. Item, Nicolaus, Nickel, Claus etc. Wir Deutschen sprechen den Namen Matthew dürr und recht aus, wie Hebräisch geschrieben wird, Matthath, *Thaf raphato, et A puro vel Italico* (das ist, mit einem Taf, das mit Raphe versehen ist, und mit einem reinen oder Italienischen A.)

124. Diesen Matthes laßt uns wohl merken, an dem liegt's, da ist Abraham und Davids Blut nahe hinnan zu Messia kommen, fast in das letzte Haus. Denn bis in dieses Matthes Haus ist Messia nun von oben herab kommen, und wir haben ihn in diesem Hause gewiß; und aus diesem Hause allein muß er kommen, hintangesetzt, was zur Seite aus Brüder oder Vetter Häuser sind, die gehen uns nichts an, in Matthes' Hause da ist er. Wenn wir nun nichts mehr hätten, denn diesen Matthes, so hätten wir reichlich genug zu antworten denen, so sich bekümmern wie Maria und Joseph eines Stammes und Hauses wären. Denn weil der Messia in Matthes' Hause ist, und aus Matthes' Hause kommen muß, so hat der Evangelist damit klar und hell beweiset, daß beide, Maria und Joseph, nicht allein von dem Stamm

Juda und aus dem Hause David sein müssen, sondern auch aus einem Hause Matthes' des Großvaters Joseph; weil aus Matthes Haus Messia kommen muß. Ist aber Messia in Matthes' Haus, so ist seine Mutter gewißlich auch drinnen, als die, eine Jungfrau, soll den Messia gebären aus Matthes', Davids, Abrahams Haus. Denn in welchem Vater oder Hause der Messia ist, in demselben muß gewißlich auch seine Mutter Maria zuvoraus sein (wie droben gesagt), das macht, sie ist Jungfrau, hat keinen Mann; die Jungfrauschaft thut's, die führt Messiam mit seiner Mutter durch alle Väter, bis auf sich selbst.

125. Woran hat's nun gemangelt, daß uns St. Matthäus nicht hat können beweisen, wie Maria und Joseph eines Stammes, Hauses und Vaters sind? Daran hat's gemangelt, daß wir nicht gemerkt haben, in welchem Vater der Messia wäre, in demselben müste auch seine Mutter sein, weil sie soll Jungfrau sein, und kann ihr Kind keinem Menschen geben, denn ihr selbst und ihrem Vater. Denn daß Hieronymus, Lyra und andere schreiben, Joseph und Maria sind daher Eines Geschlecht zu beweisen, daß er sie hat zur Ehe genommen nach dem Gesetz Mosis, 4 Mos. 36,6.7., damit die Güter nicht in fremde Stämme getrennt würden, das ist viel zu kalt und zu faul, auch zu hoch droben, über David hinauf gesucht, und hilft doch nichts; wie das auch Burgensis recht und wohl widerficht. Warum haben wir diesen Matthes nicht angesehen? da wären wir näher dazu kommen, und so nahe, daß (es) nicht näher sein kann.

126. Denn weil Messia aus Matthes' Haus und sonst nirgends her kommen muß, so laßt uns sehen, was aus demselben Hause kommt. Erstlich kommt heraus Jakob, sein Sohn, wie Matthäus schreibt. Aus dieses Jakobs Hause kommt Messia nicht, ist auch nicht drein kommen, sondern Joseph, sein Sohn, kommt heraus. Nun müssen wir wider auf Matthes' Haus sehen, was zum andernmal heraus kommt. Maria kann noch nicht heraus kommen noch seine Tochter sein, ob sie wohl drinnen ist, mit ihrem Sohn Messia; sonst würde Joseph seines Vaters Schwester oder seines Großvaters natürliche Tochter genommen haben, das GOtt durch Mosen verboten hat, 3 Mos. 18, 12. Viel weniger kann's eine andere Tochter Matthes' sein, die Messia Mutter werde, welches muß allein Maria sein. Denn die Töchter gehen aus dem Vater-Hause weg in andere Häuser, darum zählt die Schrift keine Frauenschnur. So muß nun Matthes noch einen Sohn (zum wenigsten) haben, in welchem von ihm der Messia kommt, der ist Eli, wie Lucas schreibt. Dieser zeugte eine Tochter, Maria Jakobi, die ist's nicht; und darnach eine jüngere Tochter die ist's. Hat er mehr Söhne oder Töchter, das gehe seinen Weg; denn Messia muß von einer Jungfrau, des Eli Tochter, kommen.

127. Hie haben wir nun die Mutter des Messia, die ist mit Joseph Geschwisterkind, und sind beides Niftel eines Großvaters, Matthes. Also, meine ich, sei stark genug beweist, daß Maria und Joseph Eines Stammes und Geblüts sind, weil sie eines Großvaters Niftel, zweier Brüder Kinder, und nicht näher sein können, sie wären denn leibliche Brüder und Schwester. Es war aber durch Mose in diesem Volk zugelassen, daß Geschwisterkinder sich zur Ehe nehmen möchten, das ist, ein Großvater möchte seine zwei Niftel oder zween Brüder möchten ihre Kinder

zusammen geben in diesem Volk, daß auch der Evangelist darum Joseph Marien Mann, und Maria Josephs Braut nennt; als wollte er sagen: Weil ihr hört, daß Joseph Marien Mann ist, so kennt ihr sie ja wohl, daß sie nach gemeiner Weise Eines Geblüts, und Geschwisterkinder sind.

128. Also hat der Evangelist den Messiam, seine Mutter mit ihm, von oben an, durch aller Väter Häuser, bis in Matthes' Haus, darnach in Eli Haus, und von dannen in Josephs Haus bracht, darinnen er geboren und erzogen ist; nicht von seinem Leibe, sondern von seiner ehelichen Braut Leibe, oder in seinem Ehestande, und ist Messia sein ehelicher Sohn, und Joseph sein ehelicher Vater, doch allein von der Jungfrau Maria. Weil wir nun so viel haben, daß Joseph und Maria Niftel sind des großen Vaters Metthes, haben wir genug, und ist gewiß, das Maria vom Hause Davids ist mit Joseph. Wer nun weiter will klügeln über den zween Brüdern Jakob und Eli, ob Jakob habe seines Bruders Tochter, Maria, zu sich genommen und seinem Sohn Joseph gegeben, oder ob Eli, seines Bruders Sohn, Joseph, zu sich genommen und ihn seiner Tochter Maria gegeben habe, der mag's thun; uns ist hierin auch genug, daß sie, die beiden Väter Josephs und Maria, des Matthes Söhne gewest sind.

129. Daß Hieronymus schreibt, Jakob sei Joseph's natürlicher Vater nach St. Matthäus' Schnur, aber Eli, den er auch Eliakin und Joakim nennt (denn es sollen alle drei Ein Name sein, wie bei uns Nicolaus, Nickel, Claus), sei sein Vater nach Lucas' Schnur, das ist sein Schwäher oder Vetter nach der Weise, da Tochter-Mann auch Sohn, und Sohns-Weib auch Tochter heißt, und nach dem Gesetz, da ein Bruder muß sich seines verstorbenen Bruders Kinder Vater lassen nennen und sein. Das gefällt mir wohl, und besser denn Eusebius mit Lyra, der meint, Jakob habe seines Bruders Eli Wittwe genommen, und mit derselben Joseph gezeugt. Da würde Maria (Joakim oder Eli Tochter) und Joseph einerlei Mutter Kinder und natürliche Geschwister sein, das leidet Mose nicht, 3 Mos.18,6.

130. Hie fällt hierein die alte Frage: Welcher Evangelist unter den beiden, Matthäus und Lucas, die väterliche Schnur beschreibe, weil es offenbar ist daß Matthäus von Salomo herab bis auf Ochosias die brüderliche Schnur führt, wie droben ist beweist. Erstlich muß man hie lassen Lyram und sein Theil fahren mit ihrer Meinung, denn sie gehen zu fern vom Wege, also daß er auch hält, Nathan sei nicht Davids natürlicher Sohn, sondern der Prophet (der wohl so alt gewest, als David selbst.) und sei mit den andern zween Brüdern, Simea und Sobab, 1 Chron. 3,5. von Uria und Bethsaba herkommen, die David hernach erwählt habe zu Körkindern, und allein Salomo sei Bethsaba Sohn von David; dahin führt er den Spruch, Sprüchw. 4,3.: "Ich war ein einiger Sohn meiner Mutter" etc. Das ist nichts; mit der Weise würde Christus Uria's Sohn, der war Hittheus, ein Heide, wiewohl frömmer, denn viel tausend Israeliten.

131. Zum andern ist einem Christen das genug, daß beide Evangelisten eitel Davidskinder einführen, es sei Vater-oder Bruder-Schnur, und bleiben beide im Hause David, zählen keine Körkinder, oder fremd Geblüt. Von welcher nun Christus kommt, so kommt er von David her. Ich halt's mit denen, so Lucas die

väterliche Schnur geben, bis auf Eli; denn da sich die Schnur von Matthes, dem Großvater, zwieset ein Theil auf Jakob, das andere auf Eli, da muß er wohl Joseph, Eli Sohn, das ist, Eidam, setzen, aus der Ursache, wie er selbst sagt, daß Joseph sei, *putativus pater*, vermeinter Vater Christi, nicht natürlicher Vater, wie es die Schnur wohl gefordert hätte, wo Maria, seine Braut, nicht Jungfrau-Mutter gewest wäre, und der Schrift weise nicht leidet, die Frauen-Schnur zu führen; noch ist er *putative*, vermeinter Weise, Ein Leib mit seiner Braut Maria, wie er auch vermeinter Vater Christi ist. Summa, wie, gesagt, der große Vater Matthes macht's alles schlecht, daß Maria und JEsus Eines Hauses und Vaters Kinder sind.

132. Es bewegt jene, daß Matthäus immer sagt, *genuit, genuit*, er hat den gezeugt oder geboren; darum halten sie, Matthäus rede von der natürlichen Schnur, die aus der Geburt folgt vom Vater auf den Sohn für und für; Lucas aber rede von der brüderlichen oder väterlichen Schnur, die sie *legalem* nennen, nicht *adoptivam* wie Lyra meint, sondern, da ein Bruder nach dem Gesetze (wie gesagt ist) sich muß seines verstorbenen Bruders Kinder annehmen, als wäre er ihr Vater. Dies glaube ich nicht, St. Matthäus glaubt's selber nicht und hält nichts davon. Denn er läßt wissentlich unter den Königen wohl drei Glieder außen und spricht: Joram zeugt Usia; welches unmöglich ist, weil Usia im vierten Glied von Joram bei 100 Jahren nach Jorams Tode geboren ist, dazu in der brüderlichen Schnur von Nathan, nicht von Salomo, herkommt, da doch Joram herkommen ist. Desgleichen thut er unter den Fürsten nach der babylonischen Gefängniß, da er viel außen läßt, allein vierzen zählt, so Lucas wohl zweiundzwanzig zählt, und nicht heißen könnte: Asar zeugte Zaddok, so vielleicht dazwischen zween oder drei ausgelassen sind; darum thut das *genuit* nichts hiezu, daß Matthäus sollte die väterliche Schnur führen.

133. Er hat seine Weise also zu reden, *genuit*, er zeugte ihn etc. Damit er nichts anders will denn: er ist von ihm her oder von seinem Geblüt geboren, wie wir's auf Deutsch auch reden: Carolus ist von Maximiliam herkommen oder geboren. Das zeigt er auch mit diesen Worten im Titel: "Das ist das Buch von der Geburt Jesus Christi, des Sohns Davids, des Sohns Abrahams." Christus ist ja nicht geboren noch gezeugt von David; noch ist er sein Sohn, weil er von ihm herkommt nach dem Geblüt. So kann ja Geburt hie nicht heißen allein die persönliche Geburt Christi, so er wohl vierzig Geburt zählt seiner Vorfahren. Lucas aber führt die väterliche Schnur. Denn er rühmt sich im Anfange, er habe sich alles fleißig erkundet und wolle es ordentlich schreiben, dem müssen wir glauben, weil wir daß Größere und alles Andere glauben. Denn solche Register sind bei den Juden wohl bekannt gewesen, haben's alles (wie ihre Weise gewest) fleißig angeschrieben, wie da stehen zwei Exempel Chronica (und) Esra; auch Mose, der Jakobs und Esau's Geschlect fleißig beschreibt.

134. Matthäus aber bekennt frei, daß er nicht so wolle alles ordentlich zählen, da er spricht, er wolle drei *Tessardecadas*, dreimal vierzehn, machen von Abraham bis auf Christum. Und weil er vierzehn Patriarchen fand, wollte er nicht mehr denn vierzehn Könige und vierzehn Fürsten nehmen. Wiewohl durch die Schreiber, ohne

des Evangelisten Schuld, Ein König, Jojakim des Jechonja Vater, ausgelassen, und nuhr dreizehn Könige da stehen, wie St. Hieronymus auch in den griechischen Büchern den Mangel zeigt. Lucas aber macht wohl viermal vierzehn, nimmt sie alle, auch die, so nicht Könige gewest sind, als Nathan und seine Nachkommen. Demselben Luca ist auch durch die Schreiber das vierte Glied nach Noah zugesetzt, nämlich Kenan, das doch nicht sein kann. Darum achte ich's eine vergebliche Mühe, alle Namen gegen einander vergleichen wollen, weil wir die Register nicht haben. Und ist uns Heiden nicht vornehmlich (sonder den Juden) geschrieben, die es wohl gewußt. Ist genug, daß wie derselben so viel vergleichen, als wir können; da magst du Joseph(us) und Philo um fragen.

135. Ich will die ganze Freudnschaft setzen, nach meiner Idee oder Begriff; wer's besser macht, der habe Dank.

Levi.				Abraham.		
Aaron.				David.		
Zadok.				Joas.		
Jojada.				Zerubabel.		
A*				Matthes.		
Zacharias	Elisabeth	Anna	Eli			Jakob.
Johannes Baptista.						
Maria Cleophä		Maria		Joseph	Salome	Zebedäus
1. Jakob	2. Simon		JESUS	1. Jacobus major		
3. Joses.**)	4. Juda			2. Johannes Evang.		

*Refers to priestly line   **Refers to royal line

136. Diese Maria, unsers HErrn Mutter-Schwester oder seine Muhme, heißt in den Evangelien Maria Jacobi, von dem Sohne; heißt auch Maria Cleophä, vom andern Mann, der noch lebte am Ostertage Christi, Lucä 24, 18. Also heißt Juda auch Jacobi, vielleicht daß er Jacobi Bruder, von Alphäo, dem ersten Mann Mariä Jacobi, ist. Diese werden unseres HErrn Brüder genannt, weil sie seiner Mutter-Schwester Kinder sind.

137. Auch spricht der Engel Gabriel, Luc. 1, 36., daß Elizabeth sei Mariä Muhme oder Gefreundtin; das kann nicht wohl anders sein, denn daß Marien Mutter sei Elisabeths Schwester gewest, die wollen wir lassen sein Anna, wie sie überall genannt ist. Weil aber Elisabeth aus dem Priesterstamm ist, wie der Engel sagt, aus den Töchtern Aaron, darum setze ich die zwo Schwestern, Anna und Elisabeth, in die Schnur Aaron, so nimmt Joachim oder Eli aus dem Stamm David die ein Schwester, Annam, und Zacharias aus dem Priesterstamm die andere, Elisabeth. So wird Maria von der Mutter her Aarons Tochter aus dem priesterlichen Stamm, und vom Vater her Davids Tochter aus dem königlichen Stamm also Christus auch beide vom königlichen und priesterlichen Geblüt. Und ist Elisabeth ihre Mume und des HErrn große Mume; so wäre Maria mit Johanne dem Täufer Geschwisterkind, und er ein naher Vetter unsers HErrn JEsu Christi im dritten Glied.

138. Nun will die Salome etwas Sonderliches sein, vermißt sich eines Vorteils bei dem HErrn, weil sie ihn bittet, er solle ihre zween Söhne setzen, einen zur Rechten, den andern zur Linken in seinem Reich (Matth. 20,21.), daß ich halte, sie müsse ihm sehr nahe zugehört haben. Darum setze ich sie Josephs Schwester; sie hat gedacht, Maria Jacobi ist der Mutter Schwester, ich aber bin des Vaters Schwester; darum gebührt mir mit meinen Kindern der Vortritt gegen der Mutter Schwester mit ihren Kindern, Denn weil Joseph kein Kind mehr hat, sind meine beiden Söhne die nächsten Freunde JEsu, und sie denkt, JEsus sei Josephs Sohn, wie das jedermann dafür hielt zur selben Zeit (Luc. 3, 23.). Dawider murrten die andern, ohne, Zweifel der Mutter-Schwester Kinder, und vielleicht etliche mehr mit ihnen, die auch gern wollten die Größesten sein, wie wir im Evangelio lesen. Hiemit werden Jacobus der Große und Johannes Evangelista auch Vettern des HErrn, mit dem Namen so nahe, als Jacobus und Simon, Juda und Joseph, aber Eines Glieds weiter nach dem Geblüt. Denn Joseph ist nicht natürlicher Vater des HErrn, allein seine Mutter Maria und Salome sind zweier Brüder Töchter etc.

139. Hieraus sieht man, wie sich des HErrn nächste Freundlein zu ihm gethan haben nach menschlicher Weise, und wiederum stellt er sich wie ein anderer Mensch, Phil. 2,7., und hält sich auch freundlich und brüderlich zu ihnen. Und leuchtet hie kein Glanz der Majestät, sondern die äußerste knechtliche Gestalt.

140. Etliche, als Bonaventura, haben hie ihre Andacht, doch mit freiem Gewissen, daß Johannes Evangelista und Maria Magdalena seien Bräutigam und Braut gewest in der Hochzeit zu Cana, wie der Sequenz von St. Johannes Evangelista lautet. Dagegen mag ein anderer sein (doch freie) Andacht haben, es sei Simon oder Juda der Bräutigam, und die Braut auch eine nahe Mühmlein im andern oder dritten Glied gewest; denn die Evangelia nennen Simon von Cana und Juda Zeloten, das ist, von Cana. Und ist wohl zu denken, daß Braut und Bräutigam müssen der Mutter Maria nahe Freundlein gewest sein, weil sie selbst da ist und hilft regieren. Denn sie nicht so leichtfertig sich in fremde oder weiter Fruendschaft Hochzeit mengen würde, da wohl andere nähere Frauen wären.

141. Aber die endliche Meinung der Evangelisten, sonderlich Matthäi, mit solcher Schnur des Geschlechts, ist diese, daß er die unwissenden schwachen Juden will unterrichten und stärken, den halsstarrigen aber das Maul stopfen mit diesen zwei Artikeln: Jesus ist Messia, und Maria ist eine Jungfrau. Denn diese Artikel waren den frommen sehr schwer zu glauben, den Halsstarrigen aber unmöglich zu glauben; Ursach, er war zu Nazareth mit Vater, Mutter und ganzer Freundschaft sehr wohl bekannt, ganzer dreißig Jahr lang daselbst erzogen und gelebt, mit seinem Vater Joseph gezimmert, wie ein Handwerksgeselle, nicht in die Schule gegangen, nichts gelernt, desgleichen nach seines Vaters Tode sich mit seiner armen Mutter so fort genährt, nichts lassen sich sonderlich merken, sondern schlecht und allerding sich still gehalten, wie ein anderer Geselle seines Gleichen, daß sie sein gar wohl gewohnt, und in ihr Herz nicht fallen konnte, daß der ungelehrte, grobe, arme Zimmermann sein Lebenlang sollt gelehrt, schweige denn ein Prediger werden.

142. Plötzlich, da die dreißig Jahr um sind, läßt er das Handwerk, läuft davon, läßt sich mit andern auch taufen von St. Johannes, fähet an zu predigen, die Schrift zu deuten und lehren und Wunder zu thun, deß sich alle Welt entsetzt, daß gegen ihm alle Priester und Lehrer faule, kalte Lumpenprediger gehalten wurden. Das war ein seltsam unbegreiflich Ding in ihren Augen und Ohren. Noch viel seltsamer war's, daß er nicht allein ein Prophet, sondern der Messia selbst sein sollte. O wie seltsam verächtliche Reden sind darüber gefallen! Lieber, schweig stille, sollte Jesus predigen, meinst du, ich kenne ihn nicht? Ich hab dreißig Jahr mit ihm gelebt, weiß wohl, wer er ist und was er kann.

143. Nimm dich selbst zum Exempel: Wenn du mit Hans N. eines armen Bürgers Sohn von Jugend auf bis in dreißig Jahr gelebt, gearbeitet, gegessen, getrunken etc. hättest und du ihn wohl kenntest, als dich selbst daß er nie keinen Buchstaben kekannt hätte, und das selbe Jahr wegwanderte in ein ander Land, daselbst du von ihm hörtest, daß er predigte, und gelehrter wäre, denn alle Doctores der ganzen Welt, dazu Wunder thäte; da würdest du dem Ansager antworten: Bist du thöricht oder scherzest du? Meinst du ich kenne Hans N. nicht, mit dem ich dreißig Jahr Brod gegessen habe? Würde das Geschrei groß, daß etliche begännen zu glauben und zu rühmen, er wäre König oder Römischer Kaiser, würdest du sagen: Wohlan er ist thöricht worden, und die Welt ist toll und will toll sein, mich soll man deß nicht bereden, ich kenne ihn deß zu wohl. Eben so geht's hie den Nazarenen auch mit dem JEsu.

144. Da er wieder heim kommt, etwa kaum über ein halbes Jahr, geht er in die Schule, tritt auf, nimmt das Buch Jesaiä in die Hand, liest daraus, sitzt nieder, und thut eine schöne Predigt, daß sie sich alle verwundern; da sehen sie ihn alle selbst, können nich leugnen, es sei der JEsus, den sie sehr wohl kennen, fahen an und sprechen, Matth.13,54.ff.: "Woher kommt diesem solche Weisheit und Kraft?
Weisheit und Kraft? Ist er nicht eines Zimmermanns Sohn? Heißt nicht seine Mutter Maria? Und seine Brüder Jakob und Joses, Simon und Juda? und seine Schwestern, sind sie nicht alle bei uns? Woher kommt ihm denn das alles? Und ärgerten sich an ihm." Warum ärgerten sie sich? Sie konnten nicht glauben, daß es von GOtt wäre, was sie hörten und sahen. Die Person kannten sie zu wohl, und wäre zu geringe; darum dachten sie, er hätte sich dem Teufel ergeben, der müßte solch unerhört Ding durch ihn treiben. Und da er sie mit einem Wort antastet, nahmen sie ihn zur selbigen Stunde, führten ihn zur Stadt hinaus, wollten ihm den Hals, den Fels hinunter abstürzen, als einem schädlichen Menschen.

145. Denn er hatte sich in der Lection Jesaiä lassen merken, er wäre Messia, da er sagt, derselbe Spruch wäre in ihm erfüllt, Jesaiä am 61,1.: "Der Geist des HErrn ist auf mir, darum hat mich der HErr gesalbet," das ist, zum Messia gemacht, und war doch Bettler, wie sie ihn kannten. Dazu schalt er sie, als wären sie seiner Wunerthaten nicht werth, wie solches Lucas am 4.V.16., anzeigt. Da wurden sie zornig und dachten: Weg mit solchem Messia, der wird Unglück anrichten; wir wissen, daß er ein Bettler ist, und will Messia sein. Aus mit dem Buben, der neulich hat ein Haus helfen aufbauen, un mit uns Späne gelesen, und

ist so plötzlich Messia, das ist, König aller Könige, worden, und verachtet uns heiliges Volk Israel dazu, daß er nicht will thun, was uns gefällt etc.

146. Aber da ärgert sich's erst recht, da er von dem Tod auferstand und gen Himmel fuhr (sie aber meinten, er wäre nun todt, wie er verdient hätte als ein Verführer) daß sie nun sollten diesen JEsum, mit dem sie der Köten (wie man spricht) gespielt hatten, nicht allein für den rechten Messiam halten, sondern auch nach dem Tod für einen Herrn Himmels und Erden annehmen; das war ihnen eine unleidliche und unerträgliche Predigt, daran haben sie sich gestoßen und sind gefallen, der größere Haufe, bis auf diesen Tag; denn ihre Gedanken mußten recht haben, GOtt mußte lügen und unrecht haben, wie sie noch thun, und haben sich bis daher zerlogen und zermurrt wider den JEsum, daß (es) nicht zu sagen noch zu schreiben ist.

147. Ja, das ist (wie ich anfing) des Evangelisten vornehmliche endliche Arbeit, daß er den Jesum gern wollt den Juden einbilden, daß sie ihn für Messiam annähmen, und alle Aergerniß fahren und sich nicht hindern ließen, daß er die dreißig Jahr bei ihnen so verachtlich gelebt und hernach so schändlich gekreuzigt wäre. Denn er sei der Sohn Abraham, David und aller Väter, nach der Schnur hergezählt, bis auf die Mutter Maria, die von Jesaia und dem Heiligen Geist eine Jungfrau bezeugt wäre; nicht ein schlechter Sohn Davids und der Väter, wie andere mehr, als Joseph, Simon, Juda, Jakob; sondern der einige, sonderliche, wunderliche Sohn, in dem die Weissagung und Verheißung, Abraham und David und allen Propheten geschehen, erfüllt wären. Wenn sie diesen Sohn, das ist, die Erfüllung der Weissagung und Verheißung würden annehmen, so hätten sie den rechten Messiam ergriffen, da würden sie das alte Testament wohl fahren lassen, mit Beschneidung, Priesterthum, Fürstenthum, Tempel. Jerusalem und allen Gesetzen, die hierauf gehen und gehören, denn sie bedürften's nicht mehr. Dagegen würden sie das neue Testament, Taufe, Sacrament und alles, was der Messia gelehrt und geordnet hat, fröhlich annehmen, auch viel, viel heiliger halten, denn das alte Testament gewest ist, und nicht darauf stehen bleiben, daß keine heilige Schrift oder Buch mehr sei denn das alte Testament, wie sie träumen.

148. Umsonst und vergeblich hat der Evangelist nicht gearbeitet, neben anderen Aposteln und Evangelisten. Viel sind bekehrt, die den JEsum haben mit großen Freuden angenommen, sich nicht genug verwundern können, daß GOtt so wunderlich, und doch so lieblich und freundlich seine Verheißung erfüllt hat, ehe sie es verstehen konnten. Die andern haben sich gehalten und halten sich noch des Spruchs Jes. 53,2.3.: "Wir sahen ihn, aber da war keine Gestalt, daß wir sein hätten mögen begehren. Er war der Allerverachteste und Unwertheste, voller Schmerzen und Krankheit, er war so verachtet, daß man das Angesicht vor ihm verbarg: darum haben wir sein nicht geachtet" etc. Aber wer den Juden Kochab oder Messia sein will, der muß nicht also gestaltet noch anzusehen sein, sie verachten ihn gewiß, spricht hier Jesaia.

149. Daß wir zum Ende kommen, die Juden, wie gesagt, glauben leicht, daß die Schnur, so Matthäus führt, vom Abraham bis auf Jesum recht sei, und sofern

stehen sie wohl still und hören zu. Denn es sind zu der Zeit alle Manns-und Weibsbilde dess ganzen Stammes Juda, der viel tausend gewest, so wohl von Juda, und der größere Teil vom Hause Davids so wohl herkommen, als Joseph, Maria und ihr Sohn JEsus, das ficht sie freilich nicht an. Aber da der Evangelist dran hängt: "von welcher geboren ist JEsus der da heißt Messia" da prallen sie zurück, als schlüge sie der Donner darnieder, da ist kein Hören mehr, so doch der Evangelist in die Schnur so viel Glieder eingeführt hat, der er wohl weniger hätte mögen nehmen; wie er denn etliche außläst, anzuzeigen, das nicht noth sei, alle zu nennen (denn sie hörten ihr Geschlecht gar gern rühmen), daß ihnen dieser heilsame Artikel auch also mit sollte säuberlich und sanft eingehen.

150. Dazu will St. Matthäus nicht allein aus seinem Geist (wie er doch Macht, Recht und Befehl hat) sagen, daß Maria, eine Jungfrau, geboren habe, sondern führt auch mit ein den Prohpeten Jesaia, sie freundlich zu locken durch ihre eigene Schrift. Aber was hilft's bei den störrigen, knorrigen, halsstarrigen, verdammten Juden? Sie haben hier viel Marterns in diesem Spruch, wie sie in allen andern haben, und können doch nichts schaffen, ohne daß sie immer am Schlegel flicken, und eine Lüge mit sieben Lügen gern wollten wahr machen. Aber, wie droben gesagt, soll man die Juden lassen fahren und nichts darnach fragen, was der Teufel durch sie tobt. Ist etwa ein Menschenherz unter ihnen, das wird GOtt wohl finden; mit den andern heißt's nach dem Sprüchwort: Verloren wie eines Juden Seele. Darum, zu stärken und zu schmücken unsern Glauben, wollen wir sehen, wie lächerlich (doch giftig) der Teufel durch sie diesen Spruch wider St. Matthäum handelt.

Von dem Wort Alma, und der Jungfrauschaft Mariä

151. Erstlich. "Siehe (spricht Jesaias), die Jungfrau ist schwanger" etc. Hie steht das Wort Alma, davon viel andere, ich auch habe geschrieben, daß es heiße eine Jungfrau oder Magd, die noch in Haaren und im Kranze geht und keine Frau worden ist. Und kann mir ein Jude oder Hebräist weisen, daß Alma etwa in der Schrift eine Frau heiße, der soll hundert Gulden bei mir haben, GOtt gebe, wo ich sie finde. Denn viermal, und nicht mehr, steht das Wort Alma in der heiligen Schrift. Erstlich 1 Mos. 24, 16. von der Rebekka, welche mit vielen Worten daselbst Mose beschreibt, daß sie keines Mannes schuldig sei. Zum andern, 2 Mos. 2, 8., von Mosis Schwester Miriam: "da ging Alma hin, und rief ihrer Mutter" etc. Es konnte aber Mirjam nicht wohl zehn Jahr alt sein zu der Zeit, wie die Juden selbst bekennen müssen. Zum dritten, hie Jesaiä.: "Siehe, die Alma ist schwanger." An diesen drei Orten ist ein Artikel, der bedeutet *singulariter unam* und keine andere. Zum vierten, Sprüchw. 30, 18.ff.: "Drei Dinge sind mir wunderlich, und das vierte weiß ich nicht: des Adlers Weg im Himmel, des Schiffes im Meer, der Schlange Weg auf dem Felsen, und eines Manns Weg an einer Magd. Also ist der Weg einer Ehebrecherin, die verschlingt und wischt ihr Maul, und spricht: Ich hab kein Uebels gethan."

152. Hie, hie steht (sprechen sie) Alma bei einem Manne. Ich frage nicht, ob Alma da bei einem Manne stehe; denn ich sehe es selber sehr wohl, GOtt gelobt, darf keines Juden, der mir das zeige. Ich sage, man solle mir beweisen, daß Alma hie eine Frau, und nicht eine Jungfrau heiße; den Meister wollt ich gern hören, und hundert Gulden zugeben. Wie, wenn Salomo an dem Ort (wie es der verfluchte Goj, Doctor Luther, versteht, und ihm nicht wird leichtlich nehmen lassen, wenn's gleich nicht hundert Gulden gelten sollt) redete von dem verdrießlichen Unglück in der Welt? da ein "Geber," das ist, ein Ehemann, nicht kann der Frau Bett treffen in GOttes Namen, und schleicht etwa einer Magd oder Jungfrau nach, des Teufels Namen. Wiederum "Gebirah" (die Frau) nicht kann finden des Mannes Bett, in GOttes Namen, und kreucht zum Knecht oder andern Gesellen, des Teufels Namen, hat ein raum Gewissen, verschlingt den Ehebruch wie der Wolf eine Mücke, wischt darnach das Maul, und darf sie niemand eine Hure schelten. Wer will's beweisen?

153. Weil nun solches muß im Finstern gespielt und heimlich gemaust sein, da gehören wunderliche Wege, Griffe und Ränke zu, die kein Salomo noch Regent alle aussinnen, oder mit Verboten vorkommen, oder überzeugen kann, so wenig er kann dem Vogel in der Luft den Weg vorschreiben, weil der ganze Himmel sein Weg ist, und dem Schiffe das ganze Meer der Weg ist, und geht, wo der Wind hin will, und die Schlange auf dem Felsen, die auch keine Schnur noch Richtscheit hält, sie kann des Krümmen(s) zu viel. Es ist ein Jammer dieses Lebens, daß man dem heimlichen Ehebruch nicht wehren kann, und daß (leider) dem Ehemann eine Magd baß gefällt, denn die Frau, und ein Knecht der Frau lieber ist, denn der Herr; wie auch der Poet sagt: *Quod licet, ingratum est. Nitimur in vetitum. Lex occasio peccati.* Also wolle die Hure Potiphars thun dem frommen Joseph. 1 Mos. 39,7.

154. Dennoch heißt Alma hie eine Magd oder Jungfrau, welcher der Mann nachschleicht; bringt er sie zu Fall, so its sie nimmer eine Magd; ist sie fest, so bleibt sie eine Alma, wie ich der Historien wohl gehört, daß die frommen Jungfrauen haben den Frauen die geilen Männer listiglich zubracht, unter ihrem Namen. Also können die Juden nicht beweisen, daß Alma hie Jesaiä 7. eine Frau heiße, weil das Wort Alma in der ganzen Schrift eine Jungfrau oder Magd heißt; auch in *plurali numero*, Alamoth, können sie nicht beweisen, daß es anders, denn Jungfrauen oder Mägde heiße. Beweise es anders, doch fahr schön, daß ich meine hundert Gulden nicht so schändlich verlieren müsse. Und zuvoraus, daß St. Matthäus ja nicht ein Lügner werde; sonst würde sich der Heilige Geist selbst beschneiden lassen müssen; das wäre Schade um die schönen Federn, daß sie sollten jüdisch werden.

155. Zum andern, spricht Jesaia, daß solche Alma schwanger sei und das solle ein Wunder oder Zeichen sein; spricht nicht, sie wird schwanger werden, wie etliche Raben gern gedeutet hätten: sie mußten sich schämen vor ihrer eigenen *grammatica* daß Hara heißt *concepit, est praegnans* sie ist schwanger, sie hat empfangen. Aber doch wollen sie sich dahinaus drehen, daß der Prophet habe in seinem Alter ein jung Mägdlein genommen und sie geschwängert; darauf fahe er an und spricht: Siehe, ein Alma ist schwanger, und wird einen Sohn gebären, daß also die Meinung

sei: Das ist nicht das Zeichen, daß die Alma schwanger ist, das hat der Prophet schön ausgerichtet, der ist ihr Mann; sondern daß sie einen Sohn, und nicht ein Mägdlein gebiert.

156. Wem wollen wir nun glauben? GOtt spricht: Das soll ein Zeichen sein, daß die Alma schwanger ist. Der Jude spricht: O nein, GOtt leugt, das ist kein Zeichen, weil der Prophet die Alma geschwängert hat. Also haben wir hie zween Text; der Text Jesaiä steht hell und klar da: GOtt wird euch ein Zeichen geben, siehe, die Alma ist schwanger etc. Aber der Juden Text ist dieser: Siehe, die Alma hat einen Mann und ist schwanger vom Propheten, da wird euch GOtt ein Zeichen geben, daß sie einen Sohn wird gebären und nicht Tochter. Möchtest du vielleicht fragen, wo die hohe Kunst in die Juden kommen sei, daß sie den Text und GOttes Wort so meisterlich können würfeln, als wären sie aufm Doppelspiel, und das Hinterste zuvörderst setzen; auch der Alma einen Mann geben, da Jesaias nichts von schreibt, sondern sagt, die Alma sei schwanger, sagt nicht, der Prophet hab's gethan.

157. Ich verfluchter Goj kann nicht verstehen, woher sie solche hohe Kunst haben, ohne daß ich muß denken, da Judas Scharioth sich erhenkt hatte, daß ihm die Därme zerrissen, und, wie den Erhenkten geschieht, die Blase geborsten: da haben die Juden vielleicht ihre Diener mit güldnen Kannen und silbernen Schüsseln dabei gehabt, die Judas-Pisse (wie man's nennt) sammt dem anderen Heiligthum aufgefangen, darnach unternander die Merde gefressen und gesoffen, davon sie so scharfsichtige Augen kriegt, daß sie solche und dergleichen Glosse in der Schrift sehen, die weder Matthäus, noch Jesaias selbst, noch alle Engel, schweige wir verfluchten Gojim, sehen können. Oder haben ihrem Gott, dem Sched, in den Hintern guckt, und in demselben Rauchloch solches geschrieben funden. Es steht ja nicht in der Schrift, das ist gewiß; so läßt sich's nicht herausnehmen.

158. Darum müsen wir verfluchten Gojim den allerheiligsten Juden ihre himmlische Weisheit, so sie außer der Schrift, funden haben in Judas Pisse und in ihrem Judenschweiß, lassen, daß sie allein klug bleiben, und seien wir dieweil Narren mit Jesaia und Matthäo, daß wir in und bei dem armen, magern, dürren Text bleiben, da keine solche Kunst innen ist, wenn des Judas Pisse und der Juden Schweiß heraus ist, nämlich, das diese Alma schwanger sei ohne Mannes Zuthun, und einen Sohn gebäre ohne Verlust ihrer Jungfrauschaft. Denn auch in der ganzen Schrift keinem Weibsbilde ein Kind zugesprochen wird, da nicht der Mann oder Vater des Kindes genannt werde; wie man auch spricht, das Kind muß einen Vater haben, ausgenommen allein diese Alma, da wird keines Mannes gedacht, und doch ihr ein Sohn verheißen.

159. Zu verhüten freilich das böse fährliche Exempel, daß die Jungfrauen und Wittwen nicht rühmen könnten, wenn sie Kinder ohne Männer kriegten, sie hätten's, wie die und die Frau in der Schrift, die auch keine Männer gehabt hätten. Denn es sollte gar ein seltsam Wesen werden, wenn unsere Töchter, Jungfrauen und

Wittwen wollten uns das Haus voll Kinder setzen, und sagen, sie hätten's am Schnee geleckt, und hätten sonst keinen andern Vater. O nein, man leckt die Kinder nicht am Schnee. Moses sagt, 1 Mos. 1, 27., es gehöre ein Männlein und Fräulein dazu; GOtt wollte auch den Segen nicht geben zu Leibesfrucht, bis er sie beide geschaffen und zusammen gegeben hatte.

160. Aber diese einige Maria hat keinen Mann, dem sie das Kind geben könne, sondern muß da bloß allein und ohne Mann stehen, und hören, sie sei schwanger und werde einen Sohn gebären; aber es soll ein Sonderliches, ein Zeichen und Wunder sein (spricht GOtt), nicht die gemeine Weise; ja, es soll mein Zeichen sein, ich will's geben und thun, ich will Vater und Mann sein, sie soll Mutter sein. Nun weiß man wohl (es sollt's schier eine Kuh wissen), daß nicht ein Zeichen ist, wenn ein junge Ehefrau schwanger ist; was wollten oder sollten sie sonst thun, die jungen Frauen, bei ihren Ehemännern, denn daß sie schwanger würden? wozu sind sie sonst geschaffen? Man hält's für kein Zeichen noch Wunder, sondern für eine gemeine Weise und Exempel, das selten fehlen muß.

161. Also ist das auch kein Zeichen noch Wunder, daß ein schwanger Weib einen Sohn trage und gebäre, weil es die gemeine Weise ist, von GOtt geordnet; daß sie nicht eitel Töchter tragen sollen; ohn daß die Juden GOtt zu solchem leichtfertigen Narren machen wollen, daß er solle das ein Zeichen nennen, das sie nach ihrer Judaspisse ein Zeichen erdichten, da doch die Weiber selbst, und die Aerzte leichtlich rathen können, ob's ein Sohn oder Tochter sei. Doch wenn dieses Zeichen steht, daß die Alma ohne einen Mann schwanger ist, so ist's schon mit der Juden Glosse nichts denn Judaspisse und Judenschweiß; das fühlen sie selbst wohl, darum fechten sie das erste Stück an von der Schwängerung der Alma. Denn an dem liegt's das die Mutter Jungfrau sei.

162. Wenn Jesais kein Prophet, und Matthäus kein Evangelist wären, welchen man von GOttes wegen schuldig ist zu glauben, sondern schlechte Historienschreiber, so sollte man ihnen billig glauben, wie man Joseph und Philo thut, und mehr, denn den verlogenen, lästerlichen, verstockten Juden, die in der ganzen Schrift nun schier bei zweitausend Jahren sich geflissen und geübt haben, eine Lüge auf die andere zu erdichten, daß man ihnen billig kein Wort glauben soll. Denn einem verlogenen Maul glaubt man nichts, wenn er gleich die Wahrheit sagt (wie man spricht), wenn ihm GOtt gleich ein wahr Wort beschert, so glaubt's doch niemand. *Et illiud: Si mentiris, etiam, quod verum dicis, mentiris.* Christus, unser Herr, wollte die Teufel auch nicht reden lassen, ob sie wohl die Wahrheit sagten; also soll man die Juden auch halten, schlecht verlogen wie die Teufel, zuvoraus wo zween fromme ehrliche Männe oder *historici* anders sagen; wie viel mehr, wo ein Prophet und Evangelist anders sagen. Denn es taugt nicht, daß man Judas-pisse und der Juden Schweiß über die Salbe des Heiligen Geists hebe.

163. Auch ist's nicht Isaias allein, der die Mutter Christi eine Jungfrau verkündigt. Es hat's Gott am Anfang der Welt, nach dem Fall Adam, da er die erst Verheißung des neuen Testaments oder Evangelii gab, verkündigt, da er sprach:

"Ich will Feindschaft setzen zwischen dir und einem Weibe, zwischen deinem Samen und ihrem Samen, der selbe soll dir den Kopf zertreten, und du wirst ihn in die Ferse stechen" etc. (1 Mos. 3, 15.) GOtt der HErr könnte freilich wohl so viel Redens, daß er hätte mögen sagen: Eines Mannes Same soll dir den Kopf zertreten, oder doch den Mann nennen, deß das Weib wäre; aber nun schweigt er des Mannes und gibt das Kind oder Samen allein dem Weibe; das kann niemand sein, denn Maria, die Mutter Christi; denn alle Kinder und Samen werden sonst den Männern zugreschrieben.

164. Ob nun wohl alle Heiligen von Adam her, und wir Christen bis ans Ende auch solcher Same sind, die dem Teufel den Kopf zertreten, so sind wir's doch nicht von uns selbst, sondern von dem Samen des Weibs, an den wir glauben, gleichwie wir nach ihm Christen und GOttes Kinder heißen und auch sind, weil wir in ihm, das ist, in Christo und GOttes Sohn bleiben; wir müssen ihm gleich werden. Durch solchen Glauben des verheißenen Samens ist zur selben Zeit Adam, Eva, Abel von der Schlange Gewalt wieder aufkommen, und seine Kopftreter worden. Was nun hie etliche Väter in diesem Spruch spielen mit Allegorien, lassen wir fahren. Denn einen Teils taugen gar nichts: als, daß Adam solle sein *portio superior rationes*, Eva *inferior portio*. Solche *philosophia* gehört hier her nichts. Eines Theils machen aus Eva die Kirche, die Christen ihren Samen. Aber das ist ein Stück vom rechten Verstand, nämlich, wie gesagt, daß all Heiligen auch solcher Same sind durch den Glauben an den einigen Samen des einigen Weibes. Und ob jemand wollte vorgehen, hiemit wäre noch nicht beweist, daß das Weib müsse eine Jungfrau sein, könnte wohl eine Wittwe sein: wohlan, GOtt hat's nicht alles wollen auf einmal herausschütten, sondern mit der Zeit klarer und klarer verkündigen; es ist jetzt genug, daß Christus solle eines Weibes Same sein ohne Mannes Samen; da ist die Jungfrauschaft angezeigt. An dem Samen liegt's alles. Hernach soll's Jesaias ausdrücken, daß (es) eine Alma, Jungfrau sei. Das Neue Testament soll helle frei heraussagen, sie heiße Jungfrau Maria zu Nazareth, Josephs Braut und Christi Mutter.

165. Hierher sieht (wie uns die *Grammatici* Hebräisten vermahnen) der Patriarcha Jakob mit dem Wort Silo, 1 Mos. 49,10.: "Der Scepter Juda soll nicht wegkommen, bis Silo kommt." Denn es sehr gut zu rechnen ist, daß die Väter von Adam her die Verheißung von des Weibes Samen täglich und wohl geübt haben, als der ihr Leben und Seligkeit gewest ist, nach dem Jammer und Fall Adams. Silo aber kommt her von Silva oder Siljah (wie sie sagen), und soll heißen *secundinam*, da das Kind in Mutterlieb inne liegt, oder neulich geboren Kindlein, *continens pro contento* wie das 5 Mos. am 28. V. 53. scheint, da er den Juden solchen Jammer dräuet, daß ein Weib vor großem Hunger werde ihr Siljah fressen, die von ihrem Leibe ausgehen, das ist, ihr Kindlein, neulich geboren, *per Synecdochen*, welche Figur in allen Sprachen gemein ist. Als wenn wir sagen, der kann ein Faß aussaufen, einen Topf ausfressen, so man doch nicht faß noch Töpfe, sondern das drinnen ist, säuft und frißt. Item: "Jerusalem, Jerusalem, du schlägest die Propheten todt" (Matth. 23,37.), so doch die Steine und Holz solches nicht thaten, sondern die Leute, so drinnen sind. Item, das ist ein bös Haus, wenn böse Leute drinnen sind.

166. Also will nun Jakob sagen: bis daß Silo kommt, das ist, bis ihr(der Frau, nicht des Mannes) Kind kommt, das sie allein in ihem Leibe empfangen, getragen und geboren hat, davon unserm Vater Adam gesagt ist: eines Weibes Same etc., auf Deutsch, bis daß der Jungfrauen Sohn kommt. Denn er sollte nicht in Sünden empfangen und geboren werden, wie andere Adamskinder; darum mußte seine Mutter eine Jungfrau sein, die kein Mann berührt hatte, auch keine Wittwe, welche zuvor einen Mann gehabt, und zu der Erbsünde zu mehren gedient und geholfen hat. Psalm 51, 7.

167. Und wenn der Teufel diese Ursache hätte mögen haben, daß Maria eine Wittwe wäre, sollte er uns so viel Christos gemacht haben, als eine Wittwe möchte Kinder getragen haben, daß wir nicht gewußt hätten, welcher's wäre, und damit unter so vielen Söhnen den rechten einigen verloren hätten. Es hat sonst Mühe gehabt, daß wir den einigen behalten haben vor seinem Wüthen. Denn er fing durch seinen Manichäum schon an, einen andern Christum zu machen, der Mariä nicht natürlichen Sohn, sondern ein Gespenst von ihr kommen wäre. So wollte Helvidius, der Narr, auch Marien mehr Söhne nach Christo geben, aus diesen Worten des Evangelisten: "und Joseph erkannte seine Braut Maria nicht, bis sie ihren ersten Sohn gebar"; solches wollte er verstehen, als hätte sie nach dem ersten Sohn mehr Söhne gehabt; der grobe Narr. Dem hat St. Hyronymus fein geantwortet. Summa, er ist dem Samen des Weibes feind, wollte ihn gern zunicht oder doch ungewiß machen. Daher (wie gehört) die Evanglisten die Schnur des Geschlechts so fleißig beschrieben, daß die Juden (sich) nicht sollten ärgern und denken, es müßte ein anderer Jesus sein, von dem solche großen Dinge gesagt würden, dieser (den sie wohl kennten), Marien Sohn, könnt's nicht sein. Ach ja (sprechen sie), es ist derselbige, der einige Jesus, der Sohn Mariä, der Sohn David, Abraham und aller Vorfahren.

168. Darum war es noth, daß seine Mutter wäre eine Jungfrau, eine junge Jungfrau, eine heilige Jungrfrau, die von der Erbsünde erlöst und gereinigt durch den Heiligen Geist, nicht mehr dem einen Sohn, Einen Jesum trüge, er ihr Siljah, Frucht, ihres Leibes Samens, ohne Vater ein einiger Christus uns gewiß sein könnte. Aber hie ist nicht Zeit, solches auszustreichen; denn ich müßte predigen, wie des Weibes Same müße ein Segen sein, Abrahä verheißen, das ist, wie er müßte Gott sein. Ich habe anderswo davon geschrieben und geredet, darum lass ich's jetzt so genug sein.

169. Daß die Rabbinen dringen möchten auf das He und Cholem im Silo, ficht mich nichts an, kann das Cholem wohl wegthun: wenn gleich Silo nicht sollt Silah zu lesen sein, *feminino genere*, dennoch wäre die Frucht des Weibes allein, weil kein Mann da ist, und müßte heißen der Jungfrauen Sohn von Juda, oder des Juda. Aber 5 Mos. 28, 53. steht der Mann bei der Frau, die ihre Kinder frißt; hie steht allein des Weibes Frucht, Silo, ohne Mann. Hievon werden gar viel feiner Predigt geschehen, und Bücher geschrieben sein, die mit der Zeit sind vergessen und verloren; wie wir jetzt sehen, daß ein gut Buch oder Predigt kaum ein Jahr währt, und, wie man sagt, ein neu Lied singt man Ein Jahr, ohne was wenig Leute sind, die solches behalten auf ihre Nachkommen; der Haufe läßt's vorüber laufen, und

wartet immer auf ein Neues; damit behält der Teufel die Welt immer für und für in Irrthum, der kleine Haufe bleibt bei dem, das er empfangen hat, Joh. 8, 31. Also ist's geschehen, also geht's von Anfang bis zu Ende der Welt, daß große Dinge geschehen, und doch wenig des achten; die andern lassen's fahren und vergessen's.

170. Dennoch wäre nun Jesaias ein feiner *Vocabularius*, der uns als ein Mesiter das Wort Silo, und des Weibes Samen hätte ausgelegt, als sollte er sagen: Wollt ihr wissen, was Silo, was Weibs Same heißt? ich will's euch sagen: Es ist das Wunderzeichen, daß Messiah soll sein einer Jungfrauen Sohn seine Mutter soll eine Alma sein, die in ihrem jungfräulichen Siljah oder Leibe empfähet ohne Manns Zuthun. St. Elisabeth geht auch fein gleich zu, da sie Mariam fröhlich empfing und sprach: "Gebenedeiet ist die Frucht deines Leibes" (Luc.1.,42.), das ist Silo, die Frucht *matricis tuae*, deiner Siljah, oder deines Leibes allein, und keines Mannes; denn meines Leibes Kind hat einen Vater, Zacharia genannt.

171. Also singt auch David Psalm 22, 10. in der Person Christi: "Du hast mich aus meiner Mutter Leibe gezogen." Hie nennt er sich selbst Silo, der aus seiner Mutter Leibe (nicht aus seines Vaters Lenden, wie alle anderen Kinder) gezogen sei. Item V.11.: "Auf dich bin ich geworfen aus Mutter Leibe, du bist mein GOtt von meiner Mutter Leibe an." Solches kann kein Kind Adams sagen, die alle in Zorn und Sünden, und ohne GOtt geboren werden, Ps. 51,7. Allein dieser Einige ist GOttes Kind und in Gnaden, des Augenblicks, da er von seiner Mutter Leibe genommen wird, und muß doch so große Marter leiden, der eitel Gnade würdig ist etc.

172. Weiter spricht David Psalm 110, 3.: "Aus der Mutter, aus der Morgenröhte, so kommt deine Geburt aus der Mutter (Mutter heißt hier nicht die ganze Person des Weibs, wie im vierten Gebot, sondern das die Frauen Mutter heißen in ihrem Leibe, *matricem* oder Siljah).

Nun fällt der Thau vom Himmel ohne aller Menschen zuthun, Mich. 5,6., ja, auch ohne Wolken, auch wenn der Himmel hell und die Morgenröhte am schönsten ist, so fällt er am allerlieblichsten; kann niemand sagen, woher, oder wo er anfähet zu fallen. Also ist auch Christus kommen aus der Mutter, die in der Jungfrauen Maria Leibe ist, daß kein Vater drum weiß, ja, kein Mensch, noch sie selbst sagen noch wissen kann, wie es zugangen sei, daß dieser schöne Tau, Christus, in ihrer Mutter oder Leib empfangen und geboren sei. Er heißt: vom Heiligen Geist, von oben herab, empfangen.

173. Demnach heißen nun auch alle Christen "geboren wie der Thau vom Himel," Mich. 5,6. Denn weil wir an ihn glauben, werden wir ihm gleich gemacht und geachtet. Joh. 1,12.: "Er gab ihnen Macht, GOttes Kinder zu werden, die nicht aus dem Geblüte, sondern aus GOtt geboren sind." Denn niemand kann sagen noch wissen, wo ein Christ herkommt; "denn er wird aus Geist und Wasser geboren," Joh. 3,5. Das Wasser sieht man, wie man den Thau fühlt, aber die Geburt sieht niemand. Also sind wir auch Kinder, aus dem Heiligen Geist

empfangen und geboren, Christo gleich, ohn daß wir aus Gnaden und um seinetwillen dazu kommen; er aber hat's seiner Person halben, darum, daß er GOttes Sohn, nicht durft anderweit geboren werden, ist in der alten Geburt der Sünden und Todes nicht gesteckt, wie wir verlorene Adamskinder.

174. Hiezu führen wir auch den Spruch Jeremiä am 31,22.: "Der Herr wird ein Neues schaffen auf Erden, ein Weib wird einen Mann umgeben." Das hat man in der ganzen Christenheit gelesen und verstanden von Christo und der Jungfrau Marien, seiner Mutter wie recht und billig ist. "Es soll ein Neues sein," spricht er, das nicht gewest ist zuvor auf Erden. Es sind von Anfang Kinder geboren, Regiment gewest, böse und gute Leute gelebt, sich gebessert und verbösert, wie es noch jetzt geht, und bis an der Welt Ende gehen wird: aber hie soll das neue Wunder geschehen, das vor nie geschehen ist, nämlich eine Nekefa, ein Weib, die nicht ein Mann ist, solle einen Mann umgeben, das ist, Maria soll GOttes Sohn empfangen und gebären.

175. Denn das muß sein, so unser Glaube recht sein soll, daß Christus, unser HErr, in dem Augenblick, da Maria dem Engel Gabriel ihr Vollwort gab und sprach: "Mir geschehe nach deinem Wort," ist zugleich GOtt und vollkommener Mensch gewest in Einer Person, wie das die lieben Väter im Concilio Ephesino wider dem Nestorium erhalten haben. Denn wo das nicht sein sollte, so wäre sie nicht *theotocos*, GOttes=Mutter, zu nennen, noch Christus ihr Sohn zu nennen; davon anderswo disputirt, und hie zu lang ist zu handeln. Laß mir nun das einen neuen seltsamen Mann sein, der zugleich GOtt und Mensch, in Mutterleibe ein Kindlein ist, es sei wie klein es wolle. Klein muß er gewest sein, wie die Doctores, Damascenus, und mehr hernach, dasselbe ausrechnen. Demnach nennt Elisabeth Mariam des HErrn Mutter aus vollem Geist, so doch Maria vielleicht kaum vierzehn Tage dazumal schwanger gewest ist, um welche Zeit kein Kind in andern Weibern leben kann; wie man weiß.

176. Zuletzt kann ich's nicht lassen, ich muß anzeigen, welche feine Gedanken St. Bernhard, aus Mose spinnt, 3 Mos. 1, 2. da er spricht: "Wenn ein Weib besamt wird, und ein Knäblein gebiert, soll sie sieben Tage unrein sein" etc. Hie verwundert sich St. Bernhard, warum Mose seinen Mund läst übergehen mit solchen vergeblichen Worten: wenn ein Weib besamt wird; warum spricht er nicht kurz also: Ein jeglich Weib, das ein Knäblein gebiert, soll unrein sein sieben Tage? Weiß man doch wohl, daß alle Weiber müssen besamt werden, sollen sie Kinder tragen, und keine trägt ein Kind, die unbesamt ist. Da schleußt er, daß Mose habe seinen Mund wollen verwahren, und sich nicht verbrennen an der Mutter des HErrn, die er hiemit will ausgenommen haben von seinem Gesetze, daß sie nicht soll den andern Weibern gleich unrein sein; damit verkündigt, es würde einmal kommen die Mutter, so ein Knäblein gebären würde, unbesamt, das ist, die den Silo, ein Mutterkind ohne Vater tragen würde.

177. Solches alles will ich diesmal geschrieben haben unserm lieben HErrn zu Ehren, Lob und Dank, zu stärken unsern Glauben, zu Hohn und Verdrieß dem leidigen Teufel, und seinen beschnittenen Heiligen. Denn ich sehr wohl weiß, wie

sie diese eingeführten Sprüche shänden und lästern, damit niemand dürfte sagen, und ich wüßte ihr Ding nicht, verdammt sie unverhört, und ich würde nicht so freveln wider sie, wenn ich ihren Verstand wüßte. Nein, (GOtt gelobt), ich weiß wohl was ihre Weisheit ist in der Schrift, hab's in jenem Büchlein beweiset, in dem Spruch Jakob 1 Mos. 49. Haggai 2 Daniel 9. und im Artikel von der Beschneidung und von dem Adel des Geblüts; in diesem Büchlein im Scham Haperes, Jesaiä 9. und dergleichen. Ich hab nichts Unbewußtes handeln wollen.

178. Will auch wohl ihre Kunst im Spruch Jeremiä 31,22. noch anzeigen, da sie sagen: "Ein Weib wird einen Mann umgeben" solle heißen so viel: das Volk Israel ist das Weib, GOtt der Mann. Nun ist Israel eine Hure gewest in der Abgötterei; darnach hat sie sich bekehrt und bereuet, damit den Mann, das ist, GOtt, wieder umgeben und versöhnt. Wenn nun gleich die Worte das könnten geben, als nicht sein kann, wie kann solches ein Neues auf Erden geschaffen heißen? Ist das Volk Israel niemal eine solche Hure gewest und wieder bekehrt worden? Da frage das Buch der Richter um. Hie will's doch dahin kommen, daß, was ein Rabbin neu heißt, das ist neu, was er alt heißt, das ist alt, wie droben die Regel gibt von der linken und rechten Hand.

179. Aber das ist noch viel höhere, feinere Kunst; an diesem Ort sprechen sie, das Weib sei die Hure Israel zu verstehen; wenn sie aber Hochzeit haben, führen sie die Braut dreimal um den Bräutigam, auf das sie diesem Spruch Jeremiä genug thun, ein Weib umgibt den Mann. Hie muß Nekefa, das Weib, eine Jungfrau heißen, dort eine Hure. Warum? Darum, daß die Rabbinen nicht fehlen können, wenn sie sagen, eine Hure ist eine Jungfrau, und eine Jungfrau ist eine Hure, nach der Regel, daß die linke Hand recht ist wenn sie ein Rabe recht heißt. Und muß auch vor nie ein solch Ding geschehen sein, wenn ein Weib oder Braut um den Mann dreimal geführt wird, denn Jeremias spricht: "es solle ein Neues sein auf Erden, vom HErrn geschaffen." Aber hie hat ein Rabbin der Sache bald geholfen und gesagt was er neu heiße, das ist neu, was er aber alt heiße, das ist alt, *ut supra*.

180. Summa, verzweifelten Teufels Lügenmäuler meinen nichts anders, denn die heilige Schrift sei ihr eigen, wie ein Papier, deraus sie Männlein, Vögelein, Häuslein, Katzenstühlein schnitzen möchten, wie sie wollen; und was sie sagen, das sollen beide, ihre Juden und wir Christen, für recht annehmen.

181. Darum will ich hiemit wiederum ein Urtheil über die verfluchten Rabbinen sprechen. Erstlich also: Die heilige Schrift ist nicht der Juden, nicht der Heiden, auch nicht der Engel, viel weniger der Teufel, sondern allein GOttes, der hat sie allein gesprochen und geschrieben, der soll sie auch allein deuten und auslegen, wo es noth ist; Teufel und Menschen sollen Schüler und Zuhörer sein.

182. Zum andern, ist uns Christen verboten bei Verlust göttlicher Gnaden und ewigen Lebens, der Rabbinen Verstand und Glossen in der Schrift zu glauben, oder für recht zu halten. Lesen mögen wir's, zu sehen, was sie verdammt Teufelswerk bei sich treiben, uns davor zu hüten. Denn so spricht Mose, 5 Mos. 28, 28.: "Gott wird dich schlagen mit Wahnsinn, Blindheit und rasenden Herzen."

Solches hat Mose nicht von den verfluchten Gojim gesagt, sondern von seinen beschnittenen Heiligen, dem edlen Blut, Fürsten Himmels und der Erden, die sich Israel nennen. Hiemit ist aber von GOtt selbst verdammt all ihr Verstand, Glosse und Auslegung in der Schrift als eitel Wahnsinn, Blindheit, Raserei, daß alles, was sie diese 1500 Jahr in der Schrift gearbeitet haben das spricht und urtheilt GOtt selbst nicht allein falsch und Lügen, sondern auch eitel Blindheit, rasend, wahnsinnig Ding. Und wie solch Urtheil lautet, so findet's sich auch in dem Werk und in der That, wie du droben gesehen hast im Spruch Jakobs 1 Mos. 49, 10. Hagg. 2,7. Dan. 9,24 im Schem Hamphoras; Jes. 7, 14. von der Alma; Jer. 31,22. von der Nekefa. Summa, dergleichen thun sie in allen Sprüchen, so vom Messia und rechtem Glauben reden. Ein rasender Mensch muß rasen.

183. Solch Urtheil bestätigt Jes. 29, 13.14.: "Darum, daß dies Volk zu mir nahet mit seinem Munde, und mit seinen Lippen mich ehrt, aber ihr Herz fern von mir ist, und mich fürchten nach Menschen Gebot, die sie lehren, so will ich auch mit diesem Volk wunderlich umgehen, aufs wunderlichste und seltsamste, daß die Weisheit seiner Weisen soll untergehen, und der Verstand seiner Klugen soll sich verbergen." Das ist auch nicht von uns Gojim, sondern vom Volk Israel gesagt, welches treffliche, weise, kluge Leute und Propheten gehabt, und derselben Bücher noch haben; aber weil sie ein falsch, heuchel Lügenvolk sind worden, die GOtt mit dem Maul rühmen, und mit dem Herzen zum Teufel fahren sollen sie die Weisheit und Verstand der Propheten auch verlieren und nicht haben, sondern, wie sie GOtt mit dem Maul (das ist mit den Hülsen) bezahlen, und mit dem Herzen (das ist, mit dem Kern) dem Teufel dienen, so sollen sie wiederum auch die Buchstaben (die ledigen Schalen) in der Schrift haben, aber den Kern, den rechten Verstand sollen sie nicht riechen.

184. Hart davor im selben Capitel, V. 11., spricht er: "Es sollen euch aller Propheten Weissagungen sein, wie die Worte eines versiegelten Buchs oder Briefes, welchen man gebe zu lesen (einem), der da lesen könne oder nicht; (er) muß sagen, ich kann sein nicht lesen, denn er ist versiegelt" etc. Solches gibt auch das Werk in den blinden rasenden Juden; denn sie das Buch wohl haben, aber da ist kein Verstand, weder vom Messia, noch Gesetz Mosis in einigem Vers, das die Heiden und Poeten viel besser Ding lehren, weder die Juden, da sie auch am besten sind. Der Sprüche sind viel mehr in den Propheten, sonderlich der Psalm 69, 23. f., den St. Paulus einführt Röm. 11, 9.: "Ihr Tisch müsse vor ihnen zum Stricke werden, zur Vergeltung, und zur Falle. Ihre Angesicht müsse finster werden, daß sie nicht sehen" etc.

185. Aber 2 Cor. 3, 14. 15. 16. malt sie St. Paulus ja recht, da er von diesen Juden sint der Zeit Christi her redet (denn es kann von niemand anders verstanden werden).: "Bis auf diesen heutigen Tag, wenn Moses gelesen wird, bleibt die Decke über ihrem Herzen; denn ihre Sinne sind verstockt. Wenn sie sich aber zu dem HErrn bekehrten, würde die Decke abgethan." Also hat ihnen der HErr selbst auch verkündigt Matth. 8,12.: "Die Kinder des Reichs werden in Finsternis herausgeworfen werden"; und Joh. 8,21.: "Ich gehe dahin, und ihr werdet mich suchen und in euren Sünden sterben; denn da ich hingehe, könnet ihr nicht hinkommen."

Und was treibt St. Paulus in allen Episteln, denn daß er die Juden Hunde, Zerschneidung, und ganz verblendet und verstockt schilt, vor denen man sich hüten solle?

186. Wenn nun über solch Urtheil und Verdammniß der Juden ein Christ will bei den Juden Verstand in der Schrift suchen, was thut er anders, denn der bei einem Blinden das Gesicht, bei dem Rasenden Klugheit, bei dem Tod das Leben, bei dem Teufel Gnade und Wahrheit sucht? Recht geschieht ihm, so er auch wahnsinnig, blind und rasend wird, wie seine Meister sind, von GOtt verdammt. Das man die Sprache und Grammatica von ihnen lernt, das ist fein und wohl gethan, gleichwie sie auch thun, lernen von uns die deutsche Sprache, von Walen die welsche, und wo sie sind da lernen sie des Landes Sprache; aber unsern Glauben und Verstand der Schrift lernen sie nicht. Also sollen wir auch die Sprache von ihnen lernen; aber ihren Glauben und Verstand, von GOtt verdammt, meiden.

187. Darum sollten unsere Hebräisten (darum ich sie auch hiermit will um GOttes willen gebeten haben) lassen ihnen diese Arbeit befohlen und angelegen sein, die heilige alte Bibel von der Juden Peres und Judaspisse zu reinigen, wo sie die Punkte, Distinction, Conjugation, Construction, Signification, und was mehr die Grammatica hat, könnten ändern, und von der Juden Verstand wenden, daß sich's zum und mit dem neuen Testament reimte, daß sie solches getrost und mit Freuden thäten, wie St. Paulus Röm. 12,7. lehrt, daß die *prophetia* soll *analoga*, ähnlich sein dem Glauben. Denn so haben sie uns, das ist, der Bibel gethan diese 1500 Jahr. Wo sie die Bibel mit Punkten, Distinction, Conjugation etc. haben können von unserm Messia und Glauben wenden, und dem Neuen Testament unähnlich machen, das haben sie mit großem und rasendem Fleiß gethan, wie droben in den Exempeln 1 Mos. 49, 10. Haggai 2,7. Daniel 9, 24. Jesaiä 7, 14. und der gleichen zu sehen ist.

188. Als, Jesaiä 9,5., da sie den Text also machen, Vajikra, Schemo, Pele etc.: Es wird der Wunderbar, Rath GOtt, Held, ewiger Vater den Messiam nennen Friedfürst. Hie sieht man ihren Muthwillen, darum soll man ihre Punkte und Construction verwerfen, und lesen, wie wir's lesen, weil es die Grammatica der Buchstaben gerne gibt, so man für Vayikra lieset Vayikare, und alle Namen im Nominativo stehen können. Solches werden die Hebräisten wohl mehr finden, auf daß man den Dieben wieder mit Ehren nehme, das sie mit Schanden gestohlen haben diese 1500 Jahr, vielleicht auch wohl länger. Denn das Hauptstück muß wahr sein, daß die alte heilige Schrift auf Messiam und unseren Glauben gehe und zeuge; wer sie dahin nicht versteht, der kann sie nicht haben.

189. Darum hab ich gesagt, daß Mose und die Schrift bei den jetzigen Juden nicht kenntlich, noch der rechte alte Mose ist, so schändlich haben sie ihn besudelt mit ihrer Judaspisse. Denn Mose will traun des Messiä Zeuge sein, das ist gewiß. Aber weil sie den Messiam so schändlich zurichten, ist's unmöglich, daß sie sollten Mose in einem Pasuk recht verstehen. Diese Arbeit wollt ich gern aufgeladen sehen meinem lieben Herrn und Freunde, M. Bernhard Ziegler zu Leipzig, hebräischem Professor, daß er auch einmal sich hervor thäte, wie die andern Hebräisten (GOtt

Lob) nicht ohne große Frucht sich haben lassen sehen; den er ist sonderlich der jüdischen Judaspisse feind, und vermöchte wohl etwas, zöge die andern Hebräisten zu sich, und reinigten uns die Hebräische Bibel. Denn soll sie rein und wieder gut Hebräisch werden, so müssen's die Christen thun, die den Verstand haben des Messia, wie Paulus sagt, 1 Cor. 1,24., "wir haben den Sinn Messiä," und Luc. 23, 45.: "Er that ihnen den Sinn auf, daß sie die Schrift verstanden"; und Matth. 13, 11.: "Euch ist's gegeben, zu verstehen das Geheimniß des Himmelreichs."

190. Ob man müßte mich angreifen und tadeln, der ich zuweilen in der Dolmetschung gefehlt hätte, das will ich mit Dank annehmen. Denn wie oft hat Hieronymus gefehlt! Und ich sehe, wie die zween feinen Männer, Sanctes und Münster haben *studio incredibili et diligentia inimitabili* die Bibel verdolmetscht, viel Gutes damit gethan. Aber die Rabbinen sind ihrer etwa zu mächtig, daß sie auch der analogia des Glaubens gefehlt, der Rabbinen Glosse zu viel nachgehängt haben. Denn ich auch selbst ihrer Translation etwa zu viel gefolgt, daß ich muß widerrufen, sonderlich 2 Sam. 23., in *verbis novissimis David* wie ich bald thun will.

191. Mit dieser Weise könnte man der Juden Verstand in der Bibel fein schwächen, und ist das Vortheil da, daß Mose und die Propheten nicht haben mit Punkten geschrieben, welches ein neu Menschenfündlein, nach ihrer Zeit aufbracht; darum nicht noth ist, die selben so steif zu halten, als die Juden gerne wollten, sonderlich wo sie dem neuen Testament zuwider gebraucht werden. Ebenso soll man auch mit der *aequivocatio* und *distinctio* thun wo sie wider das Neue Testament dienen. Die Juden haben doch Lust alle ihr Ding zweifelhaftig und nichts Gewisses zu machen. Darum, wo sich die *aequivocatio* in einem *vocabulo* begibt, so nehme man die *significatio,* die mit dem Neuen Testament stimmt, so wird sie gewiß; und die rechte *significatio* hat einen starken Zeugen und Beistand am Neuen Testament; so bleibt den Juden die andere *sinificatio,* das ist, die ledige Hülse und Peres, ohne Zeugen und Beistand.

192. Solches sei den Hebräisten befohlen. Hie will ich's lassen und mit den Juden nicht mehr zu thun haben, noch weiter von ihnen, oder wider sie schreiben; sie haben's genug. Welche sie bekehren wollen, da gebe GOtt seine Gnade zu, daß sie (doch etliche) mit uns erkennen und loben GOtt den Vater, unsern Schöpfer, sammt unserm HErrn JEsu Christo, und dem Heiligen Geist in Ewigkeit, Amen.

C

Pastoral Letter on the Occasion of the 25th Anniversary of the Proclamation of the Conciliar Declaration "Nostra Aetate"

Dear Brothers and Sisters in Christ,

We address you today about the very important issue of our relationship to the Jewish people and to the Mosaic religion, with which we Christians are uniquely linked. We do this on the occasion of the 25th anniversary of the proclamation of the Conciliar Declaration "Nostra Aetate," in which the Church defined more precisely its relations to non–Christian religions, among them, the Jewish religion. This Declaration, adopted on October 27, 1965, has lost none of its importance or contemporary value today. Our Holy Father John Paul II has repeated this on numerous occasions, saying "I would like to confirm with the deepest conviction that the teaching of the Church, given during the Second Vatican Council in the Declaration "Nostra Aetate" ... always remains for us, for the Catholic Church, for the episcopate ... and for the Pope, a teaching to which one must adhere, a teaching which one must accept not only as something relevant but even more, as an expression of faith, as an inspiration of the Holy Spirit, as a word of Divine Wisdom" (speech to the Jewish community in Venezuela, January 15, 1985).

The Conciliar Declaration points out first and foremost the multiplicity and diversity of ties that exist between the Church, the Jewish religion and the Jewish people. There is no other religion with which the Church has such close relations, nor is there any other people with which it is so closely linked. "The church of Christ," write the Fathers of the Council, "acknowledges that, in God's plan of salvation the beginning of her faith and election is to be found in the patriarchs, Moses, and the prophets" ("Nostra Aetate," no. 4). Therefore, John Paul II, who after St. Peter, was the first of his successors to visit a synagogue, having visited the

Read on January 20, 1991. Trans. by Prof. Thomas E. Bird, Queens College, New York, at the Interreligious Affairs Department of the American Jewish Committee.

synagogue in Rome on April 13, 1986, could address the Jews as "our elder brothers" in the faith.

The Church is rooted in the Jewish people and in the faith of the Jews most of all because of the fact that Jesus Christ, according to the flesh, came from that people. This central event in the history of salvation was from its very inception intended by God in his original plan of salvation. To that people God disclosed His Name and made a covenant with them. This election was not only an exclusive privilege but also a great commitment to the faith and fidelity to the one God including the testimony of suffering and, quite often, of death as well. To this people God entrusted the special mission of uniting everyone in the true faith in one God and awaiting the Messiah, the Savior. When the time was fulfilled, the Eternally true Word of God, the only begotten son of the Father took flesh from the Virgin Mary, a daughter of the Jewish people. Announced by the prophets and awaited by his own people, Jesus Christ was born in Bethlehem, as "a son of David, a son of Abraham" (*Matthew 1, 1*). From the Jewish people came also "the Apostles, the pillars on which the Church stands, as are many of those early disciples who proclaimed the Gospel of Christ to the world" ("Nostra Aetate," *ibid.*).

The Church, as God's people of the new election and covenant, did not disinherit God's people of the first election and covenant of the gifts received from God. As St. Paul teaches, the Israelites, because of their forefathers, are the subject of love (*Romans 11, 28*) and therefore, the gift of grace and the calling of God are irrevocable (*Romans, 11, 29*). To them belong also "the sonship, the glory, the covenants, the giving of the Law, the worship and the promises" (*Romans 9, 4*). God thus has not revoked his selection of the Jewish people as the chosen people, but continues to bestow his love. He and only He, the Almighty and Merciful God, knows the day "when all people will call on God with one voice and serve Him shoulder to shoulder ("Nostra Aetate," *ibid.*).

The Fathers of the Council, in the Declaration, deny in a clear and decisive manner the main accusation that all Jews bear responsibility for the death of Christ. The Declaration states, "Although the Jewish authorities and their supporters demanded the death of Christ, what was committed during His passion, cannot be ascribed to all Jews without distinction who lived at that time, nor to present-day Jews" ("Nostra Aetate," *ibid.*). Some people, however, quoting the words of St. Matthew's Gospel, "Let his blood be upon us, and upon our children," (*Matthew 27, 25*) accuse the Jews of the death of Christ. In reality, these words mean: We accept the full responsibility for that death. But it was not the entire Jewish people who said this, only the unruly crowd gathered in front of Pilate's palace. One should not forget that for these people, as for all of us, Jesus prayed on the cross: "Father, forgive them, for they know now what they do" (*Luke 23, 34*).

The Catechism of the Council of Trent treats the question of the responsibility for the death of Christ as follows: "Christian sinners are more responsible for the death of Christ in comparison with certain Jews who participated in it. The latter really 'did not know what they did, whereas we know only too well'" (pars I, cap. v, questio IX). The Declaration "Nostra Aetate" reminds us of the traditional teaching of the Church that Christ ... accepted his passion and death voluntarily with unlimited love for the sins of all people" ("Nostra Aetate," *ibid.*).

The teaching of the Church in that Declaration was developed in later documents of the Apostolic See. Especially important is a document of 1985 entitled "The Jews and Judaism in Spreading the Word of God in Catechesis of the Catholic Church." This deserves the widest possible dissemination, especially among pastors and catechists.

With the Jewish people we Poles have particular ties as early as from the first centuries of our history. Poland became for many Jews a second fatherland. The majority of Jews living in the world today are by origin from the territories of the previous and current Polish Commonwealth. Unfortunately, in our century this particular land became the grave for several million Jews. Not by our wish, and not by our hands. Here is what Our Holy Father said recently, on September 26 of this year, about our common history. "There is still one other nation, one particular people: the people of the Patriarchs, of Moses, and the Prophets, the inheritors of the faith of Abraham.... This people lived side by side with us for generations, on the same land, which became as it were, a new fatherland of their diaspora. This people underwent the terrible death of millions of their sons and daughters. At first they were stigmatized in a particular way. Later, they were pushed into the ghetto in separate neighborhoods. Then they were taken to the gas-chambers, they underwent death—only because they were children of this people. Murderers did this on our land—perhaps in order to dishonor it. One cannot dishonor a land by the death of innocent victims. Through such death a land becomes a sacred relic" (speech to the Poles during a Wednesday audience, September 26, 1990).

During his historic meeting in 1987 with the few Jews living in Poland, in Warsaw, the Holy Father said, "Be assured, dear brothers, that the Poles, this Church in Poland, who view at close range the ignoble reality of the ruthless annihilation of your people, planned and carried out, commiserated in a spirit of deep solidarity with you. Your danger was our danger. Our danger did not reach the same extent, there was not time for it to reach the same extent. That awful sacrifice of destruction you bore, one might say, bore it for others, who were also slated for annihilation" (Circular Letter of the Press Office of the Polish Episcopate 28/1987/179).

Many Poles saved Jews during the last war. Hundreds, if not thousands, paid for this with their own lives and the lives of their loved ones. For each of the Jews saved there was a whole chain of hearts of people of good will and helping hands. The express testimony of that help to Jews in the years of the Hitler occupation are many trees dedicated to Poles in the place of national memory, Yad Vashem, in Jerusalem with the honored title, "Just Among the Nations," given to many Poles. In spite of so many heroic examples of help on the part of Polish Christians, there were also people who remained indifferent to this incomprehensible tragedy. We are especially disheartened by those among the Catholics who in some way were the cause of the death of Jews. They will forever gnaw at our conscience on the social plane. If only one Christian could have helped and did not stretch out a helping hand to a Jew during the time of danger or caused his death, we must ask for forgiveness of our Jewish brothers and sisters. We are aware that many of our compatriots still remember the injustices and injuries committed by the post-war Communist authorities, in which people of Jewish origin also took part. We must acknowledge, however, that the source of inspiration of their activity was clearly neither their origin nor religion but the Communist ideology, from which the Jews themselves, in fact, suffered many injustices.

We express our sincere regret for all the incidents of anti-Semitism which were committed at any time or by any one on Polish soil. We do this with the deep conviction that all incidents of anti-Semitism are contrary to the spirit of the Gospel and,—as Pope John Paul II recently emphasized—"remain opposed to the Christian vision of human dignity" (John Paul II on the occasion of the 50th anniversary of the outbreak of the war).

In expressing our sorrow for all the injustices and harm done to Jews, we cannot forget that we consider untrue and deeply harmful the use by many of the concept of what is called Polish anti-Semitism, as an especially threatening form of that anti-Semitism; and in addition, frequently connecting the concentration camps not with those who were actually involved with them but with Poles in a Poland occupied by the Germans. Speaking of the unprecedented extermination of Jews, one cannot forget and even less pass over in silence the fact that the Poles as a nation were one of the first victims of the same criminal racist ideology of Hitler's Nazism.

The same land, which for centuries was the common fatherland of Poles and Jews, of blood spilled together, the sea of horrific suffering and of injuries shared—should not divide us but unite us. For this commonality cries out to us—especially the places of execution and, in many cases, common graves. We, Christians and Jews, are also united in our belief in one God, the Creator and Lord of the entire universe, who created man in his image and likeness. We are united by the commonly accepted ethical principles included in the Ten Commandments, crowned by the love of God and neighbor. We are united in our respect for the biblical books of the Old Testament as the Word of God and by common traditions of prayer. Lastly, we are united in the common hope of the final coming of the Reign of God. Together we await the Messiah, the Savior, although we, believing that He is Jesus Christ of Nazareth—await not His first but His final coming, no more in the poverty of the manger in Bethlehem, but in power and glory.

The most important way to overcome the difficulties that still exist today is the establishment of a dialogue which would lead to the elimination of distrust, prejudices, and stereotypes, and to mutual acquaintance and understanding based on respect for our separate religious traditions as well as opening the way to cooperation in many fields. It is important, moreover, that while doing this, we learn to experience and appreciate the proper religious contexts of Jews and Christians, as they are lived by Jews and Christians themselves.

We conclude our pastoral homily, dear Brothers and Sisters, recalling the recent statement of the Holy Father about our common temporal and final destinies: "The [Jewish] people who lived with us for many generations, remained with us after the terrible death of many millions of their sons and daughters. Together we wait for the day of Judgment and Resurrection" (Speech to the Poles during the Wednesday audience, September 26, 1990).

Commending to the merciful God all the victims of force and hatred, we bless you from our hearts, praying that "the God of peace may be always with you" (*Philippians 4,9*).

The 244th Plenary Conference of the Episcopate of Poland
Czestochowa, November 30, 1990

(signed)
All the Cardinals, Archbishops and Bishops present at the Conference

D

Resolution 3–09, "To Clarify Position on Anti–Semitism," of the Missouri Synod of the Lutheran Church (July 1983)

Whereas, Anti–Semitism and other forms of racism are a continuing problem in our world; and

WHEREAS, Some of Luther's intemperate remarks about the Jews are often cited in this connection; and

WHEREAS, It is widely but falsely assumed that Luther's personal writings and opinions have some official status among us (thus, sometimes implying the responsibility of contemporary Lutheranism for those statements, if not complicity in them); but also

WHEREAS, It is plain from Scripture that the Gospel must be proclaimed to all people—that is, to Jews also, no more and no less than to others (Matt. 28: 18–20); and

WHEREAS, This Scriptural mandate is sometimes confused with anti-Semitism; therefore be it

Resolved, That we condemn any and all discrimination against others on account of race or religion or any coercion on that account and pledge ourselves to work and witness against such sins; and be it further

Resolved, That we reaffirm that the bases of our doctrine and practice are the Scriptures and the Lutheran Confessions and not Luther, as such; and be it further

Resolved, That while, on the one hand, we are deeply indebted to Luther for his rediscovery and enunciation of the Gospel, on the other hand, we deplore and disassociate ourselves from Luther's negative statements about the Jewish people, and, by the same token, we deplore the use today of such sentiments by Luther to incite anti–Christians and/or anti–Lutheran sentiment; and be it further

Resolved, That in our teaching and preaching we take care not to confuse the religion of the Old Testament (often labeled "Yahwism") with the subsequent

Judaism, nor misleadingly speak about "Jews" in the Old Testament ("Israelites" or "Hebrews" being much more accurate terms), lest we obscure the basic claim of the New Testament and of the Gospel to being in substantial continuity with the Old Testament and that the fulfillment of the ancient promises came in Jesus Christ; and be it further

Resolved, That we avoid the recurring pitfall of recrimination (as illustrated by the remarks of Luther and many of the early church fathers) against those who do not respond positively to our evangelistic efforts; and be it finally

Resolved, That, in that light, we personally and individually adopt Luther's final attitude toward the Jewish people, as evidenced in his last sermon: "We want to treat them with Christian love and to pray for them, so that they might become converted and would receive the Lord" (Weimar edition, Vol. 51, p. 195).

Action: *Adopted (10).*

Bibliography

Articles

Arnal, L. Oscar, "Luther and the Peasants: A Lutheran Reassessment," *Science and Society*, Vol. XLIV, No. 4, Winter 1980.
Barth, Karl, "Die Judenfrage und ihre christliche Beantwortung," *Judaica*, Vol. 6, 1952.
Cohen, Carl, "Martin Luther and his Jewish Contemporaries," *Jewish Social Studies*, Vol. 25, No. 3, July 1963.
Davies, Allen, "Racism and German Protestant Theology," *The Annals of the American Academy of Political and Social Science*, Vol. 450, July 1980.
Eckardt, Roy A., "Can There Be a Jewish-Christian Relationship?" *The Journal of Bible and Religion*, April 1965.
Erickson, F. Willis, "A Parish Pastor's Reflections on Christian-Jewish Relations," *The Lutheran Quarterly*, Vol. XX, No. 3, August 1968.
Estes, Joseph R., "Jewish-Christian Dialogue as Mission," *Review and Expositor*, Vol. LXVII, No. 1, Winter 1971.
Foster, R. Claude, "Historical Antecedents: Why the Holocaust?" *Annals of the American Academy of Political and Social Science*, Vol. 40, No. 7, 1980.
Gilbert, Arthur, "Jewish Resistance to Dialogue," *The Journal of Ecumenical Studies*, Vol. 4, No. 2, Spring 1967.
Heschel, Abraham J., "No Religion Is an Island," *The Union Seminary Quarterly Review*, Vol. XXI, No. 2, Part I, January 1966.
Karsten, Robert E., "What Stance for Lutherans?" *The Lutheran Quarterly*, Vol. XX, No. 3, August 1968.
Liebeschütz, H., "Judaism and Jewry in the Social Doctrine of Thomas Aquinas," *The Journal of Jewish Social Studies*, Vol. 13, 1962.
Lindbeck, George A., "The Jews, Renewal and Ecumenism," *The Journal of Ecumenical Studies*, Vol. 2, No. 1, Winter 1965.
Littell, Franklin H., "Politics, Theology and the Jews," *The Journal of Ecumenical Studies*, Vol. 2, No. 1, Winter 1965.
Meyer, Heinrich, "The Church and the Jewish People: Report on a Consultation," *The Lutheran Quarterly*, Vol. 21, No. 4, November 1969.

Moltmann, Jurgen, "Israel's 'No': Jews and Jesus in an Unredeemed World," *The Christian Century*, Vol. 107, No. 32, November 7, 1990.

Neumann, Matthias, "Confessions of a 20th Century Christian Judaizer," *America*, Vol. 163, No. 13, November 3, 1990.

Pawlikowski, John T., "A Challenge to Jewish Attitudes," *Moment*, Vol. 15, No. 4, August 1990.

Poppel, Stephan, "New Views on Jewish Integration in Germany," *Central European History*, Vol. 9, No. 1, 1976.

Rowan, Steven, "Luther, Bucer and Eck on the Jews," *The Sixteenth Century Journal*, Vol. XVI, No. 1, Spring 1985.

Shannon, William J., "Thomas Merton and Judaism," *America*, Vol. 163, No. 9, October 6, 1990.

Swidler, Leonard, "Vatican II and the Jews—A New Hochhuth?" *The Journal of Ecumenical Studies*, Vol. 2, No. 1, Winter 1965.

Sykes, Gresham, and David Matza, "Techniques of Neutralization: A Theory of Delinquency," *The American Sociological Review*, Vol. 22, No. 6, December 1957.

Toynbee, Arnold, "Jewish Rights in Palestine," *The Jewish Quarterly Review*, Vol. LII, No. 1, 1962.

Willis, Robert E., "Why Christian Liturgy Needs an Enduring Jewish Presence," *The Journal of Ecumenical Studies*, Vol. XXV, No. 1, Winter 1988.

Books

Abbott, F. George, *Israel in Europe*, New York, Macmillan, 1907.

Abbott, Walter M., ed., *The Documents of Vatican II*, New York, Association, 1966.

Agus, Jacob B., ed., *Judaism and Christianity*, New York, Arno, 1973.

Alexander, Robert and James Donaldson, eds., *The Ante–Nicene Fathers: Translations of the Writings of the Fathers Down to A.D. 325*, Grand Rapids, Mich., Eerdmans, 1885.

Allport, Gordon, *The Nature of Prejudice*, Reading, Mass., Addison, Wesley, 1954.

Anderson, Floyd, ed., *Council Day Book*, Vatican II, Sessions One and Two, D.C., National Catholic Welfare Conference, 1965.

Aquinas, Thomas, *Opera Omnia*, Paris, Ludovicum Vivès, 1889.

———. *Summa Theologicae*, New York, McGraw-Hill, 1975.

Augustine, *The City of God*, Whitney J. Oates, ed., *The Basic Writings of Saint Augustine*, Vol. 2, New York, Random House, 1948.

Ausubel, Nathan, *The Book of Jewish Knowledge*, New York, Crown, 1964.

Baron, Saul, *A Social and Religious History of the Jews*, Vol. I, New York, Columbia University Press, 1951–1965.

Barth, Karl, *Church Dogmatics*, Vol. IV, Edinburgh, Clark, 1962.

Baum, Gregory, *Is the New Testament Anti–Semitic?* Glen Rock, N.J., Deus, Paulist, 1965.

Becon, Thomas, S.T.P., *Prayers and Other Pieces*, Cambridge, The Univeristy Press, 1844.

Blau, Bruno, *Das Ausnahmerecht für die Juden in Deutschland*, Düsseldorf, Verlag Algemeine Wochenzeitung, 1965.
Blumenkranz, Bernhard, *Die Judenpredigt Augustins*, Basel, Switzerland, von Helbing und Lichtenhahn, 1946.
Bonhoeffer, Dietrich, *No Rusty Swords: Letters, Lectures and Notes, 1928-1936*, Vol. 1, Edwin H. Robertson and John Bowden, transl., New York, Harper & Row, 1947.
Bornkamm, Heinrich, *Luther and the Old Testament*, Eric W. Gritsch and Ruth C. Gritsch, transl., Philadelphia, Fortress, 1969.
Brecht, Martin, *Martin Luther: 2. Band, Ordnung und Abgrenzung der Reformation*, Stuttgart, Calwer Verlag, 1987.
_____, *Martin Luther: Die Erhaltung der Kirche, 1532-1546*, 3ter Band, Stuttgart, Calwer Verlag, 1987.
Brosseder, Johannes, *Luthers Stellung zu den Juden im Spiegel seiner Interpreten*, München, Max Hueber Verlag, 1972.
Brown, Robert McAfee, *The Ecumenical Revolution*, Garden City, N.Y., Doubleday, 1967.
Browning, Robert, *The Poems and Plays of Robert Browning*, Bennet A. Cerf and Donald Klopfer, eds., New York, The Modern Library, 1934.
Bultmann, Rudolf, *Jesus and the Word*, New York, Scribner's, 1934.
Burleigh, John S., *Augustin: Early Writings*, Philadelphia, Westminster, 1980, pp. 231 and 241.
Calfhill, James, *An Answer to John Martiall's Treatise of the Cross*, Cambridge, The University Press, 1846.
Clemen, Otto, *Flugschriften aus den ersten Jahren der Reformation*, Nieuwkoop, Netherlands, de Graaf, 1967, pp. 375-377.
Cordier, Leopold, *Die Evangelische Jugend und ihre Bunde Schwerin in Mecklenburg*, Friedrich Bahn Verlag, 1927.
Cranmer, Thomas, *Letters of Thomas Cranmer*, John E. Cox, ed., The Parker Society, Cambridge, The University Press, 1846.
Cummings, D., transl., *The Rudder (Pedalion) of the Metaphorical Ship of the One Holy Catholic and Apostolic Church*, Chicago, The Orthodox Christian Educational Society, 1957.
Davies, Plan T., *Anti-Semitism and the Christian Mind*, New York, Herder and Herder, 1969.
Dawidowicz, Lucy, *The War Against the Jews*, New York, Holt, Rinehart and Winston, 1975.
Dawson, J.G., *Aquinas Selected Political Writings*, New York, Barnes and Noble, 1959.
De Corneille, Roland, *Christians and Jews: The Tragic Past and the Hopeful Future*, New York, Harper & Row, 1966.
Deferrari, Roy Joseph, ed., *The Fathers of the Church*, Vol. 12, Saint Augustine, Treatises on Marriage and Other Subjects, New York, Fathers of the Church, 1955.
Dobnow, S. M., *History of the Jews in Russia and Poland, from the Earliest Times to the Present Day*, I. Friedlander, transl., Philadelphia, The Jewish Publication Society of America, 1916.

Dubnov, Simon, *The History of the Jews*, Vol. 2, Moshe Spiegel, transl., London, Thomas Yoseloff, 1968.
Durant, Will, *The Age of Faith*, New York, Simon and Schuster, 1950.
_____, *The Reformation*, New York, Simon and Schuster, 1957.
Durkheim, Emile, *The Elementary Forms of the Religious Life*, New York, The Free Press, 1948.
_____, *The Rules of the Sociological Method*, Glencoe, Ill., The Free Press, 1895, 1950.
Eckardt, Roy A., *Your People, My People*, New York, Quadrangle, 1974.
_____ and Alice Eckardt, *Elder Brother, Younger Brother*, New York, Scribner's, 1967.
Edwards, Jonathan, *Original Sin*, New Haven and London, Yale University Press, 1970.
Edwards, Mark, and George Tavard, *Luther: A Reformer for the Churches, An Ecumenical Study Guide*, Philadelphia, Fortress, 1983.
Edwards, Mark U., *Luther's Last Battles, Politics and Polemics, 1531–46*, Ithaca, N.Y., Cornell University Press, 1983.
Encyclopedia of Philosophy, New York, Macmillan, 1967.
Erikson, Kai T., *Wayward Puritans: A Study in the Sociology of Deviance*, New York, Wiley, 1966.
Fackenheim, Emil, *God's Presence in History*, New York, New York University Press, 1970.
Falk, Gerhard, *Murder: An Analysis of Its Forms, Conditions and Causes*, Jefferson, N.C., McFarland, 1990.
Feldman, Leon A., *Ancient and Medieval History*, New Brunswick, N.J., Rutgers University Press, 1972.
Fichte, Johann Gottlieb, *Addresses to the German Nation*, R.F. Jones and G.H. Turnbull, trans., New York, Open Court, 1922.
Fishman, Hertzel, *American Protestantism and a Jewish State*, Detroit, Wayne State University Press, 1973.
Flannery, Edward, *The Anguish of the Jews*, New York, Macmillan, 1964.
Fleischner, Eva, *Judaism in German Christian Theology*, Metuchen, N.J., Scarecrow, 1975.
Foxe, John, *The Acts and Monuments*, George Townsend, ed., New York, AMS, 1965.
Frazier, George, *The Golden Bough*, Macmillan, 1922, 1960.
Freud, Sigmund, *Moses and Monotheism*, New York, Knopf, 1939.
Gaines, David P., *The World Council of Churches: A Study of Its Background and History*, New York, Richard R. Smith, 1966.
Gamm, H. J., *Judentumskunde*, 4th ed., Frankfurt, 1962.
Gellner, Ernest, *Legitimation of Belief*, London, The Cambridge University Press, 1974.
Gilbert, Arthur, *The Vatican Council and the Jews*, New York, World, 1968.
Gilbert, Martin, *The Holocaust*, New York, Holt, 1985.
Gilson, Etienne, *The Christian Philosophy of St. Thomas Aquinas*, New York, Random House, 1975.
Gorschenek, Gunter, and Stephen Reimers, eds., *Offene Wunden-Brennende Fragen*,

Juden in Deutschland von 1938 bis Heute, Frankfurt a.M., Joseph Knecht, 1989.
Gradewitz, Otto, *Vocabularium Jurisprudentiae Romanae*, Berlin Savigny Stiftung, 1903.
Graetz, Heinrich, *History of the Jews*, Philadelphia, The Jewish Publication Society, 1891-1898.
―――, *History of the Jews*, Vol. II, Philadelphia, The Jewish Publication Society, 1898.
Grant, M. Robert, *A Short History of the Interpretation of the Bible*, New York, Macmillan, 1963.
Grayzel, Solomon, *A History of the Jews*, Philadelphia, The Jewish Publication Society of America, 1947.
Guttmann, J., *Das Verhältniss des Thomas von Aquinos zum Judenthum und zur jüdischen Literatur*, Göttingen, Vandenhoeck & Ruprecht's Verlag, 1891.
Harkins, Paul W., transl., *Saint John Chrysostom, Discourses Against Judaizing Christians*, Washington, D.C., The Catholic University of America, 1977.
Hay, Malcolm, *Thy Brother's Blood, The Roots of Christian Anti-Semitism*, New York, Hart, 1975.
Hegel, Friedrich, *On Christianity*, T.M. Knox, transl., New York, Harper, Row, 1948.
Hertz, C. H., *The Pentateuchs and Haftorahs*, 2nd ed., Soncino, 1961.
Hilberg, Raul, *The Destruction of the European Jews*, New York, Octagon, 1978.
Hocking, William E., *Types of Philosophy*, 3rd ed., New York, Scribner's, 1959.
Isaac, Jules, *Has Anti-Semitism Roots in Christianity?* New York, National Conference of Christians and Jews, n.d.
Katz, David S., *Philo-Semitism and the Readmission of the Jews to England*, Oxford, Clarendon, 1982.
Kisch, Guido, *Erasmus Stellung zu Juden und Judentum*, Tübingen, J.C.B. Mohr, 1969.
Klein, Charlotte, *Anti-Judaism in Christian Theology*, Philadelphia, Fortress, 1975.
Knox, John, *The Works*, David Laing, ed., Edinburgh, Bannatyne Club, 1854, and New York, AMS, 1966.
Küng, Hans, *Projekt Weltethos*, München, R. Piper, 1990.
Lamberti, Marjorie, *Jewish Activism in Imperial Germany*, New Haven, Yale University Press, 1978.
Latimer, Hugh, *Works*, Cambridge, The University Press, 1845.
Latourelle, Renée, *Vatican II, Assessment and Perspectives*, Vol. 3, New York, Paulist, 1989.
Lessing, Gotthold Ephraim, *Lessing's Werke*, Richard Gosche, ed., Berlin, 1884.
Levin, Nora, *The Holocaust*, New York, Schocken, 1973.
Lewis, T., *A Latin Dictionary*, Oxford, Clarendon, 1980.
Linder, Amnon, *The Jews in Roman Imperial Legislation*, Detroit, Wayne State University Press, 1987.
Lipsky, Abram, *Martin Luther, Germany's Angry Man*, New York, Frederick A. Stokes, 1933.
Littell, Franklin H. and Hubert G. Locke, eds., *The German Church Struggle and the Holocaust*, Detroit, Wayne State University Press, 1973.

Locke, John, *A Letter Concerning Toleration*, Mario Montuori, ed., The Hague, Martinus Nijhoff, 1963.
Luther, Martin, *On the Jews and Their Lies*, in Helmut Lehman, gen. ed., Franklin Sherman, ed., *Luther's Works*, Volume 47, The Christian in Society, Philadelphia, Fortress, 1971.
Luther, Martinus, "Vom Schem Hamphoras und vom Geschlecht Christi," *D. Martin Luthers Werke, Kritische Gesammtausgabe*, Weimar, Herman Bohlhaus, Nachfolger, 1920.
McHugh and Callan, eds., *Catechism of the Council of Trent for Parish Priests*, New York, Joseph F. Wagner, 1923.
Mann, Thomas, *Politische Schriften und Reden*, Dritter Band, Frankfurt a.M., Fischer Bücherei, 1960.
Margolis, Max, and Alexander Marx, *A History of the Jewish People*, New York, Meridian, 1958.
Maritain, Jacques, *A Christian Looks at the Jewish Question*, New York, Longmans, Green, 1939.
Markish, Shimon, *Erasmus and the Jews*, Chicago and London, The University of Chicago Press, 1986.
Maurer, Wilhelm, *Kirche und Synagogue*, Stuttgart, 1953.
Merton, Thomas, *Conjectures of a Guilty Bystander*, Garden City, N.Y., Doubleday, 1966.
Miller, John H., ed., *Vatican II—An Interfaith Appraisal*, New York, Association, 1966.
Muller, Herbert J., *The Uses of the Past*, New York, Oxford University Press, 1952.
Mussner, Franz, *Tractate on the Jews: The Significance of Judaism for Christian Faith*, Philadelphia, Fortress, 1984.
Newman, Louis Israel, *The Jewish Influence on Christian Reform Movements*, New York, Columbia University Press, 1925.
Parker Society, *The Works of the Fathers and Early Writers of the Reformed English Church*, Cambridge, The University Press, 1849.
Parkes, James, *Prelude to Dialogue*, London, Vallentine, Mitchel, 1969.
Pawlikowski, John T., *The Challenge of the Holocaust for Christian Theology*, New York, The Center for Studies of the Holocaust, 1978.
Petuchowski, Jakob J., ed. *When Jews and Christians Meet*, Albany, N.Y., The State University of New York Press, 1988.
Pfisterer, Rudolf, *Im Schatten des Kreuzes*, Hamburg, Herbert Reich Evangelischer Verlag, G.m.b.H., 1966.
———, *Juden und Christen: Getrennt, Versöhnt*, Neukirchen-Vluyn, Aussaht und Schriftenmissions Verlag, 1973.
Rahner, Karl, *Theological Dictionary*, Richard Strahan, transl., New York, Herder and Herder, 1961.
Richarz, Monika, *Jüdisches Leben in Deutschland*, Augsburg, Deutsche Verlagsanstalt, 1976.
Ross, Ralph, and Ernest van den Haag, *The Fabric of Society*, New York, Harcourt Brace, 1957.
Ruether, Rosemary, and Herman J. Ruether, *The Wrath of Jonah*, New York, Harper & Row, 1983.

Sartre, Jean-Paul, *Anti-Semite and Jew*, George J. Becker, transl., New York, Grove, 1948.
Schaff, Phillip, and Henry Wace, eds., *A Select Library of Nicene and Post Nicene Fathers of the Christian Church*, Vol. 5, Grand Rapids, Mich., Eerdmans, 1892.
Schleiermacher, Friedrich, *The Christian Faith*, New York, Harper & Row, 1963.
Shirer, William, *The Rise and Fall of the Third Reich: A History of Nazi Germany*, New York, Simon and Schuster, 1960, p. 430.
Simon, Merrill, *Jerry Falwell and the Jews*, New York, Jonathan David, 1984.
Simon, Ulrich, *A Theology of Auschwitz*, Atlanta, John Knox, 1979.
Smith, Preserved and Charles M. Jacobs, *Luther's Correspondence and Other Contemporary Letters*, St. Louis & Chicago, Lutheran Publication Society, 1918.
Soloviev, Vladimir, in Zhaba: *Russkie Mysleteli o Rossii i Chelovechestve—Antologiia Russkoi Obshchestvennoi Mysli*, Georg Vid Tomashevich, transl., Paris, YMCA Press, 1954.
Stern, Selma, *Joel Rosenheim*, Gertrude Hirschler, transl., Philadelphia, The Jewish Publication Society of America, 1965.
Stone, Kenneth R., ed., *The Church and the Jews in the Thirteenth Century*, Detroit, Wayne State University Press, 1989.
Stow, Kenneth R., *Catholic Thought and Papal Jewry Policy*, New York, The Jewish Theological Seminary, 1977.
Stupperich, Robert, ed., *Martini Buceri Opera Omnia*, Series I, Vol. 7, Paris, Presses Universitaires de France, 1964.
Swidler, Leonard, ed., *Breaking Down the Wall*, Lanham, Md., The University Press, 1987, p. 115.
Tannenbaum, Marc, Marvin R. Wilson and A. James Rudin, *Evangelicals and Jews in Conversation on Scripture, Theology and History*, Grand Rapids, Mich., Baker, 1978.
Tappert, Theodore G., ed., *Luther: Letters of Spiritual Counsel*, Philadelphia, Westminster, 1970.
Thoma, Clemens, *A Christian Theology of Judaism*, Helga Croner, transl., New York, Paulist, 1980.
Thomas, William I., *Essays on Research in the Social Sciences*, Washington, D.C., The Brookings Institution, 1931.
Thompson, James W. and Nathaniel Johnson, *An Introduction to Medieval Europe*, New York, Norton, 1937.
Thompson, R. Craig, *The Colloquies of Erasmus*, Chicago, The University of Chicago Press, 1965.
Tolstoy, Leo, *War and Peace*, Louise and Aylmer Maude, transl., New York, Norton, 1966.
Torrance, David W., and Thomas F. Torrance, eds., *Calvin's Commentaries on The Epistle of Paul the Apostle to the Romans*, Grand Rapids, Mich., Eerdmans, 1960.
Tyler, Edward B., *Religion in Primitive Culture*, New York, Harper, 1958.
U.S. Government, *Trial of the Major War Criminals*, in *Nazi Conspiracy and Aggression*, Washington, D.C., Government Printing Office, 1951.
Van der Zanden, James, *American Minority Relations*, New York, Ronald Press, 1972.

Von Hefele, Joseph C., *Concilgeschichte*, Freiburg, Herder'sche Verlagshandlung, 1873.
Von Ingen, Ferdinand and Gerd Labraisse, *Luther Bilder im 20ten Jahrhundert*, Amsterdam, Rodopi, b.V., 1984.
Von Kues, Nicholaus, *Philosophische-Theologische Schriften*, Leo Gabriel, ed., Vienna, Verlag Herder, 1967.
Wagener, Hans, ed., *Gegenswartliteratur und Drittes Reich*, Stuttgart, Phillip Reclam, Jr., 1977.
Weber, Max, *The Theory of Social and Economic Organization* (1925), Talcott Parsons, ed., New York, The Free Press, 1964.
Wilken, Robert L., *John Chrysostom and the Jews*, Berkeley, The University of California Press, 1983.
Williams, Robin, *The Stranger Next Door*, Englewood Cliffs, N.J., Prentice-Hall, 1964.
Wissowa, Georg, ed., *Realencyclopedie der Classischen Altertumswissenschaft*, Stuttgart, Alfred Druckenmüller Verlag, 1905.
Wolzogue, Louis D., *Dictionnaire Wolzogue*, Paris, Universelle de Philosophie Sacrée, 1846.
World Council of Churches, Third Assembly, *The New Delhi Report*, New York, Association, 1961.
Yzermans, Vincent A., ed., *American Participation in the Second Vatican Council*, New York, Sheed and Ward, 1967.

Newspapers

Buffalo Jewish Review
Buffalo News
New York Times

Personal Communications

Cjajkowski, Michael

Index

Abraham 7
Adam and Eve 216
"Adonai" 181
Aelia Capitolina 167
Against the Jews and Their Lies 166
Agnus Dei 177
Agobard, Archbishop of Lyon 35
Albrecht of Saxony, Count 194
Aleander, Jerome 55
Alexander the Great 187
Al-Koran 194
Allah 194
Alma 169, 212, 213
Amsterdam Assembly 116
Anabaptists 61
Andrews, Lancelot 91
Angel Gabriel 208
angels 201
anti–Judaism 1, 6, 8, 9, 13, 14, 16, 17, 28, 30, 31, 35, 39, 49, 50, 61, 63, 64, 71, 74, 75, 76, 82, 90, 94, 97, 110, 111, 112, 114, 115, 121, 123, 124, 130, 132, 136, 138, 143, 146, 147, 148, 154
Antioch 11, 12
anti–Semitism 31, 50, 71, 102, 105, 106, 107, 110, 114, 115, 116, 117, 121, 131, 133, 134, 135, 136, 138, 148, 280, 281
anti–Zionism 105, 144
The Apostate 191
Apostolic Canons 29
Apostolic Constitution 200
Appolinaris of Hieapolis, Bishop 8, 51
Aquinas, Thomas *see* Thomas of Aquinas
Arian Heresy 28
Ark of the Lord 168
Artemis, Temple of 6
Aryan clause 110
Aryan Race 11, 125
Asar 207
Aschaffenburg, Synod of 43

Ashkenazi tradition 203–04
assassin 194
Athens 194
Augustine, Aurelius (Saint) 15, 16, 65
Auschwitz 122, 123, 124
Avignon, Synod of 36

Baal Zebub 166
Bad Schwalbach Proposals 113
Bale, John 91
Balfour, Arthur 141
Baptism 211
"Baptisma" 176
Bar Kochba, Simeon 167, 181
Barnabas 3
Barth, Karl 109, 110, 139
Baum, Father Gregory 135
Becon, Thomas 88
Beelzebub 166, 168
"Beggarbook" 195
Benoit, Pierre 111
Bernard (Saint) 220
Bertholet, Alfred 111
Beziers, Synod of 3
Blomjous, Bishop of Tanganyika 114
Blumenkranz, Bernhard 15
Bonaventura (Saint) 209
Bonhoeffer, Dietrich 109
Book of Daniel 60
Book of Judges 220
Boole, George 56
Bornkamm, Gunther 108
Breviarum 19
Brown, Robert McAfee 132
Buber, Martin 137
Bucer, Martin 54, 83–87
Buddhism 4
Bultmann, Rudolf 107
Byzantium 27

292 Index

Cain 196
Calvin, John 83–85
Calvinists 61
Cana 209
Canaan 195
Carthage, Synod of 32
Chair of Grace 201
Chalcedon, Council of 18
Challaye, Felicien 177
cherubim 201
chriein 167
Christ 3, 5, 7, 166, 167
Christ Killers 11, 13, 14, 16, 22, 64, 83, 142, 154, 190
Christian Century 143
Chronicles 207
Chrysostom, John (Saint) 11, 12, 13, 14, 17, 29
Church Councils: of Chalcedon 18; of Elvira 17, 21; of Nicea 17, 18, 30, 97; of Trent 44; of Trullo 18
Church Fathers 3–25
Cicero 4
circumcision 175
Clemens of Alexandria 8
Codes of Justinian 20
codes of law, Roman 17
Cohen, Arthur A. 50
Conciliar Declaration "Nostra Aetate" 129, 145, 277–80
Congregation of Notre Dame de Sion 113
Constantinople 183
Cooper, Anthony Arthur 141
Coptic Church 117
Corinthians 222
Covenant 5
Cranmer, Thomas 88, 89
Cromwell, Oliver 92, 141
crusades 38
Cullman, Oscar 112
Cushing, Richard Cardinal 119

Damacenes 219
Daniel 220
David 169, 192, 218
Declaration of the German Bishops 138
Declaration on Non-Christians 120
Declaration on the Jews 120
Decline and Fall of the Roman Empire 181
de Lyra, Nicholaus 186
The Depression [1930s] 122
Deuteronomy 206
Devil 166, 221
Diabolos 166
Dibelius, Martin 107

Dioceses of the German Republic, Synod of the 139
Dopfner, Cardinal 131
Durkheim, Emile 16, 28
Dygrammaton 188

Eck, Johann 54, 66
Eckardt, A. Roy 133, 143
Ecumenical Council 111
Edict of Milan 11
Edroshe 192
Edward VI 89
Edwards, Jonathan 93
Edwards, Mark U. 224
Egyptians 178
Eichmann, Adolf 113, 114
Einstein, Albert 57
Eli 205
Elijah 7
Elizabeth 208
Elohim 172
emperors, Roman: Arcadius 18; Constantine 11, 17; Hadrian 7, 167; Honorius 18; Julian 14, 15; Theodosius II 18; Vespasian 167
Encyclopedia of Unbelief 166
English Reformation 92
Epaon, Synod of 32
Ephesus 6; Council of 219
Epistle 5
Erasmus, Desiderius 49–53
Erickson, Willis 135
Esau 207
Estes, Joseph R. 135
Eusebius 10
Eusibius, Hieronymous Sophronius 187, 204, 205
Evangelium 65
Evanston Assembly 117, 133
Exodus 178

Falwell, Jerry 125
Faust 166
Fichte, Johann 93
Five Books of Moses 59, 63
Flannery, Edward 114, 133
Flavius Josephus 215
Fourth Lateran Council 82
Foxe, John 89
Frazier, Sir Robert 175
Fredrick of Saxony, Count 195
Freemasons 31
French Revolution 97

Index

Freud, Sigmund 104
fundamentalists 115

Galilee 167, 170
Genesis 172
German Law 11
Germany 20, 32, 36, 37, 38, 67, 69, 71, 75, 93, 94, 97, 103, 112, 130, 139, 143, 204; *see also* Nazi movement *and* Nazis
Gestapo (Geheime Staats Polizei) 112
Gevirah 212
Geyer, Alan 144
Gibbon, Edward 181
Gilbert, Rabbi Arthur 134
Giovanni di Fidenza 209
God 189; names of 188
The Golden Bough 175
Golden Rule 200
Goppelt, Leonhard 111
Gospels 175
goyim 172, 182, 214, 221
Grayzel, Solomon 181
Great Depression 122
Greeks 178
Gregory of Nyssa (Saint) 16
Grundmann, Walter 107
Gulden 184
gypsies 194

Ha Nozri (the Nazarene) 174
Haggai 220
Halani, Queen 169
Hamdan ibn al-Ashrath 194
Harvard University 182
Hay, Malcolm 12
Hebraists 222
Hebrew 61, 62, 172, 180, 223
Hebrew letters 178, 185
Hegel, Georg Wilhelm Friedrich 94
Helena (Helen), Queen of Adiabane 168, 172
Hell 221
Heller, Celia vii
Helmsing, Charles (Bishop of Kansas City) 119
Helvidius 217
Heschel, Rabbi Abraham 119, 132
Hexagrammaton 188
"Hidden" Name 181; *see also Shem Hamphoras*
Hindus 166
Hitler, Adolf 11, 17, 55, 89
Hittite 206

Holocaust 5, 22, 97, 109, 148, 175, 187; *see also* Nazi movement *and* Nazis
Holy Ghost 177
Holy Land 115
Holy Scriptures 196, 221
Holy Week 158
Holy Writ 196
Hosea 169
House of David 191, 205
House of Matthes 204
Hyppolytus of Rome 9

Ignatius 5, 6
Inferno 209
Innocent III 38
Isaiah 168, 189, 218
Iscariot 173
Ish Kariot 173
Ismaelites 194
Israel 7, 8, 9, 16, 30, 33, 64, 68, 75, 84, 85, 86, 87, 88, 92, 96, 106, 107, 108, 110, 111, 112, 115, 116, 117, 118, 119, 124, 125, 130, 133, 138, 139, 140, 141, 142, 143, 144, 145, 146, 147, 148, 160, 169, 172, 173, 175, 178, 181, 183, 186, 188, 193, 198, 201, 202, 204, 210, 220, 221
Israelites 201
Izates 168

James I of Aragon 38
Jehovah 188
Jeremiah 171, 198, 220
Jerome (Saint) 197, 217
Jerusalem 7, 115, 167, 187, 211
Jerusalem Bible 169, 188, 197
Jesiah 210
Jews of Lincoln 90
Joan of Arc 171
John 177, 202
John the Baptist 209
John XXIII 118
Joram 207
Joseph 191
Judah 192
Judaizer 13, 14, 31, 61, 147
Judaizing 14, 17, 75, 84, 159
Judas Iscariot 170
Judea 167
Julianus, Flavius Claudius *see* The Apostate
Justin 6, 7, 8
Justinian, Codes of 20

Index

Karsten, Robert 134
Katterman, Gerhard 166
Kelso, James L. 144
Kielce massacres 66
Kisch, Guido 50, 53
Kittel, Gerhard 107
Klein, Charlotte 105
Knox, John 91
Kung, Hans 112, 159, 160

Lactantius 9
Last Supper 158
The Last Words of David 223
Latimer, Hugh 90
Lessing, Gotthold 93
Levirate 206
Leviticus 200
Linder, Amnon 21, 24
Lister, Joseph 57
Locke, John 92
The Logos 215
Lord of Heaven and Earth 210
Lord of the Flies *see* Baal Zebub and Beelzebub
Luckner, Gertrud 112
Luke 195
Luke (Saint) 193
Luther, Martin viii, 17, 35, 55–76
Lutheran Position re Anti-Semitism 281–282
Luther's Last Battle 224
Lyra 204

Macon, Synod of 33
Mainz, Synod of 43
Malachi 7
Mann, Thomas 71
Margareth of Antioch (Saint) 171
Margarit, Antonius 178
Maria Jacobi 205
Maritain, Jacques 106
Markish, Shimon 50
Marr, Wilhelm 50
Marranos 104
Marx, Karl 95
Mary [mother of Christ] 191, 192, 212; virginity of 169
Mary Magdalene 209
Mary of Nazareth 216
Matthew 171
Matthew (Saint) 193, 211
Melanchthon (Schwarzerde) 62
Mephistopheles 166

Merton, Father Thomas 119
Messiah 169, 181, 202, 221
Messianic Age 156
Meyer, Albert Cardinal 119
Meyer, Eduard 111
Micah 198
Middle Ages 182, 204
Middle East 167
minor prophets 202
Miriam 212
Mohammed 194
Moltmann, Jurgen 137
Monobaz I 168
Moses 167, 173, 180, 197, 221
Moses, Law of 4, 7
Moses ben Maimon 42, 156
Mother of God 219
Mussner, Franz 138, 139
Muszinski, Bishop Henryk 148

Nasser, Gamal Abdel 143
National Socialist German Workers Party 11
Nazarenes 6, 168
Nazareth 175, 176, 203
Nazi movement 17, 20, 37, 70, 71, 72, 104, 106, 107, 108, 109, 110, 113, 115, 118, 123, 124, 139, 142, 143, 147, 148, 187, 195, 280; *see also* Holocaust
Nazis vii, 19, 28, 38, 74, 95, 107, 109, 121, 122, 147, 175
nekefa 219
Nestor 219
Nestorian Heresy 219
Neumann, Matthias 147
New Covenant 158
New Covenant Church 199
New Delhi Assembly 117, 133
New Testament 10, 13, 62, 190, 193, 198, 222, 224
Newton, John 141
Nicea, Council of 17, 18, 30, 97
Nicholas of Cusa 43
Noah 207
Nyeshavah, Statute of 57

Oberman, Heiko 224
Old Testament 59, 62, 198, 211, 224
Origen 8
Orthodox Church 29, 32
Oursel, Masson 177

Parsis of Iran 166
passion play 131
Passover Seder 158
Pasteur, Louis 57
pasuik 223
Paul (Saint) 52, 183, 193
Paul IV 81
Paul of Burgensis 186
Pawlikowski, John T. 157
pele 223
Peres Shema 183
Pfefferkorn, Johann 44, 54
Pfisterer, Rudolf 125
Philo of Alexandria 215
Phoenecians 166
Pilkington, James 91
Pius V 45
Pliny 6
Poland 148
Polish Episcopate Commission for Dialogue with Judaism 148
Pontifical Commission for Peace and Justice 144
Pontifical Council for Christian Unity 148
popes 38, 45, 81, 118
Porchetus (Purchetis, Purchetus) Salvaticus 166, 168
Potiphar 213
priestly line 208
Prince of Peace 223
Principle of Legitimacy 5
Promised Land 118
prophets 167; Jewish 7, 8
Protocols of the Elders of Zion 91, 184
Psalms 169, 186

rabbis 173
Rahner, Karl 130
Ranke, Leopold 181
Rashi *see* Shlomo ben Yitz'hak
Reform liturgy 158
Reuchlin, Johann 44, 54
Ritter, Joseph Cardinal 119
Roman religion 191
Rosenzweig, Franz 158
royal line 208
Ruether, Rosemary Radford 144

Sabbatarians 61
saints 11, 12, 13, 14, 15, 16, 17, 29, 39–42, 52, 65, 171, 183, 193, 197, 209, 211, 220
Sandmel, Rabbi Samuel 135

Sartre, Jean-Paul 104
Satan 166, 221
"Scape Goat" 177
Schacter, Rabbi Zalman 119
Schism, the Great 27
Schreiner, Stefan 137
Schurer, Emil 111
scripture 4, 201
secularists 155
Secundae Partus 216
Seeligsberg Conference 112, 114
Sefarad 204
Serbia 194
Shadai 214
Shakespeare, William 87
Shem Hamphoras 166, 169, 170; *see also* "Hidden" Name
Shiloh 192
Shlomo ben Yitz'hak 186
Shirer, William 71
Shoah 148; *see also* Holocaust
Shom Haperes 183, 192; *see also Shem Hamphoras*
Shoton 166
shtetls 103
Sigismund, King of Poland 29
Silo 191
Sinaitic Legislation 40
Singer, Isaak Bashevis 195
Six Day War 141, 143
social processes 153
Soloviev, Vladimir 96
Sons of God 7
Spain 32
Spinoza 175
Stocker, Adolf 58
Stow, Kenneth 81
Stransky, Thomas 119
Streicher, Julius 58
Der Sturmer 58
synagogues 11, 20, 21, 35, 38, 43, 69, 70, 90, 92, 156, 277
synecdochen 216

Taft, Charles 117
Talmud 96, 134, 182
Talmudists 198
Tannenbaum, Rabbi Marc 129
Tartars 194
Tavard, George 112
Te Deum Laudamus 171
Teachings of the Twelve Apostles 200
techniques of neutralization 37, 68, 75
Ten Commandments 197, 202
Tertullian 9, 65

Tetragrammaton 181
Theodosius, Codes of 20, 21
theologians, English 87
theotocos 219
Third Reich 111; *see also* Nazis
Thoma, Clemens 124, 138
Thomas, William I. iv, vii
Thomas of Aquinas (Saint) 39–42
Toledo, Synod of 33, 34
Tolstoy, Leo 56
Tomashevich, George Vid 166
Tomb of the Kings 168
Tora 199
Toulouse, Synod of 35
Toynbee, Arnold 143
Tractatus Theologico Politicus 175
Trent, Council of 44
Trier, Cathedral at 183
Trigrammaton 188
Trinity 69
Troullos, Council of 29
Trullo, Council of 18

Unity, Christian 154
Urban II 38
Uria 206

van Buren, Paul 144, 147
van Dusen, Henry 143
Vatican 111

Vatican Council 131
Vatican II 45, 96, 119, 120, 121, 131, 132, 145, 147, 153
vayikra and *shemose* 222
Vennes, Synod of 32
Victoria 166
Vienna, Synod of 36
Vienna, University of 178
Visigothic Code of Law 33
Vom Schem Hamphoras viii, 63, 72, 73, 74, 79, 194
von Hefele, Carl 32
Weber, Max 108
Wesley Brothers 141
Wilberforce, William 141
Wilhelm II, Kaiser 89
witchcraft 67
Wittenberg 182
World Council of Churches 111, 116
World Ethos 159, 160
World War II 97

Yesha Yahu 189
Yiddish 103, 172, 195

Zacharia 7, 198, 208, 218
Zadok 207
Zasius, Ulrich 54
Ziegler, M. Bernhard 223
Zionism 120, 140–44, 198

www.ingramcontent.com/pod-product-compliance
Lightning Source LLC
Chambersburg PA
CBHW051210300426
44116CB00006B/510